CAPITALISM AND ITS ECONOMICS

CAPITALISM
AND ITS ECONOMICS
A CRITICAL HISTORY

NEW EDITION

Douglas Dowd

Pluto Press

LONDON • ANN ARBOR, MI

First published 2000 by Pluto Press
345 Archway Road, London N6 5AA
and 839 Greene Street, Ann Arbor, MI 48106

New edition 2004

www.plutobooks.com

British Library Cataloguing in Publication Data
A catalogue record for this book is available from
the British Library

ISBN 0 7453 2280 8 hbk
ISBN 0 7453 2279 4 pbk

Library of Congress Cataloging in Publication Data
Dowd, Douglas Fitzgerald, 1919–
    Capitalism and its economics: a critical history / Douglas Dowd
        p.   cm.
    Includes bibliographical references and index.
    ISBN 0–7453–2280–8
        1. Capitalism—History. 2. Economic history. I. Title.

HB501.D68 2000
330.12'2—dc21   00–020283

10   9   8   7   6   5   4   3   2   1

Designed, typeset and produced for Pluto Press by
Chase Publishing Services, Fortescue, Sidmouth, EX10 9QG, England
Printed in the European Union by
Antony Rowe Ltd, Chippenham and Eastbourne, England

With deep gratitude and affection,
this book is dedicated to
Robert A. Brady (1901–63), M.M. Knight (1887–1981),
and Leo Rogin (1893–1947):
wonderful teachers, whose passion for understanding
and contempt for ideology
have served as a continuing inspiration

Contents

Preface to the First Edition

As the twentieth century ended, two sets of economic facts stood in stark and disturbing contrast. First, for the first time in history, existing resources and technology taken together had made it possible for all 6 billion of the earth's inhabitants – now or within a generation – to be at least adequately fed, housed, clothed, educated, and their health cared for. And second, instead, well over half of that population was malnourished (with numberless millions starving), ill-housed, ill-clothed, ill-educated, in precarious health, and stricken by infant mortality rates and average life-spans belonging to the era of the early industrial revolution – when there were no more than 2 billion people.

The contrasts between the possible and the actual illuminate the disgraceful realities of that century. Yet, as this is written, capitalism – "the market system" – and its economic theory stride arm in arm on parade, celebrating their joint triumph, aloof and oblivious to these ugly facts.

But many who are neither capitalists nor economists know or sense much or all of those realities, and feel something other than triumph. They are alarmed at what exists and fearful of what edges over the horizon, and baffled, stupefied, or angered by what passes for economic wisdom. Using only good sense, these uneasy or indignant people see contemporary capitalism as producing a set of ongoing and imminent disasters for most people and much of nature: and they could rightly see economists serving not as society's economic doctors but as cheerleaders for business and finance.

*

This book, a critical analysis of the dynamically interdependent histories of capitalism and economic theory, contends that the "many" are right, and sets out to show why. To do so, it is necessary to examine the dynamic *interaction* of two processes – the historical realities of capitalism and the evolution of the economic theory that supports it. Both have been thoroughly studied over many years (if with diverse aims), and many of those inquiries will be referred to as we proceed.

In most histories emphasizing one or another or both processes, attention has not always been paid to our concern: their interaction. Even when the latter has received considerable attention, a serious gap remains; namely, the relevance of understanding that interaction for our own time. This work, as often with histories, has been prompted by present issues. Among the most pressing of the latter is that economists now celebrate capitalism in ways that make it reasonable to classify them as ideologues – and to put them in their place.

The book's discussions of both socioeconomic and analytical histories will necessarily be summary and, to meet present purposes, selective, both for capitalist history and its economic theories: summary, to keep its length within reason; selective in terms of which nations and which economists are discussed. The book's purposes neither require nor allow an encyclopedic treatise; its failure or success will be measured in the degree to which it meets the need of "the many" to shake off the hypnotic effects of contemporary ideology and economic theory.

Much of what industrial capitalism has meant can, of course, be seen as achievements. They will be duly noted, as will the valuable analytical work of the relatively few exemplary economists over the whole period of this study. But our examination, when placed against the social values and scientific standards of our formal culture, will also reveal considerably more in capitalism's past and present that must be seen as tragedy, verging all too often on criminality.

Significantly, it will be found that those few mainstream economists (as distinct from radicals and reformers) who *have* made serviceable studies of capitalist processes and relationships have rarely if ever had their contributions integrated into the corpus of thought known as economic theory more than briefly. Least of all has such analysis been incorporated in the economic theory that today guides and rationalizes economic policies.

In less gentle words, the relationships between capitalism and economics – unsurprisingly, as will be seen – have rarely been at "scientific" arm's length; they have always been incestuous to some degree, and most shamelessly so as we approach the present. In consequence, the shared flaws of economics and capitalism have been aggravated and now become downright lethal – a term here used advisedly. This work is meant to support that strong language. It will be noted that Part I covers a time span more than twice that of Part II. The reasons for that difference are discussed in the Prologue. The latter provides a bare summation of the period within which both capitalism and economics first took hold. After an analysis of the core elements of capitalist development, there follows a synoptic analysis of the nature of economic thought and how and why it has evolved over the capitalist era.

The three chapters of Part I treat of the distinctive periods bringing us up through World War II, and do so by an examination of the leading economies of each period – Britain in Chapter 1, plus the United States, Germany, and Japan in Chapter 2, and their and others' mutual breakdown in Chapter 3. It will also be noted that Chapters 2 and 3 are more than twice the length of most others. That is because, in addition to a continuing examination of the functioning of the "analytical quartet" that ties this book together – capitalism, industrialism, nationalism, and imperialism – there is an examination of the "historical quartet" that led the way. That is, the "quartet" that were becoming and still are the four most powerful industrial capitalist nations: Britain, the United States, Germany, and Japan. Those chapters might seem interminably long to the reader; to the writer it was a constant problem to keep them from becoming even longer, if superficiality were to be avoided.

Part II critically examines the past half-century, and suggests alternatives both to its socioeconomic realities and current trends and to the economic theory guiding them.

What might seem a lopsided emphasis on recent decades is by no means accidental, for they have "made" our present, and are the years that most require our understanding. The emergence in recent years of impending and frightening socioeconomic and ecological crises – with every reason to believe that what underlies them is accelerating – mandates that closer look.

The intended audience for this work are the concerned members of the reading public, academic and otherwise, who suspect or know in their *bones* that something is terribly wrong with our socioeconomy, but are unable to counter the abstruse arguments of mainstream professionals and their political counterparts.

With that public in mind, this book's intention is to serve as a useful step toward unlearning the dangerous arguments now guiding economic policy, while also *learning* how capitalism, despite and because of its innumerable changes over the years, serves more as a wrecking crew than as a builder. It will conclude with a very brief set of possible and desirable alternatives.

Neither this nor any other book, nor reading alone, can suffice for such large purposes. But reading is essential for understanding. Scandalously, such understanding of the economy is unlikely to be gained in a typical economics classroom or text: quite the opposite. Beginning with the undergraduate major, and made worse at the graduate level, the economics student is required to master theoretical technique, not to understand the economy. The consequence is what has been called a "trained incapacity" to comprehend economic realities.

Because I have been a professor of economics and economic history for about 50 years, it is probable that, despite my good intentions, I have not successfully overcome the "professorial" tone. It will be seen that there are numerous notes. Where they are not simply for documentation they are meant to elaborate on and support the generalizations in the text. There are many references for further reading in those notes, also placed there with the hope that they will be pursued. For the reader who is deterred by notes, I add that the text can be read with no reference whatsoever to them; they may be ignored or, for those interested, be read at a later time.

Many of the observations, analyses, and data to follow were developed in various of my previous publications, and are used here again in a somewhat or greatly different context. It seemed it would be foolish to work out different ways of saying things I had said before, unless I had changed my mind. The source in which the original occurred is given.

Finally, I wish to offer my deep thanks to those who have assisted in the processes of getting this book written and published. In the midst of its first draft, I was much helped by the solicited criticisms of James Cypher, Michael Keaton, and Fred Doe (the latter currently studying economics at Berkeley). As the work went on, I was gratified by the various forms of assistance provided by Edward S. Herman, Howard Zinn, and, again, Michael Keaton. When Pluto Press accepted the manuscript, the subsequent and numerous suggestions of Roger van Zwanenberg of Pluto were vital in leading to a substantial revision. And I can never sufficiently express my gratitude for the constant encouragement and help of my wife, Anna.

Bologna,
November, 1999

Preface to the New Edition

In the few short years since this book's initial publication, the world has been shaken by a connected series of minor earthquakes in its economic, military, and political realms. It is a main theme of the book that such was to be expected, as the ineluctable outcome of what are seen as contemporary capitalism's triumphs – the ubiquitous free markets and hyper-technology and extraordinary productivities of globalization. However, and as with the much-marveled successes of nineteenth-century imperialism, globalization has had a negative side to it; and, also as with imperialism, that negative side has been essential to what has been seen as the system's successes.

History does not and cannot repeat itself; the social process is made of too many interdependent changes in all spheres of social existence to allow constancy of any sort; from our era's failures we cannot expect a repetition of the eruptions of the early twentieth century, or the chaos, destruction, and disasters that ensued. What lies ahead will be very different; unfortunately, it may well be considerably worse, in both its quantitative and qualitative dimensions. How and why?

The hallmark of the past half century has been an ever-tighter integration of all elements of social existence over the entire globe: obviously in its economic affairs; also, however, and as a functional accompaniment and requirement of that integration there has also been an integration of the world's cultural, military, political and, not least, its environmental behavior. This is to say something else: Contemporary globalization, like the imperialism of the nineteenth century, could not have come into being without the dominance of a single power: Britain in the nineteenth century, for a while; the United States for the past half century, up to the present. It was what were deemed its successes that brought Britain down; the first stages of that same process as affecting the U.S. now seem well underway.

The explication and support for the foregoing generalizations are put forth in the newly-written Chapter 6, "The Unfolding Crises of the Twenty-first Century." Its contents represent an "updating" of processes already considered in the first edition – an "updating," however, which may be compared with the reportage of new earthquakes following the earlier rumbling of an underground volcano.

Prologue

WHAT HAS CAPITALISM DONE FOR US? TO US?

And how does it get away with it? "Get away with *what*?" a large percentage of well-off (and even some not well-off) would respond, in the United States and elsewhere. But for those whose hearts and minds have yet to be fully won over by capitalism, whose brains and eyes and feelings remain relatively intact; for those who have not lost all sense of the connectedness of each with all, of the need for and rewards of human solidarity – for us, whether comfortable or not, the world too often can seem like a nightmare without end.

It is a world in which, except for perhaps 15 per cent of its 6 billion people, each day involves a desperate struggle, more for survival than comfort. Even the privileged percentage could well shrink soon. Its members too could be engulfed by the economic, ecological, and social calamities capitalism necessarily entails (or produces as "side-effects").

Before the 1930s, capitalism was touted without irony as a society where "It's each for himself, and God for all" – until the Great Depression made that a bad joke. That slogan has yet to revive, but another and older phrase threatens to fit the social cruelties now spreading and deepening: a war of all against all. Notwithstanding, the paeans to capitalism have never been so loud as now, nor so unabashed. Never has capitalism been praised so fulsomely for its presumed virtues and its vices passed over so lightly, or – more to the point – trumpeted as virtues, thus heaping insult on mountains of injury.

The injuries have been, are, and will be of all sorts, always deeper, always more widespread. They have endured capitalism's more than two centuries, covering many of what economists call "long runs" – in which a better world for all perpetually awaits. Less bedazzled observers worry that the continuation of capitalism through the twenty-first century is more likely to finish us all off.

Capitalism's record has two sides to it. *Of course* it has meant improvements in most areas of human existence for some, whether measured in comfort, education, health, productivity, or income levels. But there is the other side, whose components are casually ignored or brushed aside by mainstream opinion-makers. Two centuries ago there were fewer than 1 billion people in the world.[1] Now more than 3 billion people live in a state of misery and deprivation. In the prehistoric, ancient, medieval, and early modern worlds the means for universal well-being did not exist; now they do. Nor should it be forgotten that primitive peoples – whatever the dangers and hardships of their existence – very probably were better fed, clothed, and housed and more secure in their lives than the several billions who have been or are now being uprooted from their traditional ways of life as a result of capitalism's conquests.

In that primitive past there were innumerable tribes. What exists now instead are *"two* tribes" (to adopt Disraeli's words): one relatively small and *very* rich, one enormously large and *very* poor. Both despite and because of what is generally seen as "progress," the gap between them has not narrowed, but has widened, and does so ever more rapidly.[2]

The accelerating damages through capitalism's existence have destroyed or ruined innumerable millions of people and whole cultures and societies, and have pulverized the mortar of social traditions that protect human beings from the worst within and between us. Doubtless some of what was lost is better so; but also lost was much of great value when set against the culture of commercialism that now rules.

As if that were not bad enough, capitalism's pressures for unremitting economic growth hold as permanent hostage the flora and fauna, the air, the soil, and the water of the planet – never to be freed, fated to succumb to capital's voraciousness and the "free market's" heedlessness.

The millennia preceding industrial capitalism too often made for Hobbesian lives – "nasty, brutish, and short." Nonetheless, our, and other, species survived and flourished over those millennia. Among the achievements of the modern world are many which none would wish to see lost; but taken as a whole, the results of those "achievements" threaten the survival of most species, including our own.

How is it, then, that with such a dubious record – and such dire prospects – capitalism is less resisted and more popular than ever? One answer lies in the sources and uses of capitalist power. That power is manifested in the economic, political, and cultural dimensions of our existence, and it strengthens in line with technological advance. For capitalism's ongoing purposes and my present concern, those advances that help to shape thought and feeling, those in communications are most relevant: they have facilitated the processes by which our "cultural space" becomes totally dominated by commercialism, serving most especially the super-corporations and their "boughten" political cohorts.

Thus, in the three "dimensions" just noted, and in addition to the power that has brute force or sheer money behind it (as between rich and poor nations, or employers and employees, for example), there is the power of supporting ideas. The latter function in all the components of the media and, among other areas and most pertinently to what follows, not least in the economics profession.[3]

In the realm of ideas and ideology, the focus of this book will be considerably more on the role of economists than of historians, sociologists, and political scientists. That is not meant to slight the latters' substantial contributions – for better and for worse – to the understanding (and misunderstanding) of contemporary capitalism.

Underlying the analysis here is the view that history is the *sine qua non* for understanding economic life;[4] that the structures and relationships of society (most especially those of power, usually seen as a political concept) determine the quantitative and qualitative aspects of our existence; that in a *capitalist* society economic structures and relationships are critical; that moving within social processes – economic, cultural, political, scientific – are *ideas* produced by and producing changes in *all* those structures and relationships; and that, finally, among such sets of ideas in a capitalist society, economic arguments naturally tend to carry the most weight.[5]

*

The three chapters that comprise Part I[6] trace out the intricate relationship between capitalist development and concurrent economic thought from the mid-eighteenth century to the end of World War II. What became the economics profession almost always served to support capitalism, while obscuring its harmful consequences – with, only now and then, voices of reform or opposition.

Part II, which examines the decades from 1945 to the present, continues the examination of the customary symbiotic relationships between capitalism and economics, and focuses on the developments that have taken us to the present period of intense globalization. The book concludes with a critique of contemporary capitalism and its supportive theory, and briefly suggests alternatives.

The remainder of this Prologue provides a bird's-eye view of that complex set of developments. Its objective is to give the reader an early and overall sense of the shape and directions and "feel" of the book.

Beginning with Adam Smith (1723–90) and the British industrial revolution we first turn to the socioeconomic processes that made capitalism possible and note the imperatives capitalism must meet in order to survive, let alone to flourish, and let the devil take the hindmost – which the devil invariably does.

THE DYNAMICS OF CAPITALIST DEVELOPMENT

Capitalism and economics, of course, both had an embryonic existence before 1750, but neither possessed the dynamism or the strength underway by 1800 – a swiftness of change, as will be seen, intrinsic to the capitalist process. Hindsight informs us that by 1800 the rise of industrial capitalism had become irreversible in Britain. Also by then the socioeconomic foundations of what became "classical political economy" had been put in place by the three earliest of its main thinkers: Adam Smith, Thomas Robert Malthus (1766–1834), and Jeremy Bentham (1748–1832).

Then, in 1817, capitalism's development brought forth the key theoretical treatise of David Ricardo (1772–1823); in 1848, John Stuart Mill (1806–1873) synthesized the main elements of classical political economy, in what was the last major work of that body of thought. In that same year, Karl Marx's (1818–83) and Friedrich Engels' (1820–95) portentous *Communist Manifesto* exploded into existence.

Taken together, the efforts of Smith, Malthus, and Bentham, followed by those of Ricardo, Mill, and Marx, laid the foundations for the arguments which to this day support or oppose capitalism's maintenance, spread, reform, or dissolution. The main elements of all these will be analyzed in the following chapter. Here we examine the when, the whys, and the wherefores of this most dynamic of social systems.

Capitalism's nature and nurture

Some scholars contend that capitalism first took hold in medieval Italy, or in seventeenth-century Holland, rather than in Britain. But if capitalism is taken as meaning *both* economic *and* social processes and relationships going well beyond production and trade for profit, eighteenth-century Britain commands our attention.[7]

There and then capitalism had developed the momentum and depth essential to a sturdy birth and survival. It was unlikely to end except by forces external to it,[8] or by revolution.

The momentum of the capitalist process was driven by efforts seeking to satisfy its three systemic imperatives: expansion, exploitation, and oligarchic rule. Capitalism could only meet *those* imperatives within a larger context of three overlapping developments that it strengthened and was in turn strengthened by: colonialism (which became imperialism, and has now become globalization),[9] industrialization, and nationalism.

Taken together, the meeting of these imperatives, joined with a satisfactory development of the foregoing elements, provide the basis for capitalism's viability. Yet that same set of processes and relationships inexorably produces an intermittent burst of crises – threats to its survival that have all too often became ugly realities.

We shall see that Adam Smith was the first conscious proponent for what was becoming a capitalist society. Marx, in becoming the first to posit capitalism's "economic laws of motion," also became its first profound critic. His arguments remain fundamental to successive critiques. The following historically precocious passages from his and Engels' *Communist Manifesto* (1848) can serve as a vivid introduction to our discussion of the ravenous appetites of the capitalist process, words that fit today's processes at least as much as those of his own time:

> The bourgeoisie cannot exist without constantly revolutionizing the instruments of production, and thereby the relations of production, and with them the whole relations of society. Conservation of the old modes of production in unaltered form, was on the contrary, the first condition of existence for all earlier industrial classes. Constant revolutionizing of production, uninterrupted disturbance of all social conditions, ever-lasting uncertainty and agitation distinguish the bourgeois epoch from all earlier ones. All fixed, fast-frozen relations, with their train of ancient and venerable prejudices and opinions, are swept away, all new-formed ones become antiquated before they can ossify. All that is solid melts into air, all that is holy is profaned, and man is at last compelled to face with sober senses his real conditions of life and his relations with his kind.
>
> The need of a constantly expanding market for its products chases the bourgeoisie over the whole surface of the globe. It must nestle everywhere, settle everywhere, establish connexions everywhere. (1967c, 38)[10]

But *why* must capitalism always expand and exploit, as it rules oligarchically? And, assuming there are good answers to those questions, why are neither the questions nor the answers part of "economics"? (Where, indeed, the term "capitalism" – as distinct from the bland images of "free enterprise" or "free markets" – seldom if ever raises its controversial head.) Before progressing , here is a brief set of responses to the "why" of capitalism's life processes.

The heart of the matter: expansion and exploitation[11]

Throughout its history, capitalist profitability has required, and capitalist rule has provided, ever-changing means and areas of exploitation (where "areas" signify both geographic and social "space," as will be seen). The central relationship making this possible is the ownership and control of productive property: a small group that owns and controls, and a great majority that does not, and whose resulting powerlessness requires them to work for wages simply to survive. Those social relations between these two classes are the basis vital for capitalist development.

Given those social relations, the strengths of each capitalist enterprise and nation, and of global capitalism, vary in accordance with the volume, scope, and rate of capital accumulation: that is, the expansion of the capitalist's capital. This refers to the driving force of capitalist development, the "ploughing back of profits" (or, as Marx saw it, of "surplus value"[12]), which converts those profits into additional capital. Capitalists as such are not driven by the desire for higher consumption – given that their consumption is normally at the social maximum – but by the passion for wealth. Marx put it succinctly in this famous passage:

> he shares with the miser the passion for wealth as wealth. But that which in the miser is a mere idiosyncrasy, is, in the capitalist, the effect of the social mechanism of which he is but one of the wheels. Moreover, the development of capitalist production makes it constantly necessary to keep increasing the amount of the capital ... in a given industrial undertaking, and competition makes the immanent laws of capitalist production to be felt by each individual capitalist, as external coercive laws. It compels him to keep constantly extending his capital, in order to preserve it, but extend it he cannot, except by means of progressive accumulation. (1867a, 649)[13]

Capital accumulation for present purposes may be seen as the basis for *economic* growth or expansion. That has always been tightly interwoven with processes of extensive and intensive *geographic* expansion – most intensively in its contemporary expression as "globalization."

It is useful to think of economic and geographic expansion as being, respectively, *vertical* (the economy expanding "upward") and *horizontal* (national capitalism expanding its power outward over weaker societies), the former requiring and always pressing for the latter.

The two forms of expansion taken together may be seen as the essence of the capitalist *process*, its "heartbeat." In turn, they depend on capital's ability to exploit labor and the State's cooperation in external expansion – capitalism's "muscles." And the "brain" of the capitalist process, the third member of the triad, is rule – direct and indirect – by capital.

But how can that be, especially when it is understood that political democracy normally follows in capitalism's path? To answer that requires a pause for a brief discussion of the limitations of political democracy. Then we return to the processes of expansion.

Oligarchic rule?

Taking account of modern economic and social history helps to confront that seeming paradox. The "democracy" that capitalism brings in its path – that, indeed, it has required – is *political* democracy; that is, the formal right on the part of the citizenry to install and remove those who make up their governments, through the electoral process. But that process is predictably contaminated when it coexists with capitalism's essential stratifications of income, wealth, and power – all three of which are characterized by substantial inequality, enabling the members of the higher levels of income and wealth to maintain or increase the inequality of power and to initiate policies favoring them. Or, just as important, to effectively veto those that do not. Such has always been the case, throughout recorded history.

Oligarchic rule was the norm before capitalism, of course; but its continuity in the modern era within political democracies constitutes a puzzle: until one thinks about it. As Robert McChesney (in keeping with many others) points out:

> Capitalism benefits from having a formally democratic system, but capitalism works best when elites make most fundamental decisions and the bulk of the population is depoliticized. (1999, 3)

Throughout the capitalist era, whether in the United States or elsewhere, power has (so to speak) been "bought." Not for nothing, for example, was the U.S. Senate called "the rich man's club" in the years termed "the gilded age," or "the great barbecue" when there was no direct election of senators. But when that changed, means were found to bring about the same result, with respect to the Senate as with other areas of government – in keeping with Woodrow Wilson's remark (made in 1912) that "When the government becomes important, it becomes important to control the government."

In one variation or another, at all levels of sociopolitical power and irrespective of nation, that has been so. This is not to overlook the instances (most especially after World War II) when, in the richest capitalist nations, socioeconomic policies were put in place favoring, also, the lower 80 per cent of the population. But, as will be discussed at length in Part II, those developments – the social democracies of Britain and Western Europe, and the "corporate liberalism" of the United States – were also economically beneficial to those at the top. When they ceased to seem so, in the 1970s, the "corporate counterattack"[14] took hold. That about-face was much facilitated, indeed made possible, by the role and control of the media, which has now become so common (and continues to grow). That role, the indirect use of power, has now been joined to raw money – where, more often than not, it is one faction at the top vying with another faction, also at the top. But quite apart from (although it never *is* apart from) the purchasing of politics, politicians, and power, the ugly truth behind the capitalist fig leaf of political democracy is that the overwhelming majority of the population is without means of support, except insofar as they earn their incomes on the terms of those who own and control the means of production. If there is any difference between the past and the present, it resides in the existence of populations in the politically democratic countries who have been so mesmerized – or trapped, or lost – in the jungles of consumerism that force is no longer necessary to gain their acquiescence in an exploitative and otherwise harmful social system.

That takes us back to *expansion*. The true nature and consequences of capitalism's need for inequality – of income, wealth, status, and power – and the exploitation enabling it, have been effectively obscured in the leading industrial capitalist nations proportionate to the degree that the needs for expansion have been met. This has been most effectively so in the United States, and remains one of the several qualities of U.S. capitalist development making for the comparative absence of class consciousness and conflict in the United States as compared with Europe.[15]

What exploitation?

It is important to digress here to examine the matter of "exploitation," a concept that does not *exist* in contemporary economics. We take a moment now to pursue a few central points, which will be elaborated in later chapters when appropriate.

Economics provides no plausible explanation for the most crucial question, "Where do profits come from?"[16] Instead, all recipients of incomes – interest, profits, rents, and wages – are seen as receiving a return for their contribution to production: thus, for example, profits are normally discussed as "earnings."

However, when we examine two fundamental works of classical political economy – those of Adam Smith and David Ricardo – we see that they took exploitation as normal and necessary, but the term itself was not used. What *was* used was a presumption that workers ought naturally to receive subsistence wages, unconnected to their production or productivity, wages sufficient only to keep them alive, reproducing, and working.

What Smith took for granted, Ricardo pursued (though not for our purposes). He saw wages and profits as having an inverse relationship – if one went up, the other had to go down – and showed that existing protective tariffs on imported grain (called "corn" in Britain), by raising the price of bread, therefore raised wages, and lowered profits. The advantage went to the landed gentry, at the expense of the incipient industry Ricardo championed. He called such agricultural gains "rents" or "unearned income."

Marx took the logic of Ricardo's argument on rent and applied it just as rigorously against profits. In doing so, he had placed a land-mine in classical political economy. Avoiding that was a major reason for the subsequent replacement of classical by "neoclassical" economics. The latter's dreamlike abstractions allowed profits to be "earned."

But surely, the exploitation Marx saw as essential to capitalist development has – even in the rich democracies – been much lowered, even disappeared? Not quite. Contemporary data regarding exploitation and employment noted in Chapter 5 reveal that after the substantial *reduction* of worker exploitation of the 1950s and 1960s, there ensued a steady and pervasive *increase* in exploitation of workers in both the commodity and service sectors in the advanced industrial nations – led by the United States.

And in the "emerging economies"? The harrowing condition of workers of the early industrial revolution have been outstripped by those in the developing countries. Furthermore, the numbers of those harmed are a large multiple of the earlier period – with, moreover, no surcease to be found in any conceivable "long run."

Capitalist development, and the nature and evolution of classical political economy and subsequent transformation to neoclassicism, will be examined in the first two chapters of Part I; the collapse of capitalism and that economics occupies Chapter 3. Part II studies the rebirth and mutations of capitalism and the concomitant mutations of economics up to the present.

Of all that, more later. Now we return to our previous focus on expansion to elaborate somewhat on the crucial question of "horizontal" expansion. The Prologue concludes with some observations on the whys and wherefores of economic theorizing, as distinct from the theories themselves.

"Trade and the flag": Which follows which?

Capitalism and the nation-state had their formative years in the sixteenth and seventeenth centuries, with each feeding on and strengthening the other. It was a period of permanent warfare fought mostly on the high seas, over who would control which part(s) of the expanding "overseas empire." Without military protection merchants could barely survive, let alone prosper from, an expedition to the areas fought over by many nations.

The overseas expansion that began with Portugal and Spain in the 1500s – both holdover feudal societies obsessed with "cross and flag" – continued with the very practical Dutch in the 1600s. That took the conflict into the eighteenth century, where it became a seemingly endless bloody struggle between the British and the French.

Holland, France, and Britain were bent on winning out in a fierce conflict requiring military strength and yielding economic gain: and it was believed that for the latter to rise, so also must the former; and vice versa: the essence of "mercantilism." Those doctrines and practices were the target of Adam Smith in his *Wealth of Nations* (1776).[17]

The economic side of the pre-capitalist period had many elements to it. First, economic strength was essential for military strength, which in its turn was essential for the nation's survival *as* a nation (in the seventeenth century there was international war in all but four years). Second, the era was one in which the economy's main dynamism came from foreign trade (with production and finance dependent). And third, the most gainful aspect of trade was in such overseas products as "spices" (of which there were several hundred, including both food and medicinal products), tobacco, cotton, and, increasingly important over the period, slaves; it was the epoch of "beggar thy neighbor."[18] Marx called the associated processes "primitive accumulation":

> The discovery of gold and silver in America, the extirpation, enslavement and entombment in mines of the aboriginal population, the beginnings of the conquest and looting of the East Indies, the turning of Africa into a warren for the hunting of black-skins, signalised the rosy dawn of the era of capitalist production. These idyllic proceedings are the chief momenta of primitive accumulation. (1967a, 751)

Given worker exploitation, this leaves unanswered the question "Why are economic and geographic expansion necessary for capitalist profitability?" Once again, where do profits come from? When "capitalists" *manage* an enterprise (which, except for small businesses, they do not), they earn an income for that contribution to production. But profits are something in addition. They are a return to the *ownership* and control of capital, of the means of production – that is, of the means of life. In this they are the same as interest on borrowed money, or rent for the ownership of land. The following words from John Maynard Keynes (1883–1946) might well have been written by Ricardo:[19]

> Interest to-day rewards no genuine sacrifice, any more than does the rent of land. The owner of capital can obtain interest because capital is scarce, just as the owner of land can obtain rent because land is scarce. But whilst there may be intrinsic reasons for the scarcity of land, there are no intrinsic reasons for the scarcity of capital. (1936, 376)

As we will see in subsequent chapters, Keynes went on to argue that the industrialization process brings about levels of productive capacity which – under existing conditions of the inequality of income and wealth, and therefore of limited purchasing power – reduce capital's scarcity. Hence, the justification for the reward to capital dwindles to vanishing point. Keynes, though a reluctant supporter of capitalism (as the lesser of all evils), became infamous to the financial class when he argued that the abundance of capital should lead to "the euthanasia of the rentier, and, consequently, the euthanasia of the cumulative oppressive power of the capitalist to exploit the scarcity-value of capital" (ibid.).

In the absence of governmental policies for what Keynes called social consumption (public housing, and so on), and social investment (highways, bridges, schools),[20] capital "scarcity" can be maintained or created, if at all, only by further private investment, increasing sales for the industries producing materials and equipment but *also* adding to already excess productive capacities; or by increasing exports.[21] Clearly, these latter will ultimately run into a wall. They did so in the 1930s, and led Keynes to develop his reformist perspective on capitalism.

There are, of course, other seeming means for continuous expansion: 1) that created by substantial technological change, and 2) expansion enabled by always rising consumer debt. Together, they explain much of the great expansions since World War II. But the wall exists for them also, as we shall see in the discussion in Part II. There an even more forbidding ecological wall looms and will also come into focus.

These have been very large generalizations. In our examination of the history of capitalism since 1750 it will be seen that differences and complexities have been numerous among capitalist nations and in any one nation over time. Through that jungle of complexities, the basic characteristics of capitalism remain decisive – even as this most volatile of social formations changes in many ways for many reasons, endlessly and heedlessly producing and requiring, wracked and nourished by, alterations in all quarters of social existence: everywhere.

In sum

Capitalist expansion processes may be seen as something like the progress of a tightrope walker, precariously poised along an always shifting path of balance and imbalance. This is the path of what used to be called "the trade (or business) cycle" – one process of expansion and contraction (or "recession") after another: until, that is, the 1920s and 1930s, when one *economy* after another crashed. The world was soon thereafter ravaged by the violence of the worst war ever.

That two-decade period was framed by two world wars, the first a product of all the competition, tension, and conflicts – economic, political, global – that give the modern world its dynamism; the second, a consequence of the inability of that chaos to be resolved other than by massive destruction. By 1945, only one major power stood standing, the United States: it could and had to create a new and quite different global economy, if capitalism was to be brought back to life. We shall see that *two* different global economies were created – both by the United States. The first extended through the 1950s into the 1970s, very much dominated by the effects of World War II and the ensuing Cold War, and the second the considerably more intensified and "financialized" global economy, whose hold began to tighten in the 1980s, and increasingly so through the 1990s. In examining those two major developments, we will see that, however much they differed from prior developments and from each other, they shared two characteristics with their predecessors: 1) tendencies toward greatly rising production and productivity and rapid social change and an always greater interdependence within and between societies – for better and for worse, and 2) the creation of a supporting ideology, propagated not least (if not seen as such) by the economics profession.

We conclude this Prologue with a general – overall, abstract – discussion of the ways in which "economics" has dealt with, influenced, and has been influenced by – or stayed aloof from – the processes of capitalist-dominated history. In doing so, we enter the exotic realms of "methodology," realms which for economics have more often than not been difficult to distinguish from those of ideology.

THE SOCIOLOGY OF ECONOMIC THEORY[22]

Methodology may be seen as the systematic analysis of theory; more exactly, it explores the whys and wherefores, aims and means, and validity of a particular theory, or even a whole school of thought. Its defining characteristic is not so much a concern with the *content* of analysis as with the how and the why by which that content is selected, organized, and used to construct (in our case) economic theories and, by extension, the manner in which they lead to (or are occasioned by) associated policies. Something like the concern of an optometrist, who is not interested in what you look at but whether you see it clearly; and if not, why not.

Among the matters relevant to such inquiries are those that entail questions of abstraction, factuality, and focus: what is abstracted *from* and on what level (and why), what elements are focused *upon*, and how closely, leaving what are to become the theory's "variables" (and why). Both the "whats" and the "whys" are important.

Earlier, it was insisted that economic understanding requires *at least,* but not only, history, the study of social connections over time. No economic relationships or processes can be adequately understood unless approached historically; nor can they be understood except in their dynamic connections with other aspects of social existence (political, technological, cultural): the very term "economy" is itself an abstraction invented so as to allow "economic analysis." There are many questions to be answered before one can decide that a particular theorizing process is or is not valid, and some of those will be faced in ensuing chapters. Here let us examine those regarding "history" and the "economy." In the very first course I took in economic history, and in its very first meeting, the professor raised these questions: "Supposing that historical understanding is essential for social understanding, then which history? When, and where, and *why* should we study *that* history? Should one choose to study France in the eighteenth century? And if so, how do you decide between an inquiry into Voltaire's laundry tags, rather than, say, the processes leading up the French Revolution? Or should something else be chosen? Is there a theory of history that enables one to choose? How does one choose that and not some other theory of history?"[23] To which may be added, and *who* does the choosing? And why? We will return to those questions more than once in later chapters.

"The economy"

Just as economics came into being with capitalism, so did the notion of "an economy." *Of course* there were "economic" activities before capitalism (Aristotle was only the most notable among those discussing them). They took place in social formations – ancient, medieval, early modern – in which those activities were always pursued *within* a set of primary institutions and social values rather than set off from or dominating the larger social process. As will be seen, Adam Smith was the first to propose that an "economic system" could be "left to itself," the origin of the term *laissez-faire* (now called "a free market economy"). The shocking quality of that notion for other than modern times was clearly portrayed in the following passage from R.H. Tawney's perennially illuminating masterpiece, *Religion and the Rise of Capitalism*:

> to found a science of society upon the assumption that the appetite for economic gain is a constant and measurable force, to be accepted, like other natural forces, as an inevitable and self-evident *datum* would have appeared to the medieval thinker as hardly less irrational or less immoral than to make the premise of social philosophy the unrestrained operation of such necessary human attributes as pugnacity or the sexual instinct.[24]

Objectivity and neutrality

So then, what has usually engendered conventional economic theory? The view that seems to me most persuasive holds that "policy precedes theory." That is, the efforts and ideas involved in developing theory are driven and guided by sociopolitical problems and possibilities that the theorist envisions, senses, grapples with, is troubled or inspired by. These (or other attitudes or feelings) in turn stimulate the thinker to identify particular social processes as being crucial, and as requiring certain changes which, when made, will permit desirable conditions to persist, eliminate undesirable conditions, and/or make way for a better social order.

The preceding generalizations most obviously apply to the political "tracts" of the "mercantilist" seventeenth and eighteenth centuries. Those tracts were normally addressed to the State to begin, modify, or end a particular policy (regarding trade or industry). If less obviously, the generalizations also fit the more comprehensive and profound theorists who followed – as diverse as Adam Smith, Karl Marx, and J.M. Keynes – who sought, respectively, to foster, overthrow, and save capitalism.

Though this characterization of the process of theorizing seems almost crude, it nonetheless fits all important social thinkers. The crux of the matter has to do with the difference between objectivity and neutrality.[25]

Any work claiming to meet the standards of modern science has to satisfy at least the two standards that essentially define objectivity: those of fact and logic. But one can meet those standards with total rigor, while at the same time serving an ideology. It all depends not on whether one has adhered to evidence and logic, but which questions are asked and which are *not*. That in turn depends on the theorist's experience, interests, biases, aims, values – all dominantly subjective. With all that, neutrality fades into the shadows.

Concerning social matters, nobody is "neutral." Indeed, it is fair to say that one wouldn't wish to know anyone who *is* – one, oblivious of the outcome of this, that, and the other aspect of the social process, others' wealth or poverty, health, or illness, ignorance or education, security or insecurity, and so on. We all care in one way or another about all those matters and others, of course. It might be easy occasionally to suppress or repress such concerns; nonetheless, they exist. And, the more self-conscious thinkers are about such matters, the more unlikely they are to be "objective" in even the casual use of the term.

In sum, one's position on social matters determines one's interests. If one is a "social scientist," the questions one asks of social materials – what they are, their particulars, and whether this is taken as central and that is set aside as "given" – emerge from those interests, consciously or not.

When this reasoning is applied to economic thought, the results may well be shocking, but they should not be surprising. Thus it is often alarming to note what mainstream economists do and do *not* examine, what questions they do and do *not* ask, what aspects of the economy (and important connections with the rest of the social process) they do and do *not* take into account. In this connection, it may be illuminating to contrast the approach of "the first economist," Adam Smith, and the neoclassicists of the late nineteenth century who, after being upended by the depression of the 1930s, are once more dominant.

For one as critical of capitalism as I am, there are ample grounds for criticism of Adam Smith's work, and some of those criticisms will emerge in the first chapter. Having said that, it may also be said that

Smith was not only "the first economist," but he can be seen doing in his day what economists should be expected to do, but nowadays is rarely done.

What should economists be expected to do?

We may begin by answering that the interested public needs and expects to get good answers to the question "What do we need to know about the economy?" And to the closely related question "And what can and must we do to have the economy serve our human and social and ecological needs?"

Smith sought honestly and admirably to answer at least some of those questions in his *Wealth of Nations;* so, however, did Karl Marx in *Capital* and other works. That being so, it becomes clear that these apparently simple questions are – and cannot help but be – "loaded." For if Smith and Marx were answering similar questions, it is obvious that there had to be different references for "we" and "our."

For Smith the reference was to the incipient industrial capitalist; for Marx it was the working class. Nor is it uninteresting to note that both Smith and Marx assumed that the exploitation of workers was essential to the functioning of capitalism, but Smith's audience was largely those who were (or would be) doing the exploitation, Marx's the exploited. Both answered the questions, well and honorably: that they did so in quite different ways points to the critical difference between "objectivity" and "neutrality." Both were objective, stretching neither fact nor logic, neither was neutral: they spoke to contrasting social interests.

But neoclassical economics does not answer the questions noted above, from *any* standpoint. It starts with a set of assumptions and values (muted or taken for granted) and proceeds, using only logic, to assert (through assumptions) what is not so and to follow that with a set of analyses and prescriptions which, although they serve the interests of those holding power in the capitalist status quo, are put forth as equally valid for the society as a whole.

Neoclassical economists do not treat economics as a discipline seeking to inform the public "what it needs to know about the economy," for their economics says *nothing* about the economy.[26] Instead, its definition of economics is "the science of allocating scarce resources to unlimited wants." But the reality is that resources are *not* scarce and human wants are *not* unlimited – except in the sense that resources are *made* to be scarce through some combination of frivolous and wasteful patterns of consumption and production, and that wants are *induced* through advertising to become unlimited.[27]

All that will be examined more fully as we proceed, as will the consequences of the policies recommended by the neoclassical economists, past and present.

As we now move ahead to Chapter 1 and its consideration of the first century of industrialism and political economy, a last "methodological" observation seems appropriate. Adam Smith's great work was a study of complex historical processes *over* time at particular key points *in* time. Connections between business and politics, technology and business, between all that and the material conditions of diverse groups – "classes," Smith called them – were a major focus. That method of inquiry came to be termed "political economy." From the 1860s onward, economic thought became "modern." In that process, one after another – and ultimately all – of those "connections" were set aside, taken as "given" – that is, left unexamined, ignored, even seen as not having meaning.

During and in the aftermath of the depression of the 1930s, such economics lurked fecklessly in the shadows. Now it is back again. And its eager and vociferous cohorts seem close to having defined out of existence the "political economy" that once did and still should form the bedrock of economics as a discipline.

Smith, the first economist, had studied how (almost) all matters relevant for his analysis functioned and interacted. It may be wondered how many mainstream economists today – while claiming *The Wealth of Nations* as the basis for "free market economics" – have studied any, let alone all, of the relevant connections. Indeed, it may be wondered how many of them have ever even read Smith, and if they have, what their reactions were to Smith's view of "businessmen":

> an order of men whose interest is never exactly the same with that of the public, who have generally an interest to deceive and even to oppress the public, and who have, upon many occasions, both deceived and oppressed it. (1776, 250)

Yet, Smith's work was seminal in facilitating the triumph of precisely that "order of men" over any and all other social forces. How and why Smith could come to such seemingly conflicting conclusions is part of what we next consider.

Part I: 1750–1945

1 Birth: The Industrial Revolution and Classical Political Economy, 1750–1850

THE START OF SOMETHING BIG

Just as Medieval Europe grew out of the decayed remnants of the Roman Empire, and did so in consequence of innumerable and diverse struggles over long stretches of time and space, so did capitalism thrust its way into history over the enfeebled elements of monarchical–mercantilist Europe. But, as noted in the Prologue, capitalism could do so only in dynamic, uneven, and often explosive relationships with its siblings – colonialism, nationalism, and industrialism.

The ensuing centuries, whether viewed in quantitative or qualitative, in economic, social, cultural, political, technological or military terms, or as a set of achievements and disasters or both, made all preceding epochs seem quaint in comparison.

That the industrial revolution and robust capitalism took hold first in Britain is now rarely disputed; nor, any longer, are the reasons why it all took place there and then, and not elsewhere. The reasons are many – the appropriate resources, a long history of pre-modern industry, of involvement in global commerce and extensive colonial holdings and finally and critically, a relatively fluid social process compared to others at that time.

Capitalism lives by change, produces it as no other social formation, and *needs* it as no other, as Marx had seen in 1848: "Constant revolutionizing of production, uninterrupted disturbance of all social conditions ... " But its very birth required much in the way of changes, also. To understand how and why that requirement was met first in Great Britain it is pertinent to expand on generalizations made in the Prologue by comparing Britain with France – a seemingly likely competitor for becoming an industrial capitalist nation. In the event, however, France trailed Britain by more than a century.

Why Britain took the lead

A casual look at France's relevant characteristics in the seventeenth and eighteenth centuries would suggest a different outcome, for it too appeared to possess the prerequisites. In addition to being the oldest and the strongest of nation-states, France claimed a substantial empire and excellent natural resources, had a relatively large population, and it too was dotted by thriving pre-modern industries. But, a closer look – most notably that of John U. Nef, in *Industry and Government in France and England, 1540–1640* (1940) – shows that France lagged behind not only Britain throughout the nineteenth century but also the as yet non-existent Germany[1] and the new United States – not because France lacked the vital material bases for industrial capitalism, but because of the social framework and standards that led to the misuse of its advantages.

That this would be so had its roots most especially in what happened as regards the State in England but did *not* happen in France – and why – most pointedly in the seventeenth century. As the 1640s began, England was entering a new period of institutional transformation, which broke the ground for the socioeconomic flexibility enabling modern industry and capitalist rule to come into being. France, meanwhile, though richer and more powerful than England, was developing increased socoioeconomic rigidities. Thus, to mention "1640" in England would elicit the likely response: "Puritan Revolution." For the French the response (setting the arts aside) would focus instead on the splendor of the court and the military prowess of Louis XIV's France; and his first minister, Colbert, was the most insistent and the most coherent of all "mercantilists" – the main target of Smith's *Wealth of Nations*. In the very years when Britain was moving toward industrial capitalism, Napoleon was expanding east and south, through Europe and into the Mediterranean.

Seemingly unbeknownst to the French, the strengthening of British industry would also bring military superiority, on land and sea; meanwhile, the French derided them as becoming "a nation of shopkeepers." When the stodgy British defeated Napoleon at Waterloo, they also gained a growing hegemony over the economic development (among other matters) of Europe. The added strength engendered more of the same, sufficient to allow Britain to "rule the waves" – both literally and figuratively – for the rest of the century.

The Puritan Revolution has often been seen as being more "bourgeois" than "Puritan," but the division is more usefully viewed as one between traditionalists and republicans.[2] Its main consequence (for present purposes) was the breaking up of debilitating remnants of feudalism and the codification of limits on the power of the Crown. By the mid-eighteenth century that meant more leeway for unfettered *private* power.

Commodification as revolution

The key element in that freeing-up process – wherein traditions of social control and stability were displaced by commercial criteria and violent change – was the "enclosure movement" of the late eighteenth century.[3] What was being "enclosed" were the agricultural lands of Britain, whether for the grazing of sheep or the cultivation of grains.

The most important result of the enclosures was the commodification of both land and labor: the transformation of countless thousands of small farms into (by 1790) giant holdings (2,000–3,000 large landlords owning 75 per cent of the cultivable acreage). "Commodification" meant that all goods and services would be up for sale; thus it also meant the elimination of traditional social protections. A major result of all this was a class of powerless, dispossessed farmers, able to survive only by "welfare" or *de facto* slave labor.[4]

The resulting conditions for what had been "a bold peasantry" were considerably worse than those just noted, cruel though they were. The whole way of life of a large percentage of the population was destroyed; and though traditional rural life often (though not in all respects or always) deserved Marx's characterization of "idiocy" (to which could be added brutality), it had its virtues as well. Be that as it may, the fate of what had been rural people in the century stretching from 1750 to 1850 became for several generations a living urban hell – a hell made of cotton.

Before pursuing the important direct and indirect role of cotton in British development and the distribution of its benefits and costs, it is more than simply relevant to undertake a specific statement on the role of the State in the industrial capitalist processes of Britain. This, not only because that role *was* important, but because the role the State has played in the economic development of *all* nations has been (and remains) so generally ignored, denigrated, or denied – or simply misunderstood. Rarely is that the case for economic historians. Usually it is the case for economic theorists and the ideologues of capitalism (often the same people): one of the larger sets of "misunderstandings" prompting this book.[5]

THE STATE: NOW YOU SEE IT, NOW YOU DON'T

All agree that what the State has or has not done has been and remains of great importance in the development of society. Beyond that simple statement, disagreement begins and becomes sharp. When has the State's role been beneficial and when harmful? When vital and when of small consequence? What is the "composition" of the State, as between public and private institutions (or even persons)? These and other such questions place an examination of the role of the State in a context of both theoretical and ideological dispute, while raising still another, analytically more intricate question. To what degree and in what ways does the relationship of the State to economic development reveal and in what ways conceal the changing structure and functions of social *power*?

Virtually all the debate over these highly charged questions between those who wish to minimize and those who wish to extend the State's role centers on easily discernible, specific policies: statutes, regulations, fiscal and monetary and commercial policies, subsidies, welfare, and the like. But a minimal understanding of the State's role requires that we also comprehend what the State has forced or allowed to be prevented or *undone* and, among other matters, what the State has been responsible for that did not appear in specific actions; that did not, often, "appear" at all.

To appreciate the complications – and the importance – of this point would of course require going well beyond what is practical here. But an initial grasp of the important confusions may be had by a study of the quote that follows, a statement made by a reputable mainstream economic historian of both Britain and Germany, W.O. Henderson. He declares of Britain that

> In the age of *laissez-faire* the role of government in economic affairs was a passive one ... The social evils in town and countryside that followed in the wake of the Industrial Revolution might have been alleviated at an earlier date if the governing classes had been better informed about the great changes that were taking place in the mines and factories ... The government was inactive because it saw no good reason why it should do anything.[6]

The "passivity" and "inactivity" of the "government" and "governing classes" are the key terms here. They stand in most minds for the role of the British "State" in the industrial revolution, as they did in Henderson here (and elsewhere in his writing). But, meticulous researcher that he was, he *could* surely have learned that "the governing classes," far from being passive and inactive, were the prime movers, and, as well, the prime beneficiaries of the "social evils" and the "great changes" of the time. Furthermore, that their "inactivity" and inability to see any "good reason" why they "should do anything" are explicable in terms of their combination of private self-interest and public power.

The government of Britain in the "age of *laissez-faire*" – whether in the Commons or the Lords – was made up largely of landed gentry and nobility and those (some being in the latter groups also) incipient or emerging "Whigs" whose power and aspirations centered on those dreadful and always deepening and expanding coal mines and hoped-for expanding trade (not least with colonies, where conditions were made at least as bad) and industry. Those public and private "roles," taken together (and setting aside the always weakening Crown), were then tantamount to much of what can be meant by "the State": then and there, and, in different detail, here and now.

There are surface differences between the evictions of "a once bold peasantry" from their copyholds during the Enclosures (where the agency was Parliament and the "judge" was the prime power in the locality), and the conditions in the mills and coal mines.[7] Similarly, there were differences between British conditions and those of German and U.S. workers (among others) in their economic processes. But there is more that is common than diverse as between those conditions: in all cases, those who were the State or whose voices resounded in its figurative halls were – as they are still – prominent among those directly responsible for and profiting from those same conditions.

It seems necessary – especially in a capitalist society – repeatedly to remind ourselves that the links between economic and political power are forged of the most durable steel. Indeed, that necessity grows always stronger in the modern world: as democracy has grown, so has the need – and the ability – for those in power to develop and to use direct and indirect modes of disinformation and misinformation, and to suppress plain information regarding those links of power. The generic term for all this has become "spin," with the media its stage, TV its star performer. Of that, much more in Part II.

As we now return to Britain's industrial revolution, and the disruption and horrors thus entailed for the largest part of the population, we may note in passing that the absence of democracy in that period very much simplified the tasks of the State at home. Within Britain, the use of force was perennial, with violence only intermittently necessary; abroad, both force and violence were the routine tasks of the State, if there was to be an expanding British Empire.

EMPEROR COTTON

The wool trade had been important in England since medieval times. Its production and trade grew in importance as the eighteenth century progressed; by its end, wool had long been vital to British economic strength. But with the emergence of the modern factory system, signaled by the first factory in 1815, cotton more than took wool's place. In the eighteenth century, wool production was not located in factories (as we understand the term) but in rural homes – "cottage industry" – usually as an integral complement of an agricultural family's work.

In the first years of the eighteenth century, the spinning wheel and the hand-loom were the technology of wool production. That the weaving was more efficient than the spinning (with the gap widening from the 1730s on) stimulated the invention of the spinning jenny; by the 1760s the "water frame" had been invented; in the 1780s the jenny and the water frame were combined in the "mule." That development effectively made cottage industry a thing of the past, bringing water-powered wool mills into being. Weaving, having fallen behind in efficiency, then developed the power loom as the nineteenth century opened. Watt's workable steam engine had been devised by 1776, and by 1815 that was combined with the mule and the power loom for cotton textiles to become the world's first modern factory.

The foregoing is an instance of capitalism's fusion with industrialization; all along that way, colonialism and nationalism were also doing their part. Wool was "grown" in English acres; cotton came from British colonies – first from the slave plantations of the British West Indies, then from their counterparts in North America – as, surprisingly, did most of the markets. As Hobsbawm points out,

> Until 1770 over ninety per cent of British cotton exports went to colonial markets ... mainly to Africa. The vast expansion of exports after 1750 gave the industry its impetus; between then and 1850 cotton exports multiplied ten times over. Cotton thus acquired its characteristic link with the underdeveloped world, which it retained and strengthened through all the various fluctuations of fortune. (1968, 41)

The first cotton factory using steam power, as noted, was not created until 1815. Following upon that, the cotton industry became the principal motive force of the industrial revolution – and, thus, of Britain's commercial, financial, and military dominance of the world, for many decades.

Hell on earth

The working conditions and wages of that first and of ensuing mills – to say nothing of coal mines and other new industries – were simply dreadful: "satanic," as the poet William Blake put it. But at least, by then, there *was* work. The dispossessed rural families from the mid-eighteenth to the second quarter of the nineteenth century mostly had *no* work. In consequence, as the industrial revolution took hold in Britain in the early nineteenth century, something like half of its population were not only very poor and powerless, its men, women, and children were quite simply demoralized: a social disaster now being repeated (in larger numbers) in today's "emerging economies."

The "choices" of a substantial portion of the population were few and stark: to work 12–14 hours a day for a wage barely allowing survival,[8] or to be effectively imprisoned in a "workhouse" or mine or mill (husbands and wives and children separated from each other – like slaves – often permanently), or to starve.[9]

But that picture is taken from a distance. Moving closer, we see children (aged four to ten years) working[10] in the cotton mills, where their small hands could manipulate thread and spindle better than adults. Alongside small women, we see them working in coal mines, pulling what we might call "kiddy-carts" of coal through tunnels that could be smaller in diameter (and thus less costly) than those for a full-grown man. That such women and children, once *in* the mines might never escape from them alive (or un-abused), was of course common. As the Hammonds remarked, referring to Britain's role in the slave trade as the industrial revolution evolved:

> the steam engine was invented too soon for the happiness of man; it was too great a power to put in the hands of men who still bought and sold their helpless fellow creatures.[11]

In the world of ideas, then as now, there were advocates of lunging industrial capitalism who possessed the moral ingenuity to cheer it on, no matter what. One such in industrialism's infancy was Jeremy Bentham, whose "utilitarianism" and "science of moral arithmetic" will be discussed below. Bentham, referring to small children, argued that the new industrial technology of the cotton mills demonstrated that "infant man, a drug at present so much worse than worthless, may be endowed with an indubitable and universal value" (Stark, 1954). An early instance of what is now called "tough love."

Given the dynamic relationships between capitalism, colonialism, and industrialism, that with nationalism is conclusively affirmed when we ex-amine its role in the emergence of the cotton industry, and of the latter in Britain's rise to eminence and power – economically, politically, militarily. "Whoever says Industrial Revolution says cotton," began Hobsbawm in his chapter on the period (1968, 40); and whoever says cotton must also note the role of the State in taking Britain along that path. Before cotton, wool was the prime industry for England, going well back into the medieval period.[12] The English wool trade was a mighty political force, for it included merchants, the woolen cloth producers, and those raising the sheep. In 1700 the English wool interests prevailed upon the State to ban *all* imports of cotton ("cali-coes") from India – then the leading cotton *cloth* producer in the world.[13] Though initially meant to serve the woolen industry, and given relevant matters earlier noted, it was the chief element in insuring that the infancy and early developments of the cotton industry would be fully protected from competition. This, of course, in the nation that, with Ricardo, came to be the principal voice for "free trade."

INDUSTRIALISM IN THE SADDLE

Preceding, nourishing, and nourished by the "revolutionary" transforma-tion and expansion of the cotton industry was, of course, a whole host of other transformed and much-expanded industries: the potteries, metallurgy and metal products, coal mining and transportation. The drama was most obvious in transportation. Its modernization was of immense significance, not only to all of industry and trade, but to the larger developments of global industrialization, and, not least, for the evolution of colonialism toward the deeper penetration and powers of imperialism.

It was the steam engine that was critical to virtually all these developments: its use required quantum leaps in coal production, gave rise to railroads and steamships, spawned giant factories (for that time) with their belching smokestacks; required, also, a great leap ahead in the nature and production of machine tools – the often unnoticed but key ingredient of modern productive efficiency.

But it was in transportation that the effects were most important. The railroad gave rise to sprawling networks of internal transportation and along with the steamship tied whole continents together quickly and cheaply.[14]

When one ponders the full meaning of expanded steam-powered transit, it soon appears that the requirements for the carriers alone (the steamships, the rolling stock and rails for trains) constituted a massive market for a host of vital industries – coal, steel, machinery, construction, etc. That impact would not be equaled until the twentieth century, and the direct and indirect meaning of the automobile industry – if then.

As will be detailed in Chapter 2, the larger economic meaning of all this emerged in the last half of the nineteenth century: the possibilities and necessities of large-scale, mass production and rapid transportation yielded massive increases in agricultural and industrial production – because of *cheap* steel, *cheap* food, *cheap* machinery, and much else – and the relentless beginnings of giant corporations, an integrated global economy, and imperialism. All that enabled and required what has been called a second industrial revolution – which, in its turn became the basis for the industrial revolution(s) of the twentieth century.

Such enormous economic changes could not occur without changes at least as enormous in social (including cultural) and political life. Whatever positive meanings that may have carried for the upper layer of society up to 1850, it constituted a grave and many-dimensioned setback for the lives of the majority in Great Britain – whether English, Irish, Scottish, or Welsh. In all those societies, cities and factories and mines grew like weeds – poisonous weeds for well over half of their populations.

The merciless conditions of work in the mines and mills have been suggested above.[15] That could not have happened without the disruption of what had constituted the traditional existence of the majority of the British population – most drastically, of what became its working class.[16]

If the horrible conditions and stresses and horrors connected with the passing of one way of life and the forceful passage to another and unwanted existence were not enough, there was also a deterioration in the quantitative measures of existence. Hobsbawm, after a careful study of the available data and the public statements of the time (from high and low, from conservatives and radicals), comes to the considered conclusion that Sidney Webb, leader of the Fabian (moderate socialist) Society as the nineteenth century ended, was correct when he said:

> If the Chartists in 1837 had called for a comparison of their time with 1787, and had obtained a fair account of the actual social life of the working-man in the two periods, it is almost certain that they would have recorded a positive decline in the standard of life of large classes of the population.[17]

The Chartist movement was but one of several efforts to change the direction of British socioeconomic development in the first half of the nineteenth century. Preceding it were the periods of protest and unrest marked by the Luddites ("machine-breakers"), the Peterloo Massacre of 1819, and various attempts to reform by workers by forming unions, political efforts toward factory and Poor Law reform and, throughout the 1840s, the Chartist movement for greater political representation of the working class. All these will be examined in one degree or another in the next chapter, when we focus upon labor and socialist movements.

Returning to the "narrower" economic development of British industrial capitalism, it had become clear by mid-century that it would be unable to maintain or increase its momentum without a simultaneously changing and expanding world economy.

In addition to the advantages to Britain of its empire, its economy could flourish over time only with rising exports of commodities and of capital. The latter, used for investment by (for example) Germany and the United States – Britain's main debtors in the nineteenth century – ineluctably meant that Britain's prosperity depended on the creation of what became stiff market competition. By the end of the century the contest was becoming deadly.

Clearly, the period extending from 1750 to 1850 was amazing in both its quantitative and qualitative characteristics. Naturally, then, those developments were accompanied by a flourishing of thought and theory on the whole range of economic, political, and social processes brought forth and required by (especially) British industrial capitalism. Much of that, which came to be called classical political economy, sought to facilitate those processes; some of it, most obviously that of Marx and Engels, stood in opposition. We now turn to a brief critical analysis of the main elements of both sets of arguments.

THE BRAINS TRUST

Adam Smith was the prime inspiration for the theoretical framework for classical political economy, which shortly evolved into capitalism's ideology. In his *Wealth of Nations*, he provided the main arguments against the political obstacles holding back industrial capitalism, and the claim that the "wealth of the nation" would be enhanced by their removal and the emergence of freely competitive markets.

Ideas compatible with Smith's had been proposed earlier – Locke on property, Defoe on labor, Petty on trade, for example. But it was Smith who first constructed a comprehensive attack on "the mercantile system" still dominant in his time, and matched that with a coherent analysis of the possibilities of a *"laissez-faire"* economy.[18]

Comprehensive though he was, and as is to be expected with all innovators, Smith had provided "only" a framework. First, Smith's main arguments will be examined. Then, more briefly, we take up the leading ideas of Ricardo, Malthus, Bentham, Jean-Baptiste Say (1767–1832), and Mill. They pursued Smith's reasoning and completed the structure with more particular analyses: Ricardo on foreign trade, Malthus with a pseudo-scientific rationale for social harshness,[19] Bentham (in addition to his two cheers for child labor) the theory of human nature that still underlies economic theory, Say the basis for the "macroeconomic theory" (or, more accurately, the rationale for its absence, until Keynes), and Mill the synthesis (and what may be seen as the requiem) for classical political economy.

Following Mill, in the 1850s and 1860s, what was taking hold as an economics profession sought both to rid itself of the weapons (especially the labor theory of value) classical political economy had provided to the likes of Marx and, as well, to smooth the way for the industrial capitalism Smith had argued for and that by 1850 in Britain was in place. The outcome was "neoclassical economics," (see Chapter 2). First we turn to Adam Smith's great work.

Adam Smith

A professor of moral philosophy, Smith became the first "economist," as distinct from the earlier "tract" writers – who proposed or opposed *particular* economic policies – preceding him in the long mercantilist epoch. Given the breadth of his sweeping program for socioeconomic reform, Smith reasonably felt impelled to support his arguments with something of a theory of human nature.

In keeping with much of the social thought of his time, Smith posited an inherent "natural order," an order best left to itself – which, for Smith, meant removing the power of the State from the economic process: letting things be. The basis of his presumed natural order was human nature; that in turn for Smith consisted of six "motives": self-love, sympathy, the desire to be free, a sense of propriety, the habit of labor, and "the propensity to truck, barter, and exchange."

Whatever its limitations, Smith's view was considerably more sensible than what came to be and remains the bedrock of economic theory: "homo economicus."[20] Let people be, argued Smith, and the beneficence of Providence will provide that social order which, though far from perfect, is the best to be had.

Assume that all the motives Smith noted do in fact exist in most of us (at least in western culture). But so do many other motives, just as "natural." Many of the latter are irrational, some are downright ugly: "the seven deadly sins,"[21] plus fear, shame, hate, and others. The world advocated by Smith and, considerably more, that championed today by mainstream economists, a world in which all social traditions are set aside by "the free market" for everything,[22] would yield a society which, although we are perilously close to it, has yet to be fully experienced.

Be that as it may, it was not Smith's notions of human nature that accounted for the impact of his work, but his political economy. His critical emphasis was on the entrenched barriers standing in the way of technological progress and what today is called "venture capital" then struggling to gain momentum. Those barriers were at the center of what Smith called "the mercantile system."

That system had begun to take hold more than two centuries earlier, when capitalism and industrialism were still in embryonic form. The world then was caught up in constant warfare between the several rising nation-states, all of them scrambling for territorial advantage in Europe and overseas. The State needed merchants, financiers, and industries (not least those for ships and arms), and the "businessmen" of that time needed the State: tariff protection at home, naval protection on the seas and at their overseas destinations, and monopolistic privileges in both trade and industry (such as, respectively, the East India Company and the Batteries Royal). All that and more were essential for economic and national survival in that early modern period. By 1776, however, the very successes of that system had become sand in the economic gears, gears in any case rusted by many decades of corruption.

Thus, when Smith presented his case it was at a time and place such that British political and business support – outside the charmed circle surrounding George III, that is – grew quickly. Within a generation or so the first modern factory, which had been institutionally impossible in 1776, was in place; and the sociopolitical context Smith had argued for was being forced into existence. The stage for modern economies and their economics was set.

Smith's critique of the cupidity and stupidities accompanying mercantilist ways and means was fully justified; his hope that industrialization
would over time bring meaningful improvements to the lot of ordinary
people was much less so. He did not foresee the deterioration of life that
would be experienced by generations of workers as *all* barriers to capital's
self-interest were removed. Nor could he anticipate that industrialization
would bring about the disappearance of the "invisible hand" of competition he depended on to transform "individual self-seeking into social
well-being." In retrospect it is easy to see that innumerable small firms
would be brushed aside or swallowed up by giants, and supplant
competitive pressures by monopolistic arrangements. Expanded efficiency
indeed there was; its benefits went mostly to the top of the social
pyramid.[23]

Obliviousness to the "side-effects of successful industrialization" may
be forgiven in Smith;[24] it is quite another matter to forgive the indifference of today's economists to the facts of the realized past and of the
present: their ignorance, one may say, is cultivated – an element of their
training.

"Invisible hand" or "invisible fist"?

The competition lauded by mainstream economists and business has
been replaced by rivalry in the key sectors of the economy, and is very
close to the opposite of what Smith hoped for. The ubiquitously small
firms of a "Smithian" competitive market perforce would strive always to
reduce costs and would be powerless to set their prices above those
sufficient only to meet labor and materials costs, "managerial wages," and
interest payments.

Today, in sharp contrast, the rivalry between giant firms (GM, Ford,
Chrysler, amongst others) is manifested largely in costly advertising and
equally costly product differentiation (including "deliberate obsolescence"). The costs are passed on as higher consumer prices, enabled by the
agreements made among and between the small number of companies
("oligopolies") which are characteristic of modern industry in all nations.[25] Smith's critical focus was appropriately on the misuse of State
power; he did not anticipate the baronial power that would be sought and
gained by the enormous companies industrialization facilitated – and that
a compliant State has allowed.

Smith's *Wealth of Nations* is regularly cited as a support for the free
marketry that now rules economics. Those who do so needs must ignore
(or be entirely ignorant of) Smith's negative views of businessmen,
including those cited in our Prologue.[26]

Given Smith's time, place, and social framework, his book may be
seen as a master work. It combines a coherent historical, political, and

economic analysis with a social philosophy to a remarkable degree. And it may be seen as being as much a scientific work as is reasonable to expect of social analysis – where "scientific" is meant to comprise some combination of observed fact, logic, and testable hypotheses. There have been all too few others in the mainstream tradition who have worked in comparable terms.

Comprehensive as Smith's *Wealth* was though, it slighted at least two major economic processes: those that became the province of foreign trade and of macroeconomic theory. The former was soon taken up by Ricardo; the latter (presumably) by Jean-Baptiste Say.[27] Ricardo, as we will now see, left his mark not only on trade theory, but on the process of theorizing itself. In both respects his ideas continue to dominate economics and economic policy today – if anything, more so than in his own time.

David Ricardo

As the term "scientific" has been used above, Ricardo qualifies, but only barely.[28] Science combines inductive with deductive reasoning. Induction generalizes from observable realities; deduction depends on logic – conclusions derived from a set of definitions, premises, assumptions, and inferences.

Ricardo argued within his innovative (and long-lived) framework of abstract, deductive theory. Unlike many theorists today, Ricardo was not ignorant of economic realities. He had spent much of his adult life in the world of finance, and successfully so; and he had a keen sense of the economic strategy that would most benefit Great Britain: global free trade.

As with Smith, Ricardo's ideas had their predecessors. Principally, in his case, those of Grotius, in – and for – seventeenth-century Holland (from where Ricardo's parents had emigrated). Ricardo's *Principles of Political Economy and Taxation* came out in 1817 and its policies triumphed in Britain in the 1840s, after a bitter struggle over "the Corn Laws." As we now examine that issue and Ricardo's theory, both the reasons for his theory and its triumph will emerge. Considerably more important (and difficult) to comprehend is why a theory enunciated so long ago would remain virtually intact today, both in form and content, in a world so utterly different.

Just as Smith was able to discern the possibilities of modern industrialization in its embryonic beginnings of his own time, so too was Ricardo prescient in seeing that Britain was on the verge of becoming an industrial economy (as distinct from an economy with some industry in it) and that, as such, it would have to import ever-increasing volumes of always more diverse commodities, and would need rising exports to help pay for those imports. The imports would consist increasingly of foodstuffs and industrial raw materials, the exports of industrial commodities (coal, cotton cloth, machinery, etc.). And, to the degree that there was no hindrance to exports *or* imports by tariffs (taxes on imports), Britain's industrialization would proceed apace. The latter was also Smith's goal, of course, but it was sufficient to his purposes to emphasize economic freedom in general.

The gospel of free trade

The most important obstacles to free trade in Ricardo's day were the seventeenth-century "Corn Laws." They provided a protective tariff on imported grains. By 1817 those laws protected *all* farmers – small and inefficient, large and efficient. The latter were the politically powerful landed gentry, and the main beneficiaries of the tariff.[29] The tariff on imported corn meant a handsome "rent" – or, as Ricardo used the term, an unearned income – a return not to production but to power.[30]

The larger significance of this lay in the fact that the main item of "subsistence" for workers, and thus of costs of production, was food (in turn, largely, bread) the price of which was artificially inflated by the tariff. Thus the enhancement of landowners' profits implied a rise of workers' (money, not real) wages. That, Ricardo argued, meant lower (money *and* real) profits and thus the retardation of industry – to the benefit of the landed gentry. The latter were the main political power in 1817; by 1846, after a major political struggle the Corn Laws were repealed, for the rising business class was then sufficiently in the ascendant to swing Parliament its way.

The key theory underlying Ricardo's argument for free trade was "the principle of comparative advantage." Adherence to the policy implied by that principle – the abolition of *all* barriers to trade – would, "other things being equal" (about which more in a moment) – bring about maximum efficiency in global production, and thus the highest possible level of life for *all*. Very soon after the repeal of the Corn Laws, Marx (in a speech delivered before the Democratic Association of Brussels, January 9, 1848) made an observation that might as easily – and as accurately – be made today:

> Every one of the destructive phenomena which unlimited competition gives rise to within any one nation is reproduced in more gigantic proportions in the market of the world.
>
> If the Free Traders cannot understand how one nation can grow rich at the expense of another, we need not wonder, since these same gentlemen also refuse to understand how in the same country one class can enrich itself at the expense of another.

Ricardo's theory still holds sway, with always greater force, always greater damage. To even begin to grasp why that is so, it is essential to pause to explore those "other things" and their "setting aside," which became and remains the life-support system of economic theory.

Abstract theory versus earthy realities

The "other things" are the nesting-place of abstract economic theory's assumptions which, to the degree – and *only* to the degree – they are reasonably approximated in reality, give the theory any validity it might possess.[31] But the devil, always, is in the details.

Such details made Ricardo's theory problematic even in his own century; and considerably more so today. Whether then or now, the meaning of such detail emerges mainly from what it reveals about the sources and consequences of power. This in mind, let us examine his "principle" in his time (and again, in Part II, for our own time).

The gist of the principle is that each *nation* should produce that in which it is *relatively* most efficient. Ricardo's now classic example was for wine and cloth, Portugal and Britain. Thus, even assuming that Britain could produce both cloth and wine more efficiently than Portugal, but produce cloth with relatively greater efficiency than wine, then Britain should *specialize* in cloth and import wine; and Portugal should stick with – even if that meant getting stuck with – wine.

What, for Portugal and Britain, were the other things that were to be taken as "equal" – that is, set aside, left unexamined, to be ignored? Among them is that Portugal would never produce anything *but* wine (or other agricultural products), while Britain would produce *all* the cloth and – given the dynamic qualities of industrialization – develop in such a manner as to produce many (or all) other industrial commodities over time.

Thus Britain would *logically* become *the* paramount industrial nation. In doing so, it would also become increasingly powerful, "modern" (in terms of education, health, politics, military strength, etc.); meanwhile, Portugal (and its like) would remain hewers of wood and drawers of water – and an economic colony of Britain (which, in fact, Portugal became); or worse. Rule Britannia.

Ricardo may or may not have been conscious of the implications of his principled theory; policy-makers in all other countries strong enough to act with relative independence *were* conscious of those implications. Accordingly, they acted to protect their economies from Britain's otherwise unbeatable competition: they surrounded themselves with protective tariffs and subsidized their industries (among other devices) to "level the playing field."

First among those countries was, of course, the United States. Its national ("Hamiltonian") policies became a major element leading to the Civil War – the American South Smithian/Ricardian (Britain its principal customer for cotton, rice, and tobacco, and its source of imports), the

North Hamiltonian, seeking to protect what the latter had dubbed its "infant industries." And thus it went throughout the nineteenth century, for Germany,[32] France, Italy, Japan, *allowing* them to become (with Britain and Canada), today's dominating "Group of Seven."

The gist of Smith's and Ricardo's economic arguments will be examined again in later chapters when their application to the contemporary world's economic processes is critically examined. Shortly there will be a discussion of Malthus and Bentham, the two main architects of the ideas underpinning the social policies and social philosophy (if such it can be called) of capitalism throughout its full-blown existence, and with awful and renewed vigor even today. But first a brief look at a minor economic notion that had a major existence, the non-macroeconomics of Say.

Jean-Baptiste Say

Followers of Adam Smith had a rough ride on the Continent, and most especially in Say's France. (For a brief while, it seemed to catch on in Germany, where it was called "Smithianismus," but the Prussians put an end to that.) Although Say deviated in important analytical respects from Smith,[33] he may be seen as one of the most ardent and useful voices for "free markets." That he failed dismally in France, despite strong efforts in the first quarter of the nineteenth century, was unavoidable, for France was the most avidly mercantilist nation in Europe.

His lasting contribution was not in the analytical realm he pressed for most ("utility"), but in his enduring "law of markets" which applied to what is now seen as the macroeconomy. Although, as will be seen, "Say's Law" was given a belated death sentence by Keynes in the 1930s, it was reprieved in the Reagan era, and is now very much alive and kicking.

Depression is impossible

For present purposes, the nub of Say's "law of markets" was that overproduction cannot happen: "supply creates its own demand." Say never put it as succinctly as that, but that was the gist of his position. Accepting his idea leads easily to the firm stand that it is *never* necessary or desirable to interfere with "markets" whatever trouble they may seem to have brought. Trouble – whether of failed businesses or long lines of unemployed – will ultimately take care of itself; trying to speed up the process only introduces distortions to the economic process.

As with Smith and Ricardo, Say's analytical failings may be "forgiven" in part when we understand that he was writing in the very first stages of industrialization, with a whole world yet to walk that path. Much of the world has yet to do so; but when Say wrote his *Treatise on Political Economy* (1803) only one small part of the world – Britain – was moving strongly toward doing so. When, as the nineteenth century unrolled, industrialization spread from Britain to the Continent, the United States, and Japan, there seemed a certain credibility to Say's notion – a credibility dependent on, however, global industrialization being in its *early* stages.

Thus, there were processes of expansion and contraction throughout the century ("business cycles") which indeed did "correct themselves." Both the expanding and contracting phases went on without governmental intervention in the form of the monetary or fiscal policies now associated with Keynesian theory. But that "bounce" did not exist for the reasons Say posited, those having to do with the *impossibility* of their being production that would not be taken off the market at a reasonable price. Instead, and in somewhat more technical language, throughout the nineteenth century there was a relative *shortage* of capital and savings for the amount and kinds of industrialization under way.

By contrast, in the years leading up to and following World War I, there was a shortage of *buyers* – whether of capital or consumer goods – a *surplus* of capital and of savings: that is, there was what Say had seen as impossible: overproduction (or "underconsumption") or, a third term coming to much the same meaning, excess productive capacity.

When, in the 1930s, the depression dragged on, the economics profession (most especially in the United States) clung to Say's Law, and argued that the cause of depression and unemployment was that workers were demanding excessive wages: the very workers who were standing in those long bread lines, their families near starvation, sinking into misery. Stubborn, stubborn workers: *dummkopfen.*

Say's wishful thinking was replaced with Keynesian theory in 1936, by which time the depression had made Say's "law of markets" appear to be a joke in very bad taste – as will be discussed at length in Chapter 3.[34]

Now it is time to examine the ideas of Malthus and Bentham, who – although not in accord with what may be seen as Smith's social values or philosophy – were both well suited to capitalism's needs and the emerging economics that rationalized them.

Thomas Robert Malthus

For reasons soon to become apparent, Malthus was opposed to industrialization; it is thus a major irony that his social theories did much to ease its way – both in his century and ours. Implicitly or explicitly those ideas are today at the center of the rationalizations used to justify social savagery against the poor.

As the son of a landed gentry family, Malthus enjoyed a very comfortable life from birth: he graduated from Cambridge University, was a parson and a professor, and spent much of his time writing. In the first period of his writings (twenty years or so beginning in 1798) he developed diverse variations on his obsessive "theory" that seeking to help the poor hurts them and everyone else – a position that led him, as will shortly be seen, to advocate their deliberate elimination – by any means short of murder (preferably starvation or disease).

His later work, in his continuing spirit of anti-industrialization, sought to show that industrial capitalism was an unstable economic system, subject to what he called "gluts" – supplanting what he saw as a stable (and more desirable) agrarian society. The passage of time proved him right, though not for the reasons he imagined.

First, his cold-blooded advice about the poor. His fundamental "theoretical" position is of course famous: population has a tendency to increase at a geometric rate, food resources only arithmetically: 1, 2, 4, 8, 16, ... versus 1, 2, 3, 4, 5, ... On the population side of that extraordinarily counter-factual theorem, Malthus contended, the fault lay with the poor. It helps us to understand Malthus's attitudes if we recall that in 1798, when he wrote his (first) *Essay on Population* (1970),[35] there was considerable social unrest and agitation, prompted by the socioeconomic devastations following the enclosure movement (heated up more than a little by the hysteria crossing the Channel from revolutionary France).

The Poor Laws (dating back to medieval England, and revised in Elizabeth's reign), where "poor" signifies unemployed, required that the poor in each parish be assisted through what we would call local taxation, levied principally on the landed gentry of that same parish: the very social class of which Malthus was a member. It is crude, perhaps, but not too crude, to suggest that Malthus's social ideas were at least in some degree influenced by his social position.

Instead of indicating the details of his analytical and policy positions, it seems sufficient to provide the encompassing long quote that follows. If Malthus possesses any virtue at all, it resides in the brutal honesty revealing his *hatred* of the poor. To his credit, at least he did not, as is so common now, put forth circumlocutions culminating in cute phrases such as Daniel Moynihan's 1960s "benign neglect" and its 1990s successor, "tough love." Now hear this:

> It is an evident truth that, whatever may be the rate of increase in the means of subsistence, the increase in population must be limited by it, at least after the food has once been divided into the smallest shares that will support life ... All the children born, beyond what would be required to keep up the population to this level, must necessarily perish, unless room be made for them by the deaths of grown persons ... *To act consistently,* therefore, we should facilitate, instead of foolishly and vainly endeavouring to impede, the operation of nature in producing this mortality; and if we dread the too frequent visitation of the horrid form of famine, *we should sedulously encourage* the other

forms of destruction, which we compel nature to use. Instead of recommending cleanliness to the poor, we should encourage contrary habits. In our towns we should make the streets narrower, crowd more people into the houses, and court the return of the plague. In the country, we should build our villages near stagnant pools, and particularly encourage settlements in all marshy and unwholesome situations. But above all, we should reprobate[36] specific remedies for ravaging diseases ... If by these and similar means the annual mortality were increased ... we might probably every one of us marry at the age of puberty, and yet few be absolutely starved. (1970, 2:179–80; emphases added)

Not quite what Jesus had in mind, one may believe, when he said, "Suffer the little children."

Malthusian ideas about population and food supplies, and of the responsibility of the poor for their plight, are as lively today as ever; perhaps more so. But not with relevant members of the scientific community: demographers, biologists, and many others (including some studious economists) are in agreement that from the moment Malthus first wrote, up to and including the present, food supplies over the globe have *always* grown more rapidly than the population.[37]

Reality has been unkind to Malthusian *theory*; but that has not dampened the enthusiasm for his policies against the poor.[38] We have not, of course deliberately brought on "plagues" (at least not of the medieval sort he envisaged which, of course, smite the rich as well as the poor).[39] But, and except for an interval after the 1950s, Malthusian policies have been in place (again, most especially or only in the United Kingdom and United States), in the specific sense that economically plausible steps to lower the percentage of poor among us – or to eliminate poverty entirely – have been at best halting and hesitant, have always stigmatized the poor in the process,[40] and have most recently been for all practical purposes abandoned – with, it must be added, a certain glee in many quarters. Nor should it be forgotten that the continuing existence of a sizable percentage of poor and powerless people suits the political economy of capitalism. They serve as a warning to those workers *not* poor and, all too often (and among other "uses"), serve as a target upon which to vent frustrations – especially when, as is common, they combine with racist attitudes.[41]

Before turning to Bentham, a few sentences about the Malthusian theory of "gluts." Analytically, Malthus anticipated Keynes in important ways, most especially in arguing (in his *Principles of Political Economy* [1820]) that there could be periods of what Keynes called "inadequate effective demand," and associated depression.

Like Keynes, Malthus was seeking to keep his society from plunging into a chaos prompted by economic disaster. But Keynes was concerned to preserve capitalism from committing suicide; Malthus sought to stave off industrial capitalism, which he saw as destroying the "one true and socially useful [that is, his] class": the landed gentry.

For the landed gentry, Malthus had a sweet argument to make his case for "gluts." He saw three classes: workers, capitalists, and the landed gentry. Of them, only the gentry consumed adequately. Workers had just enough to survive; capitalists (this is before industrial corporations) put as much of their profits/income into further investment as possible; only the leisured gentry had both the incomes above subsistence *and* the desire to spend it on consumption. But industrialization ground away at the very existence of the landed gentry. Solution: slow the processes of industrial capitalism (even better: roll them back!).

Unsurprisingly, little attention was paid to that set of Malthus's ideas: they suited the powers of a dying, not a rising socioeconomic system. All the more revealing, then, that this anti-industrialist's ideas on population and poverty survived and strengthened as industrialization proceeded. That survival was aided and abetted by Bentham, however – indirectly, and whether or not unintentionally.

Jeremy Bentham

Generally seen as the effective originator of "Utilitarianism," Bentham's life-span (1748–1832) almost coincides with the period of the industrial revolution; and his 60 productive years as a published thinker overlapped with the formative years of classical political economy. His principal contribution to economic thought was what came to be called utility theory – the bedrock of the economics that took hold in the 1860s and that has come to dominate once again in our own time.

That theory, as noted earlier (and as will be discussed further in Chapter 2 and again in Part II), first emerged in the 1850s, a full generation after Bentham's death. That he was the initiator of those theories is among the intricate puzzles of intellectual development; but that his arguments came to be embraced is easily explicable in terms of capitalist political economy.[42]

The theory of human nature standing at the center of Bentham's utilitarianism was contained in his *An Introduction to the Principles of Morals and Legislation* (1780). There he set out his "principle of utility": human beings are governed by the striving after pleasure and the avoidance of pain: "in all we do, in all we say, in all we think." Sounds fine, until you reflect on it. Except tautologically, much that is done voluntarily has little or nothing to do with pleasure; and much that is done voluntarily brings us much pain (childbirth; raising children). Much that we do, more generally – except tautologically – has little to do with *either* pleasure *or* pain.[43] This philosophical notion became the basis for what was called "psychological hedonism" – itself the basis for neoclassical "utility theory."

That this theory became lastingly important well after Bentham's death is not difficult to explain. Classical political economy had at its theoretical heart the so-called labor theory of value. It was expressed loosely by Adam Smith and carefully by Ricardo. Nor, in this connection, is it unimportant to remember that Ricardo, in the very first paragraph of his *Principles*, gave primary importance to understanding the "laws" of income and wealth distribution – as between the three classes of the population:

> The produce of the earth – all that is derived from its surface by the united application of labour, machinery, and capital, is divided among three classes of the community, namely, the proprietor of the land, the owner of the stock or capital necessary for its cultivation, and the labourers by whose industry it is cultivated. But in different stages of society, the proportions of the whole produce of the earth which will be allotted to each of these classes, under the names of rent, profit, and wages, will be essentially different ... To determine the laws which regulate this distribution is the principal problem in Political Economy ...[44]

As the industrial revolution and capitalism moved toward mid-century, the class struggles over what those "laws" would be were three-fold: "capitalists" versus the landed gentry (the struggle which concerned Ricardo in his work), the capitalists versus the industrial workers, and the workers versus both the landed and industrial powers. By mid-century, the gentry had effectively lost power (except for what was an occasional veto in the Parliament); what remained was an increasingly bitter struggle between workers and the capitalists of mine, mill, dockside, rail, and ships.

In such a world, the less discussion of class (of any sort), the better. Utilitarianism and its offspring, the utility theory of economics, shifted the focus away from such matters – matters of production – and toward the psychological/mental states of all economic "units" – consuming, working, business, whatever, "units" – and "the market," where things (all commodities, including work "units") are bought and sold, and where the buyers and sellers behave in response to anticipated pleasure or pain.

In the next chapter I discuss this doctrine more fully. It is one that depends on everyone, everywhere, all the time, being calculating, rational human beings: no classes, no history, no past, no tomorrow (that could be right); just buying and selling, rationally, all of us, all the time. And a cigar, Dr. Freud, is just a cigar.

John Stuart Mill

Of Mill, the enthusiasts of free market capitalism, both in his own time and ours, could well cite the wry complaint "with friends like him, we have no need of enemies." Mill's *Principles of Political Economy* was published in 1848,[45] "the year of revolutions" – more exactly, clamorous uprisings in major *cities* (Paris, Vienna, Berlin, Frankfurt, Milan, as distinct from France, Austria, Germany, Italy). London, too had its upheavals, but of a different sort.

On the Continent, although workers were much involved, the tumult and shouting were aimed more at moving toward political freedoms and bourgeois rule than, as in England – already long under "bourgeois" rule – where, led by the Chartists, better lives and more power for the working class were the central element.

J.S. Mill's father James was one of the most intransigent of the classical political economists; and he raised his son very deliberately to follow in his footsteps – beginning at the age of three with the study of the classics, in the original Greek and Latin. But, as Eric Roll has put it, J.S. Mill's work can only be understood against the background of the increasing challenge of socialism (1946, 389). That is, in Britain the already strong hold of industrial capitalism had brought forth the first prominent manifestations of modern class struggle. J.S. was an ardent supporter of *laissez-faire* ... but. The "but" had to do with his equally firm belief that the free market should *not* be left to itself, that it required governmental intervention to protect labor and the land: the core of the system, of course. Consider this famous (among capitalist converts, infamous) statement:

> If, therefore, the choice were to be made between Communism with all its chances, and the present state of society [1848] with all its sufferings and injustices; if the institution of private property necessarily carried with it as a consequence, that the produce of labour should be apportioned as we now see it, almost in an inverse ratio to the labour – the largest portions to those who have never worked at all, the next largest to those whose work is almost nominal, and so in a descending scale, the remuneration dwindling as the work grows harder and more disagreeable, until the most fatiguing and exhausting bodily labour cannot count with certainty on being able to earn even the necessaries of life; if this, or Communism, were the alternative, all the difficulties, great or small, of Communism, would be but as dust in the balance.[46]

Whatever one might think of that entire quotation, it remains cogent as regards the inverse relationships between work and income. Those who accuse the poor of being lazy have failed to observe that those they demean almost always work harder, longer, and at totally unenviable jobs than those whose incomes are one multiple or another of that of the poor. Thus, there breathe no professors with senses so dull that they would envy the workload or its content of the janitors in their buildings; but had they had the same life-opportunities from birth as the professors – and unless one believes that janitors are constrained to be so only or mostly by mental incapacities – one doubts there are janitors who would not trade places with the professors. (To say nothing about the comparisons one could make with the janitors who work for millionaire Wall St. speculators.)[47]

But back to Mill. His synthesis of classical political economy was from its beginnings marked by analytical confusion and contradictions – occasioned not by lack of intelligence (of which he had an abundance) but by his inability to have his thoughts dominated by the ideology implicit or explicit in classical political economy.

His conflicts with received doctrine were analytical as well as "political." Thus, he argued – contrary to his acknowledged master, Ricardo – that wages were not unavoidably determined by the level of subsistence, but that, rather, their level was *set* by the owners of the means of production at what they considered a desirable rate of total profits (less their own consumption standards). It was not some abstract market, but *power* that set wages; just as, for Ricardo, wages rise and fall in keeping with the power of the landed gentry to set tariffs. And so on. It was of course this very nexus on which Marx was to focus (not in 1848, but in *Capital* [1867]).

In the final pages of *Principles*, Mill, this time in agreement with Ricardo, argued that there is a relentless tendency for the rate of profit to fall – an argument reiterated by Marx and, in his own way, by Keynes. But, Mill saw – here anticipating (of all people) Lenin – that this otherwise ineluctable tendency could be "profitably" interrupted by exporting that which moved toward surplus: capital.

That dry notion had very juicy implications and ramifications, many of them summed up in the term "imperialism." The grip of the latter became serious from the 1860s on. Support profit rates (and lift wages in Britain) though it did, it also made unavoidable the most destructive war in history – until World War II, imperialism's offspring.

So, you can see that J.S. Mill was willy-nilly something more than the synthesizer of classical political economy: he also came close to writing its obituary. After his death, and as the nineteenth century drew to a close and the socialist movement gained strength, it was Mill's rather than Marx's thought that guided socialism in England.[48] The economists after

Mill, those who constructed neoclassical economics, willingly gave up the ghost of classical political economy. Its analytical core – the labor theory of value – had become an albatross hanging round the neck of capitalism, and therefore that of economics. Off with it!

And Karl Marx

As readers of *Capital* (1867) will know, the theoretical core of Marxian economic theory was the labor theory of value. What had become awkward well before then had thus become an onus for the economists; and the theory was abandoned. That process will be examined in Chapter 2. Here we confine our discussion to "the early Marx," and to his understanding of human nature.

The Marx who turned classical theory against itself labored away for about a quarter of a century – beginning in the 1840s – to produce what became Volume I of *Capital*.[49] In the 1840s he was very much a beginning student of capitalism – prompted to be so by Engels, who became his lifelong friend, confidant, and co-worker. But, as sometimes happens, the student overtook his teacher. From the start Marx ascertained the key relationships of economic processes, those that center on the control of the means of life. Under capitalism that control depends on private ownership of the means of production, made to function with profit as its end.

Marx's first examination of this matter pierced through to its inescapable meaning for those *without* control over the means of production – those powerless to maintain their lives except as "alienated" persons. As we soon quote Marx on this, it is necessary to keep in mind that the words "work" and "labor" had quite different – vitally different – meanings as he used the terms (in a tradition with its beginnings in the ancient world).[50] "Work" is life-maintaining – be it farming, building, fabricating – done under the worker's control; labor is done under the control of another (an employer, slave-owner), the class of those who decide what is done, when, how, where, and why – *and* decides as well the division of the resulting income and wealth. "Labor" characterizes the condition of the working class in capitalist society. And it is a main (though not the only) source of what Marx called "the alienation of labor."

> What constitutes the alienation of labour? First, that the work is *external* to the worker, that it is not part of his nature; and that, consequently, he does not fulfil himself in his work but denies himself, has a feeling of misery rather than well-being, does not develop freely his mental and physical energies but is physically exhausted and mentally debased. The worker, therefore, feels himself at home only during his leisure time, whereas at work he feels homeless. His work is not voluntary but imposed, *forced labour*. It is not the satisfaction of a

need, but only a *means* for satisfying other needs. Its alien character is clearly shown by the fact that as soon as there is no physical or other compulsion it is avoided at all costs. External labour, labour in which man alienates himself, is a labour of self-sacrifice, of mortification ... not his own work but work for someone else ... in work he does not belong to himself but to another person ... [The] worker feels himself to be freely active only in his animal functions – eating, drinking and procreating, or at most also in his dwelling and personal adornment – while in his human functions he is reduced to an animal.[51]

That was written in 1844. *The Communist Manifesto*[52] was written in December 1847 and was first published in February 1848. It preceded as well as nourished the widespread turmoil in Europe of 1848 – among the hopes Marx and Engels pinned on the document. We quote but a few of the early sentences (taken from its 30+ pages), beginning with its first ringing words – which, accurate or inaccurate as they turned out to be in their own time, certainly raised a few hairs in 1848. They are effectively unknown to all but a few today; hence the long quote:

A spectre is haunting Europe – the spectre of Communism. All the Powers of old Europe have entered into a holy alliance to exorcise this spectre: Pope and Czar, Metternich and Guizot, French Radicals and German police spies ...

The history of all hitherto existing society is the history of class struggles. Freeman and slave, patrician and plebeian, lord and serf, guildmaster and journeyman, in a word, oppressor and oppressed, stood in constant opposition to one another, carried on an uninter-rupted, now hidden, now open fight, a fight that each time ended, either in a revolutionary re-constitution of society at large, or in the common ruin of the contending classes.

... [The] modern bourgeoisie is itself the product of a long course of development, of a series of revolutions in the modes of production and exchange ... The bourgeoisie has stripped of its halo every occupation hitherto honoured and looked up to with reverent awe. It has converted the physician, the lawyer, the priest, the poet, the man of science, into its paid wage-labourers. [It] has torn away from the family its sentimental veil, and has reduced the family relation to a mere money relation.

The bourgeoisie keeps more and more doing away with the scattered state of the population, of the means of production, and of property. It has agglomerated population, centralised means of production, and has concentrated property in a few hands. The necessary consequence of this was political centralisation.

The bourgeoisie, during its rule of scarce one hundred years, has created more massive and more colossal productive forces than have all preceding generations together. Subjection of Nature's forces to man, machinery, application of chemistry to industry and agriculture, steam-navigation, railways, electric telegraphs, clearing of whole continents for cultivation, canalisation of rivers, whole populations conjured out of the ground – what earlier century had even a presentiment that such productive forces slumbered in the lap of social labour?[53]

After many more pages of history and analysis *The Manifesto* closes with the admonition to workers that they "have nothing to lose but their chains ... [and] have a world to win" and shouts its still unfulfilled imperative: "WORKING MEN OF ALL COUNTRIES, UNITE!" Still sounds like a very good idea – especially when amended to read "WORKING MEN, WOMEN, AND CHILDREN OF ALL COLORS AND ORIGINS," there being still, as then, so many of the latter needing that unity and needed for that unity.

The Manifesto by itself had a lasting impact; more so, it has been estimated, than that subsequently made by *Capital* and its supporting analyses. Be that as it may, and along with much else, the political economy of *Capital* will be examined in the next chapter.

2 Maturation: Global Capitalism and Neoclassical Economics: 1850–1914

AND BRITISH INDUSTRY SHALL RULE THE WORLD: FOR A WHILE

Every epoch has its hallmark. For the nineteenth century, it was industrialization – along with, of course, its supportive connections with capitalism (first and foremost), nationalism, and imperialism. The three latter "clusters" had been the emerging movers and shakers of the social process in the preceding two centuries; industry strengthened and matured in the nineteenth, dramatically so in its latter half, under the leadership of the world's first industrial power, Great Britain.

From the 1850s on, industrialization was building new societies and tearing apart old ones; and, as the new century opened, it led to what became the most destructive war ever. It was intrinsic to the processes of *capitalist* industrialization that the elements making for and entailed by the spread and deepening of industrialization outward from Britain (to the United States, Germany, France, Italy, and Japan) would be the very elements bringing about the explosive breakdown of that same new world.

In the examination of Great Britain that follows, we shall see why. In doing that, what will also be revealed will be a major component of the "economic laws of motion of capitalism."

Throughout its history, going back at least to medieval times, Europe has had " fairs" – fairs of all kinds, but not least in importance, trade fairs: in 1965, for example, Leipzig celebrated the 800th anniversary of its first such fair. The Great Exhibition of 1851 ("Crystal Palace") in England – a world fair – had virtually everything on display, but it was the first such fair in history to celebrate both industrial products *and* free trade. By then, Britain was already far in the lead in both respects.

For the era under consideration in this chapter, Great Britain played an even more dominating role in the global economy than the United States did after World War II. Although the two "hegemons" achieved that position for reasons in many ways similar, the dissimilarities were even weightier. A summary listing of the bases for Britain's ascendancy in itself suggests some of both:

the geographical advantages of the British isles; the stable yet evolutionary and adaptable nature of British political institutions in contrast with those of the Continent; the accumulation of surplus capital and the long and varied experience of economic organizations in its utilization; the superior competitive power accruing from the industrial revolution; and the comparative freedom of the British Isles from the disruptive effects of the wars and revolutions characteristic of Continental states.[1]

When we examine the post-World War II decades, we will see that among the several and important differences in the origins of the strength of the two hegemons, one that stands out markedly is that concerning wars. Although both nations were relatively unharmed by, and even benefited from, intermittent wars as they gained strength up to 1900, there was a decisive difference in the twentieth century. Great Britain was very much weakened by the first of the two world wars and flattened by the second. Much the opposite was true for the United States. The U.S. role as a major supplier to the Allied Powers before and during its military participation staved off what would have been a serious recession and became instead a basis for strengthening the economy during and, even more, after the first war. It is unquestionably true that World War II was the means by which the U.S. escaped from the depression and, with the destruction of Europe and Japan, that gave it an unassailable position of strength.[2]

Politics, the accumulation of capital, and the industrial revolution

Given the importance of Britain's relatively flexible sociopolitical institutions during the industrial revolution, the phrase that commands most attention in the quotation above is "accumulation of surplus capital." That became apparent in the 1830s as the first (textile) base of British industrialization was moving to its limits. An exploration of that "superabundance" of capital – aptly described as "vast" [3] – will take us directly to the remarkable expansion of Britain's trade and empire and to *their* explanations.

The surges of trade and empire were mutually reinforcing; and both accelerated rapidly as the seventeenth century ended and the eighteenth began. "Trade" refers to foreign trade, of course; and such trade required ships and shipping. In the preceding chapter we saw why Britain, rather than France, became the first industrial capitalist society. Even more curious is why it was *not* the Dutch who did so.

Throughout the seventeenth century, the Dutch ruled over both the production and the use of ships, which in turn served as the basis for their primacy in trade with the societies bordering the North Sea and, increasingly over time, with southern Africa, the West and East Indies, and Japan.[4]

The English and Dutch had the largest fleets of combined merchant and naval vessels, but the Dutch outnumbered the English by a good four to one, so assuring their control over what became the most fruitful of trading colonies, the Dutch East Indies. Conscious efforts to alter that balance began in England in 1651, with the so-called " Navigation Acts." All the emerging nations in that period were "mercantilist," but the mercantilism of England was the most successful, and those "Acts" stood at the center of that success.

As the eighteenth century unrolled, British colonies were established in all quarters of the globe. Before the end of the next century, Britain possessed history's most extensive, and, up to then, most profitable empire: "the sun never set on the Union Jack." That development was made possible by and continually stimulated Britain's production and use of sea vessels, much aided and abetted by the trading Acts.

Vital to the numerous provisions of the latter was the requirement concerning colonies. All exports *from* British colonies had to be carried in ships owned, built, and manned by Englishmen; many colonial "enumerated" commodities (tobacco, cotton, rice, sugar, and products used for ship construction and repair) could be exported only *to* England; with few exceptions, all imports *into* the colonies had to be shipped from or via England; most imports *not* from their colonies had to arrive in England in English ships; all coastwise shipping had to be in English boats. And so it went on.[5]

It is not difficult to imagine what all that (and related mercantilist provisions, such as the subsidization of shipbuilding and arms production) meant in terms of stimulating British trade and industry, colonization, and what Marx termed "primitive" (that is, pre-industrial) capital accumulation – especially when one puts back in the picture the other items noted in the earlier quotation.[6]

It has already been noted that in Adam Smith's time France was institutionally ill-equipped to move toward becoming a capitalist society.[7] Even less so, except for the Dutch, were the other European nations ready to "develop." But how can we explain that it was not Holland – the richest, most successful trading and *industrial* society of the seventeenth century – but Britain that was the birthplace of the industrial revolution?

What the British were to become by the end of the nineteenth century – by far the world's principal creditor – was the role occupied in the late eighteenth century by the Dutch, whose wealth by then was accruing more from finance than from trade and industry.[8] The explanation lies in what made for strength in the pre-industrial as contrasted with the industrial epoch.

Among those differences for industrialization, sheer *size* counted heavily; and both the population and geographic area of the Netherlands were quite small. Its lands were almost devoid of the resources relevant to industrial or any other production. Their dikes were built not only to prevent flooding, but to create cultivable land. Its estimated population of 1.1 million in 1700 was a fraction of the United Kingdom's 8.6 million; by 1846, the Dutch still had but 2.5 million, against Britain's more than 27 million. And, although Britain is tiny and its resources accordingly slight when set against those of the United States, its coal and iron, and wool and food crops, were just right for the industrial revolution that began in the mid-eighteenth century.

A century later, Britain had completed *the* industrial revolution. What lay ahead was the second step of that process – what came to be called "the second industrial revolution." Underlying that major development was how Britain had put its "superabundant" capital to use, first and foremost in the direct and indirect effects of its railways.

It is generally agreed that the networks of canals and roads[9] in place in Britain by 1830 and for at least another quarter-century served its transportation needs well. Nonetheless, there were two "bursts" of railway development in that same quarter-century. That such development, as expensive as it was novel, should occur is explicable mostly – perhaps only – by the abundance of capital then finding no sufficiently profitable outlet. The early investors could have had no idea of just how profitable that railway investment would prove to be, both directly and indirectly. The impact of the automobile on the U.S. economy in the twentieth century is the only comparable development.

THE SECOND INDUSTRIAL REVOLUTION

By 1840 the cotton mills of England were technologically backward, but "the English railways had reached a standard of performance not seriously improved upon until the abandonment of steam in the mid-twentieth century" (Hobsbawm, 89). Between 1850 and 1900 it became increasingly clear that the provision of more efficient transportation was by no means the most important contribution of the railroad.

The production and use of railroad technology served as what economists came to term "a growing point," not only, nor even principally, for the economy of Great Britain. It was the foundation for the "second industrial revolution." This in turn served as the basis for an unprecedented set of developments, only the most obvious of which were the direct *consequences* of the use of railroads and steamships: the penetration of all continents and their tying together by relatively inexpensive transportation and (as noted earlier), using the same and related technologies and discoveries (for example, oil), providing the world's economies with *cheap* metals and machinery, *cheap* fuels and lubricants, *cheap* power, and not least important for rising industry and its labor force, *cheap* foodstuffs. All these interacted to provide a powerful push for always deeper, always more ubiquitous industrialization.

Industrialization at the gallop

As the nineteenth century ended and the twentieth began, there emerged what may be seen as a *third* industrial revolution, centering on what Veblen called "the technology of physics and chemistry." This allowed steam power to be supplemented by cheaper and more flexible electric power and ultimately whole new industries making electrical products. Developments in chemistry led first to the heavy chemicals industry and then to innumerable products dependent upon chemical synthesis. Both developments had their first results as capital goods; before long the consequences had spread throughout consumer durable goods and services (telephones, and so on) to be followed in our time by a *fourth* industrial revolution, transforming communications, transportation, everything.

Thus it was that between the 1860s and World War I the mass production of both capital and consumer goods, the defining characteristics of the modern era, became both possible and necessary. But, as will be seen, that such mass consumption became necessary and possible did not insure that it would become real – except for the United States. Its great size, population, and high incomes (even though its also high inequality limited purchasing power) allowed the first steps. That did not help Europe, though. What lay ahead was an ever-deepening crisis and war.

All that from the railroad? The answer is yes, in the same sense that a towering sequoia emerges from its roots. This is not the place to plunge into the relevant details. The point may be made by looking only at the locomotive and the steamship, which came into use in the proximate decades.

Those mobile steam engines were of course fueled by coal, and either moved on or in what required much in the way of steel (plus rolling stock, modern docks, and so on). The steam engine itself was a fundamental stimulus to the proliferation of machine tools and other machinery throughout the nineteenth century, as well as, of course, to the intensification and modernization of mining for massive quantities of coal and iron. But a dangerous fuse had been lit.

The Pandora's box of imperialism

The new land and ocean transportation opened up vast new needs and opportunities. In the process it also transformed colonialism into imperialism, whose differences were determined essentially by the technologies of the two epochs. The most critical of those differences have been aptly summarized by Maurice Dobb, in the long quotation that follows:

> Imperialism required, as the colonial system of earlier centuries did not, a large measure of political control over the *internal* relations and structure of the colonial economy. This it requires, not merely to "protect property" and to ensure that the profit of the investment is not offset by political risks, but actually to create the essential conditions for the profitable investment of capital.
>
> Among these conditions is the existence of a proletariat sufficient to provide a plentiful and cheap labour-supply; and where this does not exist, suitable modifications of pre-existent social forms will need to be enforced (of which the reduction of tribal land-reserves and the introduction of differential taxation on the natives living in the tribal reserve in East and South Africa are examples).
>
> Thus the political logic of imperialism is to graduate from "economic penetration" to "spheres of influence" to protectorates or indirect control, and from protectorates *via* military occupation to annexation.[10]

That is an apt summation of what " imperialism *required*." It is also important to understand why imperialism *was* " required" by the nations that were, or sought to become, major powers.[11] To be a major power in the late nineteenth century meant to be an industrial power. Given the resource inadequacies of all the European nations and Japan, that in turn entailed the acquisition of assured sources of raw materials. Less urgently, but urgent nonetheless, it also meant privileged access to markets provided by empire and – key to the hopes and fears of all those powers in a world in which war was a constant[12] – strategic locations for positioning military forces and refueling warships. We return for a fuller consideration of imperialism in a later section of this chapter.

In general, thus was laid the basis for always increasing conflict and competition between the Great Powers, and an explosive ending to the fabled "century of peace." Before examining the specific processes leading to World War I, it is appropriate to examine the ways in which what became the other principal industrial nations – the United States, Germany, and Japan – achieved their status.[13] They will be examined separately and in that order, then considered together for a discussion of the outbreak of war. Not only the diversity of the paths taken by those nations will be noted but, as well, how very different each path was from that taken by the mother of industrial capitalism, Great Britain.[14]

Because Britain had been the first nation to industrialize it was able to reap the benefits with great ease – "in a fit of absentmindedness," it has been said – by comparison with its Continental rivals. Those benefits could be counted not only in Britain's cheap and easy access to foodstuffs and industrial raw materials imported from its enormous empire, but growing markets for its own industrial exports (including manufactured consumer and capital goods and, always more importantly, coal).

Less obviously, but not less importantly, in the second half of the century Britain had supplanted the Dutch as the world's major creditor, and to a stunning degree. By 1913, Britain had standing investments exceeding £4 billion in the rest of the world.[15] Although Britain was importing more than half of its foodstuffs and seven-eighths of its raw material needs (excluding coal), they were easily paid for by the returns from its foreign investments. As will be seen in Part II, the United States now has a substantial, always rising and already spectacular, import surplus, not as a creditor but as a *debtor* nation, whose obligations to the rest of the world have increased sharply in the past 20 years.[16]

*

Now it is time to turn to the role played by the other major powers in this development, beginning with the United States and Germany (thence to Japan), who were Britain's main debtors in the nineteenth century and had become its main competitors by the twentieth – and economically powerful. By 1913, Germany was producing 50 per cent more steel than Britain, the United States four times as much (Mathias, 233).

THE UNITED STATES

Of all the nations now to be examined, the economics and the ideology of the United States have followed more closely those of Great Britain than have any other nation. Indeed, the rhetoric of "free market capitalism" in the United States has gone beyond that of Britain more often than not; also more often than not, the rhetoric has been confounded by the realities of U.S. economic development. When we examine the history of the Continental nations and of Japan, we will see that not even the rhetoric applied – until, perhaps, the past decade or so.

Had the United States adhered strictly to the principles of "*laissez-faire* capitalism" in either half of the nineteenth century (as Britain did, from the 1840s on), its socioeconomic development would have been drastically different. This is not to say that the United States would not then have industrialized successfully. So abundant were the blessings of time and space and circumstance, it may be said unequivocally that there was no set of *conceivable* economic policies that could have held back U.S. industrial capitalism. Put differently, when ways and means acting as obstacles to capitalist development in the U.S. did exist, they were brushed aside – by any means necessary.

Slavery is an important case in point. The slave system of the South and its exports (cotton, rice, sugar, and tobacco) were crucial to the larger economic development of the entire society throughout the second century of its colonial period and the first half-century of its nationhood. What had changed by the mid-nineteenth century was not the morality of slavery, but (as seen by northern industry) the negative meanings of the power over national economic policy which the slave-holders of the South exerted[17] – exporting agricultural products (mostly) to Great Britain, while importing manufactures. And all within a free market, including the freedom to purchase and sell slaves.

Not only were slave-holders profiting from the system; at least as much were the slave *traders* of the Northeast, centered largely in New England. The British had outlawed the slave trade in 1816; all the better for the slave traders of the new American nation. Veblen's comment on the ethical niceties involved deserves a lengthy quotation:

> The slave-trade was never a "nice" occupation or an altogether unexceptionable investment – "balanced on the edge of the permissible." But even though it may have been distasteful to one and another of its New-England men of affairs, and though there always was a suspicion of moral obliquity attached to the slave-trade, yet it had the fortune to be drawn into the service of the greater good. In conjunction with its running-mate, the rum-trade, it laid the foundations of some very reputable fortunes at that focus of commercial enterprise that presently became the center of American culture, and so gave rise to some of the country's Best People. At least so they say. Perhaps also it was, in some part, in this early pursuit of gain in this moral penumbra that American business enterprise learned how not to let its right hand know what its left hand is doing; and there is always something to be done that is best done with the left hand.[18]

With respect to both its foreign trade and domestic industry, the United States began with a struggle between warring Jeffersonian (Smithian) and "infant industries" against the otherwise overpowering competition of Great Britain – arguments at which the United States sniffs today when they are raised by "emerging market economies." The South was Jeffersonian from the beginning; the Northeast took the Hamiltonian position.[19] The Civil War is usually seen as having abolition of slavery as its prime (or only) focus, just as World War II is viewed as having been principally a war against fascism. But without the issue of who was to control the economic policies of the United States energizing the most powerful business interests of the North, it may be wondered when, if ever, there would have been a war whose basis as well as whose effect was abolition.[20]

Put more broadly, during the Civil War and for decades after, the

United States pursued what can be seen as a national economic policy supporting industrialization: 1) subsidization of the entire railroad network (at least two-thirds of whose costs were paid directly or indirectly by the federal government), 2) the great (and ongoing) give-away of immense amounts of natural resources (timber, various mineral deposits, cultivable lands, and so on), 3) a protectionist tariff policy and, not least in importance, 4) a government that placed property rights first and treated workers' rights as effectively nonexistent. In short, a capitalist paradise.

The importance of being lucky

All that may be seen as benefits for industry (and business in general) that were (as the saying goes) "man-made." Of equal or greater importance for facilitating the ultimate triumph of the United States was provided by a geography that gave it the most abundant resource base of all, while surrounding it with vast oceans insulating it from foreign wars. And then there was the timing of the U.S.'s entrance into history as a national economy, when imported capital (funds and equipment) and manufactures were increasingly abundant and cheap, and U.S. exports always more desired (not least those manna from heaven: gold and silver and oil).

To that add something less obvious, but no less vital for the relatively "easy" development of capitalism in the United States. By comparison with all others, the U.S. was devoid of a history of formalized class relationships and of the connected institutions that, elsewhere, had been protective of both land and labor. Although these had existed in colonial America to some extent, they had become a memory by the time Jefferson and Hamilton were quarreling over economic policy.

Implicit in the foregoing, but of critical importance in establishing both its absolute and relative strengths, is that concerned with the struggle for empire. That struggle, which occupied the energies of all the European powers (and Japan) from the 1870s until the outbreak of World War I, was unavoidable for all of them, for within their borders none had the resources essential for industrialization or – just as vital – for feeding the military strength whose need became increasingly obvious with each year. In those respects, as in so many others, the United States stood in sharp contrast. It was the one nation sitting on (and pushing aside anyone in the way to) everything relevant to economic development, with plenty left over to export.

Nonetheless, in the late 1890s, the United States also embarked on the imperialist path[21] – in the Caribbean and Central America, in the Pacific. But it was not from need – not, at least, as that word might be defined for the other powers. Rather, it was from a set of processes prompted by opportunity – or, less politely, greed and rapacity.[22]

The great physical size and wealth of natural resources which made overseas imperialism less essential for the United States meant something else even more important. They attracted and supported what also became the largest population among the new industrial powers, and allowed it to become the unchallenged center for the mass production of both capital and consumer goods, with parallel developments in agriculture.[23]

The key elements of mass production are the techniques yielding standardized, "interchangeable" products for articles consisting of many parts. A moment's reflection will show that such standardization implies a mass market for such products. The most important work along these lines initially took place in the United States.

It was accomplished by Eli Whitney and Simeon North, for producing firearms used in the war of 1812. The "mass market," of course, was the U.S. government. Such techniques slowly but surely came to be used (first and foremost in Connecticut, where they had begun) in a whole variety of industries. By the end of the Civil War they had become the norm in the United States – in agricultural implements, in the machinery industries, in metallurgy, and so on.[24]

Big, bigger, biggest

The railroad sat at the center of economic development (ranging between 15 and 25 percent of real investment in the last half of the century). All the machinery, rolling stock, and steel of that development – yielding 200,000 miles of track by 1900 – was a boon to the many contributing industries. But it also allowed and required a spreading-out of an always growing population – and of urbanization. The real investment requirements of the numerous cities – housing, streets, utilities, shops, plants – were enormous.

From all of that and much else unmentioned the United States became the first economy of mass production *par excellence* – just as Britain had become the first industrial nation. As we shall see in the next section, Germany, both despite and because of its severely limited resource base, had, by the end of the century, become the technologically most advanced nation in the world.

By 1900, although Britain was rich and growing richer, it was clear that the United States and Germany were becoming, or had already become, the strongest industrial nations in the world. The United States, by virtue of its size, resources, and population (the latter twice that of Germany), had an aggregate strength far greater than Germany, but Germany's "technology of physics and chemistry" was more advanced.[25] Both nations had now overtaken Britain.

That achievement was an instance of a "law of development" that Veblen had made much of; namely, "the penalty of taking the lead, and the advantages of borrowing." Thus, he saw England as having borrowed the handicraft technology from the Continent after 1600, and gone on to higher levels than those who had "taken the lead." But both Germany and the United States had done the same with industrial technology, taking it to new heights both qualitatively and quantitatively, while Britain relaxed with its wealth and old-fashioned economic ways and means.[26]

Two other major accompaniments of industrial capitalist development remain to be considered: the tendency toward giant firms and monopoly, and the response of workers to their exploitation, which led to unionization and socialist movements. Like imperialism, the latter will be taken up toward the end of this chapter, where both phenomena will be analyzed for all the major powers. Here we turn to the consolidation of business in the United States, which took hold late in the nineteenth century. Subsequently it will be seen that the other industrialized countries followed similar paths in the same direction, though with important variations.

In our discussion of Great Britain we made no mention of a movement toward giant firms, consolidation, monopoly, or the like. That is not because nothing of the sort occurred, but that what did occur was slower and on a smaller scale than elsewhere. That in turn, like its technological backwardness by the time of (say) 1910, can be explained by Britain having "taken the lead" in industrialization. Powerful, wealthy, and industrialized though Britain was by 1900, in comparison with the United States and Germany, most especially, it was still the home of relatively "small business."

That the United States was the first home of mass production ineluctably led to its becoming the first home of giant firms. The processes of combination took hold first in the railroads; in manufacturing it was prompted by the spread of mass production[27] – first and foremost in metallurgy. What Microsoft has come to mean for the computer industry is something of a replay of what happened in both railroads and the steel industry. This includes the major pressures toward monopolization which were much strengthened by the spread of excess productive capacities and the reality or threat of price competition – the bane of industry, ideology notwithstanding.

That began to be a problem in the 1870s. For the next two decades or so, as industry spread throughout an emerging economy that was growing too rapidly to be controlled, productive capacities increased and prices fell, leading to what businesses term "destructive competition." This was intense in the steel industry. The leader in its "combinations" was Andrew Carnegie. By 1900, Carnegie Steel had combined 750 steel companies into one; by 1901 it had combined the other eleven largest firms into the United States Steel Corporation (USS), the first $1 billion company, and the largest steel company in the world.

Those processes were only the most dramatic of a larger movement. In the years before 1905, over 5,000 firms in diverse industries (copper, oil, steel, whisky, amongst others) had merged into 318: taken together, they constituted the powerful heart of the economy, matched by an equivalent concentration in the financial world. The latter, led by J.P. Morgan, added to its profits (as still today) by organizing the mergers for a substantial fee (and, often, a share of the equity).[28]

Thus began the era stretching to the present in which the term "competition," whose theoretical function is to increase efficiency and lower prices while keeping economic power diffuse, was increasingly replaced by "rivalry," whose monopolistic pricing, advertising, and trivial product changes take the economy (and society) in the opposite direction in all three respects. Not quite what Adam Smith had in mind. Veblen saw the truly competitive years as having begun their exit in the 1870s; by the early twentieth century, it was something else:

> Competition as it runs under the rule of this decayed competitive system is chiefly the competition between the business concerns that control production, on the one side, and the consuming public on the other side; the chief expedients in this business-like competition being salesmanship and sabotage. Salesmanship in this connection means little else than prevarication, and sabotage means a business-like curtailment of output.[29]

The decades in which this first merger movement took place in the United States produced what was then a novel business form and structure: the giant corporation, functioning side by side with a few other giants in the same industry. The result was an industrial structure economists came to call "oligopoly": an industry dominated by a few large companies, few enough to make (illegal) agreements to maintain (or raise) prices in unison, and/or to restrict output in order to maintain (or raise) prices. This is different in form from "monopoly" – that is, one firm only in an industry – but its consequences have been even more undesirable in practice. For even though the appearance of competition is maintained through advertising and other forms of rivalry,[30] whereas honest price and cost competition *reduces* prices to the consumer for a given quality, "non-price competition" raises costs (through advertising and superficial product changes and packaging). These are passed on to the buyer, and that involves a considerable and always rising amount of waste, much of it destructive (to be discussed in Part II).

The organizational response to industrialization on the Continent throughout the nineteenth century, and up to World War I, was both similar and different. Small firms tended to persist alongside larger – but not giant – firms, but they controlled their markets against competition by organizing into what the Germans called "cartels." The member firms retained their individuality as owners, but had to follow a common price and output policy, and shared the profits.[31]

In the course of the nineteenth century the world had been transformed, more rapidly and in more ways than could have been imagined in 1800 – if in wildly varying ways and degrees, and with cruelly diverse consequences among and between societies and classes. It may be asserted that the drama thus suggested was more electrifying for the United States than any other. As has been noted, the U.S. was simultaneously the best served by nature, and the least restrained by history, for better or worse. Some of both "the better and the worse" are captured by Du Boff, when he notes that

> The accumulation process ... had moved the economy out of a long era of increases in living standards that were tiny and reckoned in centuries (when they were discernible at all) to a new age of productivity-generated advances in mass purchasing power. No sooner was the brave new age begun, however, than it was being undermined by science-based gains in efficiency that permitted huge expansions in productive capacity that tended to overshoot actual levels of private demand. The main problem lay in a system that encouraged efficiency gains but discouraged a distribution of income that could assure commensurate gains in worker purchasing power. (Du Boff, 42)

Though this reference is to the close of the preceding century, it could equally well have been written to describe the state of affairs as the twenty-first century began.

Now we turn our attention to Germany, the heavyweight of European economic, military, and social development. After that, we examine Japan, which consciously walked in Germany's footsteps, and in more ways than one.

GERMANY

When the nineteenth century began, there were Germans, a German language and culture, and there was German history; but there was neither a German economy nor a German nation. Among the provisions of the Treaty of Westphalia (1648) was one which, in order to hamstring Germany, rendered it into a patchwork of over 300 principalities. The Treaty of Vienna (1815) reversed that, reducing the sprawling group to under 40. Most powerful among them were the Prussians east of the Elbe. Already strong before 1815, their strength was much enhanced by the Treaty. It allowed the agricultural Prussia of the east to annex the more highly developed Rhenish lands to the west. At the stroke of a pen, the new Prussia thus became the undisputed major power both economically and militarily of the still fragmented German lands. It also became the driving force that transformed the rhetorical "Germany" into a true nation with a modern economy.

Prussian political economy

The first step was taken in 1818, when Prussia introduced the Maassen Tariff, the purpose of which was to eliminate barriers between its eastern and western territories. Then in 1834 it initiated the *Zollverein*, a customs union eliminating tariff barriers among and between most of the remaining and expanded principalities, while creating barriers against the rest of the world.[32] By 1866–67 all of what at the same time became Germany belonged to the union; and, with the triumphant conclusion of the Franco-Prussian war, Germany became Imperial Germany in 1871.

The Prussian tariff initiatives were a vital first step toward modernization. But a major problem was the geographic separation of East and West Prussia. However, the *Zollverein*, in enlarging the German market for all member states, also made the railroad more realistic and more compelling. From their virtually simultaneous beginning, the Prussians (guided by the coherent program of Friedrich List) saw the tariff and the railroad as the twins of the industrialization process: the *Zollverein* in 1834, the first German railroad in 1835; "the railroad era" of the 1840s.[33]

Accompanying the growth of the railroad in Germany (as elsewhere) was the classic pattern of growth and interaction of related industries: in mining, metallurgy, machinery, and the transportation industries themselves, with secondary stimulating effects in light industry, trade, and finance. Thus was "Germany" thrust toward national industrialization, with Prussia leading the way. At first glance, this would seem to have been an unlikely development. The ruling power in Prussia was a feudal nobility of militaristic landlords (the *Junkers*). Anti-industrial, anti-capitalist, not at all "pan-German," they were most comfortable when handling rye or drilling soldiers. But despite their particularistic outlook, it was nevertheless this anachronistic coterie of feudalistic farmers[34] that willy-nilly marched the crooked path that led them from their unpromising sandy soils to where they became the makers and rulers of a united, an industrial, and an imperious Germany.

By the end of the nineteenth century, the Prussians had come to preside over the strongest nation and most powerful economy on the Continent. The land that had produced Bach and Beethoven, Schiller and Goethe, Lassalle and Marx, came to be ruled by the spirit of Fichte, List, von Bismarck and von Moltke, found its symbols in a fierce eagle and a spiked helmet, controlled its economy through protective tariffs and cartels, and sang of blood and iron and soil.

German science and technology

This was a new Germany, more worrisome than ever to those both within and outside its borders; and understandably so, when one absorbs Brady's characterization of the deepening predicament of Germany as it "grew the economic limbs of a giant only to be confined in space fit for a pigmy [;] ... bottled up, a highly industrialized Germany would explode." [35]

German industrial development was a striking case of making the most of very little, a process also generously embellished with serendipity. The "little" had to do with their resources; the "serendipity" connected both with their creative response to their deficiencies and, as well, with the fact that their railroad system, hastened and designed with military defense and aggression in mind, was the prime mover of the most compressed industrialization process ever.[36] But first, let us take a closer look at Germany's relatively meager natural resources.

Although German soils and forests and potash are abundant, other natural resources (non-ferrous metals, wool, cotton, petroleum, and rubber) are non-existent or problematic. Yet, as Brady put it, "no other major industrial country has developed a large-scale heavy industry with the raw materials under its own political and economic control forming so limited and narrow a base." [37]

In mid-century, petroleum and rubber were not yet vital;[38] but wool and cotton were important, and coal and iron were crucial. Coal was in ample supply, but its quality was poor, largely lignite ("brown coal"), rather than the bituminous and anthracite coals essential for modern industry. Its iron ore supply, in contrast, was of good enough quality (in Upper Silesia) but inadequate quantity; and was located perilously close to its borders. After the conclusion of the Franco-Prussian War, however, Germany controlled the best iron ore deposits in Europe, those of Lorraine, which it had annexed from France. That major trophy of their victory over France brought with it also Alsace and its well-developed textile industry.

Valuable though Alsace-Lorraine was for Germany, its economic development both before and after 1870 allows one to hazard that although it doubtless would have been slowed without the war, that would not have been critical. The key "resource" for German economic development may be seen as their thoroughgoing application of science to technology and production, along with their resource-saving organizational and planning patterns[39] – the levels and the combination of which set Germany apart from all others. As we shall see, both were dramatically evidenced directly and indirectly in the production and organization of the coal industry.

The ultimately advanced state of German science had its seeds in Germany's sociopolitical "backwardness"; its organizationally concentrated political economy resulted from the all-important Prussian direction, able and necessary to be exercised because of social atavism and resource weaknesses.[40]

The sociopolitical backwardness of Germany compared to the other leading European nations of the early nineteenth century was a consequence of its fragmentation into hundreds of mini-nations, the end of which was one of the aims of the *Zollverein*. But that very separation and its innumerable bureaucratic entities served as the primary explanation for Germany's people having been the best-educated in Europe. Each principality had its own government and (usually) its own tariffs and thus the need for a highly disproportionate percentage of its people who could read and write and count, by comparison with other "nations."

Also, anachronistically protected by tariffs in these numerous principalities were craft workers (in metal and textile and paper products, for example) whose skills were as much prized inside "Germany" as their products were outside (as some of them still are). As industrialization took hold, their skills were easily transformed for application in modern industry at the highest levels of the working force, up to and including engineering.

The nation with two faces

The confirmation of this cultural and economic uniqueness – in addition to its meanings for Germany's spectacular industrialization – was evidenced in the 1920s. By 1928, say, Germany was *the* scientific and intellectual Mecca, to which scientists, artists, writers, film-makers, musicians from across the world flocked for inspiration, education, or joy. There has been no such place like it since. Nor anything like the Hell that followed it.

To capture the distinctive character of German industrial development of the late nineteenth and early twentieth centuries, note the portions of the following characterization by Brady I have emphasized, and their sharp contrasts with British processes:

> The bulk of the [German] industries ... were not only devoted to *mass production*, but they also turned out *producers'* goods predominately ... [and] *even* the industries producing *consumers'* goods were in large part *tied directly to the big coal, steel, chemical, machine and engineering firms*, either through vertical consolidations, through dependence upon a common source of *raw materials largely under the control of the industrial giants*, or – as with *pharmaceuticals, fertilizers, synthetic dies and fibers* – because of dependence upon one or more of the leading *by-products* of the new complex operations which characterized the heavy industries.[41]

This is to say that Germany's development centered on the "heavy industries." In an important sense those industries produced for *industrialization* rather than "for the market," least of all for the consumer goods market.[42] This is another way of repeating what was said differently somewhat earlier: German industrial development was "guided," as neither British nor U.S. development was – by the Prussians and their willing allies in big business and finance.

Nor was there ever much in the way of innocence concerning what the ultimate uses of all this productive capacity would be. No later than 1910, German business and political leaders were acutely conscious of two unsettling facts: their heavy industries were easily capable of satisfying the needs of all of Europe for such production; and the capital goods markets of both Europe and the rest of the world were effectively closed to them. Other nations were producing and protecting their own capital goods industries or, in the case of colonies, forbidden to buy except from the home country. The danger inherent to those realities was known to all concerned; namely, that heavy industry is the indispensable economic weapon for war.

The producers' goods industries of Germany included metallurgy, machinery, and shipbuilding, of course; and it was Germany, beginning in the 1890s, that led the world in building what became modern navies, prompting Britain to rethink and rebuild its own navy[43] – an early "cold war" soon to become hot. The following quotation was written in 1897:

A million petty disputes build up the greatest cause of war the world has ever seen. If Germany were extinguished tomorrow, the day after tomorrow there is not an Englishman in the world who would not be the richer. Nations have fought for years over a city or a right of succession; must they not fight for two hundred and fifty million pounds of yearly commerce?[44]

In addition, it was German science that laid the foundations for modern chemical industries and – most importantly in this context – their vast array of synthetic products. Given the probabilities for war, the most relevant of the innovative processes centered upon coal tar derivatives, the basis for the modern explosives industry, with I.G. Farbenindustrie its major beneficiary for both peaceful and war products.

This was but an instance, albeit a very important one, of the general development of *ersatz* ("substitute") products by German industry, of which the contemporary world's array of plastics, synthetic fabrics, dyes, pharmaceuticals, and the like, are direct descendants.[45] But the coal industry had as one of its products coke, which is essential in the production of steel. And steel is essential to the production of, for example, steel rails and steel machinery (and the machinery for making steel), and so on.

It was this set of interdependent connections that led Germany to develop not just concentrated and overlapping business formations (cartels within industries, close ties between finance and industry) as a means of control, but something else less well recognized also took hold in Germany (and only there, in this period). As the new heavy industries expanded:

> they showed a tendency to draw together – to *agglutinate*, to employ a favorite German expression – in a number of ways. They were tied together by the raw materials on which they were based and partly through the swift growth of vertically integrated plants, partly by the rapid spread of the chemical industry ... Common basic raw materials, and what might be called "successive-stages" materials – in which the finished good or the by-products of one chemical process became the raw material for succeeding chemical processes – encouraged direct, physical interlinking of plants and of the firms owning them ... There gradually emerged, from the eighties on, definite patterns of regionally interlaced, nuclear industrial groupings. (Brady, 1943a, 114)

As Brady goes on to show, the comprehensive outlook rationalizing the close functional connections between science, engineering, production, location, and organizational concentration was easily translated into an outlook embracing all that was relevant to Germany's economic *and* its political/military processes, needs, and possibilities. In the closing decades of the nineteenth century, Germany was already what it has been ever since, if in quite diverse ways: a nation impatient with barriers of any kind – economic, geographic, political, or social; and one that has found it easy to move (or to seek to move) through those barriers as a dominating power – economically, politically and, when necessary, militarily.

It is highly likely that the Germany of today is no longer that Germany; its crushing defeat in history's two most horrific wars quite probably also effectively crushed that set of inclinations. Surely most Germans join the rest of us in hoping that is so.

Which prompts the digression that now follows.

A DIGRESSION ON THE CASTING OF STONES

With those comments on Germany and similar ones soon to follow concerning Japan, it seems appropriate to take heed of the biblical injunction "Judge not, that ye not be judged" and to remark at least briefly on its application to the dirty bottoms of modern history.

It will be seen that Japan's industrialization process mimicked Germany's in many ways; and that it also led inexorably to repeated wars, fascism, and related horrors. But neither Germany nor Japan developed in a vacuum. As noted earlier and as will be examined more closely later (and with only our epoch in mind), their economies changed and industrialized in a world of "dog eat dog," a world rife with conflict and competition – class against class, business against business, nation against nation – in which not to win was to lose.

It is tempting, but inaccurate, to say "'twas ever thus."

The pressures for nations and large numbers of their people to resort to force and violence and other atrocities within and beyond their borders has varied and has never been absent in history. But there has never been anything like the acceleration of their types and magnitudes of the past few centuries.

From the sixteenth century on, such pressures intensified in ways previously unrivaled, whether in degree or kind. Attila the Hun was an amateur in comparison with his modern counterparts – not because Attila was of relatively good character, but because his world had not created and could not give rise to the needs or possibilities that became common in recent centuries.

The source of the latter is to be found in the functioning of the "analytical quartet" that ties this book together, the dynamics of capitalism, industrialism, nationalism, and imperialism. Each one of these sets of institutions and processes alone contains within it stimuli that transform the normal search for wealth and power into voraciousness; their *interaction*, whatever their positive consequences might have been, assured a precipitous descent into social disasters – accentuated horribly by the powers of modern technology.

That descent has been shared throughout two centuries or so of the mutual existence of the "four clusters" – not only to or by the obvious villains, Germany and Japan; to and by all nations, in one degree or another, in one way another, at one time or another, for one set of reasons or another.

Germany and Japan with Italy in the twentieth century became the Big Three of fascism. Is it not also relevant that in modern history's dogfights they were also the Big Three of the "have-not nations"? The " haves" – Britain, France, and the United States – do not see themselves as also having been " snarling dogs." But they were. That point receives considerable support when it is applied to the United States – " the land of the free and the home of the brave" – the modern society in which the blessings of nature and location reduced "needs" to a very low level relative to other nations, and for which positive possibilities always lay within easy reach, able to be grasped within the framework of human decency.

Yet – and looking only at this – U.S. history was stained by its addiction to slavery for more than two centuries. Nor has the U.S. by any reasonable standard eradicated the racism that grew alongside slavery, nor all that slavery and racism have meant to millions for centuries. Moreover, although it has received much less attention, the U.S. has been just as much stained by its variation on imperial savagery, stained by the means with which it created its " internal empire" at the cost to Native Americans of their culture, their livelihood, their dignity.

Looking only at those two elements of U.S. history we are speaking of millions of deaths and the ruination of countless survivors and descendants over the period stretching from the colonial period to the present.[46] But, and among other disturbing questions, in how many ways has that history silently poisoned the entire social process? And how many Americans have ever had such matters even discussed in school?

No reference will be made to other, large or small, nations – France, Belgium, China, Italy, Russia, Holland – none of which has clean hands. None of us has the right to cast the first stone. This does not mean that all crimes against humanity are equal; but they are all crimes. It is to say that the crimes of our epoch are not to be explained principally by "national character." The latter has to be explained, and can be – in large part – by the intertwined and cruel histories of that epoch.

Such arguments can be and have been expressed better and more fully by others.[47] For us, here, enough.

We turn now to Japan, whose industrialization stands as much in contrast with Britain's and the United States' as does Germany, perhaps even more, generated by similar as well as different needs.

JAPAN[48]

Among the many things common to the economic development of Imperial Japan and Imperial Germany, one was a fervent nationalism, whose origins, however, were greatly dissimilar. Germany's was much nourished by its having been effectively dismembered in the seventeenth century. By contrast, of all modern nations, Japan was until the mid-nineteenth century uniquely and almost entirely isolated – culturally, politically, economically – and made so by its conscious adoption of a "seclusion policy" in the seventeenth century.

Japan was ruled by a classically feudal regime, the Tokugawa shogunate (military government). Its isolation was prompted in large part by the European overseas explorations of the sixteenth century; its end was the consequence of the pressures against it of western imperialism in the nineteenth century.

As the sixteenth century ended and the seventeenth began, the Japanese had expelled the first European presence (the Portuguese) and had ruled out the presence of any others – except (with severe limits) the Dutch, who were given trading privileges at Japan's southernmost port, Nagasaki.

In the ensuing centuries Japan's isolation produced a society which, compared with all others in that long period, remained unchanged. But from the very beginnings of the nineteenth century, Japan's hermitage began to be assailed. As Peter Duus puts it:

> The exclusion policy worked as well as it did for nearly two centuries because the Westerners had as little interest in getting into Japan as the Japanese had in letting them in ... [But] the arrival of four American gunboats in July 1853 was hardly a surprise to the Japanese authorities.[49]

And, Duus goes on to note:

> The dogged, humorless, and imperious American commander, Matthew Perry, was determined to succeed in browbeating the Japanese, whom he viewed as vindictive and deceitful. [!] He sailed his "black ships" under the guns of forts guarding the entrance to Edo [Tokyo] Bay, plunging the city into consternation and implying his willingness to use force in negotiating a treaty with Japan.[50]

When Perry left in 1853 he vowed to return, and did so, in the spring of 1854. Despite considerable discord and confusion, the ruling military clique then made two fateful decisions: to avoid hostilities, and to open two remote ports to the Americans.

The camel's nose was in the tent, shortly to be followed by its body, and those of other camels: first the United States, then Britain ... just as had happened in China.[51] All this took place under the centuries-old Tokugawa regime. Its downfall followed shortly after, with the "Meiji restoration" of 1868. This was achieved through a military *coup d'état* led by the *samurai*. What then ensued was the emergence of a hybrid society mixing the utmost in modernization with the functioning remnants of a feudal order.

In prior decades there had been a slow movement toward commercialization and some industry; its acceleration was one of the main aims of the new regime. The developments were swift and pervasive, and produced an industrial capitalist nation within the enduring sociopolitical framework of a feudal culture. The latter's viability, though diluted, had a major shaping influence on the entire process.

Feudalism had been formally abolished, but its "spirit" continued to rule (and in some ways does still). Specifically, its abolition meant modifications in land tenure, the lifting or reduction of restrictions on transportation, communications and trade, and the revision of the institutions of property and class mobility to suit the emerging new society.

At the same time, the State – ruled over by lords (daimyo) and those beholden to them – took an active role in aiding, encouraging, and subsidizing developments in transportation, agriculture, finance, education, foreign travel and trade, and (if only temporarily) in the ownership and development of certain industries strategic to military strength.

As E.H. Norman has shown, Japan thus reversed the structural development of other industrializing nations (with the partial exception of Germany) – from heavy to light industries and from military to consumer goods.

> It was the Meiji policy to bring under governmental control the arsenals, foundries, shipyards, and mines formerly scattered among [feudal] domains, then to centralize and develop them until they reached a high level of technical efficiency, while at the same time initiating other strategic enterprises such as chemical industries ... and the last step was to sell a large portion of these industries to the handful of trusted financial oligarchs. But control over the most vitally strategic enterprises, such as arsenals, shipyards, and some sectors of mining, was kept in government hands ...[52]

"The handful of trusted financial oligarchs" came to constitute the core of those who controlled – and most benefited from – Japanese economic development, the zaibatsu.[53] The latter were the power structure not only for industry but agriculture and trade, transportation and banking. That structure was one of pervasive cartelization and monopolization; the zaibatsu presiding over it was in turn led and dominated by the four largest groupings among them: the Mitsui, Mitsubishi, Sumitomo, and Yasuda – household names still today.[54]

Between 1895 and 1905 Japan had achieved great industrial strength; in terms of its gross national product, it ranked behind only Britain, Germany, and the United States. Its economy was unique to Asia; the Pacific Ocean to its east and the great land mass to its west gave it that kind of spatial defense enjoyed by the United States throughout its existence; and which both permits and encourages aggressive expansion against those within reach (and weaker).

Thus the Sino-Japanese and Russo-Japanese wars of 1895 and 1905 (respectively) – with more to come, but only (as will be seen), under circumstances not likely to continue – the circumstances that captured Veblen's attention in the years when he was studying German development.

In the Japan of the last quarter of the nineteenth century, where public interest began and private ended was much more obscure than elsewhere, except Germany. Writing in 1915, Veblen mused on Japan as follows:

> power vests in a self-appointed, self-authenticated aristocratic cabinet ... with the advice, but without the consent of a "parliament" endowed with advisory power. This bureaucratic organ of control is still animated with the "Spirit of Old Japan," and it still rests upon and draws its force from a population animated with the same feudalistic spirit ... It is only in respect of its material ways and means, its technological equipment and information, that the New Japan differs from the old.[55]

Veblen goes on to observe[56] that the industrialization process is not an old wine that can be poured into a new bottle; the wine of modern industry requires – indeed, Veblen argues, *produces* – its own bottle:

> The "Spirit of Old Japan" is an institutional matter; that is to say it is a matter of acquired habits of thought, of tradition and training, rather than of native endowment peculiar to the race ... [As] Japan has with great facility and effect taken over the occidental state of the industrial arts, so should its population be due, presently and expeditiously, to fall in with the peculiar habits of thought that make the faults and qualities of the western culture – the spiritual outlook and the principles of conduct and ethical values that have been induced by the exacting discipline of this same state of the industrial arts among the technologically more advanced and mature of the western peoples. For good or ill ... the modern industrial system ... is in the long run incompatible with the prepossessions of medievalism.[57]

That could be read as a dry academic observation on the connections between industry and society; but Veblen had much more than that in mind. Writing just as World War I had broken out, Veblen argued that Japan's future as a great power would be an outcome of how the balance between the culture of the old and that of the new would fall. His "Opportunity for Japan" thought it "still safe" to see the "deterioration" of the feudal culture and its discipline as *not yet* having advanced to the point of endangering the Meiji elite's plans to have industry "serve the turn for the dynastic aggrandizement."

> However, its industrial strength ... must be turned to account before the cumulatively accelerating rate of institutional deterioration overtakes and neutralizes the cumulatively declining rate of gain in material efficiency: which should, humanly speaking, mean that Japan must strike ... within the effective lifetime of the [present] generation

... must throw all its available force, without reservation, into one headlong rush; since in the nature of the case no second opportunity of the kind is to be looked for. (Veblen, 266)

Even though Japan had fought two successful wars (against China in 1895 and against Russia in 1905) it was still seen as a quaint and backward nation in the West. "Within the effective lifetime of that generation" (as the 1930s opened) Japan had struck victoriously into China and annexed Manchuria and its rich mineral deposits. Not much later it was spreading south and west in Asian lands and was making its plans to bomb Pearl Harbor.

World War I was beneficial to Japan, increasing its exports and strengthening its relative strategic position in Asia as the other powers (the United States excepted) were weakened. By the late 1920s Japan was among those suffering from a disintegrating world economy. Its heavy industry needed both raw materials and markets. It had also had to contend with – and suppress – labor and socialist movements both before and after the war: labor and socialist movements that were but one outcome of industrial capitalist development in Japan – and everywhere else. By 1930, following Italy and preceding Germany, for reasons both somewhat similar and very different, Japan became the second major fascist nation, thereby realizing Veblen's prediction.

*

This survey of the industrial capitalist developments of what by 1914 were the major economic powers in the world (let alone the other industrializing, or non-industrializing, societies) is not intended to be comprehensive.[58] The national discussions have sought to illuminate several major (among other) points: 1) the nature of the quite diverse paths taken by the countries examined; 2) the major reasons they were enabled or led to take such different paths; and 3) a somewhat different matter; to provide the historical background for subsequent analyses of the *economics* that developed in the period 1850–1914. That background will show that, with rare exceptions, the economics profession was inexcusably – though explicably – aloof from obvious economic realities throughout the entire period – except for the small group that included Marx and Veblen.

Before turning to the evolution of neoclassical economics – those who shaped it and those who criticized it – it is essential to examine two important developments reacting to, supporting, or ultimately serving to push the processes of capitalist industrialization to the destruction of world war, and thence to the chaos and convulsions that produced the next and even more destructive war: the emergence of labor and socialist movements, and the spread and nature of global imperialism.

ARISE, YE PRISONERS OF STARVATION![59]

Because industrial capitalism took hold first in Britain, Britain was also the first home of what may be seen as a broad variety of attempts to slow or redirect its pace, and to redress the balance between its prime beneficiaries and the great mass of losers – in a word, to reform it as it went on its way. Note "reform," rather than " revolution" as the aim. That was the nature of virtually all efforts in *Britain* up to 1918. On the Continent matters were different, and the United States and Japan were different again, compared to the British and the Europeans, as well as with each other. Britain first.

As was noted in Chapter 1, even before modern industrialization began, the consequences of the enclosure movement for the majority of agricultural workers were severe. For them, the best that can be said for the half-century before 1800 is that it was better than the coming of the factory system,: ruthless and dangerous treatment for all – young or old, man, woman, or child. Consider this, taken not from a work critical but accepting of capitalism:

> The nature of the mass of evidence concerning the status of factory workers under *laissez faire* and unrestricted competition may be illustrated by the testimony before a Parliamentary committee in 1816. A cotton manufacturer stated that children as young as five years of age were employed; that the usual hours of work were fourteen, some mills requiring fifteen; and that some mills allowed no intermission for meals. A magistrate testified that the warm, humid, unventilated mills, with cotton lint ... polluting the air, induced a condition that required the frequent administration of emetics. A physician whose father-in-law owned a large mill testified "with the greatest reluctance" that the children, when they first came to the mills, with the close, humid atmosphere and high temperature, were seized with a mild fever and were subject to a subsequent debility. There was no protection from the machinery, and he had "too often" seen workers crushed to death, and the mangling of the hands of the children was "a very common thing." He stated further that children ... were never allowed to sit down during working hours; that they frequently walked two miles from their homes to the mills; and that the factories in his community usually operated from 6 o'clock in the morning until 7 o'clock at night in the summer, and from 7 until 8 in the winter ... and consumption [is] extremely common. (BKU, 433–4)

That discussion of this and related matters took place in conjunction with its authors' summary of the Factory Acts – legislation meant to curb the foregoing (and many other such) outrages, which typified the years after 1800, when all protections of labor had been extinguished. Several points are noted by the authors concerning the Factory Acts passed in 1802, 1819, 1833, 1842, 1844, and 1847, which were designed to improve the sanitation, hours, and safety conditions of children and women in the mills and mines. First, "men were excluded out of deference to the principles of *laissez faire* and freedom of contract"; second (and this noted more than once), "the most significant fact regarding the law was that it remained from the beginning virtually a dead letter" or "this law also was not enforced"; and, third, they cite Richard Arkwright (the first textile factory master) as remarking that in the 14 years of the relevant Act, "his factory had been visited only twice" (ibid.).

"Don't waste any time in mourning. Organize"[60]

Those realities for the years 1800–50 are representative of a larger and darker picture.[61] Together they go far to explain why in those and subsequent decades the workers (and religious and lay reformers such as Robert Owen) in Britain sought to form effective trade unions, instigate reforms, to initiate a socialist movement and the British Labour Party.[62]

The first half of the century was turbulent, and the propertied classes were nervous more often than not – as well they might have been. First, they were surrounded and much outnumbered by a large and always growing and more desperate class of "proletarians" – defined as those whose very survival (unlike their predecessors or themselves) had come to depend on subsistence wages received from generally heartless strangers. Second, the ways and means of factory work (to say nothing of that in the mines) stood in sharp and usually awful contrast to the pre-industrial lives of this impoverished working mass and not only could, but occasionally did, have an incendiary effect because of the combined impact of its regularity, its routines, its monotony, its dangers, and – as Marx saw it – its "alienation."[63]

Moreover, all these people were not only *not* living in the countryside, they *were* "living" in cities and, as Hobsbawm exclaims, "what cities!"

It was not merely that smoke hung over them and filth impregnated them, that the elementary public services – water-supply, sanitation, street-cleaning, open spaces, etc. – could not keep pace with the mass migration of men into the cities, thus producing, especially after 1830, epidemics of cholera, typhoid and an appalling constant toll of the two great groups of nineteenth-century urban killers – air pollution and water pollution, or respiratory and intestinal disease ... (Hobsbawm, 1968, 67)

"Not merely" all that. For it was taking place in a society where the poor masses were constantly reminded of the rich few – Disraeli's "two worlds" – for whom the desperate *knew* they were producing great wealth, the basis for which they could *see* with their own eyes as it left the factories and mines, could *see* the private form it took – what Veblen came to call "conspicuous consumption, conspicuous display, and conspicuous waste"[64] – *see* their great houses and horses and carriages and servants, *see* their finery, *see* their grand balls and their monuments. See all this and more, as they starved, as their families were split apart, as they died prematurely. Who could be rich and *not* worry?

But the Establishment – the polite English term for "ruling class" – got away with it, for the usual reasons. First, the State was always there to make any recalcitrants pay a very high price – prison, deportation, execution; second, to form a union or a co-op, or to organize a movement such as the Luddites ("the machine breakers")[65] or the Chartists required overcoming the obstacles of fear and division and confusion inside the group, as well as to withstand the powerful opposition from outside. It's hard to do such things in our time and place; it was much harder then and there.[66]

The harshness of life for most *before* 1850 can be imagined when it is noted that subsequently, after the so-called "golden years" of the 1870s and up to the end of the century, it was estimated that in London and York "about forty per cent of the working class lived in poverty," with no more than 15 percent of the working class – usually called the "aristocracy of labor" – living in comfort (Hobsbawm, 1968, 134).

Perhaps what that can mean in terms of one's physical existence (among much else) is more than symbolized by another set of facts:

In the 1870s eleven- to twelve-year-old boys from the upper class public schools were on average *five inches taller* than boys from industrial schools, and at all teen-ages three inches taller than the sons of artisans.[67] (ibid., Hobsbawm's emphasis)

It is testament to the power of the State that despite these conditions of exploitation and repression – and because of them – the British trade union movement had trouble getting off the ground before 1850 and only began to move toward its modern forms in the early 1870s, when there was a spurt in organization. But no more than that.

It was only when "hard times" appeared at the very end of the century that unionism finally became significant in industry and in Britain's politics – aided by the formation of a socialist movement (with two parts – one radical, and the other and larger group, moderate) – all of which managed to become the basis of an increasingly significant Labour Party before World War I.[68]

Socialist movements in Europe

Workers' struggles against capitalism on the Continent stood in sharp contrast to those in Britain. On the Continent industrialization did not take hold until well into the last half of the nineteenth century, with Germany leading the way, followed by France and Italy.[69] In all three countries there emerged a complex of trade union movements that soon politicized, incorporating the theoretical frameworks of Marxian socialism, anarchism (or syndicalism), and, very much in response to those, Christian socialism – ultimately to become Socialist, Communist, or Christian Socialist parties.[70]

Why the continental nations should differ as sharply as they did from Britain is of course a matter too complicated to be explained briefly; but the main elements making for differences can at least be noted. First, although capital and labor were sharply set off from each other in Britain, the class structure there was less entrenched than for France and the others. Next, Britain *had* come first, and by the 1870s (when the continental developments had begun to take their ultimate shape), Britain, benefiting from its "lead" and the accumulating loot from its empire, was able to begin "sharing the wealth" to some degree with at least parts of the working class ("the golden years"). Finally, the three continental nations were just as much "behind" as Britain was "ahead," and had much less social leeway.

For the foregoing and connected reasons, it is both relevant and interesting to note, Marx expected that socialism would come to power first in Britain or the United States,[71] and would do so peacefully. Too bad he was wrong.[72]

And the United States?

Has the U.S. not also had a class struggle between capital and labor? Of course it has, even if awareness of that struggle more often than not has been from the top down rather than from the bottom up. Gabriel Kolko loosens the knot of confusion somewhat on this matter in what follows:

> American society could ... be understood as a class structure without *decisive* class conflict, a society that had conflict limited to smaller issues that were not crucial to the existing order, and on which the price of satisfying opposition was relatively modest from the viewpoint of continuation of the social system. In brief, a static class structure serving class ends might be frozen into American society even if the interest and values served were those of a ruling class.[73]

In addition to those (and still other) reasons why American workers would be less class-conscious than workers elsewhere, the major factor has been that they have been (and are) "paid the wages of whiteness," as Roediger puts it. Those "wages" have not been mostly in money but in support of self-destructive attitudes combining superiority, fear, and hatred – cultivated attitudes decisive for the sustenance (and worsening) of the status quo.

Given all that, U.S. trade unions have been relatively conservative from their beginnings, with impermanent or rare shifts toward New Deal liberalism or radicalism. In terms of continuity, the American Federation of Labor (AFL) was the bedrock of U.S. unionism. Although before World War I about one-third of its members were also members of the American Socialist Party (led by Eugene Debs), the official anti-socialist position of the AFL was set in the 1890s, and has not wavered since.

The AFL's greatest crisis came in the 1930s, when it was challenged by the newly-formed Congress of Industrial Organizations (CIO), which sought to make it feasible to organize workers in mass-production industries such as autos, steel, and rubber. Before and for a brief period after World War I, workers had their strongest connection with radicalism. The greatest numbers were with the American Socialist Party (ASP); less numerous but more radical were those in Industrial Workers of the World (IWW). Whatever else set them apart from their European and British counterparts, these two groups stood gloriously alone in one critical issue: they both opposed U.S. entrance into World War I.

For that Debs himself and other Socialists as well as many Wobblies were sent to prison (or deported); in addition, after the war it became all too common for Wobblies to be lynched, as often by AFL members as by war veterans. (And as will be seen, the "Red Scare" of the 1920s virtually ended both groups' meaningful existence, while also severely weakening trade unions.)

More than the unionism of any other nation, that of the United States earned the name "business unionism," a term usually used without derision. What it signified early in the century and still does is that the concerns of U.S. unions are confined to better wages and working conditions (which in the 1960s came to mean pensions, health care, and paid vacations), and almost always for their own unions only.

Necessary though such efforts are, of course, they do little to improve the larger social process. This stands in contrast to the ubiquitous efforts of the British and European unions to seek political power through affiliated parties, power that could be (and has been used) for broader purposes. (We return to those matters in Part II. Suffice it to say here that both before and since World War I, American workers have given almost all their votes to the Democratic Party, whether because of its virtues or as the lesser evil – until Reagan's ability to sell irrationality made many workers willing victims of the anti-union GOP.)

Japan and Germany (again)

As we have seen, Japan stood almost alone in its developmental qualities before World War I – with, as always, some similarities with Germany. Because of the combination of the long-standing strength of militarism in its culture, and the great powers of the *zaibatsu* both in and outside the State (in addition to other reasons), the difficulties of organizing unions in Japan were more imposing than in any other industrial country. Lockwood summarizes those difficulties as follows:

> the power of the zaibatsu concerns in the labor market, where they were careful to maintain a common front, helped to stifle the growth of a vigorous trade union movement. There were other obstacles to trade unionism, to be sure – the pressure of population, the prevalence of female labor in factory industry, the wide dispersion of small enterprise throughout the countryside, the lack of experience in democratic mass organization. But the weakness of collective bargaining, even at its height in the twenties, and especially Japan's lagging progress in factory and social legislation, must be attributed in large measure to the intense opposition, led by business interests, which greeted every proposal for advance in these fields. Whatever the business rivalries of big firms, here they closed ranks and presented a solid front. In the political realm, as well, the existence of concentrated business power retarded the growth of democratic movements at home, while providing a pliant instrument for military aggression abroad.[74]

In concluding this discussion of labor and socialist movements before World War I, it is interesting to contrast Germany's experience with that of others, most especially with that of Japan – with whom its similarities were greatest.

In Germany too there was great repression, both of efforts to unionize and even more of socialists – who were outlawed. But the stark differences between the desperate lives of most German workers on the one hand, and, on the other, their productive efficiency (as noted, the highest in the world, in the late nineteenth century) combined with their overall desperation to maintain continuous pressures for more and effective organization.

Bismarck, the Iron Chancellor, in comparison with his counterparts of other times and places, was a "relative conservative." Thus it was he who, in order to "kill the socialist movement with kindness," in 1881 introduced the first social legislation of the modern era, the beginnings of the first comprehensive "social security program" in the industrial capitalist world.

It worked in the 1880s; but by the end of the 1890s the rigors of their lives prodded the workers to form in Germany what soon became the largest socialist party in the world. With its strong unions and its many seats in the Reichstag, the German socialists seemed on the way to fulfilling at least some of Marx's expectations. But the German Left had an Achilles' heel. This was early perceived by Veblen when, writing in 1907, he put forth the following analysis:

with the passage of time and the habituation to warlike politics and military discipline, the infection of jingoism [has] gradually permeated the body of Social Democrats, until they have now reached such a pitch of enthusiastic loyalty as they would not patiently hear a truthful characterization ... The relative importance of the national and international ideals in German socialist professions has been reversed since the seventies ... The Social Democrats have come to be German patriots first and socialists second, which comes to saying that they are a political party working for the maintenance of the existing order, with modifications.[75]

Seven years later, German socialists sitting in the Reichstag voted for the "war credits" that financed Germany's entrance to World War I, as their socialist counterparts were doing in the parliaments of France and Britain.

Veblen's gloomy conclusions to the foregoing observations were all too applicable to what lay ahead not just for the next few years but for the rest of the century – applicable, unfortunately to U.S. labor (among others), which all too cheerfully lent its patriotic weight to the Cold War (wittingly or not, in exchange for material gains):

The imperial policy seems in a fair way to get the better of revolutionary socialism [in Germany], not by repressing it, but by force of the discipline in imperialistic ways of thinking to which it subjects all classes of the population. How far a similar process of sterilization is under way, or likely to overtake the socialist movement in other countries is an obscure question ... (Veblen, 456)

Now to those "imperial policies," which, in conjunction with ongoing industrial capitalism, took the world to the havoc of war.[76]

A PLACE IN THE SUN

That phrase served as the slogan for Germany's imperialist thrust. Its energies, along with those of all the other industrial capitalist nations, began their rise to fever pitch in the 1880s. Even though well before then Britain's colonial empire was vast, it too joined the imperialist scramble across the globe. The term "imperialism" requires amplification – not only because so many economists and even some historians deny its existence, and reduce it to euphemism, but because those who acknowledge it do so with analytical differences.[77]

The first to approach imperialism systematically was the British economist J.A. Hobson (1858–1940) in his book *Imperialism: A Study* (1902). In terms of U.S. political classifications, Hobson would be seen not as a radical or Marxist, but as something of a New Deal liberal. His central theme was that British unemployment (then high) was a result principally of the inadequate purchasing power of the general population; that in turn was a consequence of the inequality of income. He posited that such inequality, and its high savings rates among the rich, required and led to substantial investment abroad to keep the national economy relatively buoyant – albeit at the cost of high unemployment.[78] The remedy was to reduce the inequality of income, raise the purchasing power of the working class, and eliminate the need for imperialism.

Whatever was missing or wrong about his analysis, it is generally agreed that it stimulated and furnished the starting-point for Rosa Luxemburg's *The Accumulation of Capital* (1913) and Lenin's *Imperialism: The Highest Stage of Capitalism* (1916). They in turn provided the basis for subsequent (and continuing) Marxist analyses and debates over imperialism, as well as the mainstream position that the phenomenon does not exist – or, if it does, it has always done so, and has no integral connection with capitalism as such.

Most of the mainstream rejection of imperialism as an outgrowth of maturing capitalism has been conducted by historians; the only mainstream economist who took the arguments seriously – as he did Marxism in general – was Joseph A. Schumpeter (1883–1950).[79] It is not irrelevant to note that Schumpeter, like Veblen, is often seen as a sociologist and historian, as well as an economist; that to be a trustworthy economist *should* also mean – irrespective of one's political position – to be seriously familiar with relevant sociological and historical studies is rarely remarked.

Schumpeter's critique of Marxian imperialist theory is largely sociological. He does not deny the ugly nature of the "facts" of the imperialism of the half-century preceding his study (as most other mainstream thinkers did). His point was that far from being an outgrowth of capitalism, it was intrinsically *opposed* to the very nature of capitalism: a "bourgeois," rational system for organizing economic life, as he saw it. The contradiction between the realities of the capitalist era and his view of capitalism's intrinsic nature were resolved by his belief that

> from the earliest times to the twentieth century men have been governed by drives of an irrational and instinctive kind which have cut across the rational pursuit of material interest assumed by the model [of pure capitalism] ... drives expressing themselves in the *political* sphere.

This provides the basis for his definition: "Imperialism is the objectless disposition on the part of the state to unlimited forcible expansion." [80]

Implicit in the disagreements of the foregoing discussion is a theory of power, or, more narrowly, a theory of the State. Are the powers of the State largely independent of other areas of power – specifically (here) those of the economic arena? If so, one could accept Schumpeter's argument (which he made more fully than above). But if, as is assumed here (in consonance with, among others, Marx and Veblen), the powers of the State are organically linked with those of capital, and that where one begins and the other ends in the capitalist process is perhaps impossible to perceive, then Marxian theory and others of its sort become plausible. It could allow one to believe, for example, that the powers of the State and of business are one and the same, only in different forms. That is not assumed here, nor was it by Veblen or by most Marxists. The latter indeed have been and remain in conflict with each other, not only because the relationships and processes are as intricate as they are numerous, but because one of the major gaps in Marxian theory has been and remains its theory of the State – a gap begun to be filled in recent decades.

Leaving that discussion now, in what follows it will be assumed that imperialism – as distinct from colonialism – emerged during the last half of the nineteenth century, that it was not the policy of a particular nation so much as that of *all* the industrial capitalist nations, and that it was just as integral to capitalist development as industrialism, the combination of which was to become disastrous in its effects.

Now to some of the high (or low) points.

The rat race begins

The imperialist phase of capitalist expansion was initiated by the "scramble for China" in mid-century, the turbulence that had jolted Japan back into the world. By the 1880s it became more intense and more dangerous with the "partition of Africa," a carving-up in which others than the already present British, French, and Dutch sought to have a slice.

Setting aside Belgium,[81] what they (mostly the Germans and the Italians) got was more in the nature of slivers than slices.

But that process, picking up where the slave trade and related predations on what ambiguously was called "the dark continent" had left off, carried on over the centuries with both quantitative and qualitative jumps in its military violence and social destruction. Seldom is it remarked that the widespread and seemingly endless tragedies in that continent – now *formally* freed of western power – have been and remain today the inevitable consequence of the "carving-up" process. In addition to the death and destruction each step along the 500-year path, the ancient and "natural" forms of social organization of the numerous peoples of Africa were comprehensively "reorganized" to fit within the boundaries set by the imperialists. Numerous tribes found themselves compressed organizationally into a nation and, frequently, separated by borders entirely artificial to them. These borders, within which the government, the ruling religion, the economy, the military strength, everything resided, were in the hands of foreigners who knew nothing of their language, their customs, their needs, their lives – and furthermore couldn't have cared less.[82]

... And speeds up

While the Europeans were busying themselves in the Middle East and Africa (and elsewhere), from the 1880s on, Japan and the United States, both geographically isolated from any serious military conflict with the Europeans, were picking up small or large chunks of empire for themselves with impunity.

Japan made a foray into Formosa (now Taiwan) in the 1870s, was booted out (with the help of the French in the 1880s), and returned to stay until 1945 as part of its gains from the Sino–Japanese war of 1895. It began its first moves into mainland China as a dividend of the Russo–Japanese war of 1904–05, which poised Japan on the edge of Korea and Manchuria – taking formal control of the former in 1910, and making its successful invasion of the latter (with its strong resources in coal, iron, and oil, as well as its agriculture) in 1931, while also paving the way for its larger invasion of 1937.

As for the United States from the 1870s to 1914, the historian William Appleman Williams records 25 "American interventions excluding declared wars" in those years. There were, of course, also some declared wars, most importantly the Spanish–American war.[83] The stated reason for that intervention in what began as a revolution in Cuba to oust the Spanish was to help the Cubans do so; the consequence was that the Spanish were kicked out and the U.S. moved in (until kicked out in turn by Fidel Castro).

The U.S. picked up not only Cuba, but other bits and pieces of the Caribbean, the largest bit being Puerto Rico. At the same time, and for the same reasons, the U.S. helped the Filipinos rid themselves of the Spanish, only to find themselves confronted by the Americans in a war in which, it was conservatively estimated, 300,000 Filipinos were killed. They then became an *American* colony.

In short, it is not the Africans who are the cause of today's deadly problems in Africa, but their historical invaders. The same is, has been and remains equally the case in Latin America and the Caribbean, in Asia and the Pacific islands, in the Middle East and the Mediterranean littoral, in the Balkans, in Eastern Europe. What was done to the Native Americans has already been discussed.[84]

... Then explodes

It is revealing to examine one process in one geographic area, as a microcosm of imperialism and its proclivity for fomenting war. This process centered in the Middle East and on what might seem to be a simple matter of transportation, " the Berlin to Baghdad Railway."

It all started with a concession given by Turkey to Germany to build a railroad connecting Istanbul (Constantinople) with Ankara (both in Turkey), with branch lines into, among other areas, Persia (now Iran). Soon however, the financing and the control of the project became a tangle of conflicting business and national interests, with each of the major powers (rightly) fearful that its interests would be compromised or broken. Britain, as the major sea power in the Mediterranean and with control of the Suez Canal and thus trade with the East, adamantly opposed *any* competition by rail. Russia, with its long-standing enmity with Turkey, was nervous about the possibilities of increased German influence. France worried that its substantial but increasingly fragile position in the Middle East would break down. And so it went. Tempers frayed, fears rose, conflicts multiplied, battles began to break out – hither, thither, and yon: small at first, rising both in number and importance over time.[85]

Then, on a sunny afternoon in June 1914, and seemingly quite irrationally, a student in Sarajevo shot and killed Archduke Ferdinand of Austria. And the festering wounds turned gangrenous.

Keynes, in the opening pages of his *The Economic Consequences of the Peace*, memorialized that moment in his (perhaps sardonically) elegant way when he exclaimed: "What an extraordinary episode in the economic progress of man that age was which came to an end in August 1914!" He went on to note the much-celebrated accomplishments of that "episode" for "the greater part of the population" for several paragraphs, before concluding:

But most important of all, he ["the inhabitant of London"] regarded this state of affairs as normal, certain, and permanent, and any deviation from it as aberrant, scandalous, and avoidable. The projects and politics of militarism and imperialism, of racial and cultural rivalries, of monopolies, restriction, and exclusion, which were to play the serpent to this paradise, were little more than the amusements of his daily newspaper, and appeared to exercise almost no influence at all on the ordinary course of social and economic life, the international-isation of which was nearly complete in practice.[86]

The "projects, politics, and rivalries" that played "the serpent to this paradise" were not in the nature of warts, but the bone, meat, and gristle of a world shaped by social institutions and processes that simultaneously depended upon and feverishly increased both conflict and competition. War could not be avoided in that context; at best it could be postponed for such time as economic and geographic expansion might be prolonged. But the growth of profitable markets and expansion over the planet's surface have their limits, the first set by purchasing power, the second by nature.

If there was little surprise when war broke out in 1914 there was both surprise and shock at the war's depth, its duration, its spread, and its seemingly unparalleled (up to then) savagery.

Except for the first industrial war – the Civil War of the United States – there had never been even an intimation that war could be so destructive on such a large scale, that it could endure for so long. As early as 1915, in Germany – which had "started the war" – it was being called "the endless war," by the very people who had supported it.

The damages done by the war were unprecedented. They could not be measured only in the 10 million (at least) military deaths and countless civilian dead and wounded, plus the destruction of equipment and resources. The considerably more enduring damage was social: in that realm the war's effects were those of a massive earthquake, followed by seemingly endless aftershocks – which, in an important sense, have never ceased, and may never cease.

We will see in the next chapter that those causes of the war that may be seen as economic, far from being resolved, were exacerbated. That was clear to Keynes (and was indeed a major theme of his *Consequences*). He was but one of those – Veblen was another, if with different reasoning – who warned that the end of World War I was but the prelude to World War II.

For, it may be asserted, destructive though that war was, it was not destructive *enough*; not destructive enough to weaken the principal contenders sufficiently to deter them from further social lunacy. That "sufficient destruction" was provided by World War II. At its end, among almost all the major and minor powers, only the United States was able to fend for itself – even, for a while, to feed itself.[87] Less obvious, but at least as important was that the vital heart of capitalist vitality – and thus of the viability of the entire social process – had been critically wounded. A functioning world economy no longer existed.

Thus had the dynamic interaction of capitalism, industrialism, nationalism, and imperialism – an interaction guided by the power of the "big four" economies of Britain, the United States, Germany and Japan – set the stage for the chaos and convulsion, the revolutions and counter-revolutions, the economic cataclysms, and the vast cultural and social transformations that culminated in World War II. It was the predictable (and predicted) outcome of the Peace Treaty and its "armistice," a pleasant euphemism for an armed and deeply unstable truce.

*

Had you lived from, say, 1880 to 1910, and confined your reading entirely to the works of the neoclassical economists, you would never have suspected that the world was undergoing the most rapid processes of social, economic, cultural, political, and technological change in history; or that the world was in tumult (and shouting). The bigwigs of economics sailed placidly – and all too often arrogantly – on their way, living in another world. It was the analytical smiling face of that "typical inhabitant of London" immortalized by Keynes.

ECONOMISTS IN WONDERLAND

'Twas brillig, and the slithy toves
Did gyre and gimble in the wabe:
All mimsy were the borogoves,
And the mome raths outgrabe.

The serenity of those lines, and their meaninglessness,[88] well represent what economics was coming to by the third quarter of the nineteenth century, and which – called " neoclassical economics" – had taken center stage by its end: despite all.

That " all" has been the focus of this chapter. Its materials hardly support serenity; nor, insofar as neoclassical economics became and remains the fig leaf of capitalist ideology, was it meaningless. The concealment was and is systematic, a matter of " methodology": intrinsic to its theoretical system was a group of assumptions (its "paradigm") wherein the theory " moved."

"Let us now assume ..."

What is wrong with neoclassical theory is not, of course, that it makes assumptions. All theory must do so; which is to say that theory *entails* abstracting from certain elements of reality.[89] The assumptions of a theory consist of what is taken by the theorist as not essential to the main matter to be explained and can therefore be " set aside" – *not* examined, *not* taken into account in the theory.

It should not be necessary to add that if and when the assumptions of a theory are "relaxed" and the relevant reality brought back into focus, the theory should retain its validity. Thus, when Newton assumed away friction in his model $S = \frac{1}{2}GT^2$ – his theory of gravity still held when tested in the real world of ubiquitous friction.

That is notoriously not the case when any one (let alone all!) of the neoclassical assumptions are "relaxed" – that is, when reality has jumped back over the barricades against reality. Why that is so is illuminated by an examination of when and how and why that way of thinking came into existence.

As was noted in Chapter 1, classical political economy came into being as an attack on and critique of the dying remnants of the feudal and mercantilist periods. It was an economics of change and development. As such it was concerned with processes extending over substantial time, taking on their pace, direction and forms because of the *connections* between the economy and the larger society: thus "political economy."

But neoclassical economics came into being as economists had begun to view industrial capitalism as fully *established*, most especially in Great Britain. Among the many who gave that economics its main outlines and outlook, Alfred Marshall (1842–1924), though not an originator, became pre-eminent. He synthesized the works of others and, in doing so, gave neoclassical economics its "character" – a character conservative in all meanings of the term.[90]

We have seen that economic theory concerns itself with three major areas of economic life – the functioning of particular markets (labor, commodity, financial), called "microeconomics"; the functioning of the economy as a whole, or "macroeconomics"; and its functioning in world markets, or "trade theory." The last was inherited from Ricardo, and has changed little over the decades, except to become (like economics in general) always more abstract.

Macroeconomics, we saw in Chapter 1, was brushed out of existence by Say's Law which, in asserting that "supply creates its own demand" essentially meant there was *no* problem, except to keep the government out of the economy.[91] Much attention continued to be given to the aggregative behavior of the economy in the period under examination here, for it was going through the ups and downs called business cycles. Although the theories of the cycle that came into being were of no lasting value, the empirical work often associated with them has been, not least that examined and analyzed by Schumpeter.[92]

That is, neoclassical economics may be seen almost entirely as trade theory and microeconomics, the latter's main elements constituted by "the theory of the firm," "the theory of (individual) demand," and "the theory of distribution."[93] That economics, created well over a century ago, fell into disarray in the period between the two world wars, both because it lacked a macroeconomics and because its emphases on free trade, rationality, and perfect competition – like Say's Law – stood in hilarious (or tragic) conflict with brute realities. Now it is back, even more abstract and even more absurd (and even more dangerous) than ever before: but that's another story. We now examine the original nature of microeconomics, the heart of the doctrine.

Recipes for absurdities

Part of the impulse for neoclassical economics was ideological in origin (to counter the influence of Marx, in a time of growing social tension). Part of it was "technical," seeing the function of economics as that of meeting the relatively narrow needs of the economy – meaning, generally, its business sector – at a time of increasing competition for both resources and markets. The rationale for economics was to become the "science of economizing, maximizing and efficiency and, at the same time, by removing its analysis from history and becoming a theory of "statics," it served as a theory for working within and preserving the status quo.

It became, in the words of its main "methodologist" (as distinct from theorist, which Marshall was), Sir Lionel Robbins, "the *science* which *studies* human behavior as a relationship between ends and *scarce means* which have alternative uses." [94]

But if "science" entails the checking of hypotheses against evidence, and "studies" means attention to reality, that definition of economics – which it is still [95] – adds up to what has come to be called "disinformation," a member of the ideology family.

Of course there is scarcity – of resources, of the basic necessities of life, and of much else. But, as will be argued more fully in Part II, by any reasonable measure of the use of resources, we waste a scandalous percentage of our natural resources and, therefore and as well, our human resources.[96] Furthermore, in addition to the misuse of resources, there is the deliberate *creation* of scarcity in the market (for almost everything) by the well-known techniques associated with oligopoly and monopoly – techniques designed to keep prices up in the face of what might otherwise be market abundance (and falling prices and profits). Nor can we forget that for most people the scarcities marring their lives are a consequence of deliberate policies to keep wages low while, at the same time, their prior livelihoods have been "modernized" out of existence, echoing the enclosures of eighteenth-century Britain.

When neoclassical economists paid attention to any of that at all, it was with the cheerful postscript that what may *seem* to have gone awry will take a turn for the better "in the long run." And what of the main "assumptions" of that economics, then and now? They are contained in what Stiglitz calls "the ingredients in the Basic Competitive Model," a "model" whose main elements haven't changed one iota for well over a century, except to become always more mathematized – itself something of a comment on its scientific nature, given that almost everything else *has* changed. The aforementioned ingredients summarized by Stiglitz are three:

1. Rational self-interested consumers.
2. Rational, profit-maximizing firms.
3. Competitive markets with price-taking behavior. (Stiglitz, 31)

Let's take a look at that trio in terms of realities a century ago, and a glimpse at their subsequent evolution:

1.Consumers

A century (or more) ago (when this economics started) most people were not "consumers" in the modern sense; they were wage-earners, and their wages were so low they had no choices to make, except whether to eat less bread and more potatoes (and setting aside the manner in which the *men* who worked in the mines or mills spent all too much of it on tobacco and beer). Those consumers who *could* make choices, who had some genuinely "surplus" income, were those who captured Veblen's attention and dispraise, when he classified their consuming habits as "conspicuous display and waste."[97]

The latter were what must be called "irrational choices." What the few were doing then in our age of consumerism is now being done by a general population "making choices." In other words, they are responding to essential, massive, and ubiquitous advertising specifically designed to lead to *irrational* choices: designed, as Paul Baran has put it, to "want what they don't need, and not to want what they do."[98] And to borrow beyond the point of rationality in order to do so.

2. Profit-maximizing firms

Businesses seek to make profits, but there are some quibbles to be made. If we look at small businesses – "small" in the sense of the little bookstore, the corner grocer, the shoe repairer, the barber – those very convenient, usually very hard-working souls (often families) are quite often doing what makes sense to them because the alternative is to close their shops and work for someone else (perhaps at an even higher, or at least more assured income). They are doing what might be seen as sensible and life-preserving, but it is not – as economists use the term – rational. They are not *calculating* correctly, for such calculation excludes all but *quantitative* considerations. And, it should be added, of all the businesses in the United States, the overwhelming number are very small indeed – and easily 95 per cent of the total of 15 million businesses. Not very rich, and even less secure.[99]

Big businesses are probably run with considerably more "rationality." But anyone who has worked in one will know that there's a lot of irrational sludge and drudge – called "bureaucracy" – in the big companies that is more negative than positive in its impact on profits. It exists for various reasons, and it varies from country to country – much higher levels (executive incomes) in the United States than in Japan, for example – but there it is. And, as economists measure (or should measure) such things, it is *neither* rational *nor* profit-maximizing.

3. Competition

Here we come to the factually most outrageous of the assumptions of neoclassical theory: competitive markets with price-taking behavior. As *economists* define competitive markets, they exist only in industries in which all firms produce identical products (and would thus be fools to advertise), no firm is large enough to influence market prices by withholding any of its production from the market, and all businesses (and consumers) possess all the requisite information to make rational choices.

In addition, it is assumed that the State is outside the economic process, that technological change is absent, and the social process is irrelevant. In short, both economists and their students are led to believe that "society," far from being the subject matter of the social sciences, is merely a synonym for "parameters." And that numbers – usually imagined numbers – are all that count.

"Ah," but a mainstream economist reading the foregoing would object, "you are being unfair, you are leaving out all the 'ifs ands and buts' of economics." I do so because they are treated as dirty secrets within the profession (and the study of economics) and seldom acknowledged in public.

That is, in the formulation of economic policy – whether a century ago or now – underlying the rationale for such policies is the assumption that the market is the best guide for economic policy ("Listen to the market!") *and* that "markets" are perfectly competitive – even though virtually all economists *know* (or used to) that is not so. Nor was it when the theories were being framed.[100]

In short, this is not an economics at all, but an elaborately disguised ideology; and as such, it is worse than useless. It was allowed to serve as a guide to economic policy until the 1930s, and after what was once seen as its timely death, strides the world again today. Considering the human and social costs paid in the past, and those plus its environmental costs now, it verges on a combination of criminality and madness to allow it to persist.

Now we turn all too briefly to Marx and Veblen who, for largely similar reasons, would have *none* of that "economics," whether on methodological, political, ethical, or rational/scientific grounds.

Counter-attack: Karl Marx

Some know it and some don't, but almost all of those who today seek to understand capitalism (or have sought to since his time) do so at least partially with analytical tools first forged by Marx – though they may not do so in his spirit. But this is to say something else, something stronger: to understand capitalism, it is *necessary* to use Marxian " tools" whatever else is also required.

That is not only or mostly because Marx gave capitalism its name and to perceive its nature. It was that his prior and ongoing scholarship and intellectual profundity led him to recognize that the industrial capitalism of mid-nineteenth-century Britain was a new *social formation*. That recognition drove him to seek to uncover its "economic laws of motion," and the fuels and machinery that propel it through time and space.[101]

In earlier pages, expansion, exploitation, and oligarchic rule have been singled out as the imperatives of capitalism, its *sine qua non*. Each of those – or, better, the three of them seen as one – was extricated by Marx from the complicated depths of the capitalist social process, examined at all levels of abstraction and empiricism, and, as he might have put it, "made to reveal itself."

For economic understanding there had never been anything like the corpus of Marx's work; we may assume there will never be again. Not that Marx got everything right or that he studied all that was necessary. He didn't and he couldn't – for his own time, let alone ours. And he knew it.[102]

What Marx did do was to pierce through the manifold surface appearances of the capitalist process to see them as an organic whole of "interlocking" and dynamically related "parts" with great powers and great needs and great consequences – intended or not, positive or negative (see below).

The social process

He had seen where his analysis was going in 1859, as witness the famous statement that opens his *Contribution to the Critique of Political Economy* (and note the emphasized passages, for they presage some of the key elements of what would become "Marxian theory"):

> In the *social production* which men carry on they enter into definite relations that are indispensable and independent of their will; these

relations of production correspond to a definite state of development of their *material forces of production.* The sum total of these relations of production constitutes *the economic structure of society* – the *real foundation,* on which rises a legal and political *superstructure* and to which correspond definite forms of *social consciousness. The mode of production* in material life determines the social, political and intellectual life processes *in general. It is not the consciousness of men that determines their being,* but, on the contrary, *their social being that determines their consciousness* ...[103]

Marx has been derided as being an "economic determinist." A thoughtful perusal of the phrases italicized above, not to mention the many explicit arguments to the contrary made throughout his works, shows that Marx rejects such a view. The quotation that follows is worth studying for itself; in giving due importance to that which is "transmitted from the past" (that is, history), it is of course inclusive of much that was not as well as much that was "economic":

Men make their own history, but they do not make it just as they please; they do not make it under circumstances chosen by themselves, but under circumstances directly encountered, given and transmitted from the past. The tradition of all the dead generations weighs like a nightmare on the brain of the living.[104]

Above it was said that Marx saw both negative and positive consequences of the capitalist processes. Negative, clearly; but positive? Certainly. Marx's radicalism did not inoculate him against the optimism of the nineteenth century. What he found positive about capitalism was that it was the most *progressive* of all historical systems – prising peoples and societies loose from a stultifying past; not least, though by no means only because of its ultimately liberating technology. And, though painfully, capitalism's achievements would do it in and liberate humanity. How?

The dynamics of nineteenth-century capitalist development
The intended achievements of capitalism include capital accumulation. But Marx argued that the latter *necessarily required and created* a working class thrown together to labor in large numbers under one roof and under harsh conditions; in turn, because they are human beings, they would move inexorably toward the organization they needed to empower themselves. Second, because the accumulation process would just as inexorably lead to a deep crisis of global overproduction that would at some point be met by the rising strength of the working class. Capitalism would have given birth to its own gravediggers.[105]

We should live so long. Failed predictions notwithstanding, the *analytical* apparatus of Marx was important in his own time and much of it continues to be basic to understanding today's capitalist processes; and much of it does not. Here we *very* summarily examine what (to this writer) does and does not.

First, it should be understood that Marx's economic theory is to be found in the three volumes of *Capital*; next, that those volumes – whatever their ultimate consequences – were meant as *economic theory* and (specifically as the subtitle of Volume I indicates) "a critique of classical political economy." For such a critique to be put forth required that it does so on the " territory" and in the language of what was being criticized; which meant, more than anything else, in the land of Ricardian theory.

An earlier discussion of Ricardo had him focusing on foreign trade. But his *Principles* opens with its focus on the distribution of income, and the intent of his theory was to *change* that distribution to the advantage of the industrial capitalist and to the disadvantage of the landed gentry. It is worth repeating the opening lines of his *Principles*:

> The produce of the earth – all that is derived from its surface by the united application of labour, machinery, and capital, is divided among the three classes of the community, namely, the proprietor of the land, the owner of the stock of capital necessary for its cultivation, and the labourers by whose industry it is cultivated.[106]

As has been noted earlier, Ricardo accepted the "labor theory of value," which played an important role in his own arguments; and his way of arguing was highly abstract (and ultimately became the mode of analysis for economics). Ricardo was unquestionably the most influential economist of the years in which Marx began his theoretical journey.

Marx did not create the "labor theory," but he had to deal with it. In doing so, he turned it against its makers, and did so by showing that by *accepting* Ricardo's assumptions it could be shown that the critical share of landholders' income called "rent" (we would call them excess profits) was due to their *power*, not to their contribution to production. The same was true for the "profits" of capitalists. The landholders' power was expressed in Parliament, and gave them protective tariffs; the capitalists' power came from their ownership and control of the means of life: equipment and tools. The end result for the worker was that to survive he would be *exploited*.

Of course the realities of exploitation do not need *theory* to verify them; as long as the term "exploitation" is defined in reasonable terms, all that *is* necessary is to examine the working conditions, the wages, and the power relationships between workers and employers. Marx's use of the labor theory of value does not do that as such; nor, given the "rules of the game" for theory, did he have to. Marx showed, within those "rules," what he sought to show; in many factually descriptive pages of *Capital* he showed the realities. This leads me to note that for those who have not read *Capital*, it is pertinent to say something about its table of contents.

First, it should be recognized that the theoretical core of *Capital* is largely incomprehensible except when seen as a *critique* of then contemporary theory; without knowing what that theory was, it would be difficult to give serious meaning to Marx's theoretical arguments; they take up perhaps a third of the first volume. One can, and in my mind should, read Volume I not from front to back, but something like the reverse: begin with Part VIII (its last "Part"), the excellent historical section, which shows how capitalism came into being. Then read the middle portions of the volume, especially Chapters 10, 15, and 25 – the parts from which were drawn the evidence on worker conditions cited in our preceding chapter, which go a long way toward *defining* exploitation. Then, and last, turn to Part I, Chapter 1, the very first paragraph of which is abstract theory. (It would help to have consulted a good summary of economic thought before that, from among those suggested earlier.)

It was only when economics began to find its way into its present fairyland and, at the same time, find its way toward abstracting from almost everything of consequence (or reality) that the term "exploitation" disappeared from the economic discussions. If you look for it, you'll not find it – the word, let alone the reality. If you do see the word, it will be as regards "the exploitation of nature." And only rarely will *that* exploitation be seen as grievously dangerous.

However: it is the case that much of what Marx argued theoretically cannot be taken as an adequate guide to today's capitalism. The framework of assumptions within which he argued, although they could seem meaningful in his part of the nineteenth century, cannot seem so today. They were "Ricardian" assumptions which, alarmingly, have been continued over into present-day economics (those of the sort we examined earlier in this chapter).

Today's capitalism still conforms to Marxian explanations to a substantial degree. When that is so they are *contemporary* Marxian explanations, often embedded in a group of supporting analyses (Veblenian, Keynesian), and at least partially based on the path-breaking work by Paul Baran and Paul Sweezy, *Monopoly Capital: An Essay on the American Economic and Social Order* (1966). (Note the important adjectives "American" and "social" of their title.)

Industrial capitalism in Marx's time meant Britain's (his data were *entirely* British). Today's capitalism is dominated by American ways and means. Moreover, the capitalism of Marx's time was more narrowly "economic" than now; for today's capitalism to function effectively it has had to make "capitalistic" (so to speak) all elements of social existence. As *Monopoly Capital* made clear, to the "exploitation of labor" of Marx's day the more socially embracing capitalism of today adds the effective exploitation of the consumer (through monopolistic powers on both the demand and supply sides) and of the taxpayer (where a large majority of the population pays more in taxes than it receives in benefits, and a small minority receives more in benefits than it pays in taxes). It has added also an enormous State (working with enormous corporations), which has discovered permanent militarism (paid for by taxes, producing profits) as a solution to many of the weaknesses of capitalism.

All that will be discussed at more length in Part II, where the analytical framework of *Monopoly Capital* will be analyzed. It has been emphasized that capitalism changes with always greater rapidity; thus, not only does *Capital* need "updating," but so now does *Monopoly Capital*. Accordingly, in Part II I shall seek once more to update and broaden what may be seen as the several elements of the core of Marxian political economy from its origins to the present, in order to allow it to serve for these times. In doing so, it will be argued that we may think of Monopoly Capitalism I and II (roughly 1950–75 and 1975–1990s, respectively) and, given that our present system will soon find its own crisis, that the seeds for Monopoly Capitalism III are now germinating.

I add that one may be sure that whatever the defects or virtues of that effort, it too will need updating and broadening within a decade. If not sooner.

Now let us turn to Veblen who, having learned much from Marx (and criticized him astutely), went on to create his own approach to understanding the capitalist world (some of which came to be embodied in *Monopoly Capital*).[107]

And Thorstein Veblen

Veblen was something else, different from everyone, including Marx; although, as he remarked in his critical essay on Marx, "there is no system of economic theory more logical than that of Marx."[108]

Veblen was radical in his analyses, but not at all in his politics, and least so in his language. His criticisms went deep and ranged widely – against the State and militarism, against business ways and means and the capitalist process, against organized religion, and against the corruption of (his beloved) university, against the press; pretty much everything.

Veblen never refers to "capitalism," or "the working class," or "the ruling class," or *any* class – except, of course, his ironic code-word for those who dominate, the "leisure class." His language is never sharp-edged, except insofar as one translates his irony as concealed – or, in current slang, "closet" – sharpness. His sentences were long, convoluted, and intricate, often so much as to function as camouflage. Thus, and in the same order as above: not capitalism, but "the system of business enterprise," not the working class, but "the underlying population," not concentrated power, but "the vested interests." And so on. Camouflage effectively deceives potential allies as much as existing enemies, of course. Whether Veblen cared about that is not known. Be that as it may, many managed to decipher his codes and perpetuate and expand upon his analyses – Robert A. Brady was one, Paul Sweezy, in *Monopoly Capital* one of many others.

Although there is good reason to believe that Veblen had a different and better socioeconomic system in mind ("industrial democracy"), he never *openly* espoused anything political, never engaged in politics. And although he was analytical, he rarely made use of abstraction (except in one chapter of *Business Enterprise*, and some, myself included, have seen that as an extended joke). One unfortunate consequence of his systematic *in*discipline is that his works taken together do not easily yield the coherent whole that underlies them; he makes you work at it.[109]

Human beings versus the system

Veblen was a bone-marrow skeptic; if in his writing he displayed any passion it was against those who were *not*; not least was this so as regards neoclassical theory. Having set forth his own view of human nature in his *Instinct of Workmanship* (1914), he was especially passionate, to the point of acidity, in his hilarious critique of the neoclassical economists' view of human nature, as it had evolved from Bentham to Veblen's time (and as it has remained today), when it had become what was called "psychological hedonism":

> The hedonistic conception of man is that of a lightning calculator of pleasures and pains, who oscillates like a homogeneous globule of desire of happiness under the impulse of stimuli that shift him about the area, but leave him intact. He has neither antecedent nor consequent. He is an isolated, definitive human datum, in stable equilibrium except for the buffets of the impinging forces that displace him in one direction or another. Self-imposed in elemental space, he spins symmetrically about his own spiritual axis until the parallelogram of force bears down upon him, whereupon he follows the line of the resultant. When the force of the impact is spent, he comes to rest, a self-contained globule of desire as before.[110]

As noted earlier, at the heart of Marshall's *Principles* was "the theory of the firm." That firm, whose theoretical existence went (and goes) under the name of "the representative firm" doing its "business as usual" was given its due by Veblen in this way:

> business as usual, which means working at cross-purposes as usual, waste of work and materials as usual, restriction of output as usual, unemployment as usual, labor quarrels as usual, competitive selling as usual, mendacious advertising as usual, waste of superfluities as usual by the kept classes, and privation as usual for the common man.[111]

These are but two of what could be numerous excerpts from Veblen's artillery barrages against neoclassical economics. At least as interesting and important were his numerous essays and books showing the malign consequences of almost every contemporary institution, whether at home or abroad, and irrespective of function – most heartfelt, because it was so close to *his* home, in his critiques of the educational process.[112]

Although writing in 1904 – but certainly influenced by the Spanish–American–Cuban war and all the dangerous hoopla attending it – Veblen anticipated all too well what the complex of tendencies then just appearing (including, though not noted here, the role of the media) held for the future, as note the following:

> Business interests urge an aggressive national policy and businessmen direct it. Such a policy is warlike as well as patriotic. The direct cultural value of a warlike business policy is unequivocal. It makes for a conservative animus on the part of the populace. During war time, and within the military organization at all times, under martial law, civil rights are in abeyance; and the more warfare and armament the more abeyance ... A military organization is a servile organization. Insubordination is the deadly sin. [And what is true of the military becomes so also for the civilian population.] They learn to think in warlike terms of rank, authority, and subordination, and so grow progressively more patient of encroachments upon their civil rights ... At the same stroke [patriotic ideals] direct the popular interest to other, nobler, institutionally less hazardous matters than the unequal distribution of wealth or of creature comforts.[113]

Perhaps Veblen's deepest and most general probing took place when he took it upon himself to develop, in effect, a theory of human nature. He did so in his *The Instinct of Workmanship*. There (and along with much else) he argued that our species is marked by two sets of inclinations,[114] the one predatory ("the instinct of sportsmanship"), the other life-serving ("the instinct of workmanship"); the one destructive, the other constructive. And he saw that the modern institutional complex encouraged our destructive side. When one breaks through the elaborate camouflage of his language, hiding beneath it one thus finds a deep pessimism:

> In the cases where it has happened that those instincts which make directly for the material welfare of the community, such as the parental bent and the sense of workmanship, have been present in such potent force, or where the institutional elements at variance with the continued life-interests of the community of the civilization in question have been in a sufficiently infirm state, there the bonds of custom, prescription, principles, precedent, have been broken – or loosened or shifted so as to let the current of life and cultural growth go on, with or without substantial retardation. But history records more frequent and more spectacular instances of the triumph of imbecile institutions over life and culture than of peoples who have by force of instinctive insight saved themselves alive out of a desperately precarious institutional situation, such, for instance, as now faces the people of Christendom. (1914, 24–5)

That was written with regard to the "imbecile institutions" extant in 1914; the "institutional situation" as these words are written are surely no less " desperately precarious," and the institutions are at least as imbecilic. Shall we "save ourselves alive"?

3   Death Throes: Chaos, War, Depression, War Again; Economics in Disarray, 1914–45

THE WAR TO END ALL WARS – BUT THAT DIDN'T

Never in history have there been so many bloody conflicts, seemingly without interruption, as *after* 1918 – a veritable torrent of anguish, blood, and calamity, the ABCs of the modern era in a world seemingly gone mad. What made it so, makes it so, still?

If and when such questions are put to mainstream economists, in or outside the classroom, the usual response is "Why ask us? It's not in our field." The truth in that answer is self-damning: economics has been placed in an orbit outside the social process. We have seen that mainstream economics exiles such messy matters to a permanent limbo of "all other things being equal,"[1] for those "things" are seen as ineligible for citizenship within the sacred boundaries ("parameters") of economics. "Economics looks only at markets." (It would be helpful if it did even that, instead of only making assumptions about them.)

But economists proudly proclaim themselves as scientists, see their use of abstraction as Newtonian in origin: to construct large abstractions such as "the economic system" and "the market system," and narrower (but vital) ones such as "marginal utility" or "utility" itself is to walk in a grand tradition (*pace* Isaac).

Messy world, neat economics

But Newton (and other authentic scientists) treat of an existing earth, existing space, existing weights and measures, existing friction, existing bodies. There are, of course, real markets – for food and clothing, autos and steel. And one can study such markets – how much is produced, bought, sold, or inventoried. But *the* market and *the* economy that economists analyze and "model" exist only as their invention.[2] Moreover, particular food markets (and the food market in general) exist in dynamic interaction not only with other real markets, but with real people who receive real incomes and live their lives in a real country whose many dimensions affect the entirety of their lives – including their food purchases.

Of course, you say. Of course, the economists will also say. But you and I do not and cannot ignore the connections between our food purchases and the rest of our lives; the economists should not, but *do*. They are *taught* that to do so is natural and necessary, and not to do so is to violate the rules of the game.

For the rest of us, however, to analyze "economic" processes as if they had no interaction with the "rest of the society" is a notion so breathtaking in its vapidity that one is struck speechless.

That is why the preceding chapter was a set of arguments (with others yet to be made) which might be seen as having led to the question: "Without capitalism's role in the social process before and after 1914, is it possible that World War I would (or *could*) have happened?" *Of course* it is possible; almost anything is possible. Likely? *Of course* not.

The unlikelihood concerns the connections between the functional bed-mates of the social process: capitalism, industrialism, nationalism, and imperialism. The nature and meaning of capitalism itself finds no home in the literature of economic theory (although there you will find highly abstract – and misleading – theories of "capital"). As for the other three, forget them (as the economists have).

But (for example), is anything clearer than that to take technological change as "given" is to do the same for industrialism? And they *are* taken as "given," shot into outer space, untouched by human hands. It is to weep.

Anything like a serious look at capitalist history[3] shows that capitalism's progress was dependent on economic expansion at home and abroad; that expansion in turn depended importantly upon technological developments, which in turn depended upon ...

World War I could not have *happened* without industrial capitalism: think only of the war's unprecedented scale and destructive powers. There might have been war, but *world* war? And one such as World War I?[4] And the political turmoil that rolled the world after 1917 until today? Some, but not most of it, was of course attributable to motives only minimally "economic" in nature.[5] Thus, in a later section it will be argued that the Bolshevik Revolution was unlikely to happen at all had it not been for the thoroughgoing – economic, political, and military – disasters of the war. The counter-revolutionary struggles that came to be most important were those of Italy, Germany, and Japan – the first two because of the vigor and size of their socialist/communist movements. Surely all four of those upheavals had *something* to do with capitalism?

It is clear that in both Italy and Germany the Left movements after 1918 were quite likely to move toward power in the absence of a *militarized* opposition. The latter would have been impossible in either case without support from the ruling – capitalist – power structure: thus fascism in Italy (1922) and in Germany (1933), both murderously repressive.

And in Japan, with its uninterrupted militaristic dynasties from the seventeenth century to World War II, the tensions arising from exploitation pushed workers toward organizing efforts which never had a chance: as soon as they raised their heads in the 1920s, they were lopped off.[6]

It is manifest that the so-called "Great War" was an outcome of the deep conflicts between the "Great Powers"; and that they in turn were a predictable outcome of the interaction of the four "clusters" made so much of earlier. Equally clear is that, once under way and for long afterward, war had itself become another "cluster" of relationships and processes: the functional "big four" thus became a "big five." That meant not only that all hell had broken loose, but would continue to do so; and has.

That such a war did take place announced that capitalism had ceased to function well globally; therefore it could not function well in any one nation. Unavoidably, that also meant the breaking (or cracking) of the political institutions defining the nation-state, as well as their internal and external relationships.

All the European economies were badly strained during the war; and for most of them, the strains intensified *after* the war. Inflation struck all countries, in some devastatingly so. Inflation and the accelerating weaknesses of the world economy fed on each other. The difficulties brought on by all these were much heightened by social brittleness. Briefly, and for only a few nations, we now examine some of the details.

AS YOU SOW, SO SHALL YOU REAP

Except for the United States and Japan, World War I spread and deepened the economic, political, and social troubles that had brought it about – which meant, ultimately, an end to the "good times" for Japan and the United States too. Even a cursory examination of the economic behavior of the principal economies after 1918 makes that clear.[7]

W. Arthur Lewis begins his study of the years 1919–39 by calling them "an age of dislocation, and an age of experiment" (1949, 12). Even if we were to qualify both "dislocation" and "experiment" with "unprecedented," it would seem an understatement when set against the ubiquity of social turbulence and the rapidity of change in those years – even in the relatively tranquil United States and Britain.

The chief physical damages of the war were confined "to a gash five miles wide across France and Belgium."[8] But Russia (already during the war) and Germany, along with much of the former Austro-Hungarian empire and surrounding countries, were left in a state of "hunger, exhaustion, bewilderment and economic and moral disintegration ... [and a] sense of hopelessness" (ibid.).

As happened again after World War II, a major relief effort was essential to prevent starvation and associated epidemics (and increased incitements to social upheaval). Then, as later, the United States remained most able to provide the needed assistance.[9] Relief efforts continued into the early 1920s.

War's unwholesome economic fruits

Meanwhile, other than in Central and Eastern Europe, what was at first seen as an economic "boom" took hold immediately after the war; but in almost all countries the expansion subsided after a few years.

It was fostered in Western Europe and the United States by "pent-up" consumer demand, and by the need to rebuild the depleted stocks of raw materials and to put productive equipment (in factories, mines, transportation) back into good working order after the overuse of the war years. The result was a surface prosperity, with rapidly rising demand, but even more rapidly rising prices.[10]

Inflation was everywhere, although not everywhere was it accompanied by even short-lived "good times." The inflation reached its peak and then collapsed at different times and for varying reasons from country to country. In Britain prices rose by well over 50 percent between late 1918 and early 1920; from then on the British economy was in a slump that persisted to one degree or another until the *next* war – with unemployment averaging about 10 percent in the early 1920s.

The United States

The U.S. came off better than any other nation. It had suffered relatively few battle casualties, and the opposite of war damage. Instead, its economy benefited in both qualitative and quantitative terms. Well before the U.S. entered the war in 1917 exports of both manufactures and agricultural products had grown substantially. This in turn very likely transformed what was becoming a recession by 1914 to an expansion.[11]

But the war produced qualitative benefits as well. Most important was that the technology of warfare translated easily into the consumer and producer goods of peacetime – dramatically so in the electrical and automotive realms.

Nor did it hurt that the U.S. inflation was both mild and short-lived, or that prices were level from 1921 to 1929. The war's stimuli were critical to the expansion of those years. Later it will be seen that the expansion was unequal in its benefits; but it was strong enough to give those years the name "the prosperity decade." In all the foregoing respects, the United States was unique in the world – and not for the first time nor the last.

Germany

The German economy was badly disrupted by the war, and deteriorated afterwards. Everything was in short supply and its (democratic) government was in a state of perpetual panic. Inflation broke all records, as prices rose 1 *trillion* times between 1918 and 1923.[12] The destabilizing effects rattled through every nook and cranny of the society, and most especially in the economy.[13]

Even before the war Germany's internal relationships were tumultuous; and into that turmoil were injected the terrible tensions of its incredible inflation. Those tensions were in turn rubbed raw by the quite reasonable resentments of Germans at their mistreatment by the Versailles Treaty.[14] Put all that together, and by the time the 1920s had ended so had the possibility of any calm resolution of German socioeconomic problems. Germany had polarized into a hard Right and a divided Left, and its middle had shriveled in the shadows.[15]

Japan

Japan had gained in diverse ways from the war. While the major powers (including the United States) were preoccupied with the European war, Japan's overall exports to Europe and to Asia increased. The war years left Asia more "open" to Japan than ever before, for both economic and geographic expansion. Its overall export prospects began to dim in the mid-1920s, just as the need for them to increase was more pressing – increasing Japan's territorial appetite. At home, what steps toward social modernization made by that time began to be forcibly undone.

As noted earlier, when embryonic forms of political democracy began to stir before the war, they were quickly stifled. That happened again in the 1920s. Along with the economic buoyancy during and after the war, there had begun to emerge (or re-emerge) a variety of trade unions, cooperative societies and the reawakened germs of a socialist movement – all of them, as Brady says, were "more or less 'free' of constraints exercised from above." But as the 1930s opened, such freedoms had been "worn away," until

> to all intents and purposes, freedom of association in the liberal-democratic sense no longer exist[ed] ... [All] occupational categories in industry, trade, and agriculture [were] organized into more or less all-inclusive unions, associations, federations, and guilds. But behind all such associational forms is a backdrop which represents a blend of the feudal spirit of "servile solidarity" and the patriarchal norms of an "autonomous cooptative bureaucracy."[16]

Thus did Japan breathe new life into its age-old traditions of Shinto, the official religion of Japan, and *Bushido*, the "ethic and practice of the spirit of complaisant subordination to the universal rules of status ... which includes the willingness to die at any moment at the bidding of a recognized superior."[17]

*

Thus, among the many consequences of World War I was the setting of the stage for fascism in Germany and Japan (and in Italy too). Japan moved with only a few, and bloody, twitches from being a feudalistic industrial capitalist society to being a fascist industrial society: much more of the same, though with increased repression and brutality. The route to fascism was more tortuous in Germany.

Once the hurricane of its postwar inflation had subsided, Germany entered a period of what seemed like remarkable prosperity, most marked in the years 1925–29, when it became the magnet drawing capital as well as some of the world's most talented people into its embrace. Under the surface though a volcano was rumbling and that was apparent even in the best years. However, there was no eruption until Germany edged into the 1930s.

Not until the end of the 1920s were there substantial revolutionary or counter-revolutionary confrontations with enduring consequences, except in Russia (1917) and Italy (1922). Until now, neither of these nations has received attention in these pages. They became the first communist and fascist societies; and in doing so they joined the "major players" of modern history. That requires at least a brief discussion.

The Soviet Union

Though it would not receive universal agreement, the view here is that Russia was neither a modern nor a capitalist society in 1917. It was seen as one of "the great powers" before World War I, of course. It was immense in size and population, its empire spread from Europe to Asia, it had played a significant role in European history (including having turned Napoleon back), and its *haute* culture was *à la française*; but its economy was among the most backward in Europe. To be sure, it was speckled here and there with modern industries. But the capital was British, French, or German, and Mother Russia's economy was their deformed child.

Not until the beginning of this century had modern sociopolitical institutions even begun to be attempted in Russia.[18] The war quite simply ruptured everything, whether old or new. Worse, Russia's position on the eastern fringes of Europe (and the enormous stretch through Siberia to Vladivostok) made it vulnerable to being sealed off (or, as early in the war when it "lost" Poland and its Baltic possessions, sliced up).

Even before the war Russia suffered from a weak transportation system, a defect made all the more damaging because of the unfortunate locations of its resources (all very distant from each other). Nor did it help that Russia's foreign trade (on which it was critically dependent) was severely reduced by blockade. If that were not enough to cripple it, its participation in the war drew millions of previously productive farmers and workers into a war in which they were slaughtered in staggering numbers.

At least 80 percent of the Russian people were illiterate, their lives spent in isolated villages. Already by 1916 they were in a state of bitter discontent, much heightened by the fact that their nation was ruled over by an *opera buffa* family, indulged by a (coddled) court and a rich "civilian" circle. Mix all of that with the stresses and the pains of war, and Russia provided a perfect recipe for upheaval.

The premature revolution

When it came, the insurrection was less like the hoped-for socialist revolutions of Marx than the middle-class revolutions of 1789 and 1848. But it faced more and different troubles than those earlier bourgeois upheavals:

> The Provisional Government which replaced the imperial regime in March, 1917, was faced with a problem of tremendous difficulty. Committed to a policy of continuing the war in common with the Allied Powers to a "victorious democratic peace," it had at the same time to undertake a complete reorganization of Russia along the new democratic lines. In the economic field it had to face not only the specific problems created by the war but also the persistent demands of the popular masses for immediate and drastic social reforms ... Under such [and other] conditions the Provisional Government was perhaps foredoomed to fail in its struggle against the opposition of the Bolsheviks.[19]

It was Lenin who led the Bolsheviks to overthrow the Provisional Government in November 1917, and he who almost single-handedly brought some kind of order out of genuine chaos.[20] The year 1917 in Russia had become a genuinely revolutionary situation, but with no effective direction. To emerge from that required a complex program of socioeconomic change, with or without popular support; but the popular demand was for quick and easy – and impossible – solutions.

Lenin stepped into that chaos with a sense of strategy and tactics that propelled Russia into a program of overall social change. Whatever its merits or demerits that program amounted to an enormous historical leap, from total disorder toward a new (and, as it happened, unreachable) territory: in principle and in aim, Russia was to vault from being the most backward to becoming the most advanced of the major nations.

It was to be and was a socialist revolution, but very much at the wrong time, in very much the wrong place.[21] The Bolshevik revolution seemed to promise relief from the problems provoking dissent. At first it was generally popular. Soon, however, the Bolshevik program unavoidably became a compulsory program: its aims were unrealizable without such compulsion: or, worse, with it.

It was called "Military (or "War") Communism." Whatever its positive achievements – which included sheer survival – its rigors enacted a punishing social and economic price.[22]

When Lenin recognized the dangers and increased failures of maintaining that direction, he introduced the "New Economic Policy" (NEP, which he often called "state capitalism"). It lasted from 1921 into the five-year plans initiated by Stalin in 1928. The NEP mixed private ownership and operation of small enterprises (in both agriculture and industry) with state ownership and control of transportation and the vital industries ("the commanding heights") of the economy.

The NEP unquestionably pushed the Soviet economy toward some kind of working order. But by 1928 the Soviet economy's strength was at best that of, say, the Britain of the 1860s rather than the Britain (let alone the Germany or the United States) of 1910.

Lenin died in 1924. He was in his mid-fifties. We shall never know what path the Soviet Union would have pursued had he lived longer. Nor can it be known what Soviet history might have been after 1917 had it *not* been for the many years of economic and military combat overseen and participated in by the Allied Powers throughout the Soviet Union.

Lenin's policies suffered from defects large and small, as he himself stated more than once. Their inadequacies were numerous and often serious. But it may be said that Lenin, although a revolutionary from his youth (after seeing his brother hanged for resistance to the Czarist regime) found himself prematurely thrust into a revolutionary turmoil not of his own making. By early 1917 there was no conventional exit from that chaos. It may be said that his change of strategy in 1921 came as soon as it could, when the threat from outside military intervention was subsiding. By that time, however, terrible damages of all sorts had been done.

Forced industrialization

The West must some day acknowledge that among the most serious of those damages was the Soviet's lasting and justified suspicion of the main capitalist powers. In the brutal internal struggle for power that followed Lenin's death it was, of course, Stalin who triumphed. It has been said – let us accept it for present purposes – that Stalin had a paranoid personality. But, given the events before his taking power *and* up to 1939,[23] and then from 1945 on, his suspicions of the West must be seen as "realistic paranoia." The nature of the five-year plans was very much a response to such fears.

The plans aimed at rapid industrialization and the collectivization of agriculture, and the two programs (both involving much coercion) were seen as joined at the hip: agricultural production *had* to be raised dramatically if, at the same time, industrialization was to proceed rapidly. The latter entailed the drawing-off of labor from the farms to work in mines and mills and transportation; and the former, agriculture, could only raise its productivity by increasing its efficiency. As then seen, that meant making it large-scale, and that in turn meant tractorization; in turn, that implied the manufacture of tractors on a large scale. And tractors can become tanks in the blink of an eye.

Was Stalin *unduly* suspicious? After all, military intervention had ceased. But after all, fascism was solidly in place in Italy[24] (and in Hungary and Portugal), and elsewhere fascist movements were noticeably growing by 1928. By 1924 the Nazis had won 32 seats in the German Reichstag; in France, as with the early fascist groups in postwar Italy, there were uniformed and armed proto-fascist groups (the *Croix de Feu* and the *Camelots du Roi*). In Britain Oswald Mosley was growling menacingly as he sought to form a fascist party, at which he succeeded in 1932.

Stalin's suspicions seemed all too well-grounded by the time of the Spanish Civil War, when Britain, France, and the United States – in the name of neutrality – with one hand prohibited assistance to the democratic government of Spain while with the other they helped to supply the fascists.[25] (An instance of Veblen's "right hand not knowing what the left hand is doing.")

So the Soviet Union industrialized, rapidly and successfully. And let it be acknowledged also that it was good for "the West" that it did so. There is the general agreement (including among U.S. generals) that the armed forces of Germany were beaten so comprehensively and were so thoroughly depleted by the bitter struggles over Stalingrad and Leningrad that by 1943 the war in Europe was effectively won. After that it was just a matter of time – and millions more dead.[26]

The foregoing discussion has been too short and too pointed. Even shorter and even more pointed is this generalizing conclusion: Stalin was a monstrous leader, but some share of his monstrosities must be laid at the door of the capitalist democracies – both before and after World War II. No one can say what the history of the Soviet Union would have been had the other nations simply "let it be." But this can be said: without western interference, Lenin's "military communism" would not have been anything like as militaristic as it was (if at all). And after Lenin? Would Lenin's death have produced Stalin as his successor? And would Stalin have lasted? And if so, would he have done *all* that he did?

Asking such questions (or any "what if" questions) does not lead to assured answers, of course. But it does point to the manner in which Soviet history was diverted from other possible paths to the one that it followed. It took that path in critical part in order to survive external military and economic pressures.

The nations that came to compose the power bloc of the "West" (including, of course, Japan), dominated by the United States, appear to have learned nothing from that. Or if they have, seem to think they have learned that bristling, repressive, and (overtly or covertly) militarized policies are indeed "the way to go." After all, no anti- or non-capitalist power had managed to thrive as the last century ended, had it?

Or is there some better explanation for the continued application (in due variation) of the same cruel, dangerous, and – it will be argued – mutually harmful policies applied to revolutionary Cuba, China, Vietnam, Chile, Nicaragua (among others), since the second "war to end all wars." That sorry tale, filed under the heading of "Cold War," will be told in Part II.

Fascist Italy

"Fascist" has such an inhuman, such a fierce and brutal sound to it as to make it seem totally inapplicable to the *bel paese*. That it nonetheless did apply, and for more than 20 years, is yet another warning of the fragility of the social process; not least the capitalist social process.

Fascism has always and everywhere been a cruel and vicious social system – by definition, one might say. It has been characterized as "capitalism with the gloves off,"[27] but capitalism even with the gloves (that is, political democracy) *on*, so long as it is not also economically and socially democratic (in which case it would no longer *be* capitalism) – depends critically on economic force. The gloves come off when in addition to economic force, additional forms of force *plus* violence and intense propaganda become essential to "keep the peace."

Which brings us to the whys and wherefores of Italian fascism. Why *violence*? Italy's experience supplies the answer: given the existence of revolutionary opposition to capitalism, its defeat required violence, whatever else was necessary.

The first working class?

The roots from which Italian fascism grew go back centuries before Mussolini was born. In the sixteenth century the agriculture of northern Italy was (for that time) relatively large-scale and commercialized, with a wage-earning class of peasants: it had begun to develop along capitalist lines.

The experience and the particular rigors of the late nineteenth century in Italy combined to prod agricultural workers to form "red" unions. Having done so, they also led the way to an ultimately powerful movement combining industrial and agricultural workers, militant and capable of innumerable strikes.[28] In turn, that set the stage for a bitter struggle between themselves and those who came to constitute the power base for fascism: capitalist landlords, industrialists and financiers, nationalists, disillusioned (and often unemployed) war veterans, and the Church.[29]

The main elements of power in Italy had good reason to worry. World War I had a deeply destabilizing set of effects in Italy. Its participation in the war was a disaster in terms of direct casualties.[30] Nor did it help when belief became widespread during the war that Italy had been deluded into a senseless tragedy – a belief that turned to embitterment when Italy lost out in the prize-taking from Germany and Austria after the war.[31]

The forces of the Left were powerful enough to call literally thousands of strikes before and after the war – peaking in the 1920s[32] – and to scare the power structure of Italy. But they were not powerful enough to take power. As elsewhere, from 1917 on, those contending for power from the Left were ill-equipped in almost every way: 1) they had little in the way of funds or institutional or cultural power except among themselves; 2) their strength depended upon their numbers and their ability to persuade non-(or even most other) workers; 3) they were inept at developing the tactics and strategy that could make the most of their limited resources; and 4) they were almost always badly divided by factions fighting for control over those limited resources, even as each contending group was uncertain itself as to how they should be used.

It is not that the forces of the Right were *not* divided or wise. A mere glance at the listing above – landlords, industrialists – reveals likely sources of conflict within the Right. But, and as with their counterparts today, they did need much in the way of wisdom, for their resources were substantial: inherent in each group's very existence was some significant economic, political, and/or social power (including, even, the disillusioned war veterans).

But they possessed something else; and although intangible, that something was of the deepest importance. They presided over the status quo – its habits of thought and feeling, its "common sense" (as distinct from "good sense"). They had on their side what Antonio Gramsci called "ideological hegemony." His importance, and the importance of his reasoning then and its relevance today, justify a short discussion.

Antonio Gramsci

Gramsci was deeply involved in the struggles before and after the war; in 1921 he helped to found the Communist Party of Italy, whose head he became in 1924. In 1926 he was arrested by the fascists and imprisoned. He died in 1937 (at the age of 45), after a long illness.

In short, Gramsci had been in a good position to understand the strengths, and even more the weaknesses, of the Italian Left. He was in prison when he developed his main ideas on such matters – thus the title of his most influential work, *The Prison Notebooks of Antonio Gramsci*.[33]

Gramsci was a Marxist, but not a Leninist – except in the sense that his main ideas may be said to have developed as he thought through what he saw as the inapplicability of Leninism to Italy – or, perhaps, anywhere. The main focus of his arguments dealt with the vast array of problems requiring resolution if the Left is to achieve power to use it in such a way as to *hold* it, and to do so in desirable ways. His argument circles around the concept of *hegemony*, which cries out for definition. It is

> an order in which a certain way of life and thought is dominant; in which one concept of reality is diffused throughout society in all its institutional and private manifestations, informing with its spirit all taste, morality, customs, religious and political principles, and all social relations, particularly in their intellectual and moral connotations.[34]

With this as his basic analytical concept, Gramsci argues that "the working class, *before* it seizes State power, must establish its claims to be a ruling class in the political, cultural, and 'ethical' fields" (in Cammett, 205; my emphasis). This contrasts sharply with the common revolutionary aim of "smashing the State," a relatively short-term process. Those whose aim that has been, knowingly or not, have used Lenin's and the Soviet revolution as their model: mistakenly, Gramsci argued.

Whatever may or may not have been strategically desirable in Czarist Russia, where the State "was everything, and civil society primordial", matters were critically different:

> in the West, [where] there is a proper relation between State and civil society, and when the State trembled [as in Italy] a sturdy structure of civil society was at once revealed. The State was only an outer ditch, behind which there stood a powerful system of fortresses and earthworks; more or less numerous from one State to the next, it goes without saying ...[35]

Whatever else Gramsci is asserting there (and elsewhere) he is playing down the role of *force and violence* by themselves (or even principally) as the basis of *enduring* ruling-class domination. Instead he focuses on the less obvious but equally – ultimately more – important ideological control, manipulation, and habituation: social ways and means that ultimately define for us what is called "common sense and decency."[36]

Those ways and means, habits and attitudes, must be *unlearned* if there is to be "mental and emotional room" for *learning* other ways and means, for developing other habits and attitudes. Not impossible, but certainly not the quick pushover that "smash the State" suggests.

Now, back to Italy. Like the rest of Europe, and in addition to its other troubles, it had been hard hit economically during and after the war years. Mussolini and his fascist coterie took many years to "learn their lines," and the Italian economy was pretty much a patchwork quilt throughout the 1920s: unemployment decreased, but *only* because military expend-itures increased;[37] and even though GNP in 1928 was higher than for 1922 per capita *consumption* was lower. The major change in the next decade was that many were imprisoned (if usually with less harshness than in Germany), that many died, and that many, many more were destined to die in the Italian adventures of the years leading up to and through the next war.[38]

The future casts its shadow

Virtually nothing has been said about the rest of Europe or most of the rest of the world in the 1920s; which does not mean, of course, that they were not having any history. Almost all the world in that decade or so was undergoing small or great changes, bringing small or great troubles. The major reason for such widespread change and turbulence was that the world had become something approaching one "capitalist body" from the mid-nineteenth century on: the first "globalization."

It was created through the needs and the abilities of the most powerful nations to link their economies to the rest of the world, to one important degree or another. The greater that degree, the greater the impact on the weaker societies: on their economies, of course; but on their lives *in toto* – their politics, their culture, their *being*.

And when World War I contorted the path of European history, both during and after the fighting, it also loosened the grip of the powerful countries over the rest of the world. That loosening was the key factor easing the growth of long-standing independence movements. They found the breathing space to take hold and, during the depression and the *next* war, to become so strong as to be irresistible – with or without bloodshed.[39]

Among much else, it was in the mid-1920s that what was to become the People's Republic of China first surfaced. It did so in the vicious fighting between the Kuomintang's nationalist wing (under Chiang Kai-shek) and the first leg of the "Long March" which took the Communists to power in 1949, led by Mao Tse-tung and Chou En-lai.[40]

The 1920s were not an ordinary decade. Were there a social seismograph, the socioeconomic world of those years would have registered shock after shock, as though by a global "fault." Among the most decisive of the shocks were those centering on aggravated economic weaknesses – of all sorts, everywhere. Among them the weaknesses in foreign trade (which soon became a total collapse) were of the utmost importance.

Although the "globalization" of the many decades leading up to World War I did not approach the sweep or the intensity of today's, it had been sweeping and intense enough to allow the seeds of industrial capitalism to germinate. In every society thus affected, an inevitable accompaniment was the dependence upon its foreign trade. As the latter deteriorated, the loss of exports required the curtailment of imports.

The spreading desperation of the 1920s that led to the felt need by one economy after another to "protect" itself from the imports of others meant an arithmetic that also led to the reduction of exports from all: a madman's fraternity.

Enter the United States.

The leading economist in the United States in 1928 was Harvard Professor Irving Fisher. In that year, responding to the soaring stock market rather than to underlying realities, he famously announced that the U.S. economy had solved the problem of the business cycle, and was settled "on a high plateau of endless prosperity."[41]

The "economy" that gave Fisher that illusion was – as everyone *now* knows – not settled on anything; rather, it was surfing a tidal wave of speculation. Moreover, and more to the point: funding the speculation was 1) the availability of funds from individuals with very high incomes with no profitable resting place, and 2) funds that had been going abroad as loans (most critically to Germany and Latin America) but that were pulled back for the higher gains from domestic stock market and real estate "investments." Also, and in addition to the softening of markets at home, 3) there was a credit crunch (and thus pressures on production and trade) in both Europe and Latin America. It was that set of realities that gave Lewis the basis for his opening remarks about the years 1929–39:

> Problems left by the war remained unsolved, especially the creation of a stable international currency system, the adjustment of the size of the agricultural economy, and the reorientation of Britain, of Germany and of France in the post-war world. So soon as America ceased to expand and to lend, then underlying maladjustments were to come out and to take charge.[42]

And they surely did "take charge." In doing so, a long-standing flu suddenly became double pneumonia, accompanied here and there by a broken leg. In the metaphor of the seismograph, the 1930s went off the Richter Scale.

THE BIG ONE

The depression of the 1930s was global and explicably more so than that after the 1870s, reflecting the increased "globablization" that had taken hold by the opening of the twentieth century. World War I ruptured but did not end that globality. Nothing having been "put in its place," international dependencies had become something like that of a drug addict: when the supply runs out crisis devolves toward catastrophe.

The depth and duration of the economic slide of the 1930s was unprecedented, and it was ended only by something much worse: a harrowing war, also longer and unbelievably worse than its predecessor. The years 1930–45 were so destructive of so much and in so many ways that one would think our species would have learned something from them. We did, as will be seen shortly; but not enough to create a safe and sane and decent society. What we learned was something like the observation about generals: they are always fighting the previous war. And so, as will be argued in Part II, we have moved into a considerably more precarious and threatening world with, to make matters worse, added dangers.

Among the things learned was what causes depressions, from Keynes and those who worked with and after him. Much will be said of that below. Here it should be inserted that much that was learned began to be systematically undone by the economics profession from the mid-1970s on.

Even factual memories have atrophied. Economists have "learned" to overlook not only *why* there was such a disaster, but *how* it moved from its first through its later stages – all too understandable, given that mainstream economics stands aloof from the world of fact. Such social amnesia is especially troubling at present, as the world once more hovers near the edge of economic adversities that could move to massive troubles.[43]

So we begin by recalling the depression's *history*, how it lurched from 1929 into the successive years of the next decade. The facts recounted will be those mostly of the United States.[44] It was the depression's epicenter, and more severe than elsewhere – except Germany. There the numbers were about the same, but the social consequences – examined in the section to follow – were indescribably worse.[45]

The bitter with the better

The term "prosperity decade" was applied generally to the United States in the1920s, but it was appropriate for at most a third of the population. And the other two-thirds? Like their counterparts in today's whiz-bang economy, they were in varying degrees of difficulty, strain, and hardship, or downright poor.

One of the major developments giving the 1920s their dazzle was a wave of technological changes, in both productive techniques and in products. Emerging from that were the beginnings of consumerism (and thus of advertising and *its* pizzazz). That meant cars, and 'fridges, telephones, and radios, and a large bucket of other products, mass-produced and mass-consumed (but by only one-third of the masses).

That "modernization" also meant an early version of today's "downsizing and outsourcing" and a "dual economy" – in different forms but with similar consequences. A look at the economic fine print helps to make that clear.[46]

The economy was transforming itself. The railroads, well on their way to being displaced by trucks and cars, had already begun their long decline. Coal mining, cotton textiles, and staple agriculture (grains and cotton, especially), where most of the farm population worked, were all shrinking: a large number of jobs were at stake, and many of them were lost.

Although unemployment statistics did not become even remotely reliable until the 1930s, there are usable data for the 1920s. They show that joblessness ranged from 5 to 13 percent. The significance of those raw figures is heightened when we note that average income levels and the "standard of living" then were significantly lower than now, and that there was *nothing* to break a fall: *no* unemployment or health insurance, *no* social security.

The hard times for the majority are shown by these data: in 1929 an annual family income of $2,000 (in 1929 dollars) was necessary to supply just basic necessities. But 40 percent of all families had incomes *below $1,500*, and 71 percent were under $2,500. Related to those figures are some others: between 1923 and 1929 (years of no inflation) corporate profits rose 62 percent; manufacturing wages rose only 8 percent, were stable in agriculture, and *declined* 14 percent in mining.

The two leading industries of the 1920s were automobiles and house building, heavy users of both capital goods and labor. Both depended upon reasonably well-off – or able to borrow – consumers. And borrow they did: it was the beginning of that chapter of "the American way of life." However, and quite apart from the fact that borrowing was both a relatively new idea for consumers and considerably more difficult than now:

installment buying could not obviate the eventual retardation of expansion. There was certain to come a time when all families who would utilize installment loans were loaded up with all the debt they could carry. In the long run the only possible means of keeping these industries expanding would have been to augment the *cash* purchasing power of the consumers through sufficient increases in wages and salaries or through sufficient reduction in retail prices.[47]

This meant pervasive and increasingly unused capacities in manufacturing and mining, in transportation, and in agriculture. Then (as now) much of the fuel for real estate and stock market speculation came from the high savings of the high-income groups. Their funds ceased to go into real investment (why do so, with excess capacities?), and went instead into speculation. As that happened, the prices of financial assets (then as now) rose and rose, until, like all bubbles, they popped. Crash!

The bumpy road down

And that is how the Depression is remembered – the economy suddenly collapsing, an explosive *whoosh* of air from a burst balloon: Bloody Thursday in the stock market, with prices hurtling to the bottom in a matter of days, the U.S. and the global economy skidding precipitously from prosperity to depression almost overnight. Such views are factually wrong, and deceptively so if used to measure or assess the gravity of current developments. The most astute of U.S. business cycle analysts showed this clearly:

> After the collapse of the stock market and the sharp decline in business activity in the last quarter of 1929, there was a slight abortive recovery in the early months of 1930, associated particularly with a partial recovery in automobile production and some improvement in non-residential construction ... Prices continued to decline through 1930. The rise in automobile production proved short-lived ... In the early months of 1931, the American economy again seemed to be attempting to stage a recovery ... In the late spring of 1931, the international financial structure collapsed completely, and a financial crisis starting in Europe began a new wave of liquidation through the world and deepened the depression in the United States ... [the] decline continued until the summer of 1932 ... Beginning in the third quarter [of 1932], noticeable improvement began to be evident in the United States and other countries ... In the United States the recovery was struck a sharp blow at the beginning of 1933 by an outbreak of bank closings beginning in the Middle West and spreading rapidly through the rest of the country. A final wave of hysteria undermined com-

pletely the foundation of confidence on which modern banking rests, and by the end of the first week of March all banks in the United States were closed.[48]

From peak to pit, that was *four years* on a roller coaster going down, then up a bit, then down again, and up a bit, and then ... Factually, that is how the processes of expansion and contraction *always* proceed: jaggedly. Here are some of the overall dimensions of that fall.

Individual losses for speculators were of course great, though (at least as seen here) sympathy should be reserved for others whose plight is more deserving of consideration. Between 1929 and 1933, GNP fell from $104 billion to $56 billion; per capita disposable income (what is left after taxes) fell from $678 to $360; the income of farm proprietors fell from $5.7 billion to $1.7 billion (in 1932); unemployment rose from 1.5 million to 12.8 million – 25 percent of the labor force (and that's probably an understatement).

A recession or depression is caused by and itself causes many things. Most important among those is the under-utilization of a society's productive resources – of workers, resources, and equipment. In looking at the following data for capacity utilization for the thirties, keep in mind that the optimum rate is usually seen to fall between 85 and 95 percent. Already by 1928 utilization rates had begun to fall below 85 percent. Then:[49]

1930: 66 percent 1935: 68 percent
1931: 53 percent 1936: 80 percent
1932: 42 percent 1937: 83 percent
1933: 52 percent 1938: 60 percent
1934: 58 percent 1939: 72 percent

In a capitalist society, when business is bad, it's tough (almost) all over. And unemployment of course goes up when business goes down. Note that the following figures for unemployment extend through 1941, and that even after two or three years of increased military expenditures (sold to Europe), the rate was still 9.9 percent.[50]

1930: 8.7 percent 1936: 16.9 percent
1931: 15.9 percent 1937: 14.3 percent
1932: 23.6 percent 1938: 19.0 percent
1933: 24.9 percent 1939: 17.2 percent
1934: 21.7 percent 1940: 14.6 percent
1935: 20.1 percent 1941: 9.9 percent

Global contagion

There were many striking aspects to the depression that set it apart from all earlier economic contractions. First, its duration: despite some ups, in 1939 real GNP was the same as 1929, whereas a normal rate of growth would have raised it by at least another third. Second was its depth, displayed in the two tables above. And third was its tenacity: by any normal accounting, the U.S. was still in depression 12 years after 1929 (as was the rest of the world, up to the outbreak of war in 1939). And that was so even though military expenditures had been rising since 1938.

It is when we look at the U.S. economy alone that that tenacity becomes explicable. Repeatedly, it has been emphasized that no one capitalist economy can thrive without a thriving world economy. Given our earlier discussions of the 1920s, it is clear that with so many of the major economies in trouble in those years it was only a matter of time until the whole globe went down.

When it began to do so in 1929, the already inadequate levels of world trade went into a further descent, followed soon after by falling levels of global industrial production. The problems associated with that prompted the 1931 financial crisis which, once ignited, spread like the proverbial prairie fire.

The crisis began in a small place. Its intricacies are worth a close look, if only for the light they shed on today's world:

Early in 1931 Germany and Austria announced that they wished to form a customs union [a latter-day *Zollverein*]. This proposal was resented by the ex-Allied nations, and particularly by France, which exerted pressure by withdrawing short-term funds. The withdrawal exposed the weakness of Austria. The largest bank in Austria, the Creditanstalt, was found to be insolvent in 1931. The Austrian government undertook to guarantee its liabilities ["too big to fail"],[51] an international loan was raised, and foreign creditors agreed to cease withdrawals. But this failure served to draw attention to the financial weakness of Central Europe [shades of East Asia!]. A new run developed on German foreign reserves; the Reichsbank lost gold heavily, and one of the biggest commercial banks, the Donat bank, was suspended in July. The run on Germany continued ... Austria and Germany having succumbed, confidence was lower than ever, and attention shifted to London ... [whose] short-term obligations were large ... she was also owed large short-term sums but much of these were tied up ... in Austria and Germany. The Bank of England therefore had to pay in gold, and withdrawals proceeded so rapidly that in September 1931 gold payments were suspended. Great Britain was off the Gold Standard and the pound was allowed to depreciate.[52]

The fabled international gold standard was soon relegated to history, and by 1932 the number of currencies that had been depreciated in relation to gold was down to 32. The United States dropped off gold in 1933. That left the world without any kind of international monetary mechanism until after World War II.

In reality, there had been little resembling free trade for the preceding 40–50 years, except for Britain. The protectionist assault launched by Germany and France in the 1870s became universal after 1930. That was very much stimulated by the U.S. Hawley-Smoot tariff of the latter year (the highest ever): no small matter, for the United States was by far the world's largest producer and trader.[53] Within two years, barriers to trade were – and were meant to be – insurmountable; as was the depression.

A tragedy of errors

The depression began during the Hoover Administration. Its reaction to it may be summed up in the old joke "Don't just do something, stand there." But that was also the position of Congress and the business community – a position much strengthened by the disastrous effects of the first federal intervention. It was in 1928, and was meant to assist farmers.

In that year the Federal Farm Board was created. Most farmers were in trouble throughout the 1920s, troubles much deepened by the collapsing world economy. The politically powerful farm community succeeded in obtaining a program that guaranteed minimum prices for a broad array of commodities. There were no provisions for output control. The inevitable and immediate consequence was a large increase in farm output. There was no substantial increase in market demand. Consequently, the Farm Board was soon unable to meet its mountainous obligations; and by 1930 the program was defunct.

Nor was the economics profession helpful. It lived by Say's (century-old) Law to the bitter end. Its 1932 position – which changed little throughout the depression – was that the severe unemployment was not really "unemployment." The latter, in their professional view, implies that workers wish to work at the prevailing wage but can't find it; the problem of the 1930s, as they saw it, was that workers were insisting on excessively high wages. No comment.

Hoover was beaten badly in the elections of 1932. But his replacement was almost his mirror image in terms of economic matters. Roosevelt was also a conservative; as was the Democratic Congress. Immediately upon taking office, in March 1933, he declared a bank moratorium. That meant simply closing their doors, so as to preclude long lines of frantic depositors trying to get their nonexistent money back. It made things look better.

New brooms don't always sweep clean

As for collapsing production and market demand and rising unemployment, FDR took the counsel of the strongest elements of the business community. Their ideas, unsurprisingly, reflected what they saw as their interests. And that evolved into what was called the National Recovery Administration (NRA). Some idea of its nature may be gleaned by the fact that in 1934 a delegation from Germany came to the United States with the belief that Nazi Germany had something to learn from the NRA – with good reason.[54]

The basic idea for the NRA, and developed by the then head of General Electric, Gerard Swope, was first put forward in the late 1920s as "The Swope Plan." Already in 1931 (when he was also head of the U.S. Chamber of Commerce) bills were introduced in Congress to that end. As Mitchell recounts it:

> Swope wanted trade associations, with compulsory membership, in every industry; through their activities "production and consumption should be coordinated on a broader and more intelligent basis," though this objective would obviously require revision of the Sherman [Antitrust] Act. The proposals of Swope and the Chamber of Commerce closely approximated NRA provisions ... Later, when much of business turned against the NRA, it was proper to remind that organized business had mainly inspired the measure.[55]

And what Lola wanted, Lola got. The National Industrial Recovery Act was enacted in June 1933. The trade association for the industry (membership was compulsory) administered over 800 "industry codes." The administrators were the officers of the association; in turn, they represented the strongest companies in their industry. And the codes they "administered" allowed the setting of both production and geographic quotas and the establishment of *minimum* prices.

All this was very much like the cartel systems of Europe, initiated by Germany half a century earlier, but with two big differences. The cartels usually split up the profits proportionately among the participating companies; and they had no legal backing from the State. The NRA provided that the rules of the associations would be backed up in federal courts.

And something else. The symbol of the NRA was the "blue eagle." All participating firms – on the producing and the retail level – were to display that symbol (on packages, in shop windows, and so on). "Buy Only at The Sign of The Blue Eagle!" came to be a synonym for another current slogan: "Buy American!" The head of the NRA was General Hugh Johnson, and he ran it as though he – and the country – were in the army. Lots of discipline, lots of patriotic slogans, lots of pressure, but no economic stimulus.

The U.S. Supreme Court of 1935 was composed of justices appointed for the most part in the 1920s. They were deeply conservative, and when a small poultry farmer of the New York metropolitan area protested against the NRA the Court found it to be unconstitutional – if not for the best reasons.[56]

Setting legalities and the dangers of big business aside, the NRA was economically plain wrong-headed. In the name of "recovery," it was permitting output restriction and job losses and preventing prices from falling to meet reduced demand: the opposite of what was needed. But what *was* needed?

Certainly not to have workers, to cry, as with one voice, "we'll work for less!" Many of them were, of course crying just that, trying to do just that – uselessly – preferring anything to standing in long soup lines.

In the concluding section of this chapter, the response of economists to the depression will be our concern. Here we go on to examine the important changes from the "First New Deal" (1933–35) to what became the "real" or "Second New Deal" (1935–38).

NEW DEAL

The period from 1933 into mid-1935 was one of (fortunately) failed experiments. They may be characterized as attempts to save a sinking boat by bailing out the rising water. And only that. If there was anything more imaginative, it took place in banking and finance: 1) the Federal Deposit Insurance Corporation (FDIC) – which *at least* assured small depositors that their deposits would be safe without having to stand in lines (and thus deepen the panic); 2) the Securities and Exchange Commission and its laws to curtail corruption and speculation and concentration (laws undone since the 1980s, or on their way out); 3) the strengthening of the Federal Reserve System. Whatever their desirability, however, these were protective measures only.

In agriculture, the Agricultural Adjustment Act of 1933 (AAA) went well beyond the provisions of the Federal Farm Board to require output restriction for price support eligibility. The drafters of the law could *not* have been unaware, however, that the AAA's effects would include the strengthening of big agriculture and the disappearance of small farms: the larger the output, the more can be restricted, and the greater the federal payments. And vice versa. In 1935 there were about 7 million farms; there are now fewer than 2 million. And 90 percent of the government benefits go to 10 percent of the "farmers" (now appropriately called "agribusiness").

The economic policies of the First New Deal at their best were for holding on. If the depression was to be countered, what was needed were means to *stimulate* the economy. The Second New Deal developed such means; and it also went beyond that to introduce important socioeconomic reforms.

FDR became a different kind of president from 1935 on. He was told by his closest confidants that he had to do so, and he took their advice – at first as a most astute politician; later, it seemed, as a changed man. The signs of the times were hard to miss:

1. The election of 1934 resulted in a noticeably more liberal Congress.

2. Already by 1934, and increasingly in 1935, there were major strikes, marked by fury and violence, and unions – despite laws unfavorable to them – were growing.

3. All over the nation "immoderate" movements were taking hold: Huey Long and his "Share the Wealth" in Louisiana; Upton Sinclair and "End Poverty in California" (EPIC); Father Coughlin and the fascist "Silver Shirts" in Detroit; and socialist and communist groups in many of the major cities.

Not quite Germany; but not quite the United States, either. It was time for a change; and Roosevelt was both its spokesman and symbol.[57]

Better late than never

Much of the Second New Deal had to do with stimulating the economy upward; at least as important, even more so perhaps, were the social reforms it created. We can do no more than summarize both areas.

Recovery required going beyond "the market" to provide economic stimuli. In turn, that meant federal financing of two kinds of activities, what were affectionately (or derisively) called "alphabet soup": 1) the "infrastructural" projects of the PWA (Public Works Administration) dams – roads, bridges, schools), and 2) programs providing public services, such as the WPA (Works Progress Administration), the CCC (Civilian Conservation Corps), and the NYA (National Youth Administration).

The WPA set up projects involving actors, musicians, teachers, writers, and artists which did much, finally, to liven and deepen the cultural life of the nation; the CCC provided jobs for young people on farms, in forests, and in parks. The NYA provided jobs for students in the educational institution where they were studying (assisting teaching staff, mostly). A moment's reflection shows that we could use all those activities – and more – today, whether in good times or bad.

Among the areas of reform, most important were those affecting unionization, housing, and social security. We take them up in that order.

Unions

The National Recovery Act of 1933 (Section 7(a)) required that every "code" must provide "that employees shall have the right to organize and bargain collectively through representatives of their own choosing." The provisions were made, a National Labor Board was created to enforce them, and – in practice – the provisions were ignored or violated, quite apart from the demise of the NRA.

But the wall holding back unionization had been breached. In 1935, as union strife was sweeping across much of the nation, the Wagner Act (Sen. Robert Wagner, NY) was passed. It replaced the National Labor Board with the National Labor Relations Board, brought Section 7(a) back to life and gave it teeth; despite which, however, for the next three years the principal issue for most strikes was "union recognition" – presumably *pro forma* after a successful union election. But not until the Supreme Court of 1938 upheld the meaning of the Act was that so. It was in fact the economic labor shortages of World War II that provided the major numerical stimulus to organized labor's strength.

Housing

The major action was in 1937, with the U.S. Housing Act of that year. It authorized federal assistance to local communities "to remedy the unsafe and unsanitary housing conditions and the acute shortage of decent, safe, and sanitary dwellings for families of low income." That Act was supplemented by similar legislation in 1965. Since the 1970s, as will be seen, such federal assistance has scandalously declined. Thus, it was estimated in 1983 that "approximately 50 million people live in the deteriorated and socially dysfunctional areas called slums." And since then matters have gotten worse, as Congress has steadily reduced housing subsides for poor households – while increasing for comfortable incomes.[58]

Social security

The United States was very much the latecomer in this regard – as in all matters of the "social safety net." A start was finally made in 1935, with the Social Security Act. It was a good start, because it has been vitally important over the years in substantially lowering poverty rates for the old, for survivors, and for the disabled. It was also a bad start: its financing rules were defective from the beginning, and are now the source of looming troubles (though, as will be seen, not those publicized); and there was much that should have been done that was not. But it *was* a start.

As so often with such legislation, The Act began with a compromise, one concerning how it should be funded, and who should receive what benefits. The United States is almost unique in the manner finally adopted:

1. It is based on payroll deductions, whereas elsewhere it is usually financed out of general (progressive) taxes.

2. The payroll deductions are set at the same percentage for all up to a maximum income level (now about 7.6 percent up to $62,000). That means that the richest pay the same percentage as the poorest, but only up to a small portion of their income: 7.6 percent of $62,000, *nothing* on anything beyond that, no matter how much: that is, 7.6 percent of $62,000 even if your annual income is $2,000,000.

3. The ultimate benefits are proportionate to contributions, not to need. That not only means that those poor throughout their lives receive the lowest amounts (while needing, of course, the highest), but that those who are better off receive more; and the rich, who need nothing, get the maximum.

What resulted for the United States was far better than nothing, of course. But there was not, and there is not, any *good* reason why the people of the richest country in the world should have the stingiest social security system.

But even a cursory look at what was happening elsewhere in the 1930s reveals that badly off as millions of people were in the United States, this country remained the least affected of any of the major capitalist powers. The worst off was Germany.

NAZI GERMANY

> If that the heavens do not their visible spirits
> Send quickly down to tame these vile offences,
> It will come,
> Humanity must perforce prey on itself,
> Like monsters of the deep.[59]

In the post-World War II years it has become common for Germans to condemn, explain, disavow, deny, or seek to forget the "vile offences" of the Nazi years. So be it. But there would be less cause to worry about the future of our species if the condemnations and explanations were extended beyond Germany and Germans: Nazi Germany was the monstrous child of "western civilization" as well as of Germany.

It is worth repeating an earlier comment: Germany in the late 1920s was seen as the very zenith of western civilization; and rightly so. It was the land of Thomas Mann, of Bauhaus, of Einstein, of von Stroheim, and of their counterparts in all the arts, all the sciences, and in engineering – in virtually everything connoting intellect, taste, and progress: the very epitome of "western civilization."

That same Germany had its underside – as *all* the member societies of our civilization have had (and have). In the 1920s, Germany reeked of decadence, incisively portrayed in the works of Bertold Brecht, George Grosz, Kurt Weill;[60] its economy barely survived the first half of the decade; it was rife with political conflict and violence.[61] By the end of the 1920s, Germany's seemingly healthy economy was strewn with the wreckage of the thousands of small businesses smashed by inflation, was dominated by giant companies in conflict with strong unions, and had become the nation with the largest Left and the best organized *and* most extreme Right in the world.

It would be foolish to explain that "underside" by reference to unique *German* traits – except by adopting the bizarre Nazi myth of Germans as a race aside: "Aryans." Rather, attention must be paid to the centuries in which German history was tightly entwined with that of an emerging modern Europe, in which (as emphasized in Chapter 1) Germany was deliberately segmented after a "Thirty Years' War," a war in which most of those who died were Germans: two-thirds of all Germans is a common estimate.[62]

The offenses that Nazi Germany inflicted on its own and other peoples were unimaginably vile; indubitably more vile than those inflicted on them earlier by the French, the Swedes, the Dutch, et al. But pursuing such comparisons leads to no useful conclusions. Instead it is essential to seek a proper explanation. We must establish how and why such a murderous system could come into being, and do so by gaining substantial – though by no means universal – support. Neither its specific causes nor its specific nature is likely ever to be repeated. But it is all too possible that there will be some twenty-first century variant: unless (and even if) we understand the nature of the beast.

Through a glass darkly

What made it possible for the horrors of Nazism to become *normal*? How could such heinous behavior become part of the daily existence of Germany, year after year, for more than a decade, in the society that had been the zenith of our civilization? How could the nation that produced Beethoven and Goethe also participate (or acquiesce) in Nazi crimes?

No explanation will ever suffice, and certainly not one made in a few pages; but the minimum basis for such an explanation can be identified. They were the giant forces at work in the background for *all* societies in the previous two centuries, those that have been named over and over again in these pages: capitalism, nationalism, industrialism, and colonialism. It cannot be said too often that each of those brought out the worst in all the others, the worst in all societies and their peoples. In their interaction the explanation of all the major currents of modern history are to be found: those we cherish, and those we abhor.

A serpentine line can be drawn from 1918 to Hitler's installation as Chancellor. The Nazis grew out of the German Workers' Party of 1919 – with Hitler its seventh member. Within a year, Hitler's energy, passion, and political talent were instrumental in transforming that party into the National Socialist German Workers' Party (NSDAP): the Nazis. Note "workers'."

The Nazis were a small, contentious, and unpopular party throughout most of the 1920s.[63] They became increasingly popular with the onset of the depression. In Germany, as in the United States, the depression brought a 50 percent decline in production (1929–33). That stoked a fire already fueled by "non-economic" elements during and after the war. As late as 1929 Nazi membership was only 176,000; by 1932 membership had risen more than tenfold to 2 million.

During the 1920s, Nazi hooligans were regularly arrested and jailed; from 1930 on, it became increasingly common for the brown-shirted, swastika-bearing storm troopers to roam the streets, beating up Jews and Reds while the police looked the other way; or, on the diminishing occasions when the police acted, the Courts (and the newspapers) had learned to overlook it.[64]

Fascism depends upon fear, whatever else it may "offer" in the way of hate, lust, pride, and greed. The Nazis came to power riding on fear. And once in control the Nazis' enhanced powers enabled them to make Germany a land of fear and hate and violence.

By no later than 1932 all that was ubiquitous in Germany, irrespective of class, status, or function. Most important, finally, were the fears of the powerful: the industrialists and the bankers and their political and professional kin. Their fears were of the only remaining opponents of the Nazis: the Left.[65]

For several years preceding 1932, an electoral battle had raged; in that year, the Nazi vote and the combined Communist and Social Democratic vote ran neck-and-neck. When in 1933 the Nazi vote suddenly declined and the combined Left vote rose, it seemed that time was on the side of the Left. But two developments brought a different outcome. First, as the economy continued to worsen, Brady points out:

a series of conferences were held between Hitler and various industrial and financial leaders in the Rhineland. With their support came that of the Junkers ... and the bulk of the manufacturing and shipping interests of the country. Thereafter organized business lent its support to Hitler either openly or surreptitiously.

Second, and just before that, the then governing party, "the Social Democratic Party chose to play a lone hand and to cooperate with the various centrist or so-called republican parties" (1937, 20). Moreover, Brady adds, as the party in control of the machinery of the State, the Social Democrats were timid in confrontation with the always-increasing fanaticism and brutality of the Nazis, and "did not even force the Nazis to comply with ordinary criminal law" (1937, 21).

President Hindenburg appointed Hitler as Chancellor in 1933; soon the Weimar constitution was suspended. What had been *bierstube* and rough-and-tumble politics and street terrorism became codified and institutionalized as the Third Reich. Those who had supported the Nazis or leaned in that direction became part of a fully authoritarian and totalitarian, fully militarized society; the rest – "the good Germans" – either remained silent and/or were sent to the camps to be enslaved or murdered.[66]

The key determinant of this descent into horror, Brady shows, was the combination of an economy neither structured nor inclined to bring well-being for most or stability for itself, combined with an explosive social setting. Rather than the roots of Nazism being found in a deep and pervasive anti-Semitism – all too often the customary view – it was the genius of the Nazis to convert a relatively "moderate" anti-Semitism (by comparison with France, Poland, or Russia, say) into hysteria and the Holocaust; just as they were able to convert the malign and foolish – and effectively unenforced – Versailles Treaty into a tool for building social insanity.[67]

Shortly, the analysis and policies of Keynes will be examined. It was not until after World War II that those ideas were taken seriously enough to be put into practice in Europe or the United States – except in Germany. There Hitler's economist Hjalmar Schact saw their particular uses for Nazism; he was the inventor of what came to be called "military Keynesianism."

Unemployment in Germany was the highest in Europe in 1934; by 1938 Germany was the only capitalist nation with full employment – indeed with *over*-full employment. The rise in military production and in the military and paramilitary forces required, in effect, a draft to *enlarge* the labor force: compulsory labor service for youth (*Arbeitsdienst*) and women (*Frauenwerk*), and so on.[68]

By the fall of 1938 Hitler had begun to flex Germany's muscles. A year later he was using them.

Waste Land

Germany's first two acts of territorial expansion were accomplished without a shot being fired: the annexation ("Anschluss") of Austria in March of 1938, with the cooperation of the rightist Austrian government, and Germany's successful claim to sovereignty over the Sudetenland, the area of Czechoslovakia inhabited largely by people of German descent – the latter achieved through the Munich Pact of September 1938.

That event came to be called, simply, "Munich." The principal interested powers of "Munich" – as seen by themselves (not the Czechs or the Soviets) – were France, Britain, Italy, and Germany (represented by Daladier, Chamberlain, Mussolini, and Hitler, respectively).

Its first result was that the Sudetenland was annexed by Germany. The second result involved the Soviet Union. Like France, it was a formal ally of Czechoslovakia; like the latter, it was not represented at "Munich." Stalin, with some reason, concluded that the four powers of Munich were making a "deal" with the leading anti-Soviet power for reasons incompatible with "peace in our time" (as Chamberlain had justified the agreement). On August 23, 1939, in a step that stunned the world, Molotov and von Ribbentrop signed the Nazi–Soviet mutual non-aggression pact.

Apocalypse now

On September 1 the Nazi *blitzkrieg* began to roll through Poland. Britain and France declared war on September 3, but did not follow that up with any significant military resistance. Poland was occupied in less than a month; by April, Denmark and Norway had surrendered; after seven weeks of *blitzkrieg* Holland and Belgium gave in; France fell in June. Just a year later, the Soviet Union was invaded on a 2,000-mile front. That was the end of *blitzkrieg* and the beginning of a grinding, massively destructive war.

The Japanese understandably interpreted the swift victories of the Nazis and the general indifference of the United States toward the war as signifying that Asia was theirs for the taking.[69] They intensified their activities in China and broadened their sweep into Southeast Asia. And attacked Pearl Harbor. It was that single act which overnight transformed U.S. public opinion from aloofness to war fever.

We need not linger on the six years of war, except to note some numbers: about 60 million people died in Europe alone between 1939 and 1945. The United States suffered about 400,000 deaths and 1 million wounded By comparison, Paul Kennedy estimates 13.6 million Germans dead and lost (mostly as prisoners) and 20–25 million Soviet citizens.[70] And that leaves out the Pacific War.

World War I's "five-mile gash" across Belgium and France was a path in the park compared to the destruction of World War II. The weaponry of 1914–18 was almost quaint: very slow and very vulnerable tanks firing very light ammunition, planes made of canvas dropping 50-lb bombs. Almost quaint, but not quite: poison gas was used by all parties, and often; and the war is remembered as prolonged and savage trench warfare. Madness.

World War II was also insane, but there was nothing even remotely quaint about it. The tanks were a quantum leap in strength, speed, in numbers and in their weaponry, as were the aircraft. The 50-lb bombs of World War I could be carried under a strong man's arm; in the second war a 250-lb bomb was small. By the war's end the four-engined bombers were each carrying dozens of 500-lb bombs, or a smaller number of half-ton or one ton bombs. And, at the end, Hiroshima and Nagasaki: one bomb = 20,000 tons of TNT.

Whole cities were destroyed by fire bombing before Hiroshima, only the best known of which were Dresden and Tokyo. Most of the casualties were, of course, civilians; and what was destroyed were whole factories, and the infrastructure and housing that had taken decades (even centuries) to put in place. The aim was to terrorize and to paralyze. Demented.

Business leaders and economists point with pride to the productive efficiency of industrial capitalism. The wastes of the two world wars (and those in between and subsequently) are not taken into account in that reckoning. Nor are the wastes of decades of military expenditures of the Cold War.[71]

How can they not be? The answer is simple: assume *no* relationship between economic and "non-economic" processes, where "non-economic" is defined as anything other than what takes place in the rarefied confines of "supply and demand" – a locus that contains neither the "demand" for nor the "supply" of military stuff and nonsense, or the corrupt politics accompanying them.

*

It is now more than 50 years since the defeat of the Nazis. They have been years ceaselessly marked by strife and bloodshed, provoked by distant and/or recent social agonies. Some of those conflicts were to bring release from tyranny, some to maintain it, some to impose it. The main actors have been many; the most powerful of all, and therefore the one not pushed by any demonstrable necessity, has been the United States – not least, and not only, in Southeast Asia.

Mussolini and Hitler produced some of the deepest defeats of our civilization; but there have been other defeats since then that have been all too deep. Surely our species has – *must* have – other and finer possibilities. They must be cultivated, if (as Veblen said) we are "to save ourselves alive."[72]

If we are to do so, much has to be done. Most of it will be in the political arena; some of it must be done in the realm of ideas and understanding, not least that of economists. Despite the smug obstinacy of most of the profession in the interwar period, some real progress *was* made – most importantly by Schumpeter, Keynes, Joan Robinson, and Alvin Hansen. Their work will be discussed now, very briefly, in that order (and in Part II their squelching will be examined).

ECONOMICS: ALMOST OUT WITH THE OLD, ALMOST IN WITH THE NEW

Depending on how we define "economics" and which economists we look at, the period between World War I and beyond World War II (until the 1970s) may be seen either as a stagnant pool or as a rushing river for mainstream economics.

The large majority held to Lionel Robbins's definition, noted earlier: "The science which studies human behavior as a relationship between ends and scarce means which have alternative uses" – where "studies" meant making unrealistic assumptions about this and that and the other thing. Come hell or high water, the majority clung to their raft of assumptions as the real world went swirling by.

But there were others in the mainstream who were startled into life by the ongoing turbulence. They never composed themselves into a "group." It was almost as though they were working together toward a different definition of economics, as though they were jointly seeking answers to the question: "What do we need to know about the economy and what must we do to have it serve the interests of the society now and in the future?" That is, they weren't studying "economics," they were studying "economic processes and relationships." Using diverse means and working at levels ranging from high abstraction to raw empiricism, they got some promising results.

Let us look briefly at the traditionalists first, and then go on to examine the data, analyses, and conclusions of some of those who began – finally! – to give mainstream economics a good name.

The old stamping grounds

In 1920, Marshall's *Principles* had been the Bible of economics for more than two decades. It remained so for the majority of economists of (especially) Britain and the United States until well after World War II. As late as the 1950s, when there was much else to study and being studied (as will be seen below), Marshall remained the starting-point.

As discussed in Chapter 2, Marshall was the recognized synthesizer of what became neoclassical economics in the late nineteenth century. What he synthesized was a loose bundle of analyses and techniques produced over preceding decades by thinkers as diverse as Bentham, Ricardo, Jevons, Menger, and Walras; their tools of trade were labeled utility, harmony, maximization, and equilibrium.

It was Marshall's talent to bring them all together around one focus with one aim. His main focus was the individual firm; his aim was to specify the conditions of "equilibrium."

He was successful in that he became the kingpin of economics; and successful also in that his *Principles* became the point of departure for subsequent work – attempts to fill in his gaps, or to go beyond his achievements, beginning at the turn of the century.

The gaps (as seen by like minds) were several: 1) Given that the theory of the firm was basically sound, it left unexamined the vital area of the distribution of income (as between wages, interest, profits and rent) – to be dealt with by John Bates Clark. 2) Given that the equilibrium conditions for the individual firm were established, then what about the "general equilibrium," that for the economy as a whole? Going beyond Marshall and back to Pareto and Walras, Irving Fisher sought to settle that matter (and to construct the first major steps for the application of mathematical theory to statistics: "econometrics"). Then, 3) given that these matters were coming under control, how could the model respond to the manifest reality that "perfect competition" – the focal and redeeming center of that economics and its policy positions – was more rare than common, how could that be accommodated?[73] The response was developed independently and almost simultaneously by Joan Robinson (1903–93) and Edward H. Chamberlain (1899–1967). Their books came out in 1933; both were repudiated in 1951 by Robinson.[74]

In seeking to close the gaps of these three major areas of neoclassical theory, the method (and thus its assumptions) were retained by all these thinkers and those working in their ways, except to "relax" some one or two assumptions: everyone rational, no time, no change, nothing except imagined human beings and market relationships.[75]

Cavalier though it may seem, those post-Marshallian developments will here be dismissed with very brief discussions, almost out of hand, as not being "developments" at all, but the spinning of wheels (in the air).[76]

John Bates Clark

Clark's "marginal productivity theory of distribution" was an extension of utility theory. Without factual support, it assumed that each income (wages, profits, interest, rents) is proportional to its recipient's contribution to production. The key term here is *contribution*. The classicists (Smith, et al.) assumed there was only *one* contributor to production, whoever did the work (manual, mental, or managerial); and that interest, profits, and rents were rewards to ownership (and its power), *not* to production.

Clark's contribution in adapting "marginalism" to the whole matter was to generalize Marshallian theory to distribution. With that kind and degree of obfuscation, it became virtually impossible to argue with him.[77] Although Clark died as long ago as 1918, it was his theory that from then on (and still) stands as the *only* "explanation" for either your wages or, say, Bill Gates's profits. There was little inclination to argue anyhow amongst the mainstreamers, for to do so would be to revive a key element of classical political economy: that which gave capitalism's critics a strong weapon with which to make "class harmony" implausible.

Irving Fisher

Fisher (1867–1947) appears to have been an agreeable man, and not disinterested in the facts of the real world. But like so many other economists then and now, he was tantalized by the ways in which a concern for "the economy," with its innumerable quantities of this and that – imagined or real – could be mathematized. And if that meant seeing the economy as a set of "natural" (as distinct from "social") phenomena and setting aside all other realities of an economy so as to slip into the intricacies of mathematical manipulation – well, where's the harm in that? If Fisher made any useful contribution, it was that he supplied much of the foundation for "econometrics." That has often been useful; more often it has served as still another set of techniques for sending economists off in empty space.[78]

Joan Robinson I

Called "I" here because of her transformation over the decade following her *Imperfect Competition*. She began that book by acknowledging the economist Piero Sraffa's observation that "It is necessary ... to abandon the path of free competition and turn in the opposite direction, namely, towards monopoly."[79] She goes on to note that the theory of perfect competition also includes its *alter ego*, a theory of perfect monopoly; and that both theories proceeded in the same way with the same assumptions and are in effect a mirror image of each other.

A "perfectly monopolistic" industry is one where there is but one firm. That exists (especially for public utilities), but it is rare. What is common is some *degree* of monopoly, that is, of market power (or control). To explore the ins and outs of that, complete with the usual equations and diagrams and adjusted for the more awkward situations of "imperfect competition" (and "imperfect monopoly") was what Robinson achieved – while Chamberlin was doing the same for his "monopolistic competition," with analytical variations.

Their reasoning seemed so much more reasonable than the far-fetched unrealities of perfectly competitive industries that some of the more inquiring minds in the profession (like Robinson's) thought real progress had been made. But it was the kind of progress made by one alchemist over another, when he adds a little copper to the dross which then resembles gold. If the new theories had any use at all it was for testing university students.[80]

Turning the earth

As Robinson subsequently realized in her "wrong turning" remarks, to understand the role of imperfect – or any – markets was quite impossible within the framework of static analysis – that is, an analysis assuming away *time* (among other matters):

> the lack of a comprehensible treatment of historical time and failure to specify the rules of the game in the type of economy under discussion ... render[s] the theoretical apparatus useless for the analysis of contemporary problems in the micro and macro spheres.[81]

Over time, Robinson applied that understanding to the whole of the socioeconomic process, including her collaboration with Keynes on the *General Theory*, her attempts to integrate mainstream with Marxian analysis, and her work that went beyond economic theory to broader concerns that earned her the classification of "radical." As we now turn away from the efforts of those who sought to make neoclassical theories more meaningful by sheer extension and manipulation, our attention will fall mostly upon three quite different economists – Keynes, Robinson II, and Schumpeter. They were three species of a creative genus. Not always seeking to do so, all three burst through one or more of the walls of neoclassical theory's assumptions.[82]

John Maynard Keynes

In his theorizing Keynes (1883–1946) always worked within the neoclassical framework of assumptions, but we'll see that his "vision" was often (and increasingly) in conflict with the laissez-faire capitalism it supported.

That said, it is notable that even in his path-breaking masterwork, *The General Theory of Employment, Interest, and Money* (1936) Keynes adhered to the entirety of neoclassicism, micro and macro – deviating with respect to only *one* assumption: that savings are a function of the rate of interest. If that is *not* so – if, as Keynes argued, savings are instead a function of the level of income – Say's Law collapses, as does a major pillar of the edifice of *laissez-faire* capitalism (that is, an economy free of the need for governmental intervention).

The foregoing relates to something emphasized more than once in earlier (and subsequent) pages: the decisive importance of the assumptions of a theory in allowing, indeed producing, its conclusions. But it also raises once more the question of what it is that pushes theorists to *make* or *reject* certain assumptions. And that takes us to the evolution of Keynes's thinking.

Keynes was already becoming an eminent neoclassical economist before World War I, and became more so in the years up to 1936. It is widely assumed that the depression was the "epiphany" that led to the "Keynesian revolution." But a short survey of his works reveals that from his earliest writings the elements of what would become the *General Theory* were taking shape.

In 1911 (when he was 28), he was appointed editor of what was the key publication for economists, *The Economic Journal*, a post he held until 1945 (a year before his death). In 1918 Keynes was appointed Principal Representative of the Treasury at the Versailles Peace Conference. That led to his *Economic Consequences of the Peace* (1920) whose severe criticism of the Treaty was preceded by his principled resignation in 1919.

Selections from the opening pages of that book provide an early glimpse of what was to come 16 years later:

> Europe was so organized socially and economically [before 1914] as to secure the maximum accumulation of capital. While there was some continuous improvement in the daily conditions of life of the mass of the population, Society was so framed as to throw a great part of the increased income into the control of the class least likely to consume it … In fact, it was precisely the inequality of the distribution of wealth which made possible those vast accumulations of fixed wealth and of capital improvements which distinguished that age from all others. Herein lay, in fact, the main justification of the Capitalist System.[83]

That "justification" became institutionalized into what Keynes calls economic *laissez-faire* and its supporting economic theory:

> The beauty and simplicity of such a theory are so great that it is easy to forget that it follows not from the actual facts, but from an incomplete

hypothesis introduced for the sake of simplicity ... [The] conclusion that individuals acting independently for their own advantage will produce the greatest aggregate of wealth, depends on a variety of unreal assumptions to the effect that the processes of production and consumption are in no way organic, that there exists a sufficient foreknowledge of conditions and requirements, and that there are adequate opportunities of obtaining this foreknowledge. For economists generally reserve for a later stage of their argument the complications that arise – (1) when the efficient units of production are large relatively to the units of consumption, (2) when overhead costs or joint costs are present, (3) when internal economies tend to the aggregation of production, (4) when the time required for adjustments is long, (5) when ignorance prevails over knowledge, and (6) when monopolies and combinations interfere with equality in bargaining – they reserve, that is to say, for a later stage their analysis of the actual facts. Moreover, many of those who recognise that the simplified hypothesis does not accurately correspond to fact conclude nevertheless that it does represent what is "natural" and therefore ideal. They regard the simplified hypothesis as health, and the further complications as disease.[84]

A few pages later, warming to his task, Keynes observes:

Let us clear from the ground the metaphysical or general principles upon which, from time to time, *laissez-faire* has been founded. It is *not* true that individuals possess a prescriptive "natural liberty" in their economic activities. There is *no* compact conferring perpetual rights on those who Have or on those who Acquire. The world is *not* so governed from above that private and social interests always coincide. It is *not* so managed here below so that in practice they coincide. It is *not* a correct deduction from the principles of economics that enlightened self-interest always operates in the public interest. Nor is it generally true that self-interest generally *is* enlightened ... Experience does *not* show individuals, when they make up a social unit, are always less clear-sighted than when they act separately.[85]

From those observations he moves to some that may be found in somewhat different phrasing in the *General Theory* ten years later:

Many of the greatest economic evils of our time are the fruits of risk, uncertainty, and ignorance. It is because particular individuals, fortunate in situation or in abilities, are able to take advantage of uncertainty and ignorance, and also because for the same reason big business is often a lottery, that great inequalities of wealth come about; and these same factors are also the cause of the unemployment of labour, or the disappointment of reasonable business expectations, and of the impairment of efficiency and production. Yet the cure lies outside the operations of individuals; it may even be to the interest of individuals to aggravate the disease.

Then, after proposing deliberate control of currency and credit by a central institution, he adds:

My second [proposal] relates to savings and investment. I believe some coordinated act of intelligent judgement is required as to the scale on which it is desirable that the community as a whole should save, the scale on which those savings should go abroad in the form of foreign investments, and whether the present organisation of the investment market distributes savings along the most nationally productive channels. I do not think that these matters should be left entirely to the chances of private judgement and private profits, as they are at present.[86]

After reading the above selections from Keynes's early writings (and many others not noted here), and then studying the *General Theory*, one can find easy agreement with Rogin's reasoning (noted in the Prologue) that "policy precedes theory." Now we examine the *General Theory* in its major outlines.[87]

It is useful to begin with what Keynes was arguing against; namely, Say's Law. Simply expressed it stated that "supply creates its own demand." Behind those five words was an argument that may be put this way. In any period (say, one year), the market value of total production must be equal to the total value of money incomes (wages, profits). Those incomes will either be spent on consumption, or not. If not, they are saved (and that is the *definition* of savings, for both Say and Keynes).

But, Say goes on, some income is saved due to the attractions of lending money, as manifest in the ongoing rate of interest. But what determines the rate of interest? It is the demand for loanable funds, he argued (not using just these words), which in turn is determined by the funds required for real investment (in construction, equipment, and so on). The demand for such funds will, as it rises, push up the rate of interest; that in turn *ipso facto* (as though we are looking at a seesaw) pushes savings up and consumption down (in terms of percentage of the national income). Thus: what is *not* spent on consumption *is* spent on investment goods. And demand equals supply. Q.E.D.

And there cannot *be* a depression; or, more exactly, if by a depression one means substantial unemployment, then that unemployment is not due to a failure of the economic system – which might call for non-market (governmental) interventions – but to the demand for excessively high wages on the part of those foolish workers. So, *laissez-faire*, wait a while, things will straighten out, settle down, begin to look up. Meanwhile, the workers learn a lesson. Again.

Not so, said Keynes.[88] Savings are a function of income, *not* of the rate of interest. Moreover, given the inequality of incomes, with a few at the top receiving a disproportionate share, that means that as the national income rises, savings will also, and at an increasing rate (that is, the percentage of savings to income will rise). And, inevitably, this will mean that excess productive capacities exist, and that the demand for loanable funds will level off and decline and result in depression and unemployment. The lack of "effective demand" requires non-private (that is, governmental) sources of demand (that is, governmental) to take up the slack – spending on public projects – while providing sales to businesses and jobs to workers and services of one sort or another to society.

All things considered, it was a great accomplishment. There is a big but, however, even (perhaps especially) for those who like myself praise him: as a neoclassicist – albeit a cranky one – his habit of assuming away all sorts of things allowed him also to neglect any examination of power and politics. Then as (generally) since, power was concentrated predominantly in the hands of business and they used and use it to block the very policies Keynes saw as essential.

Be that as it may, one of Keynes's main aims (as an enlightened conservative) was to save capitalism, and his ideas helped to do that after World War II – for a while. Critic of capitalism though he was, for Keynes capitalism was better than any conceivable alternative.[89] If all of that were not enough to raise the hackles of capitalists, Keynes had something else that would; and it earned him the undying hatred of the financial community: he was scornful of the financial markets.

Keynes was generally unpopular in the business world, seen as a dangerous snob of sorts. Many businessmen were smart enough to see that they would be among the beneficiaries of government spending, even if it did mean that the government was going to be too much in the picture.[90] But those who make money by *dealing* in money – whether as bankers or bondholders – could see nothing but peril in Keynesianism. After all, didn't he propose "the euthanasia of the *rentier*"?

He did indeed, and in just those words. For Keynes, the reward to capital for real (productive capacity) investment was a reward to its scarcity. But, as capitalism moved through time, that scarcity intermittently declined (causing recessions) and over the long haul it might well permanently decline. Meanwhile, real investors had to pay interest to financiers, large or small, in the form of interest on borrowed funds. The higher the rate of interest, the greater the obstacle to real investment (other things being equal).

But real investment over the long haul faced diminishing profits as capital scarcity diminished. Therefore, for the national economy to be healthy (through sufficient real investment) it was necessary for the rate of interest to be *kept* low, and *pushed* lower over time: slow death, euthanasia, for the creditor class. Who can blame them for getting upset? (But who but they should *be* upset?)

Keynes was excoriated at home; those who followed him, even modestly, as FDR did after 1935, were called "traitors to their class." Anticipating such reactions, Keynes sums up as follows:

> Whilst, therefore, the enlargement of the functions of government, involved in the task of adjusting to one another the propensity to consume and the inducement to invest [through tax and spending policies], would seem to a nineteenth-century publicist or to a contemporary American financier to be a terrific encroachment on individualism, I defend it, on the contrary, both as the only practicable means of avoiding the destruction of existing economic forms in their entirety and as the condition of the successful functioning of individual initiative. (1936, 380)

Although there is much of the foregoing "conversational" tone in the book, its "bones" are found in its abstract theory. It was left to his followers to put meat on those bones. Keynes naturally had Britain in mind. Thus 1) the great differences among nations required major adjustments; 2) though well familiar with global matters, Keynes had focused on national relationships, and foreign trade had to be given specific attention; 3) all neoclassical abstractions had to be much modified or abandoned entirely; and 4) it was essential to go beyond the artificial micro/macro/trade theorizing and to develop an analysis that integrated them – as they are in reality. We now examine a few such efforts.

Alvin Hansen

Many economists in many countries contributed in the attempts to resolve the relevant analytical (and connected policy) problems. It is both appropriate and convenient here to look at some of the work of Joan Robinson in all the foregoing regards, and of the U.S. economist Alvin Hansen (1887–1975) for an adjustment of the theory to his country. The latter's contributions will be discussed first, with Robinson's work seen as part of her larger analytical development. (Apologies are due to those not noted, and I offer them here and now.)

Hansen is generally seen as the "translator" of Keynes into "American." He did that, and more, in several books and many articles. His *Full Recovery or Stagnation?* encompassed both aims, and later works took his arguments further.[91] In the deterioration of economics that has taken place since the 1970s, one of the casualties has been a certain amnesia concerning Hansen and his works. But in the 1930s and 1940s his analyses were of great importance in both the academic and policy-making worlds.

Note the term "stagnation." Hansen, along with Alan Sweezy (older brother of Paul), developed what came to be called the "stagnation thesis" as they sought to apply Keynesian theory to the United States, expanding on mere hints in *The General Theory.*

Those hints had to do with the tendency toward depression when capital becomes abundant in supply. The stagnation thesis holds first that U.S. economic expansion from its first period of industrialization up into the 1920s had resulted from the interaction of three factors: waves of technological innovation, rapid population growth, and geographic expansion. Next, Hansen argued that the latter two stimuli by the 1920s had ceased or were slowing; and that technological change by itself was insufficient to do the job.[92]

Hansen's arguments did not begin even to be known until Europe was edging toward war, and as the U.S. economy was benefiting from that stimulus plus the stimulating effects of the Second New Deal. Put differently, because of those "non-market stimuli," the stagnation thesis was disallowed the chance of being confirmed by the kind of "equilibrium at high unemployment" posited by Keynes – although ten *years* of deep depression might have been seen by open-minded observers as confirmation of sorts, and Hansen would be seen still as a great U.S. economist.

Joan Robinson II
She is unique in having been a prominent economist within the neoclassical school, become even more prominent as a participant in "the Keynesian revolution," and gone on to work seriously as a friendly critic of and contributor to Marxian analysis and a prime mover in the always more lively bunch called "post-Keynesians."

In her remarkable career, and in addition to her teaching, Robinson wrote almost 30 books, hundreds of essays (many but not all of them put together in the five volumes of her *Collected Economic Papers*), and innumerable reviews – an enormous body of work almost all of which is still worth reading.[93]

Robinson came to the attention of the profession through her *Economics of Imperfect Competition* (1933). She began to make her many contributions to what I have called "useful" economics when she, as a member of the "Cambridge circus,"[94] reworked the proofs of what was to be the *General Theory*; and it was she, more than any other, who in her *Introduction to the Theory of Employment* (1937) succinctly transmitted the essence of the theory to the non-professionals, at the same time showing what was yet to be done.

"What was yet to be done" was still far from done 30 years later, as neoclassicism (in macro as well as micro) came stumbling out of the shadows; from then on, as Keynesian theory was being (in her words) "bastardized," it was necessary both to keep it alive *and* to strengthen its always fragile body and, at the same time, to adapt it to the then evident "rules" of monopoly capitalism. Robinson contributed greatly to that work.

For well over a century, those trained in economics have worked with "equilibrium" as a central notion – of the individual firm, of the economy as a whole, even of the individual – "that isolated, definitive human datum," as Veblen mocked the notion when cited earlier, "in stable equilibrium except for the buffets of the impinging forces ..." And the mockery applies as much to the "representative firm" and to "general equilibrium."

Those *not* trained in economics might well be puzzled as to how anyone could seriously take such a concept as central for understanding the economy. The answer lies in many areas, including those murky ones that serve the "vested interests." But there is also a less disreputable reason. The search for the "conditions of equilibrium" of this and that arose in an era much enamored by science, most especially of Newtonian physics. The method – and much of the focus – of economics developed as though it were studying the very slowly and predictably changing forces of nature instead of the relatively rapid, chaotic, and uncertain processes of society.

To repeat: neoclassical economics is in all of its dimensions *static* analysis: no time, no change, and so on. As such it also quite simply ignores the past; in doing so it cannot comprehend the present. None of that had to or has to do with stupidity; it is a matter of aims and values. The social values of those that initiated and continued the development of neoclassical economics were – doubtless unconsciously in most cases – quite simply "bourgeois." Long before Marshall's *Principles* (1890) "bourgeois" (a set of attitudes and values that preceded and assisted at the birth of industrial capitalism) had been effectively redefined to have capitalism as its hegemon.

All this being so, to get economic thinking down to earth, where it could be useful for society rather than a combination of games-playing and ideology, required examining both the *processes* and the *relationships* of the economy in their real, that is, their *historical* settings.

Mainstream economists are pleased to refer to their *dynamic* analyses, where the "dynamism" is to be found in connected mathematical equations whose elements are entirely imaginary. Robinson II saw that as essentially absurd:

> The characteristic of dynamic analysis ... is that it cannot explain how an economy behaves in given conditions without reference to past history ... The concept of equilibrium is incompatible with history. It is a metaphor based on movement in space applied to processes taking place in time. In space it is possible to go to and fro and to remedy misdirections, but in time, every day, the past is irrevocable and the future unknown.[95]

Robinson's search to develop the means to locate macroeconomic behavior in the social process began with her early association with Keynes; in 1936 she began to inquire into "the long period theory of unemployment." Her *An Essay on Marxian Economics* (1942), an attempt to "translate Marx into Keynes,"[96] is a critically friendly commentary on both; it also reveals how far her analytical outlook had moved from static analysis.

The time-frame for this chapter ends in the mid-1940s, but here a thumbnail sketch of Robinson's subsequent work is pertinent. In 1951 she wrote an introduction to Rosa Luxemburg's *Accumulation of Capital* (1913), an extension (into imperialism, pre-dating Lenin) and a critique of Marxian theory; in 1956 she wrote her own *The Accumulation of Capital*. By that time Robinson had freed herself from the silken chains of neoclassicism and her real work had begun: the work of serious socioeconomic analysis.

Joan Robinson was such a great and generous teacher, in the formal and informal sense of the term: for countless economists (and their students) her life and her works were an inspiration and vital nourishment, an oasis in the broad desert of mainstream economic analysis, always offering the hope of life. Bless her.

Joseph A. Schumpeter

Schumpeter (1883–1950) was a spectacular figure, especially so for an academic. He was aristocratic in bearing (though not by birth), had a very strong ego, and very strong drives. It seems clear he sought to be another Marx, if with an entirely different analysis. Like Marx, Schumpeter expected capitalism to do itself in; unlike Marx, he wished it were not to be so.

Schumpeter was very much at home in history, in politics, in culture, a grand and enthusiastic scholar; whether he was a sociological economist or an economic sociologist would be hard to say. By all accounts, he was a fabulous teacher, combining his immense erudition with wit and passion, and doing so with grace.

It may be noted that he and Keynes were born in the same year (and died but a few years apart, both much too young). He and Keynes came to know each other when Keynes was editor and Schumpeter the Austrian correspondent for *The Economic Journal*. But, as his wife (Elizabeth Boody Schumpeter, also an economist) delicately put it, "For some reason, not easy to explain, the relation between these two was not a close one, personally or professionally."[97]

It was somewhat worse than that, at least from Schumpeter's side. As will be seen, Schumpeter had every reason to be proud of both the quantitative and qualitative aspects of his work; but he quite clearly also nursed something very much like a grievance that not he, but Keynes, became the most celebrated economist of their time.

This comes out almost embarrassingly in his memorial essay on Keynes of September 1946. All the essays in his *Ten Great Economists* are enlightening, and very much worth reading, most especially that on Marx (which will be dealt with soon). But what is most enlightening about the Keynes article is the manner in which Schumpeter alternates between generous, even flowery characterizations of Keynes as a person or as an economist, only to dart in with critical rapier-like thrusts that can leave one gasping. Here only two examples, both referring to works that most (including this writer) consider to have been of great importance and of high quality: *Economic Consequences* and the *General Theory*.

Of the first, with which Keynes "leapt into fame," Schumpeter writes:

> Those who cannot understand how luck and merit intertwine will no doubt say that Keynes simply wrote what was on every sensible man's lips; that he was very favorably placed for making his protests resound all over the world ... that won him every ear and thousands of hearts; and that, at the moment the book appeared, the tide was already running on which it was to ride. There is truth in all this ...[98]

Then, after having thrust the blade in, Schumpeter pulls it out, and wipes it clean:

> But if we choose, on the strength of this, to deny the greatness of the feat, we had better delete this phrase altogether from the pages of history. (ibid.)

Schumpeter goes on to recount in admiring tones the numerous public and academic (and cultural) activities of Keynes's busy life, adding that

"Nature is wont to impose two distinct penalties upon those who try to beat out their stock of energy to the thinnest leaf" (p. 271). And within moments, he is considering the *General Theory*.

If one had just arrived from Mars and read Schumpeter's account of the details and the broad argument of the *Theory*, he would put down the essay wondering how so many on one planet could be fooled into thinking that theory was ... what? Original? Valuable? Sound? And our Martian would find the explanation in something very much approaching the gullibility of those who saw Keynes as having made a large accomplishment. On the last page of his essay, and after quoting a letter to himself from an economist praising Keynes for making "us better economists," he comments:[99]

> Whether we agree or not, this expresses the essential point about Keynes's achievement extremely well. In particular, it explains why hostile criticism, even if successful in its attack upon individual assumptions or propositions, is yet powerless to inflict fatal injury upon the structure as a whole. As with Marx, it is possible to admire Keynes even though one may consider his social vision to be wrong and every one of his propositions to be misleading. (ibid., 291)

In other words, Keynes was a con artist? That pettiness behind Schumpeter's view of Keynes is not to be found in his comments on *anyone* else – including Marx. Indeed, his sustained analysis of Marx[100] (as prophet, sociologist, economist, and teacher) is in its tone diametrically opposed to that of Keynes. It is almost as though Schumpeter is searching for positive ways of discussing Marx. And, along with profound differences, he finds those ways.

Schumpeter was fond of using the notion of "vision" in viewing other economists; and his own work was propelled by such vision. Schumpeter frequently makes much fun of Marx's followers; he seldom does so of Marx himself. He seldom agrees with Marx; but when he disagrees it is on what could be called collegial terms, as witness his final sentence: "To say that Marx, stripped of phrases, admits of interpretation in a conservative sense is only saying that he can be taken seriously." [101] His *Capitalism, Socialism and Democracy* does just that, agreeing, on different bases, that capitalism would destroy itself. Marx (to oversimplify greatly, of course), saw capitalism as producing "its own gravediggers" in the form of an ever-growing, ever more class-conscious and organized working class which would confront capitalism in a moment of accumulation crisis, and bring it down. Up to now, Marx has been wrong.

Schumpeter thought that prediction would hold, not because of class struggle, and despite the successful evolution of the economy. He believed that capitalism would always find its way out of any economic crisis into which it had propelled itself (through processes of "creative destruction"). But he also thought it would be done in, but for sociological rather than economic reasons: reasons centering around the loss of vitality of the capitalist class (the rise of big business, bureaucracy, and so on). Up to now, Schumpeter has also been wrong.

Our concern here is not the rightness or wrongness of predictions. The value of both Marx and Schumpeter is in what they analyzed and how they went about it: everyone can learn from both of them. But Schumpeter was also more than a historian of economic ideas and a commentator on the future of capitalism. He also did some lastingly valuable work on the history of capitalism.

He began his career with *Theory of Economic Development* (1910). Its main importance was in the analytical worryings that led him to his later conclusions about the entire capitalist process, in *Capitalism, Socialism and Democracy*. Between those two works lay what (at least) economic historians and business cycle economists consider his masterwork: *Business Cycles*.[102]

The work is an extraordinary, one may say unbelievable, combination of fact, historical analysis, and theory, of the entire capitalist epoch, for all the relevant nations. It is all the more extraordinary (as his widow informs us) in that he did all the research himself and wrote (not typed) out all his notes: scarcely what one would expect from an eminent Harvard professor – or any professor, in this day and age.

In the process of doing that kind of work, and doing it uniquely well, Schumpeter, consciously or not, had lifted himself out of the dry-as-dust world of neoclassicism. To the end he remained a devoted fan of Walras and all others who sought to mathematize and "general equilibriumize" economics; and he had the mathematical ability to do that himself.[103] Whether consciously or not, his writings in those regards were always comments on the work of others; he himself did more useful work.

A final comment. The foregoing observations on Schumpeter began on a downbeat; and, despite the subsequently more favorable tone concerning his work, anyone who has read this far in this book will have guessed that I do not see Schumpeter as a soul-mate. But I do see him as very much worth reading; very much an economist who makes arguments of the kind and in a way that provokes thought and second thoughts. And that's saying a lot – especially considering the "mainstream" from which he extricated himself: intentionally or not.[104]

Part II: 1945–2000

4 Resurrection: Global Economy II and *its* Crisis; Hopeful Stirrings in Economics: 1945–75

THE BEST OF TIMES – FOR SOME, FOR A WHILE

The 25 years between the late 1940s and the early 1970s were the most persistently and pervasively expansive in both their spread and their depth in the entire history of capitalism. Expansion manifested itself in all areas of economic activity: in per capita real consumption, most notably in consumer durables in the leading countries; in all aspects of real investment – construction and equipment for every type of production; in technological change at all levels in all sectors – consumer and producer products and techniques in industry, agriculture, and all services, most potently in transportation and finance; and in enormous increases in world investment and trade.

In the major capitalist nations those years were also unmatched in their underlying social and political stability; the widespread political strife symbolized by "1968" (in Chicago, Paris, Mexico City, and elsewhere) was itself prompted in good part by those "good times."

The processes of expansion of this period comprised both quantitative and structural economic change; that is, both growth and development. *Development* means transformation; structural economic changes both require and enable changes in the *social* process, in the institutional realm – for better or worse.

Beginning in the early 1900s, societies everywhere began to shudder from economic, political, and military upheavals, culminating in the social earthquakes that ended with World War II. Whatever else had been shattered by 1945, so too had the bases for the survival of capitalism – unless, as had happened in response to earlier (and much lesser) crises, capitalism found ways to succor itself. The ways were found by the only nation possessing both the vigor and the size to act: the United States.

As will be noted shortly, the policies and behavior of those with economic and political power – private or public, wittingly or not – interacted dynamically to produce a new "social formation": "monopoly capitalism."[1]

Monopolistic arrangements are older than capitalism itself.[2] With industrialism they became both more essential and easier to arrange. In one variation or another they were common in all industrial capitalist nations by the late nineteenth century. Throughout the twentieth century there were repeated waves of mergers and acquisitions ("M&As"). They varied in degree and kind from country to country, but with one characteristic in common: an always greater concentration of economic and political power. As the century ended, M&As within and between industries, sectors, nations had become explosive.

Capitalism has always been a *social*, not just an economic system, has always meant more than the existence of privately controlled markets for goods or services. *Monopoly* capitalism entails an increasingly pervasive subservience to the economy by the entire set of social institutions and processes.

The Big Six

The constituent elements of that metamorphosis will soon be designated as six "clusters" of relationships and processes, those centering on 1) giant corporations, 2) the State, 3) "consumerism," 4) globalization, 5) the military-industrial complex, and 6) the role of the media. Each cluster is intricately complicated in itself, and each depends to a critical degree on the existence of and interaction with all the others, in an always more integrated world economy. Separately or (even more) taken together the "six" required technological and organizational developments that neither did nor *could* exist until recently. In consequence, the joint powers of business and the State have been recast so that the economy can now function to their satisfaction only insofar as the entirety of social existence is increasingly bent to the needs and desires of capital: everywhere.[3]

A further note to keep in mind for our later discussion of the *economics* attending these developments. As we now examine the defining characteristics of monopoly capitalism, it will be obvious that they stand in shocking contrast to Smith's "invisible hand" and *laissez-faire*, as they do even more so with neoclassical economics. In recognition of that, a significant number of economists (including some who had been part of the mainstream) set to work to study and "report on" reality and to adjust theory accordingly. (Much of this book's information depends on that work.) However, the majority of economists sailed blithely on, and, with the crisis of the 1970s, were slowly but surely able to reclaim "their" temporarily lost territory, and, by the 1990s, to proclaim an almost total triumph.

Here, we return to reality. As we do so, most of the analysis and the data will center on the United States, even though this is meant to be a history of capitalism in general. Had this study been written a century ago, the emphasis would have been on Great Britain, the hegemonic power of early capitalism. Now, but considerably more so, it is the United States of contemporary capitalism – dominating not just with its economic and military power, but with its political economy, its culture, and its ways of thinking: alas, as will be argued in the book's conclusion.

BEHEMOTH CAPITALISM UNBOUND

Unevenly, and rapidly or slowly, the main elements of monopoly capitalism took shape through the late 1940s and on through the 1950s and 1960s. As each of those elements grew in strength it depended on, fed, and was fed by the strengthening of the others. Among all those, primary in importance was the vast increase in both the absolute and the relative power of *super-corporations*, which in turn required and facilitated an equally striking increase in both the quantitative and qualitative roles of the *State* in all functional and geographic areas, and at all levels.

Given that both those developments constituted a marked departure from traditional U.S. notions of what was proper, it was essential for the maintenance of socioeconomic stability that vigorous economic expansion be assured. This was made possible by the achievement of the remaining elements: the strengthening and spread of *consumerism* in the United States (and its replication in all the leading and some of the lesser economies); the recreation, transformation, deepening, and energization by the United States of an expanding global economy; based on the economic stimuli of the U.S. *military–industrial complex* and the Cold War that rationalized it.

But none of the foregoing developments – economic, social, political, military, national, or international – could have reached the levels or taken the form achieved by the 1960s had they not been facilitated, sustained, or created by the extension and refinement of the techniques of *mass communication* for selling both products and politics: the indispensable lubricant of monopoly capitalism's ways and means – not least those of the Cold War which, like its huge military expenditures, seems destined never to end, *de facto*.

Each of these will be discussed in some detail in this chapter; because of great changes in all of them since the 1970s, they will be examined in the different context of Chapter 5. Here, we begin with the attempts to deal with the manifold destruction of the war, which took the form of "rescue, rebuilding, and modernization," each merging into the others. Thus, the next section will encompass the rebuilding of a global economy and its dependence on the Cold War. Then, in order, we'll examine the power-center of those processes – big business and the State – thence to consumerism and the media, thence to the "stagflation" crisis of the 1970s. We conclude with the ups and downs of economic thought, within and outside neoclassical economics.

FROM THE ASHES ARISING ...

It is difficult now to imagine, nor is it easy to describe, the extent and gravity of destruction wrought by World War II, for all but the nations isolated either by location (as in the Western Hemisphere) or some particular political "understanding" (as in Switzerland and Sweden).

The destruction of human lives lingers in the memory longest. Less tragic, but in its way tragic enough, was the physical destruction not only of bridges, railroads, ships, and factories, and even, as noted earlier, of whole cities, hundreds of them lost to memory. To this must be added the *social* destruction, where "social" comprises the political and economic and cultural, and something just as vital but difficult to find a word for, other than "morale."

If we consider only Europe, few indeed were the families who did not lose at least one member of their family among the tens of millions dead: "in the trenches," in bombed cities, or in concentration camps. And few escaped some sort of physical incapacitation (through wounds, fire, disease, malnutrition).

Were all that not enough, there was something else that weakened morale. In one way or another, to one degree or another, it is difficult to find any important nation whose national (political and/or economic) leadership did not behave badly in the years leading up to or even during the war. After the war, that was a heavy weight to be borne by all Europeans. All this of course betokened immeasurable but surely significant political conse-quences for the European "establishment."

In the United States, in contrast, only a small minority was conscious that their record had been stained by their frequently helpful policies toward the fascist nations – Spain, Italy, Germany, and Japan.[4] Instead, public opinion was dominated by something like an opposite set of attitudes: triumph, pride, and satisfaction – diluted only by widespread worries after the war that depression would once more take hold.

As soon as the war ended, and faced with the socioeconomic collapse of Europe as a whole, the United States, as only it could, sought in different ways to breathe life back into the desperate nations' economies. Japan was treated differently, at first: the United States occupied and totally controlled it.

As the United States took the lead in all this, those with economic and political power saw the relevant policies as being in their business and/or nation's self-interest. Not doing so, it was clear, would have allowed a global drift into deep chaos. Furthermore, given the attitudes of a substantial percentage (in some cases, a majority) of the populations of Britain, France, Germany, Italy (and many smaller countries such as Greece and Holland), a decisive shift away from capitalism seemed imminent.

This was not popular opinion in the United States. If those in power perceived both the threats and the possibilities of the postwar situation, just as clear is it that the majority of the population and of the owners of millions of small businesses dwelt on neither the threats nor the possibilities. Then (as now) the average person in the United States thought little of affairs elsewhere, and considerably less so than is customary in Europe.

U.S. business heads (with some notable exceptions) had been fervent opponents of the taxes, expenditures, and social policies of the New Deal. However, by the time the postwar period opened experience had taught them that the State could be a friend as well as a foe. Most especially had that lesson been learned by those in the industries that converted from (say) autos to tanks and airplanes, from typewriters to machine guns; and so on.

The vision of those in the key industries was thus clearer than that of "the man in the street." And understanding that the U.S. depression was ended finally (perhaps only) by massive military expenditures was not a long step from comprehending the role of a revived Europe and an associated well-functioning global economy.

Thus, as the content of "rescue," and more pointedly of "rebuilding" and "modernization" and their connections with the evolution of the Cold War are examined, neither implicitly nor explicitly will there be a suggestion that a "conspiracy" gave birth to the Cold War. Rather, it is sufficient to understand the shaping of the Cold War as a convergence of diverse interests – those of business, of global-minded political figures, of militarists, and of idealists. Through that convergence, it became possible for U.S. domestic and foreign policies after 1945 to be framed in terms combining expanding markets, idealism, and the declared – if not real – need to confront a militarily threatening Soviet Union.[5]

As we turn first to "rescue" operations, there is barely a glimmer of what was to come with "rebuilding" and "modernization." Both were embodied to an important degree in the Marshall Plan (1948). Taken

together, they constituted a large step toward Global Economy II and
the Cold War.

Rescue

As used here, "rescue" refers to the provision of the bare minima for
survival (food, medicine, fuel) for the numerous nations (especially in
Europe) unable to provide for their people, many millions of whom
had been shunted around ruthlessly for years.

On its own and through the institutions of the new (1945) United
Nations, the United States supplied vast quantities of food and
clothing and medical supplies, and facilitated the relocation of the
displaced persons, from mid-1945 through 1946. The need was deep
in Britain and the Soviet Union and in the defeated nations, plus the
numerous occupied countries (Poland, Holland, Belgium) and those
allied with the Germans and Italians in Central and Eastern Europe
(Hungary, Romania, et al.). Malnutrition and its consequences were
rife, and tens of millions were often close to starvation and freezing to
death. Although there was surely self-interest in those activities, they
were done with decency and dispatch.

Rebuilding

Because of the varieties of national and business self-interest, rebuilding could not be accomplished either with dispatch or with much
decency. Serious debate and discussions began as early as 1942,
between Britain and the United States. Both within and between the
two countries, disagreements were strong, arising from different views
as to what was best for their respective country's future. In 1944, the
first agreements were signed, beginning with the International Monetary Fund (IMF) and the International Bank for Reconstruction and
Redevelopment.[6]

In order to meet the desperate needs of the British and French, in
1946 (after strenuous negotiations) loans in the billions were extended. In Havana, the following year, an international conference put
together the General Agreement on Tariffs and Trade (GATT), the
blueprint for many later trade agreements including, most recently,
the World Trade Organization (WTO). Then, as still, it was squarely
based on Ricardian doctrine; at the time, the agreement evoked the
protests of the weaker nations, as today (along with, now, protests of
workers and environmentalists).

The stated aim of those institutions was a combination of global
stability, expansion, and development. Then followed a string of
European treaties – comprising the Marshall Plan and its military
counterpart the North Atlantic Treaty Organization (NATO, 1949),

soon to be followed by the European (essentially French and German) Coal and Steel Community, the first steps toward today's European Union.

Separately or together, all the foregoing took the shape and directions desired by the United States. Its power was immense and virtually beyond dispute.[7] Since then, global institutions such as the IMF, which began with a particular task, have adapted to intermittent crises by insensibly enlarging their dominion and going beyond their original mandate.

This is another way of saying that, given the periodic crises of capitalism, the scope required to accomplish a task in one period is much enlarged in a later period. As the capitalist process moves into and out of crises, more has to be dealt with if it is to emerge from each successive crisis. It follows that the always enlarging scope of policy required to emerge from crisis also assures that the *next* crisis will extend its difficulties always more deeply into the larger social process.

In the following chapter, the examination of the presently emerging global financial turmoil will trace out that process for, among other matters, the IMF and the IBRD (or World Bank). Here, as we turn to "modernization" and its connected developments, it will be seen how and in what ways those generalizations applied.

Modernization ... and the Cold War

The institutional rebuilding of the global economy after World War II had reached substantial significance by the 1950s. Of even more importance was that the political economy of U.S. monopoly capitalism was also finding the means to keep its own and key other nations' economies on a path of economic *expansion*. As will be further detailed in the next section, sitting at the vital center of those means was the political economy of the Cold War, the *sine qua non* for postwar "modernization."

After the United States, the two most powerful and "modern" economies from the 1950s on were those of Japan and Germany. Both had been pulverized by the war, of course. But as they soon became the principal strategic bastions of the United States in its conflict with China and the Soviet Union, both were effectively "subsidized" into modernization and expansion by the Cold War. (This was true, of course, for the United States too, and, in lesser degree, for several other nations.)[8]

Japan became an immense "aircraft carrier" for the United States. It was that most obviously (and non-metaphorically) in the uses and abuses of Japan's colony Okinawa by the United States – despite vigorous objections by Okinawans from the beginning to the present.

But Japan proper served a variety of functions of at least equal importance to the United States: for example, in serving as a key manufactory for napalm during the Vietnam war, and as a (covert) storage point for U.S. nuclear weapons.

At the end of the war, Japan was demoralized, destitute, and capital-hungry – and U.S.-occupied. But an inward flow of dollars began almost immediately and after 1950, with the Korean war, rose to great heights. One unforeseen consequence was that Japan "modernized" to such an extent that by the 1960s it was the U.S.'s main competitor, notably in electronics and autos. And by the close of the 1970s, Japan was well on its way to becoming what it is now: the main creditor of the globe, including the United States.[9]

As the U.S. bastion in Europe, Germany played the same role. Like Japan in Asia, and to the fury of General de Gaulle of France, it had become Europe's largest economy. By the close of the 1950s there were at least 350,000 U.S. troops "permanently" stationed in West Germany. Quite apart from other important elements of subsidization (in transport, communications, and the like), imagine what the upkeep of those troops (in terms of housing, food, entertainment) meant to the German economy: manna from heaven. From the viewpoint of Britain, the Soviet Union, and (in some sense) France – former allies either in debt to or treated with hostility by the United States – that was an unwelcome irony. But it worked for the global economy:

> from the time that European recovery was well in progress, the world entered a spell of unusually rapid economic growth that was sustained without significant interruption for a quarter of a century. The increase in world production of agricultural goods was 32 percent between 1948 and 1958 and 20 percent between 1958 and 1968; of minerals, 40 percent ... and 58 percent ... of manufactures 60 percent ... and 100 percent in the later decade. The volume of exports of the non-communist countries grew even faster: 83 percent ... and 113 percent [to 1968].[10]

And worked even better for the United States:

> The true "American century" arrived between 1947 and 1972, the golden years of the postwar expansion. During this run, real GNP grew at a rate of 3.7 percent per year, real disposable income per person at 2.3 percent per year, civilian unemployment [was at] the lowest quarter-century average in the statistical series dating back to 1890, and ... corporate profitability ... rose substantially over most of the period, peaking in the mid-1960s.

In these times the United States was the only superpower ... [and its] economic policies could be formulated in splendid isolation ... Corporations could raise wages and benefits annually, keep the industrial peace, pay the bill out of productivity increases, and pass off any added costs in higher product prices with little fear of losing customers to new oligopolistic rivals or foreign suppliers ... Neither foreign competition nor balance of international payments constraints intruded ... in any serious way. The United States exported more than it imported, with unbroken surpluses through 1970 and net exports of goods and services well into the 1970s ...[11]

"Cry Havoc! And let slip the dogs of war"

There is considerable dispute as to how and why the Cold War began. Some see it as a response to a substantial and growing military threat from the Soviet Union and, later, China; others (like myself), saw a Soviet military threat as imagined or contrived, given the virtual destruction of the Soviet economy and the deaths of well over 20 million of its people during the war.[12]

However that controversy might be resolved, one fact is indisputable: from 1946 to this day, the direct and indirect economic elements of the Cold War undergirded both the early and subsequent economic expansion of the entire globe. Even using the systematically understated official data – for example, those of the *Economic Report of the President* – the figure for military expenditures after 1946 exceeded $9 *trillion* by 1980 and now exceeds $12 *trillion* (in 1992 dollars).

Simple numbers are neither the beginning nor the end for understanding the meaning of those expenditures, what came to be called "military Keynesianism."[13]

One set of developments originating in or stimulated by milex – those in electronics, metallurgy, transportation and nuclear energy, in particular – can be seen as both positive and negative (quite aside from the fact that such developments were likely to have emerged, if less rapidly, without war), but more generally they too can be seen as negative.[14] More clearly harmful are two important *economic* consequences from never-ending massive milex: they are purely wasteful and purely inflationary – wasteful because they serve no *economic* function;[15] inflationary because they lift incomes without increasing marketable goods and services.

In addition, there have been and remain their harmful sociopolitical accompaniments, requirements, and consequences, for the United States and the rest of the world. Although we cannot know what the United States and either its friends or its targets would have become *without* the Cold War and its various elements, we can identify the main social injuries to the U.S. economy, its politics and its culture after 1945 through their Cold War militarization.

"Excessive vigilance in the defense of freedom is no crime"

Thus spake Senator Goldwater, as he sought the presidency in 1964 – and already for many years U.S. political and military agents had been operating covertly in Vietnam and elsewhere. Politics based on anti-communism did not begin with the Cold War or in the United States, of course; but their earlier scope and damages in the United States were minor when compared to the years after 1946. Then it escalated into McCarthyism, with transforming consequences for politics and politicians at all levels, for trade unions, universities, and (among other areas), the entertainment fields.[16] The strength and penetration of those processes were such that the American people (among others) slowly but steadily learned to look the other way regarding "their" social process, allowing what had never been pristine to become always dirtier, more strident, more corruptible, sleazier; a society with always sharper edges, increasingly seeing violent means as acceptable for always more numerous ends.[17]

And our targeted enemies in those same years moved along the same path and became very well armed against internal and external enemies – real or imagined. Would they have become so irrespective of the Cold War? We can never know the answer. We can say, however, that from the end of the war (or, in the case of China, after its 1949 revolution) they were permitted no alternative – deliberately so, the CIA has proudly acknowledged. Militarization of the U.S. economy not only "saved it" from depression, but strengthened it in the global economy. The militarization of the Soviet Union brought about very much the opposite, wrecking any chances that might ever have existed for a reasonably democratic, reasonably efficient, reasonably prosperous Soviet socialism.[18]

Such generalizations cannot be pinned down as though they were facts. Nor are they easy to refute – especially when one also looks at how the politics of U.S. allies (including Italy and Japan) were corrupted or studies the cruel postwar histories of diverse countries in Latin America (Cuba, Nicaragua, El Salvador, Chile), Asia (Cambodia, Laos, Vietnam, Indonesia), and parts of the Middle East and Africa. Their relationship to the U.S. Cold War was not by any means the entire source of their difficulties; but the difficulties were made insuperable by the grudging or willing part they played in the U.S.-written scenario.

There were of course many reasons why the Cold War came to be as widely accepted as it was (and is) in the United States (and elsewhere). Ranking high among those reasons, however, was what is here called "the political economy of the Cold War." The felt (and imagined) benefits – measured in variously defined well-being – accrued to business, to politicians, and to workers/consumers. Which takes us to an examination of those elements of monopoly capitalism denoted earlier in terms of super-corporations, the State, consumerism, and the media, in that order.

BIG BUSINESS

In the industrializing world after 1860, the tendency toward always enlarging companies was well-nigh universal: industrialization *meant* big firms, in order for businesses at once to take advantage of the "economies of large-scale production" *and* to fend off price competition from other (or potential) giants. The United States led that particular parade, in part thanks to the blessings of time and space earlier noted. Connected with that, the normal positive relationship between war and big business proved to be uniquely favorable to the United States: much in the way of stimuli, little in the way of damage.

The war stimuli included those enlarging the size and strength of businesses, notably, at first, in the industrial and transportation sectors – beginning with the Civil War, and always more so with the two world wars and the Cold War.[19] This is especially true of the Cold War if one takes into account its major contribution to Global Economies II and III.

The World War I economy gave a large boost to the consolidation of business. During that war, and again in the 1940s, the State's urgent demands for the rapid delivery of mountains of military goods led it (in the name of efficiency) to encourage "cooperation," which facilitated both the merging of companies and the easing of barriers to trade unionism.[20]

Additionally, and spurred on by the boom of the 1920s, was a new and more extensive merger movement. By 1929, the assets of the largest 200 (non-banking) corporations almost doubled, rising at an annual rate of over 5 percent (while those of all other corporations rose by only 2 percent).

As would happen with the later M&A races of the 1930s, 1960s, 1980s, and 1990s, each batch of mergers involved both quantitative and qualitative changes: quantitative in terms of the numbers of mergers and the value of assets involved, qualitative as regards the movement from *horizontal* mergers (of firms in the same), to *vertical* mergers (a firm of one industry merging with one of its suppliers and/or customers in a different industry), to *conglomerate* mergers (those in different industries).

By the 1980s, and even more so in the 1990s, all that was continuing to happen *within* the industrial countries. Also, both within and *between* countries mergers were combining finance with industry with trade with media with ... anything and everything.

Next we look more carefully at the years since 1945.

The giants feed

One outcome of the M&As of the 1920s was a series of critiques of big business. A landmark of that literature was *The Modern Corporation and Private Property* (1932),[21] concerned with the 200 largest corporations. By the end of the 1930s, such concerns (along with the New Deal) led to the Temporary National Economic Committee (TNEC), which undertook dozens of studies of separate industries.[22] Those studies, comprising massive amounts of empirical data, came to serve the needs of those postwar governmental and academic economists in the United States who helped to loosen the stifling bonds of neoclassicism. Here is a sampling of what they found.

As a matter of fact ...

- In the years 1948–54 there were 1,773 mergers in mining and manufacturing, most of them mergers of one big company with another, with the process speeding up as it went along: M&As in 1954 were three times those of 1949.[23]

- In 1952 there were about 672,000 business corporations in the United States. Those with assets over $100 million, comprising 0.1 percent of all corporations, held 52.4 percent of all assets, and 7 percent owned 90 percent, while 59.1 percent held only 1.9 percent of all assets.[24]

- In 1955, *Fortune* began its annual listings of the "500 Largest Industrials." In the 1995 issue, celebrating the 40th anniversary of the "500," the editors noted that they had revenues equal to 63 percent of U.S. GDP for 1994, far exceeding the GDPs of Japan and Germany.[25]

Then in the 1960s the most spectacular M&As ever (up to then) took place. As that was occurring, a new phenomenon broke into sight: the multinational corporation (MNC), the predecessor of today's transnational corporation (TNC). The similarities between the MNC and the TNC are many; their differences, as will be seen in Chapter 5, are weightier – most vitally that although the MNCs were among the most powerful companies in their nation from (roughly) 1960 to1975, by the 1990s the TNCs were coming to "rule the world."

Technology was, of course, a key factor in the rise of the giant corporation, as it would be with the MNC and the TNC. But in the capitalist process neither technology nor any one "factor" is ever decisive. The critical factor for the MNCs and TNCs was the accelerating evolution of the most fully integrated world economy in history.

There had long been "international" companies, most especially those exploiting the natural resources outside their own countries. Already in the 1920s there were instances of production of manufactures by one company in more than one country – say, the General Motors takeover of Opel in Germany and Vauxhall in Britain (but selling the product only in the same country). With the MNC such companies became more common while their operations became more manifold. Stephen Hymer was one of the first to notice and analyze the MNC, in the 1960s:

The multinational corporation is in the first instance an American phenomenon. Its precursor is the U.S. *national corporation* created at the end of the 19th century when American capitalism developed a multi-city continent-wide marketing and manufacturing strategy ... National firms think in terms of the national market, multinational firms see the whole world as their oyster and plan manufacturing and marketing on a global scale ... closely connected to the aeronautical and electronic revolutions which made global planning possible.[26]

In keeping with the partial (but important) U.S. pressures for the "European Common Market" (established in 1957), between 1958 and 1965 over 3,000 American companies either set up (tariff-free) subsidiaries in the European Common Market or gained control over already existing firms within it.[27] By 1972, the 4,000–5,000 U.S. MNCs had 23,000 global subsidiaries, with just 157 of them holding 75 percent of the total assets of U.S. investment abroad.[28] Following in the footsteps of the U.S. MNCs were the giant companies of Europe and Japan; by the mid-1970s, every major national economy had numerous holdings in each other's economies as well as, of course, in the previously imperialized small countries – by then politically independent, but economically always more dependent.

As these super-corporations came to dominate their national economies and much of the rest of the world, for reasons associated with the Cold War, Global Economy II, and domestic politics, the State took on greater and different meanings than in the past.

SUPERSTATES

In Chapter 1 we noted that from capitalism's beginnings the State has played a key role, including in those "most capitalist" and *laissez-faire* of all societies, Great Britain and the United States. Since World War II, however, the State's role has changed both quantitatively and qualitatively – in its percentage of GNP as spender and taxer, and in the functions it performs (with, of course, significant variations among nations).

What does not vary, however, is the crucial nature of the State's role and what Marx might have seen as its "contradictions." Writing in the Marxian tradition, in his *The Fiscal Crisis of the State* (1973), the U.S. economist James O'Connor presented a complex analysis centering on the two main functions of the contemporary State, and the manner in which their interaction serves to produce a new form of capitalist crisis, combining economic with political strains. In the thumbnail sketch of his analysis that follows, it will be seen that it aptly prefigures the striking political changes of the United States of the past quarter-century, provoked by the "stagflation" of the 1970s.[29]

O'Connor argues that since World War II, the capitalist state has nourished capitalism through always rising expenditures of two kinds: on "social capital," insuring profitable capital *accumulation*, and on "social expenses," which provide capitalism's *legitimization*.[30] These substantial expenditures (about 30 percent of GNP in the United States, rising to about 50 percent in Germany), are financed through proportionately high and always more unpopular taxation (whose burden, especially in the United States, is borne always more by the bottom 80 percent of incomes).

Thus, and although the State's intended function is to provide economic stimulus and social stability, its activities become both the source and the mitigator of the tensions accompanying social crisis – and over time fail to control the problem of global excess productive capacities.

With respect to the latter, it is worth noting that in the United States until the 1970s there were *no* signs of inflation, despite the enormous expenditures of the State on both "social capital and social expenses". Rather, there were four recessions between 1948 and 1961 – even with the expanding federal budgets for the war in Indochina and the social expenses of the Kennedy and Johnson years. Moreover, when rising prices did take hold in the early 1970s, it was in the context of rising unemployment and falling profits.

The State's functioning undergirded a spectacular increase of profits and of the money incomes ("take-home pay") plus the "social wage" (pensions, health insurance, etc.) of what in the United States is called "the middle class" (in effect, those neither rich nor poor). In the United States this occurred because of the strength of organized labor from the late 1940s into the early 1970s, and was one of the elements making for "corporate – or Cold War – liberalism" (or the "warfare-welfare state"). In Europe the same (but more generous benefits) were introduced because of the strength of social democratic parties, lest a worse fate (that is, socialism) befall.

In the industrial countries there was thus a major increase in the purchasing power of the majority and of consumerism; in turn fostering accumulation *and* substantially increasing the tax base with which to finance the State's expenditures.

But capital's power, though shared as never before, was still dominant. Thus it was that from the early 1960s, especially in the United States, the taxation of corporations and of those in the top income brackets *fell* in relative terms,[31] while that of the "middle class" *rose* – not only absolutely as their incomes rose, but relatively. Meanwhile, as consumeristic individualism and household debt rose along with rising taxes, so did social expenses to placate that fifth of the population classified as living in poverty.[32]

All those changes – along with the racial tensions associated with the civil rights movement and the nationalist tensions provoked by the anti-Vietnam war movement – facilitated a steady shift among "middle-class" voters away from their majority support of the liberalism of the Kennedy/Johnson administrations to what became enthusiastic support for the covertly racist, anti-poor, jingoistic and pro-business policies that were already strong during the Carter administration (1976–80), were much stimulated in the Reagan years, and have since become entrenched.

The return of the ideology of *laissez-faire* capitalism, with the abundant if irrational assistance of "the middle class," came to coexist within the institutional realities of Monopoly Capitalism I (and later, II) – that is, alongside an ever-expanding State, increasing largesse for those on top and higher taxes and lower real incomes for those in the middle and on the bottom, hurting also if not most the largest number of voters supporting them. What also returned in the 1980s were the high poverty rates of the 1960s. The media had become as adept at selling shoddy ideas as shoddy goods.

The political basis for that set of transformations was much informed by the antagonisms anticipated in O'Connor's *Fiscal Crisis*, antagonisms that would be nourished by the economic crisis of the 1970s. We examine the latter below; first we must study the growth of consumerism along with the rising strengths of the media.

ALL TOGETHER NOW: SHOP! AND BORROW!

There have been both beneficial and harmful consequences of consumerism. Perhaps the beneficial outweighed the harmful effects into the 1970s, although that too is contentious. Without doubt, however, consumerism's harmful consequences have overwhelmed its benefits: increasingly widespread and massive amounts and kinds of waste (many of them destructive), accompanied by serious environmental and sociopolitical costs.

In this chapter, only the first years of contemporary consumerism and its close companions debt and advertising will be examined, those from the 1950s into the 1970s. As we begin, however, it is important to make some distinctions.

Consumption and consumerism are aspects of the same set of processes, of course, but only as eating and gluttony are: we must eat regularly in order to survive, but we fall into trouble if we are regularly gluttonous; similarly, eating is instinctive and essential, but habitual gluttony belongs in the realm of individual pathology. Consumerism is a form of social pathology.

Throughout history most people have been unable to meet their basic needs. Today those needs could be met for all. But by any reasonable standard, now – as during the depression when FDR uttered his famous phrase, in the United States "one third of the nation is ill-clothed, ill-fed, and ill-housed" – that is true of at least one-half of the world's people. Consumerism has done little to mitigate those problems in the U.S. or elsewhere. Indeed, its side-effects may be shown to have exacerbated the problems of the poor in the rich countries, and even more those of the rest of the world's poor. None of this could have happened without a continuous and globally spreading "big sell."

The consciousness industry[33]

As we have seen, the advertising industry was already an important player in the economy before World War II. In the years here under scrutiny – most especially because of the maturation of TV – the media and advertising's role within it were both quantitatively and qualitatively transformed.

The people of the United States had long been targets of sustained advertising designed to lead them "to want" – as Paul Baran once put it – "what they don't need and not to want what they do." But advertising, and thus consumerism, took a giant leap ahead with the 1950s.

Advertising's function is not to provide information, and consumerism has little to do with consumption – if by the latter one refers to purchases to meet customary needs or wants for food, clothing, shelter and the various pleasures of existence.[34]

Consumerism could not have come into existence without the "mind management" of advertising, in which the strengths (and defects) of television played a paramount role. It was noted earlier that Veblen saw capitalism as bringing out the worst in us; Baran made something like the same point and captured the essence of advertising's strengths when he noted:

> It is crucial to recognize that advertising and mass media programs sponsored by and related to it do not to any significant extent *create* values or *produce* attitudes but rather reflect *existing* and *exploit* prevailing attitudes. In so doing they undoubtedly re-enforce them and contribute to their propagation, but they cannot be considered to be their taproot. ... [A]dvertising campaigns succeed not if they seek to *change* people's attitudes but if they manage to find, by means of motivation research and similar procedures, a way of linking up with *existing* attitudes ... status-seeking and snobbery; social, racial, and sexual discrimination; egotism and unrelatedness to others; envy, gluttony, avarice, and ruthlessness in the drive for self-advancement – all of these attitudes are not *generated* by advertising but are made use of and appealed to in the contents of advertising material.[35]

That was accomplished in both obvious and subtle ways. Obvious in the proliferation of advertising of all sorts, everywhere, for everything; subtle in the skills used to stimulate normally latent irrationalities toward spending – illuminated by the comedian Mort Sahl in the 1960s when, after "riffing" on ostentatious automobiles, he asked "How else can you get sexual satisfaction?"

And how else pay for all those things, even with a good income, but by going into debt? Although those with the highest (10–15 percent) incomes could buy almost endlessly without going into debt, the rest of the population had to become increasingly adept at borrowing. This meant working more (and making the 2–3 wage-earner family a commonplace). Beginning in the 1920s, debt had begun to be a major part of "the American way of life" for a third of the people. By the end of the 1970s, almost everyone was "doing it": in 1979 alarms were raised when it was recognized that household debt had risen to 66.8 percent of personal income; by 1998 the figure was 98 percent and rose to 102 percent as the century ended.[36]

Consumerism as a social disease

Such wording might seem extreme, but not if one considers the tendencies connected with the social transformation(s) associated with consumerism. Consumerism by itself, no more than advertising, created undesirable social changes; they "merely" facilitated or exacerbated changes already under way. We focus very briefly on two matters only.

The family and politics

Doubtless modern society is more corrosive of the nuclear family than earlier times; and perhaps the nuclear family is not the best of worlds in any case. Be that as it may, in western society, we believe that a healthy family is an essential part of the good life. All that borrowing and spending and its whys and wherefores, among other undesirable side-effects, have meant that for a good two-thirds of the population (in the United States and, as a tendency, elsewhere) it has become essential for both parents (and sometimes the older child[ren]) to bring in an income in order to maintain its "standard of living" or, increasingly, to hold off bankruptcy.

The rhetoric venerating the family is very much at odds with the social tendency for both parents to work and leave the children to fend for themselves.[37] Even supposing that both adults are more contented that way, and even supposing that all their purchases make good sense, who will care for the children? Day care centers, if you can afford it; if not (and usually it is not), well, there's TV. In the next chapter we'll examine some of the implications of that.

As for politics, consumerism cultivates individualism; it is not the precious individualism of the spirit but selfish individualism, however, and that devolves easily into greed. In the modern world *selfish* individualism comes increasingly into conflict with *enlightened* individualism at the very time when there are always more large and small social problems requiring careful attention and thought *and* cooperative effort to be resolved. But, as Michael Ignatieff has warned:

> the allegiances that make the human world human must be beaten into our heads. We never know a thing till we have paid to know it, never know how much is enough until we have had much less than enough, never know what we need till we have been dispossessed ... Our education in the art of necessity cannot avoid tragedy.[38]

A world addicted to consumerism is one in which the realm of politics – always and everywhere corruptible – plunges into an always more precarious condition, marked by growing popular indifference and cynicism. In one way or another, most politicians have always been "up for sale." The combination of big (and well moneyed) business, the potent media, and the mesmerization of consumerism make politicians into just another commodity. There was never a paradise to be lost; but there may well be a hell on its way.

The foregoing does not mean to say that consumerism is *responsible* for our present condition; it does mean to say that to the extent that we are consumeristic the problems facing us become always deeper, always less likely to be resolved, as will be discussed in the next chapter.

We turn now to the economic crisis of the 1970s, both postponed and given its special characteristics by "Monopoly Capitalism I." The developments that took the world *out* of that crisis will be seen as "Monopoly Capitalism II" and "Global Economy III," the focus of Chapter 5.

STAGFLATION: THE MONSTER WITH TWO HEADS

The 1960s witnessed the longest combined national and global expansions ever (until that after 1991). The long quotation from Richard Du Boff on the numerous achievements of the U.S. expansion, cited some pages ago, closed with a sentence omitted there, but added here: "If this was paradise, or even an approximation, it would soon be lost." Why?

One of Veblen's oft-repeated notions was that any given social process (or, for that matter, any individual) may be seen as having "the defects of its virtues." Marx expressed something of the same idea when he referred to the "contradictions" of capitalism. The stagflation of the 1970s is a clear instance of those notions, as the following brief summary seeks to show.

In Keynesian terms, the great expansion may be seen as having been powered by an avalanche of business, consumer, and governmental spending (milex and otherwise), all powered by a mountain of debt from those same sectors. So whence the stagnation? And even more curiously, for it had never happened before, whence the inflation that endured for years alongside ubiquitous unused productive capacities and high unemployment? Whence "stagflation"?[39]

It is not difficult to explain the economic contraction of the 1970s: it is normal in the capitalist process. Every capitalist expansion *necessarily* comes to an end as a consequence of emerging and spreading excess productive capacities (that is, the inability to sell profitably at optimum use of productive facilities).

But nobody, not even Keynes, Marx or Veblen, anticipated that such a slowdown (with its high unemployment and stagnant or falling profits) would be accompanied by enduring inflation. Before it came into existence, no one did or could anticipate the intertwined characteristics of monopoly capitalism. The core of an explanation resides in the combination of the ability of super-corporations and organized labor to raise prices and wages (and benefits) in an expanding world economy supported by intrinsically inflationary military expenditures. This expansion was expected never to end – even though there was a general awareness that excess national and global productive capacities were widespread and growing. Once more, as had been thought in the late 1920s, the "business cycle had been licked" (as again today).

However: In the years 1960–64, the average annual increase in consumer prices was 1.2 percent, and in 1965–69 was 3.4 percent. In the first five years of the 1970s, the average was 6.1 percent and in the second five years it was 8.1 percent.[40] Official unemployment rates stood at 4.6 percent on average for the last five years of the 1960s, and at 6.9 percent for the late 1970s. Average real wages for the bottom 80 percent fell steadily after 1973 (not to level off and to begin a very slow rise until the *late* 1990s); and per capita disposable income, which had risen at an annual average of 2.3 percent from the 1950s and through the 1960s, slowed to 1.4 percent in 1973–87.[41] In the same years, what had long been a trade surplus became (in 1971) a merchandise trade deficit. Due in part to that and in part to high overseas investments and persistently large and growing milex abroad, a dollar drain was translated into a gold drain. President Nixon therefore closed "the gold window," effectively taking the United States off the gold standard. Also in 1971, and again in 1973, Nixon devalued the dollar (in order to increase exports and decrease imports) and invoked wage and price controls to contain a serious inflation that had begun already in 1971.

Some of the price inflation of the 1970s is seen as due to widespread crop failures and market shortages, with most weight attributed to the "oil shocks" caused by the Organization of Petroleum Exporting Countries (OPEC) in 1973 and again in 1979. The oil price increases were relevant; but it must be understood that to the degree that OPEC's decisions were based on *economic* considerations (rather than Middle East political conflicts), OPEC was reacting to the prior price inflation for their *imports*.

In short, the good times had ceased to roll, and troubles of diverse kinds lay ahead. Among them were those for organized labor's high wages and social benefits – to be nibbled away or crushed by what Du

Boff (in his Chapter 7) calls "the corporate counter-attack" that began in the mid-1970s and has yet to end.

Toward the new world order

There was another major development, very different in kind, working to the advantage of the biggest companies and the financial sector, and to the detriment of most wage-earners. As corporate profits and real investment began a long decrease in national economies, businesses (led by U.S. banks) increased their efforts in the international arena. As the 1970s ended and the 1980s began, a new global economy was being shaped, one that would be dominated by the transition from MNCs to TNCs, and by the growing dominance of finance over production, within and between economies.

Facilitating that major set of changes – given the always improving technologies of communications and transportation – was one consequence of the stagnation that had become evident in the late 1960s: falling profits and excess productive capacities within national economies meant that the financial community found itself with excess capital on hand.

This prompted a concerted movement to press governments that were providing subsidized loans with low interest rates or free grants-in-aid to the "developing countries" to cease doing so. This opened the doors for bankers – literally flying all over the world with deals in hand – to "extend" private loans (frequently with the assistance of corrupt governments and Cold War links). The private loans were not subsidized, let alone free; indeed, what came to be universal already by the early 1970s were substantial loans with "variable" interest rates, mostly payable in dollars – variable upward, as inflation took hold. In that almost all the poorer economies involved were also importers of petroleum (the prices of which escalated in that decade); this assured that from then on the indebted countries would move into and remain in deepening and spreading economic and associated political crises. As we will see in the next chapter, the stagflation crisis of the 1970s was surmounted but, as in the past, by changes whose evolution would produce its own "defects and virtues" – among them the greatest ever "triumph of the market." The "market" that triumphed was not that which was esteemed by Adam Smith, but one dominated by a giant corporations and speculators. Rather than the "euthanasia of the *rentier* class," the end of the twentieth century saw them become top dogs. In the same process, the vocabulary of economic life came to be filled with the ugly terms and realities of "downsizing, outsourcing, and derivatives." In the next chapter it will be seen that mainstream economists,

confronted with these developments, bowed even lower than before –
except that there were also importantly positive contributions from
economists who had seen themselves as part of the economics
"establishment," and, as well as from "radicals." We look first at those
useful developments.

ECONOMICS ON A SEESAW

There had been a few promising contributions early in the century.
Interestingly enough, the most useful were produced by two of
Veblen's students, J.M. Clark (son of the *very* mainstream John Bates
Clark) and Wesley Clair Mitchell. Clark wrote the still useful *Studies
in the Economics of Overhead Costs* (1923), of which more in a
moment; Mitchell's main contributions were in his *Business Cycles*
(1913) and in his major role in creating the National Bureau of
Economic Research. He is seen as one of the key figures of "institutional economics," inspired by Veblen's works.

Clark's *Studies* sought to accomplish two major tasks: to adapt the
(micro) theory of markets to the existence and functioning of modern
technology and big business, and to move toward a reality-based
integration of micro and macro theory. What he accomplished in that
pioneering book was real. Just as real was the manner in which the
economics profession ignored all elements of his work – made all the
more interesting by the fact that his father was one of the titans of
neoclassical economics.[42]

We have seen that as the 1930s opened, the large corporations were
being taken into account – in the United States by Berle and Means,
and then by the TNEC. In those years, Keynesian theory and policies
were accepted only by a minority of economists or policy-makers of
the main industrial nations; after the war, that minority had become a
majority, even in the United States (if narrowly so). The relatively
weak momentum of the late 1930s had, by the late 1940s, become
increasingly strong. It may be said that by the 1950s (at least in the
strongest universities) economists consciously seeking to displace the
dominance of neoclassical theory and policy were in the ascendant
and, for a while, solidly influential. Out of that came the "school"
called "post-Keynesian."

Post-Keynesian economics

First, the name itself: Keynes himself was concerned with aggregative,
"macro" theory, as he sought to understand and overcome the
depression. The post-Keynesians are concerned with *all* elements of
theory: macro, to be sure, but also "micro, distribution, and trade
theory." In short, the post-Keynesians have sought to develop an

integrated theory that can answer the question earlier put here as to
what should constitute economics: "What do we need to know about
the economy, and what must we do to have it serve the needs of
people, society, and nature?"

One of its most active participants has identified the post-
Keynesians well:

> Its members represent the coming together of several dissident
> traditions within economics – that of the American institutional-
> ists and the continental Marxists, as well as that of Keynes' closest
> associates. Their work, taken together, potentially offers a compre-
> hensive and coherent alternative to the prevailing orthodoxy in
> economic theory, an orthodoxy which, because of its lack of
> relevance, stands as the principal obstacle to intelligent economic
> policy.[43]

One of the major concerns of the post-Keynesians centered on
the ability of business giants (and strong unions) to control their
markets in some significant degree, rather than being controlled *by*
them. The work done in the 1930s (including that of the TNEC)
was instrumental in helping to construct a sound empirical base for
analysis; that analysis by the late 1940s was already in the process
of formation, and it centered on oligopoly.[44] That term signifies the
existence of a few firms in a given industry whose small number
enables them to make explicit (or implicit) agreements that prevent
price competition and allows them to "administer" their markets.
Such practices are totally incompatible with the theorems of
neoclassical economics, which assumes away even existence of such
structures, let alone their dominance.

The liveliness and usefulness of post-Keynesianism was effectively
shunted aside in the universities as the "corporate counter-attack"
among other things brought neoclassicism back into favor. The new
group continued and continues to function, even though without the
recognition that would give them access to significant numbers of
students and teachers, or those in the political world. That could
change for the better, if and when a new crisis emerges. Here it is
worth providing a summary of what may be seen as their working
hypotheses, as seen in the excellent study of Stephen Rousseas:

> the basic tenets of American post-Keynesian economics ... are:
> 1) the pervasiveness of uncertainty as distinct from calculable risk;
> 2) the historical time within which production and all other
> economic events take place in an irreversible fashion; 3) the

existence of a credit money economy of forward contracts in which the money supply has virtually a zero cost of production; 4) the setting of individual product prices as a mark-up over unit prime costs in the dominant oligopolistic sector operating with *planned* excess capacity; 5) the irrelevance of demand-supply analysis to labor markets, and the key dependence of the general price level on nominal wage rates determined exogenously under collective bargaining; 6) the endogenous nature of the money supply; and 7) the inherent instability of capitalism.[45]

Radical political economy

The single most stimulating work in the realm of radical analysis in this period was Baran and Sweezy's *Monopoly Capital* (1966), on which so much of the analysis of this chapter (and much of my other work) has depended. A few additional observations regarding their contribution are worth adding here.

In the years following World War II, the authors were the most influential of English-speaking Marxist economists. In order to accomplish a long-standing need to update (one may say renovate) Marxian analysis, they changed its temporal focus to the 1950s and its location from Britain to the United States. Accordingly, they also broadened the very definition of "Marxian" political economy – all of this exemplified in their title: *Monopoly Capital: An Essay on the American Economic and Social Order.*

In their analysis of the social order they stimulated a substantial number of others to push ahead more deeply into the various elements of the "social formation" constituting the capitalist process. Among the earliest and most influential of such studies were those of James O'Connor (quoted earlier in this chapter), Harry Magdoff's *The Age of Imperialism* (1969), Harry Braverman's *Labor and Monopoly Capital: The Degradation of Work in the Twentieth Century* (1974), Herbert Schiller's numerous studies of the media, including *Mass Communications and American Empire* (1971) and *The Mind Managers* (1974), and, among other works, an excellent book of broad-based readings put together by Richard C. Edwards, Michael Reich and Thomas E. Weisskopf, *The Capitalist System* (1986).[46]

In Britain, beginning earlier and continuing to the present, a "New Left" emerged.[47] As it took hold, it owed much to the works of economic historian R.H. Tawney (1880–1962), beginning with his *The Acquisitive Society* (1920) and *Religion and the Rise of Capitalism* (1926) and extending through all his writings and including his long association as a teacher with the Workers Education Association until his death in 1962.

Tawney was anti-capitalist but not a Marxist, but the New Left movement in Britain, and its journal *New Left Review* were and remain a lively source of Marxian "renovation," with important contributions from (among many others), Perry Anderson, Ralph Miliband, and Eric Hobsbawm.

The most lasting and significant development in Marxian thought in Europe – in my judgment – was the major contribution of Antonio Gramsci. His work – notably his *Prison Letters* and *The Modern Prince* – became well known only in the 1960s, when they were translated and published in Europe, Britain, and North America.[48]

Gramsci's most relevant ideas for our time will be discussed subsequently. Suffice it here to say that, perhaps uniquely among Marxists in his lifetime, Gramsci insisted on the need to go well beyond the political economy of Marx and the politics of Lenin if there is ever to be a political movement that can gain and hold power for a democratic socialist society.

Up with the old

The economic crisis of the 1970s could conceivably have led to a strengthening of left-of-center politics; instead, quite the opposite occurred. Initially led by Margaret Thatcher in Britain, there was an upsurge in conservative political strength, soon to be even more effectively voiced by Ronald Reagan in the United States. Their conservative to rightist policies were given their rationale by the doctrines of Milton Friedman and his academic and political disciples.

Already in the early 1980s, what had been substantial diversity in economics departments and in government had given way to an effectively conservative domination of both areas – much assisted by supportive changes in the tone and content of media fare. Nor did it hurt their cause that (especially, but not only in the United States) all kinds of dissent had been stultified in the academy and in politics by three decades of Cold War and variations on its surviving McCarthyism.[49]

Combining the powers of priest and mandarin, the devout supporters of *laissez-faire* vehemently opposed any influence whatsoever by government in the economy at home or abroad – except, of course, for milex and whatever was seen to assist business at home and abroad.

Friedman was already well known in the 1950s and famous in the 1960s – but mocked as much as praised at that time. His *Capitalism and Freedom* (1962), essentially his updating of Adam Smith *cum* Alfred Marshall and the right-wing Austrian Ludwig von Mises, was much spoofed when first published. As the 1980s began, it had already taken on biblical proportions. Herewith, an apt summary in 1979, by E.K. Hunt:

> Milton Friedman advocates the *elimination* of 1) taxes on corporations, 2) the graduated income tax, 3) free public education, 4) social security, 5) government regulations of the purity of food and drugs, 6) the licensing of doctors and dentists, 7) the post office monopoly, 8) government relief from natural disasters, 9) minimum wage laws, 10) ceilings on interest rates charged by usurious lenders, 11) laws prohibiting heroin sales, and nearly every other form of government intervention that goes beyond the enforcement of property rights and contract laws and the provision of national defense.[50] (emphasis added)

In the United States (if to a considerably lesser degree elsewhere – up to now) almost all that program has been adopted wholly or partially, except for one item – the one that might make sense – the legalization of heroin.

As that return to the politics of the 1920s was taking place, economics was moving in step. As the 1980s began, economists could say, "We're all good neoclassicists [again]." Those who were not, and there were many, were relegated to the sidelines (again).[51]

5 New World Order: Globalization and Financialization; and Decadent Economics, 1975–2000

INTRODUCTION AND RETROSPECT

The troubles of the early 1970s had their origins in more than the processes of the two decades just examined; they emerged also from the enduring nature of capitalism, and its imperatives of expansion, exploitation, and class rule. Those imperatives have been met intermittently in periods of growth and crisis only as the powers of capital have managed over time to move toward the achievement of an entire society created in their own image.

This study began with the period in which the first giant steps toward that were taken, when land and labor first became commodities. Now we are perilously near the point where, if capital has its way, there will be nothing and nobody without a price: *Everything for Sale*, as a recent book has put it.[1]

Withal, whether in the deep or recent past or in the future, capitalism produces periods of economic crisis the roots of which are intrinsic to the capitalist process: 1) it is a system that functions anarchically in principle, and 2) that functioning, energized as it is by a voraciousness for profits and power, inevitably produces periods of pervasive excess productive capacities. It is a system that moves through time like a vast ship heedlessly plowing through the seas and leaving a destructive wake – except that, unlike a real ship, capitalism also produces its own storms and tidal waves, as in the 1930s.

The depression of the 1930s must be seen as having begun with the socioeconomic crisis that produced World War I. That crisis was "resolved" only by World War II. As we have seen, as the only nation left with any strength at all after the war, the United States was able to take the main steps that created a new and functional capitalism – indeed, the most successful ever.

But the manifold economic, social, political and military changes allowing capitalism to come back to life and strength after the war had themselves become dysfunctional by the 1970s; the new system had the defects of its virtues. Thus 1) in the context of seemingly assured economic expansion, giant companies and organized labor acted to raise prices irrespective of market contexts; 2) the super-states became rife with inefficiency and stained by their corrupting links with business in every major economy; 3) the seemingly endless expansion that had produced rising profits and incomes carried with it duplicative and excess productive capacities over the globe and thus slowed economic growth; 4) the essential expansion of debt to unprecedentedly high levels in all quarters brought economic fragility in its wake; 5) although economic growth slowed in the late 1960s and stagnated in the 1970s, both prices and taxes continued to rise; 6) the latter, combined with rising unemployment, led to rising social tensions and facilitated a politics for decreased social expenditures in a context where urban decay and poverty were also intensifying; 7) nor did it help that all this occurred as consumerism had created whole populations whose desires for always MORE! were much frustrated by ongoing stagflation.

Du Boff captured the nasty devolution of Monopoly Capitalism I in this way:

> The impasse of American capitalism in the 1970s was defined by the tightening [of the] constraints [of] accelerating inflation led by energy and food prices, expectations of annual wage and benefit increases in the face of pressure on corporate profitability, more frequent intervention by government in ways that threatened freedom of action by business, an emerging import penetration of consumer goods markets, and the seemingly sudden loss of international hegemony symbolized by military defeat in Vietnam in 1975 in the longest, costliest, and least successful of a series of postwar interventions against the socialist and communist left all over the world.[2]

Therefore, as the 1970s moved toward their end, if crisis were to be superseded satisfactorily, it was again essential to change the rules of capitalism. There was not, of course, a committee to do so; what existed, instead, was a diverse set of needs and possibilities which, when confronted and acted upon effectively, led to still another (also temporary) stage of capitalism.

MONOPOLY CAPITALISM II

Whether as seen by its critics or its supporters, Monopoly Capitalism I seemingly embodied substantial deflections from capitalism's "true nature": expand at home and abroad and exploit (if less so in the major economies) it continued to do, but oligarchic rule was much tempered.

"Much" does not mean "entirely"; nonetheless, certain key decisions were not those of capital alone, whether those of businesses or of governments.

This was most evidently so in the 1960s in the top layer of industrial capitalist countries. The lives of a large majority of their people rose to previously undreamed of levels of real income, with parallel improvements in working conditions: capitalism had taken a turn toward social democracy in limited or substantial degree. That all this depended on military expenditures and savage warfare in the weaker countries has been noted; still, it was a capitalism that Marx would not have recognized.

What is therefore so striking about the past two decades is that the capitalism that Marx *would* have recognized has moved toward its "second coming" – not, of course, jot and tittle, but as a set of major *tendencies*, modified by contemporary technologies and business forms.

Put differently, the capitalism that marches in triumph today – *pace* Adam Smith – displays tendencies that are more capitalist than ever, a form of capitalism demanding and getting always more expansion at home and abroad, a return to heightened exploitation in the leading countries and the reproduction of the labor conditions of the first industrial revolution elsewhere, and tighter rule by capital – over the State but also over the people. More than in Marx's time, "the ruling ideas of [the] era are the ideas of its ruling class."

As those large generalizations are now elaborated, it will be pertinent to examine the manner in which the several main elements of Monopoly Capitalism I have changed to become Monopoly Capitalism II. Though the two forms are similar, there are important differences: 1) the giant corporations of today make even those of the 1950s seem relatively small, most clearly today's TNCs; 2) the State is still "super," but it functions always more at the beck and call of giant TNCs and finance and always less for social well-being; 3) the global economy is considerably more integrated *and* considerably more disruptive *and* dominated by finance than earlier *and* less dependent on the Cold War; 4) consumerism has spread and deepened all over the globe *and* (like much else) become dependent upon clearly precarious debt accumulation; and 5) the world of the media, earlier noted as the "lubricant of monopoly capitalism," has taken on forms and power that make even its great strengths in the 1960s seem paltry. When, at the conclusion of this chapter, the current state of economics is discussed, it will be seen that it has reached new heights (or depths) of subservience to the status quo.

As in the preceding chapter, the focus will be more on the United States than elsewhere. For, with some exceptions, it has taken the lead in all major economic and social changes. But it will be noted that the order in which the foregoing dimensions are examined has changed and have become intermingled, and that the relative emphasis given to each of them has altered. That is because Monopoly Capitalism II is a very different and more "integrated" creature than its predecessor: for capitalism to exit successfully from the crisis of the 1970s, it had to become so.

GIANTS ROAMING THE EARTH

Capitalism today is dominated by two interacting processes: a striking increase in the concentration of economic power, centering especially on the transnational giants, and an equally striking intensification of globalization well beyond that already accomplished by the 1970s. For those processes to take on their dynamism and velocity, it was of course essential that governments throughout the world allow or encourage them. As we now proceed to explicate some of the important elements of that extraordinary set of changes, it will be helpful to provide a summary statement:

> Globalization is both a *tendency* and an *ideology*. As an objective tendency, globalization implies a deepening and strengthening of trade, financial markets and production systems across national boundaries. Propelling this tendency we find broad institutional changes occurring, strengthening the integration of the circuits of trade, finance and production. Globalization implies a greater degree of convergence in markets and institutions, and a greater degree of homogenization of dysfunctional movements such as economic crises which quickly shift across national borders.
>
> As an ideology, globalization implies both the *inevitability* and *desirability* of the above described tendencies toward integration and the *denial* of the existence of dysfunctional movements arising from this tendency.[3]

The central role in these developments was played by the largest companies of the world, and thus our discussion will commence with the processes of growing giantism. That will necessarily take us to a discussion of the tandem growth of financialization of national and global economies. The ideological dimension noted above will be taken up in our concluding examination of contemporary economics.

As we have seen, as the twentieth century began the economic stage had become dominated by larger-than-life companies – most dramatically in metallurgy and petroleum, followed by wave after wave of M&As in all the industrial economies. The outburst of M&As of the 1960s in the United States *seemed* to have exhausted all possibilities:

> Commencing in the early 1950s, merger activity registered progressive increases and reached a frenzied pace in 1967–1970, when more than one of every five manufacturing and mining corporations with assets exceeding $10 million was acquired.[4]

But the best – or worst – was yet to come. The pressures for M&As are both positive and negative – a means to increase profits or stave off "destructive competition." As often as not, they are the result of both pressures; and both were intensified by globalization. However, there have always been other reasons for consolidations.

Those "other reasons" moved increasingly to the front after the 1970s, not infrequently taking on a life of their own: the high monetary (and ego) rewards accruing to the main actors involved – CEOs, "corporate raiders," underwriters, and lawyers.[5]

In the very first billion-dollar deal – which created U.S. Steel in 1901 – all these motives were embodied in the persons of J.P. Morgan and Andrew Carnegie. But they were unique in their time; those who follow in their footsteps in our era have become commonplace – with some variations to be noted now.

The stagflation of the 1970s combined with the business-friendly policies of the Reagan years of the 1980s to stimulate two decades of record-breaking waves of M&As, spurred on by the first stages of something new: "hostile takeovers," "leveraged buyouts," and the increased financialization of the economy.[6] In addition, the late 1970s saw the beginnings of the now common merging across national lines, led by the oil companies:

> the post-1978 mergers were a mixture of conglomerate (USX–Marathon [steel and oil], for example), vertical (Du Pont–Conoco [chemicals–oil]) and horizontal [Chevron and Texas]. For the first time in a U.S. merger movement, foreigners were important participants (British Petroleum–Standard Oil, Unilever–Cheseborough), another manifestation of the global changes in market structures in the 1980s. British firms, long the leaders in foreign investment in the United States, acquired at least 140 American enterprises worth $19 billion in 1987 alone.[7]

Leveraged buyouts began in 1983; in the ensuing five years there were over 700 just such mergers, worth over $200 billion. Major financial institutions were and are always involved as promoters and creditors in such deals. Along the way there were (and are) also numerous mergers in the financial community among and between insurance companies, investment banks, and the like.

The groundwork had been laid for the 1990s, during which the kinds and provenances and values of M&As broke new ground. Here are some data comparing 1990 with 1998, and some instances from 1999.[8]

The waltz of the toreadors

- The largest 500 U.S. industrial corporations in 1990 amounted to less than one-quarter of one percent of all industrial corporations (and, of course, an even tinier fraction of all industrial enterprises). The Top 500 made about three-quarters of all industrial *sales*, with about the same percentage of all industrial *profits*. Their sales were $2.3 trillion, and their net income (after taxes) $93.3 billion.

- The Top 100 of the 500 had 71 percent of its assets and the same percentage of its profits.

- The Top 50 had 57 percent of the Top 500's sales, 63 percent of its assets, and 52 percent of its profits; of the Top 100, the 50 had 81, 83, and 73 percent of sales, assets, and profits, respectively.

- And then there were the super-giants, the Top 10: General Motors, EXXON, Ford, IBM, Mobil, GE, Philip Morris, Du Pont and Chevron. They alone had 30 percent of the Top 500s sales, 36 percent of its assets, and 28 percent of its profits. GM, the largest company in the world then as now, had a bad year in 1990, with sales of $126 billion (and losses of $2 billion).

By 1998, signifying the great changes that had begun in the Reagan years and that had become rampant by the mid-1990s, the "Fortune 500" U.S. industrials had become the "*Global* 500 – The World's Largest Corporations." Here are some of those data (organized somewhat differently from the foregoing).

TNCs of the world, unite![9]

As noted earlier, mergers and the great size accompanying them occur for defensive as well as offensive purposes – exemplified by the performance of the 500 global giants in 1998, as presented in *Fortune*:

> For many of the world's largest companies, 1998 was a year to forget. As one market after another succumbed to the spreading

economic malaise – first in Asia and later in Russia and Latin America – the corporations of the Global 500 struggled to eke out an almost imperceptible 0.1% growth in revenues. Profits fared even worse, sinking 2.6%, the first such decline since 1992. And excluding a one-time gain at Ford (No. 3), they fell a startling 6.1%.

In 1998 there were 12,500 M&As, with a value of $1.6 trillion, a new record. The two sectors most affected were in financial services and telecommunications, both of them recently deregulated under the auspices of the World Trade Organization (WTO), the successor organization of GATT. As a result, *Fortune* remarks, "the face of the Global 500 was dramatically altered."

That was the year of DaimlerChrysler ($40 billion), Of Travelers (once just insurance) buying out Citibank ($75 billion) and becoming Citigroup (having earlier gotten directly into Wall Street with its purchase of Salomon Smith Barney). The oil industry joined in with the international merger of Amoco and BP and the first steps toward the merger of EXXON and Mobil (which once were both part of Standard Oil, until its dissolution in 1911).

Fortune adds that these mergers were just a prelude, for "in a world of limited pricing power one of the few ways giant companies can grow is by buying their rivals." In a moment, we shall note a few of the even more striking mergers of 1999; first, some summary data for 1998:

- The Global 500s' revenues: $11.5 trillion; profits: $440 billion; assets: $39 trillion; employees: 40 million.

- The Top 10 had average revenues of $122 billion (No. 1, GM's were $161 billion). The Top 10 were GM, DaimlerChrysler, Ford, Wal-Mart Stores, Mitsui, Itochu, Mitsubishi, EXXON, GE, and Toyota, in that order. (When the EXXON/Mobil merger is consummated, they will become No. 2.)

- It is interesting to note that Philip Morris (No. 27), with revenues of "only" $58 billion (about one-third of GM's) had profits of $5.4 billion (almost twice GM's). And that Royal Phillips Electronics (No. 57), with revenues of $38 billion had profits of $6.6 billion (second only to Ford).

- The Bottom 50 of the 500 had average revenues of $9.5 billion – something more than peanuts; but taken together their revenues were under 10 percent of the Top 10.

- Of the Global 500, 191 were U.S. companies; about one-third of TNCs were also registered in the United States.

The year 1999 was not yet over when this was written, but some selective mergers will provide a sense of what has been afoot. We note recent or planned mergers only in the realms of media/telecommunications and petroleum.[10]

Media/telecommunications
In 1998, Bell Atlantic had merged with GTE ($71 billion); in January, 1999 Vodafone merged with AirTouch ($66 billion); in September, Bell/GTE and Vodafone/AirTouch (USA–UK) agreed to share markets; November, Vodafone begins hostile takeover of Mannesmann (Germany) ($151 billion: new record):

- In 1998, AT&T had merged with Telecommunications Inc. ($70 billion; in April, 1999, it merged with MediaOne ($63 billion).

- In June, 1999, Owest Communications merged with US West ($49 billion).

- In September, Viacom and CBS merged ($37 billion). The two companies now represent radio, TV, film, books, theme parks, video, cable, etc.

Petroleum

- EXXON and Mobil are expected to close their deal in 1999 ($86 billion).

- BP and ARCO (UK–USA) announced merger in April, 1999 ($34 billion).

- Total Fina and Elf Aquitane (both French) announced in September ($49 billion).

"The new economy" – Who benefits, and who pays?
Economists have joined Wall Street and politicians in proclaiming a new era of always rising productivity, low or no inflation, more jobs and falling unemployment, and prospects for a future without serious (or any?) recession. Accompanying such views are regular announcements of new mergers within and/or between countries, usually followed by details of imminent layoffs. Symmetrically, the mergers are justified by expected efficiencies, increased ability to meet foreign competition, and the expectation that "in the long run all will benefit."

Setting aside that such views are ominously reminiscent of almost identical positions uttered in the United States in the 1920s, against a very similar background, we shall concern ourselves with today's merger mania. But first, a quick look at some of its background and ongoing results.

Wall Street
There can be few who are unaware that a giant bubble has been expanding the most important financial markets of the world; the most important among them being that of the United States. There, although the major stock indices (Dow Jones et al.) for the 1990s have broken all records, there are two unsettling facts. First, price/earnings ratios have also broken all records in terms of the yawning gap between the value of stocks and the performance of their respective corporations. Thus the average P/E ratio for 125 years (1871–1996) for all stocks was 14:1, but now approaches 30:1. For the NASDAQ ("technology") exchange – the boomer within the boom – the ratio at the end of 1999 was about 200:1, ten times its 1980 average.[11] Second, more than half of all the stocks have had falling prices in recent years, as distinct from the "leaders", who have taken the indices up – an arithmetic phenomenon of the same sort that allows "average family income" to rise, while most families suffer from falling real incomes.

Wages and hours
The sustained growth of the "new economy" in the 1990s has many explanations. Fundamental among them is what may be called its "new exploitation." Wages were falling or stagnant from 1973 until about 1998, since when (in the United States) they have edged up slowly. Business cannot but be pleased with the much weakened unions of the recent past. The latter helps to explain the otherwise startling fact that the average U.S. worker works 260 hours more per year than in 1989, an additional six weeks of work without anything like a proportionate wage increase. The eight-hour day, 40-hour week is becoming a memory.

Those facts are partially explained by another. For five years after 1994, 39 percent of all new jobs in the United States were taken by foreign-born workers – on tourist or student visas, or with *no* visa. Used to a higher rate of exploitation (or powerless to resist it), they have greased the down escalator for wages and benefits. To which must be added that large numbers of women coming off welfare and many other women shifting from part-time to full-time jobs are a large part of those in the job growth data. And women are more vulnerable to exploitation than men.[12]

In fact, the expected efficiencies (and even the enhanced profits) generally have *not* occurred. For the average CEO, however, we shall see that there *has* been a spectacular increase in income and wealth. Meanwhile, the average worker's income (in the United States) began a 25-year decline in the 1970s, poverty rates rose, and the overall material conditions of workers in weaker countries moved toward or into tragedy. The "long run" appears to be that noted by Keynes as when "we will all be dead."

Globalization has been a prime mover in all these processes. It will be examined directly in a later section. Now we examine the consequences of the new giantism for workers; more exactly, what stands behind the recent additions to their vocabularies: "downsizing," and "outsourcing," and, of course, TNCs.

Lean and mean
The processes of outsourcing and downsizing began to be evident in the 1970s; as their impact on labor also became evident, criticism began to mount. Alongside that, however, also mounting was the institutional advertising and the "engineering of consent" of the corporations involved, much assisted by governmental pronounce-ments, lauding the benefits to all of "the free market." Within a decade or so, such arguments held sway.

That the critiques by unions had substance to them is revealed by some income data for the United States in the decade 1977–87. Note first what happened to the median family's income: its *money* wages rose from about $16,000 in 1977 to about $28,000 ten years later, an increase of 75 percent. But that same family's income tax payments rose by 84 percent as its social security payroll deduction rose by 116 percent. Put those numbers together with the price inflation of the same years, and the after-tax income of that median family (in 1987 dollars) had *fallen* by over $2,000 – as the median family had also come to be defined as having not one but two wage earners.[13] The tendencies toward falling real wages continued up to at least 1997, when continuing expansion combined with low unemployment rates brought modestly rising wages.

But for workers in the United States and elsewhere from the 1970s to the present not only had real wages (and social benefits) fallen, there had also been a process in which good jobs were lost, probably permanently.[14]

The ways in which the TNCs outsource and downsize, and in so doing diminish the lives of workers in the most advanced countries, have been aptly called "the global labor arbitrage" by William Greider.[15] Their losses have had both quantitative and qualitative dimensions. Quantitatively, the damage done (in one respect), is well summarized by Bluestone and Harrison:

[It] is evident that somewhere between 32 and 38 *million* jobs were lost during the 1970s as the direct result of private disinvestment in American business. The chances of even a large, established manufacturing plant closing down within a given seven-year period during the last decade [1972–82] exceeded 30 percent ... As a result of plant closings in New England industries such as shoes and apparel, anywhere from two to four jobs were eliminated for every single new job created by new capital invested elsewhere in the region ... In the New England aircraft industry, 3.6 jobs were destroyed for every new one created; in the metalworking machine industry the ratio was 1.6 to 1.0.

Moreover, contrary to popular belief, the deindustrialization process has not been limited to the "Frostbelt." Almost *half* the jobs lost to plant closings (and relocations) during the 1970s occurred in the Sunbelt states of the South and the West .... Bankruptcies were responsible for some of the job losses, but a great many of the shutdowns occurred in establishments owned and operated by profitable companies.[16]

Those are aspects of the quantitative dimension. What then happens to the workers affected? Do they get other jobs? Yes, usually – except those not forced into early retirement at a pension less than half their salary. Those that continue to work, but at another job, usually in another type of work, almost always find themselves working for a lower wage at a job classified as "unskilled."

In the latter cases – evidently the most numerous – the quantitative and the qualitative become one. It takes little imagination to comprehend what it must mean to skilled workers to find themselves – say, at ages 45–55 – in a non-union job with no benefits, less or no dignity, and no future; with a family needing two full-time wage-earners in order to keep from falling further.

Those processes are at one with the others noted earlier and yet to come, as has been underlined by Bluestone and Harrison:

[C]apital – in the forms of financial resources and of real plant and equipment – has been diverted from productive investment in our basic national industries into unproductive speculation, mergers and acquisitions, and foreign investment. Left behind are shuttered factories, displaced workers, and a newly emerging group of ghost towns. (1982, 6)

All this has been effectively presented to the general public as being unavoidable, a consequence of foreign competition and, in the long run, beneficial to all. In that same process, whatever ills average workers may see besetting them have been effectively "spun" as being caused by big government, high taxes, the undeserving poor, and immigrants.

Bluestone and Harrison do much in their analysis to show that the causes lie elsewhere. Among them, and for the United States, the most important set are those having to do with the lopsided structure of jobs in U.S. companies – where "lopsided" refers to the extraordinary percentage of the U.S. workforce that spends its time not in producing but in supervising those who do. That takes us to a related discussion.

Fat and mean
This is the title of a book by David M. Gordon. Its subject is a matter rarely studied, but Gordon did so exhaustively and definitively.[17] In order to make his case about "lopsidededness," Gordon took the time to deflate other explanations for the stagnation and decline of real wages, those that "blame the victim": the so-called "skills-mismatch" problem, and the related consequences of globalization. His focus is on the United States; but as globalization (and "Americanization") intensify, what has been true in the United States becomes so elsewhere. Before turning to what Gordon sees as the main problem – bloated management – the skills and global problems will be examined briefly.

Simply put, the problem surrounding skills is seen as deriving from the swiftness of technological advance. Modern industry demands and rewards skills that are out of the reach of (especially) middle-aged or older workers. But careful studies of labor markets in all sectors and at all levels of skill do not support that thesis. Thus (and for example), Gordon shows that within *manufacturing*, "in moderately skilled occupations ... where employment increased most rapidly during the 1980s, wages were scratching rock bottom ..." He shows that the wages of computer operators (1983–93) rose by about *0.3 percent* on average each year and that those for engineering technicians *fell* about 0.1 percent annually (as those for doctors and lawyers rose by about 3 percent (ibid., 186–7).

As for globalization, the export of jobs by the United States (among other rich countries) and rising import surpluses of commodities have placed downward (or contained upward) pressures on wages. Those pressures, however, should be greatest on those areas of the economy in which foreign trade is significant. Manufacturing – the most exposed of all sectors to imports – might reasonably be expected to have suffered most in wage trends. But it did not. In the years

1979–94 these are the figures Gordon provides for the real earnings of production and non-supervisory workers (as measured in 1994 dollars): mining, –12.4 percent; construction, –20.7 percent; manufacturing, –10.1 percent; transportation and public utilities, –15.2 percent; wholesale trade, –5.8 percent; retail trade, –17.4 percent; finance, insurance and real estate, +12.1 percent; services, +2.9 percent (ibid., 191).

What stands out in that listing is the sharp difference between the financial sector and the producing sectors. They will be examined after the discussion of Gordon's "fat and mean."(The "fat" is high bureaucratic costs; the "mean" is the "wage squeeze," or what Gordon calls "the stick strategy.")

> The connection between the wage squeeze and the bureaucratic burden runs in both directions. In one direction, stagnant or falling wages create the need for intensive managerial supervision of frontline employees. If workers do not share in the fruits of the enterprise, if they are not provided a promise of job security and steady wage growth, what incentive do they have to work as hard as their bosses would like? So the corporations need to monitor the workers' effort and be able to threaten credibly to punish them if they do not perform. The corporations must wield the Stick. Eventually the Stick requires millions of Stick-wielders.
>
> In the other direction, once top-heavy corporate bureaucracies emerge, they acquire their own, virtually ineluctable expansionary dynamic. They push for more numbers in their ranks and higher salaries for their members. Where does the money come from? It can't come from dividends, since the corporations need to be able to raise money on equity markets. It can't come from interest obligations, since the corporations need to be able to borrow from lenders as well. One of the most obvious targets is frontline workers' compensation. The more powerful the corporate bureaucracy becomes, and the weaker the pressure with which employees can counter, the greater the downward pressure on production workers' wages. The wage squeeze intensifies. (ibid., 5–6)

Gordon goes on to point out that the ratio of supervisory to production workers in the United States is a multiple of that found in Western Europe – countries with higher wage gains and the smallest corporate bureaucracies *and* with more effective trade unions. Here are some numbers Gordon provides to show the dimensions of non-productive workers in the United States:

Depending on the definition, *between 15 and 20 percent* of private nonfarm employees in the United States work as managers and supervisors. In 1994 we spend $1.3 trillion on the salaries and benefits of nonproduction and supervisory workers, almost one-fifth of total gross domestic product, almost exactly the size of the revenues absorbed by the entire federal government. (ibid., 4; emphasis added)

It is also relevant to note that in the same years in which production workers' real hourly take-home pay was declining by 7 percent, after-tax CEOs' annual salaries were increasing by 66 percent (adjusted for inflation). In the years 1990–96, when the ratio of CEO incomes to production workers' wages was rising from 140:1 to 209:1, that same ratio began and remained at 7:1 in Japan; and the ratios in Western Europe are considerably closer to Japan's than to the United States (Gordon, 34–5). The data for 1997 show that average CEO pay rose by 35 percent – to $150,000 a week – while average worker pay rose 3 percent – to $424 a week: that's $7.8 million vs. $22,000 a year. And the CEO/factory wage ratio rose to 326:1.[18]

The foregoing quality of "lopsidedness" in the work and income structure in U.S. corporations, when joined to other matters earlier and soon to be discussed – globalization and financialization – have been decisive in the warping of incomes for the bottom 80 percent of the U.S. population.

These characteristics of the present period have meant troubles mostly for all but the very top. Taken together, however, they also threaten to mix the top with the rest of us in an overall economic calamity. It will have its immediate origins in the degree and ways in which globalizaton and finance now dominate virtually all economies, with the U.S as frontrunner.

THE SUPERSTATE'S NEW MASTERS

In capitalism's first stage in Britain the State's two main functions were to keep the (labor) peace at home and to pave the way for external domination, with or without peace; with substantial variations. That was also true for the other major capitalist powers before World War I.[19]

As we have seen, the State took on what must be viewed as an entirely different life after World War II – different in quantitative terms (that is, taxing and spending), but even more importantly in the new functions it performed. The latter, again with substantial variations from country to country, always included active fiscal and monetary interventions to maintain economic stability and (among other matters) social programs that (under whatever name) had the effect of blunting the harsh edges of earlier capitalism. In doing so, they also redistributed income downward in such fashion as to facilitate consumerism. That redistribution, it is vital to note, was in terms of *shares*; the *levels* of income for all rose, most especially for those on top. The stagflation of the 1970s made such ubiquitous increases in real income impossible; some had then to lose. The structure of power being what it is under capitalism made it likely that those on the top would not be among the losers.

That such would be the case as Monopoly Capitalism II took shape was not a matter of simple evolution; it was insured by the determined "corporate counter-attack" (as Du Boff has called it) against organized labor and the "welfare state." That campaign in turn was much facilitated by what had become the "softness" (and corruption) of organized labor and the active cooperation of the media – itself almost entirely under the control of giant corporations, directly through ownership and indirectly through its advertising expenditures.

All of this had been made simpler by the ideological housecleaning of the Cold War and the growing power of already powerful companies (as noted above). Such companies – most importantly, TNCs – confronted growing needs and opportunities for exploiting very low-wage unorganized labor in countries rich in natural resources, lacking environmental restrictions, and possessing governments often eager to be corrupted at bargain basement prices. And they required and received the cooperation of their governments in realizing those possibilities. The upshot was that considerably more than in its two previous stages of development, capitalist viability came to be dependent on global developments which themselves came to be controlled more through the financial than the productive sector. Naturally, one may say, this could occur only if the State were at least in some important degree at the beck and call of the main actors in the drama: financial markets and the TNCs – many of the latter wholly or in part financial in function.

In the ensuing processes, and among other major developments, the State in *all* nations has been led to pay increasing attention to the demands of central bankers and decreasing attention to internal needs of its people and its society.

It is thus analytically difficult to discuss globalization without almost continual reference to financialization, or the role of the State without referring to both. Thus, in the ensuing discussion, the three – presumably distinct – areas will be examined as though by a juggler, keeping all in focus and in motion at the same time. First, a summary look at the contemporary global economy, and then to finance. In doing so, it will be seen that the organizing institutions of Monopoly Capitalism II are verging toward their own "dysfunctionalities."

THE WORLD AS CAPITAL'S OYSTER

The capitalist process was dependent for its birth on global expansion, and has since became habituated to it. Its eggs were the trading cities of medieval Europe, its midwife the colonialism of the sixteenth century and beyond, which, to recall Marx's comment, "signalised the rosy dawn of the era of capitalist production. These idyllic proceedings are the chief momenta of primitive accumulation ..."[20]

"*Primitive*" because it was the essential basis for the "*capital accumulation*" derived from the exploitation of workers in the industrialization process. The geographic expansion of associated imperialism was much assisted by the technologies of transportation and communication of the nineteenth century. But they were both cumbersome and slow, and set firm limits to how much could be accomplished in distant places.

With today's technologies there are virtually *no* limits; indeed, the great speed and reliability of contemporary transportation and communications combine with *production* technologies that are easy to transport. Thus the lines between domestic and foreign production now tend toward obliteration.

With appropriate modifications, this applies equally to the labor force – not only as concerns the unskilled workers who assemble parts for diverse products but to skilled workers, most especially (but not only) those in the electronics fields. Thus, for example, software experts may work for U.S. firms in New Delhi as well as Silicon Valley – as well, and at much lower pay – with gratitude and no threat of unions. In 1848, such tendencies had led Marx to remark wryly:

> If the Free Traders cannot understand how one nation can grow rich at the expense of another, we need not wonder, since these same gentlemen also refuse to understand how in the same country one class can enrich itself at the expense of another.[21]

Add to this that in the poorer parts of the world – most of Asia and Latin America, and parts of Europe – in addition to the "global labor arbitrage" Greider has noted, there is "global tax arbitrage," and what may be called "environmental arbitrage." The latter means that companies whose production destroys forests, or water supplies, or the air, whatever, may easily buy their way out of any restrictions; and on a given revenue, they may be assured of exemption from taxes – with the added attraction that the existence of such possibilities in distant places means they can often be bargained for successfully at home.[22]

That such advantages to capital sooner or later may bring on problems of a global decrease in average purchasing power, and/or that the debts required to maintain economic expansion will reach their limit and contribute to a major collapse, or that environmental damage will become ubiquitous and destructive, or ..., we'll think about that tomorrow. Such has been true in all or part of capitalist history; such problems are to be confronted *after* they appear, not before. That too is in the nature of capitalism.

As also has been financial recklessness, from early modern Holland to the Crash of 1929. But today is *very* different; in Monopoly Capitalism II, everyone and everything is at risk.

THE TRIUMPH OF SPECTRONIC FINANCE[23]

We begin with some numbers from the United States, those that accompanied the rise of financialization, and continue with those signifying the triumph of finance – first in the United States, now spreading to the rest of the world.

Numbers never tell the whole story, nor are they always decisive in how the story proceeds. But their recent history and what they reveal is indeed startling, and should be even to some of those in business who now view this as "their" system.

Recall that in the late 1960s the developing slackness in the U.S. economy, both a partial cause and consequence of global excess productive capacities, reduced the incentive for investment in new productive facilities. In turn this prompted business not only to make a quantum leap in M&As from then to the present, but provided new functions and higher income levels for finance, and brought it to its present importance.

One need not be enamored of corporate profits to believe that within the framework of a capitalist economy profits going to those involved in production are more likely to be positive for the economy than incomes derived from sheer ownership of, let alone mere speculation in, financial assets. In that connection the statistical tendency after 1949 is riveting: Corporate profits were more than ten times as high as net interest in 1949; more than five times in 1959; more than two-and-half times in 1969; a quarter more in 1979; in 1989 and since corporate profits have been less than net interest.[24]

Interest payments are only one aspect of this development and probably an understatement even in their own terms.[25] Most important to consider in this connection are related developments benefiting Wall Street in the past 25 years or so. Phillips describes some steps in the ascendance of U.S. finance:

In the early 1970s ... the financial sector was subordinate to Congress and the White House, and the total of financial trades conducted by American firms or on American exchanges over an entire year was a dollar amount less than the gross national product. By the 1990s, however, through a twenty-four-hour-a-day cascade of electronic hedging and speculation, the financial sector had swollen to an annual volume of trading *thirty or forty times greater* than the dollar turnover of the "real economy"... Each *month*, several dozen huge domestic financial firms and exchanges ... electronically trade a sum in currencies, futures, derivative instruments, stocks, and bonds that exceeds the entire annual gross national product of the United States![26]

The financial sector grew mightily in response to an intersecting set of stimuli: the emerging importance of money, equity, and pension funds; the enormous increase of household, business, and governmental debt; the spread and strengthening of insurance companies (and their mergers with other financial companies); the expansion of individual financial investors; and the spectacular growth of international financial speculation in the vast and explosive derivatives market.[27]

Also striking is that so much financial expansion occurred after, indeed was facilitated by, the financial disaster of the 1980s, centered on the savings and loans scandals. Phillips summarizes that development:

when the economic bubble of the 1980s popped as the decade ended, no one should have been surprised that so few of the major financial institutions that had carried speculation to new heights were left to drown in their own failed investments. Instead, the national political power structure bailed out the shaky financial sector, and on a large enough scale that in the end the banks and S&Ls rescued through federal insurance payouts represented a higher share of the nation's deposits than the institutions forced to close their doors in the economic hurricane of the late 1920s and early 1930s! ... Financed by massive borrowing and further enlargement of the federal deficit, [the bailout] served largely to safeguard bank investors and assets. The result was not just to prop up the stock market but to allow it to keep hitting new highs, while Wall Street firms achieved new record earnings with new products, services, and speculative devices. [And] what we will call the financial economy ... continued to eat the real economy ... (1994, xvi–xvii)

Currency speculation began to draw serious attention in the 1980s, by which time its dimensions were already amazing. Thus, in 1986, the Bank for International Settlements (the global "clearing house") estimated that *daily* currency transactions were $186 *billion* and that, significantly, no more than 10 percent of that was to finance real investment or trade. By the early 1990s the figure had jumped to $800 billion (again, *daily*), with perhaps $25 billion (about 3 percent) of that for trade and investment; now the figure approaches $2 *trillion* a *day*[28] well under 2 percent of which is for trade and real investment. The rest is speculation.

Among the large speculators are the TNCs. They require diverse currencies for their trade, for "outsourced" production, and for their investments. But because they *are* producing and selling and borrowing and lending (among other activities) they need also to *speculate* in currencies. When they do so successfully, they make profits from that alone; when they do so unsuccessfully, losses result. If they refrain from speculating, however, they are forgoing the possibility of profits and bearing the risk of possible losses from ongoing currency fluctuations. Given those realities, you will find no TNC that does not have, by whatever name, its own Division of Currency Speculation.

And then there are the innumerable others – banks, brokerage houses, individuals, governments, various funds, and others – who are part of the wild frenzy. And frenzy it is, made all the more so because a large portion of foreign exchange transactions is linked to speculation in so-called "derivatives," a "market" (as noted above) with tens of *trillions* of dollars of annual activity.

The Asian financial crisis that came to attention in late 1997 and that unraveled in early 1998 had deep as well as shallow roots, depending upon which country is examined. But in all Asian countries – as in Mexico in 1994 and Russia in 1998 – and whatever the "underlying" causes, it was the actions of fleeing speculators that triggered breakdowns, from Thailand to Indonesia to South Korea to Japan.

In all the talk of free markets and the need for "transparency" in Asia in recent years, it is seldom noted that the giddy financial markets are and have been the freest and most transparent of all. Financial markets are the least regulated or constrained, the most accessible to instantized calculations and communications, the most "globalized," competitive, and integrated markets of all; indeed, they alone approximate the ideal of the mainstream economist's "perfectly competitive market."

When economists and politicians exhort us to "listen to the market," it is those markets – stock, bond, derivatives, and currency markets – to which they refer; and it is to those markets that government leaders everywhere acknowledge *they* must listen.

It is more than merely interesting that the foregoing point – obvious though it must be to those "expert" concerning finance (including economists) – is only rarely if ever made. Were the general public to be reasonably informed on this matter, however, it is quite likely most of its members would deem it risky indeed to have their economic well-being so dependent on the activities of speculators – or, in less polite terms, gamblers.

The kinds and degrees of speculation of the 1920s by comparison with today's frenzies were as a kitten to a tiger; but Keynes, writing in 1936, registered his alarm at that "kitten" both succinctly and well. It is worth repeating at some length in this context:

> Speculators may do no harm as bubbles on a steady stream of enterprise. But the position is serious when enterprise becomes the bubble on a whirlpool of speculation. When the capital development of a country becomes a by-product of the activities of a casino, the job is likely to be ill-done. The measure of success attained by Wall Street, regarded as an institution of which the proper social purpose is to direct new investment into the most profitable channels in terms of future yield, cannot be claimed as one of the outstanding triumphs of *laissez-faire* capitalism – which is not surprising, if I am right in thinking that the best brains of Wall Street have been in fact directed towards a different object. (1936, 158–9)

Even in his day, Keynes had reason to be concerned with speculation and, as well, with the ways in which the *"rentier* class" served as a weight on "enterprise." Had he our world to contemplate, his concern might well have risen to panic for two major developments *in addition to* speculation.

Earlier we noted that when the State confronts the demands of central bankers versus the needs of the society, it is the banks that win. Now we examine the great power of banks as exercised through their nations' central banks (or, for the European Union, *its* central bank), and the enormous overhang of debt.

The little old lady of Threadneedle Street and her offspring

When Britain played the role of global hegemon now exercised by the United States, the Bank of England was in effect the world's lender of last resort. As such it was able to preside over much of the rest of the world's pace and content of economic development through its variation of interest rates. Private though it was, the Bank of England thus served as something like (even stronger than) a central bank not only for Britain but for much of the world – including the United States and Germany in their early industrializing decades.

The principles to which that bank abided came to be the principles of monetary theory and the "monetarism" that was critically powerful before the depression of the 1930s, by which time every industrial nation had its own central bank, controlled either partly or entirely by the State.[29]

In the two decades or so after World War II, all major capitalist economies placed monetary (that is, central bank) policy in a role secondary to governmental fiscal (taxing and spending) policies. But a major outcome of the stagflation of the 1970s was the beginnings of a rightward shift of politics, led by Margaret Thatcher in Britain and pushed much farther during the Reagan Administration in the United States.

As globalization intensified in those same years, and as the financial community began its sharp rise to dominance, Keynesian economics – whose perspective was always broader than the business community, let alone just its financial sector – was pushed aside, and monetary policy came to rule in, however, a very different world.

This "very different world" is one where the main processes are those of globalization, and the main actors are TNCs and financial markets. By the 1990s, those main actors found themselves functioning in a context increasingly dominated by speculation in currencies, stocks and bonds, and, linked to them, derivatives.

Meanwhile trade agreements were bringing various sectors of the globe under pressure – whether those culminating in the European Union, NAFTA,[30] the WTO or – as is being attempted – the Multilateral Agreement on Investment (MAI).[31] An associated component of those pressures is to restore monetary policy to the throne it occupied in the days of the Bank of England.

That reversal was well under way in the late 1970s in the United States, when "the Fed" – ominously – was restored to its 1920s position. Now the European Central Bank is moving toward the same end. Euroland is not yet fully institutionalized, but it is almost there in practice: its 15 members already strain to keep their national debts and budgets within specified limits. An implied consequence, also already under way, is the lowering of social spending levels. As they do so, they move toward the United States as regards health care, unemployment benefits, vacation and old age benefits.

Although the member countries of the European Union for some years have had relatively low rates of growth and high rates of unemployment (averaging over 10 percent), most are not in recession. If and when recession arrives, the need to expand rather than to contract the policies of social democracy will come in sharp conflict with the unchallenged dominance of monetary policy.

Up to now, membership in the Union has been popular in most of Europe (especially in Italy). That is likely to change when "Europe" comes to mean harder times for all; and is likely to bring a revival of currently dormant left politics. That will be especially true were recession to come violently. Far from that being a remote possibility, it is quite probable.

Among the several factors making that likely are the current extraordinary mountains of debt dotting the globe, and most especially where debt is highest and counts the most.

"Is the United States Building a Debt Bomb?"

That is the title of a recent feature essay in *Business Week*.[32] The debt referred to comprises household debt, corporate debt, financial sector debt, and the U.S. external debt. Moreover, it is not only the high levels of debt, but the reasons why they have been and continue to be incurred that are troubling. First, the levels.

Household debt as a share of disposable income stood at about 62 percent in 1978; as 1999 ended it had risen to 102 percent; non-financial corporate debt as a share of corporate output rose from under 60 percent in 1978 to over 80 percent in 1999; financial sector debt as a share of GDP more than quadrupled, from under 20 percent to 80 percent; and the U.S. debt to the rest of the world, about $1 trillion in 1980, has since more than doubled, to over $2.5 trillion.

First, debt in the business community.

A report of the U.S. Comptroller of the Currency for 1998 should have been viewed as an alarm going off:

in 1995, only about 12 percent of syndicated loans went to companies already carrying heavy debt and sub par credit ratings ... By 1997, fully 17 percent ... were to such indebted borrowers. And at the end of [1998's] first quarter, that figure had soared to 31 percent.[33]

The *Business Week* of 1999 shows that quite the opposite took place as regards corporate debt:

The most alarming sign of trouble ahead may be what's happening to corporate balance sheets. Despite the huge gains in the stock market, there is a pronounced tilt in corporate financing toward debt and away from equity. Even at today's prices, companies are buying back far more stock than they are issuing. Over the past 12 months, an eye-popping 3.6% of GDP went into stock buybacks, and even with the IPO boom, nearly $500 billion in equities have been taken off the market since 1997. Making the situation even worse, some companies are borrowing to finance buybacks ... At the same time, companies have been issuing more and more debt to finance acquisitions and expansion.

That not only non-financial corporations and consumers are borrowing for such purposes, but also financial institutions, is an important part of the explanation for Wall Street's recent boom to end all booms. Those outside the financial world would be startled to learn how much borrowing (and why) those inside have been doing. It is common practice for all financial companies – banks, mortgage companies, et al. – to "repackage" the loans they have made and sell them as bonds and notes – "creating debts of their own," as *Business Week* puts it. And the numbers are huge:

> direct borrowing by financial institutions plus securitized lending held by investors has soared from $2.4 *trillion* in 1989 to $7 *trillion* today, bigger than household debt and almost double the size of nonfinancial corporate debt.

And, *Business Week* adds, quoting a financial expert, "The worry is that we might become too efficient at creating debt."

In the fall of 1998, there was a scary period accompanying the emerging markets "meltdown," which almost brought down the major derivatives firm of Long-Term Capital Management. It was saved from a multi-billion dollar bankruptcy – and who knows what other associated developments – by a last-minute bailout engineered by the Fed. Far from either the Asian (and associated) crises serving as a warning to take heed and calm down, debt rose by 8 percent in the ensuing year, "matching the savings-and-loan financed spree of the mid-1980s."

Then there is U.S. external debt. The United States in 1980 was the world's largest creditor ever; as the 1990s began it had become the world's largest-ever debtor. With the monthly trade deficit in 1999 rising beyond $24 billion in the last few months of 1999, it seems likely that the $2.3 trillion debt of 1998 will reach $3 trillion in the near future. Another way of seeing what is under way is to note that the United States now absorbs 72 percent of the entire world's savings: thus, as Greider puts it, the United States is the "world's buyer of last resort." Insofar as that buying is a major element of what keeps the world economy from softening – which would entail a withdrawal of funds – that alone is a source for great concern.

When it is additionally understood that what keeps the U.S. stock market rising is itself importantly dependent on business, financial, and consumer borrowing and that the gains from the stock market – along with household debt – are a major part of what keeps consumption high and rising, it can be seen that the present U.S. and world economies are more precariously situated today than ever before. Such concerns are scarcely lessened when it is understood that an unknowably high percentage of stock and other purchases has been financed by borrowing against mortgages. It is obvious that unless the already extraordinarily high and still rising levels of debt are adequately secured in rising incomes and productive assets, the metaphor of "bomb" is no exaggeration. That takes us back to a further look at consumers.

The addicted consumer

Consumerism can be seen as an addiction. But as with drug addiction there are two categories: those who sniff high-priced cocaine with diverse ways of protecting themselves (at least for a while); and the largely poor who are addicted to crack cocaine, and who are driven, finally, by desperation – and into prison. So it is with consumer markets for goods and services and for debts; like the distribution of income, they are highly unequal.

Generally speaking, and whatever may have been true in earlier years, nowadays the bottom 80 percent of the population slides ever deeper into debt in order to maintain its level of consumption – or to slow its fall. On the other hand, the top 20 percent and, even more clearly, the top 10 percent, buy and borrow in another world: to speculate, to buy luxury goods, to go on a world cruise. We look first at the bottom rungs of the ladder.

In addition to their consumerism having required families to adapt to two wage-earners, the three middle quintiles (the "middle class"), to say nothing of the poor, after the 1970s have found it necessary to borrow in order to pay off debt. Numerous credit cards are not only easy to obtain, they have become difficult to turn down. Virtually none requires proof of financial abilities. This helps one to understand how it is that the poorer *half* of the U.S. population "which collects only about 20 percent of all income, was responsible for 30 percent of the debt in 1995, and over 35 percent of the growth in credit card debt between 1989 and 1995." The average annual payment on credit-card debt is about 16 percent. Household debt (excluding mortgages) as a percentage of after-tax income in 1982 was about 45 percent; by 1998 the percentage had more than doubled. Unsurprisingly, the number of bankruptcies in 1982–98 rose from 2.8 to about 5 per 1,000 persons, and rises ever more steeply.[34]

It is the largest part of the "middle class" whose incomes stagnated after 1973 – but whose addiction to consumption nonetheless continued to deepen, tempted always more by the seductions of advertising. But let us also look at the comfortable to very rich residents at the top of the heap.

These are the families whose annual incomes range from $100,000 into the millions. Their debt is seldom incurred from necessity, but rather because of perceived opportunities to become richer, more prestigious, and the like. They are successful businessmen and women, doctors, lawyers, engineers and, among others, those in finance; and they constitute the great majority of individuals who participate in the stock market. In order to do so, they also constitute the major participants in the residential mortgage market.

In 1999, the market saw what *Business Week* calls a "massive" increase over the preceding year: $400 billion:

> proceeds from mortgage refinancing and home equity loans – over and above the amount used for home purchases and renovations – were used to pay off $34 billion in credit-card debt in 1998 ... Owners' equity as a percentage of residential real estate now stands at 56%, down from 66% in 1989 ... Even more dangerous is the quadrupling of margin debt – borrowing to fund stock purchases ... [which] has tripled in only five years ... If the market plunges, much of that debt will immediately have to be paid back.

And so?

Putting together all the foregoing elements – those comprising speculation and the several mountains of debt – what seems to lie ahead? Using the analytical framework of the late and much-respected post-Keynesian Hyman Minsky, the economist James Cypher argues that

> any substantial change in either the interest rate (+), the value of equities (–), or the growth of sales (–), in the context of a credit-driven expansion will reveal widespread financial fragility.[35]

It is generally agreed that an upward shift of interest rates is not a matter of whether but when, and that this alone will push stock prices down. That decline is more likely to be drastic than moderate, considering what has allowed interest rates to be relatively low and stocks and – at least partially – therefore consumption to be high and rising: booms in stocks and consumption, low prices and even lower unemployment.[36]

Nor is it of minor concern that both directly and indirectly the percentage of the population both deeply in debt and vulnerable to a stock market decline is considerably higher than ever. Earlier we saw that household debt as a percentage of after-tax income had reached 102 percent; and it is reliably estimated that one in two families now own securities.[37]

What has been described in the foregoing pages could be seen by the proverbial man from Mars as a world losing its senses. It would be more accurate to say that our sense has been lured away from us, its place taken by "wanting." To be sure, as the earlier Baran quote on advertising argues, we have been all too easy to seduce. But living in a capitalist society does little to stimulate and much to discourage seeking after alternatives – to "get some satisfaction." Especially when the role of the always more ingenious and audacious – and concentrated – media are taken into account.

THE MEDIA: AMUSING OURSELVES TO DEATH

A century ago, the word "media" was not used; had it been, it would have referred to newspapers and magazines. Then came films and, after World War I, commercial radio, as billboards proliferated along with automobiles. The technology of television was invented in the 1920s, but not until the 1950s did it reach a mass audience – first in the United States, then in Europe. The latest addition to the media is the use of computers for entertainment (in increasing ways). Except for films, the media were funded by commercial advertising; since World War II it has come to be vital for selling ideology and politicians.[38]

All along the way, as in other sectors, M&As brought the media world toward domination by an always smaller number of companies, a process which continues to accelerate (as noted in our earlier discussion of giants firms). As of 1997, the media world was presided over by

> ten or so vertically integrated media conglomerates, most of which are based in the United States ... [along] with another thirty or forty significant supporting firms ... They compete vigorously on a non-price basis, but their competition is softened not only by common interests..., but also by a vast array of joint ventures, strategic alliances, and cross-ownership ... [with their]

financial underpinnings in advertising and its thoroughgoing commercialism.[39]

Advertising has always been central to the media; now it is TNC advertising that is coming to dominate, not only nationally (because the TNCs are also the largest national firms) but globally:

> It is TNC advertising that has fueled the rise of commercial television across the world, accounting, for example, for over one-half the advertising on the ABN-CNBC Asia network, which is co-owned by Dow Jones and General Electric ... In 1999, the United States still accounted for nearly one-half of the world's ... advertising. Even in the developed markets of western Europe most nations still spend no more than one-half the U.S. amount on advertising per capita [and its] 2.1 to 2.4 percent of GDP going toward advertising ... [But] European commercial television is growing at more than a 10 percent annual rate, twice the U.S. average.[40]

Of all these, TV engages its viewers for the most hours (as "online" viewing is growing rapidly). Directly or indirectly, TV has had the most powerful impact on thoughts and feelings and behavior – whether what is being screened is a sports event, a film, a talk or game show, a political ad or music. In what follows, therefore, it will suffice to confine our attention to TV.

In a moment, some numbers will be examined. But it is not merely or mostly the quantitative dimension of the TV phenomenon that counts, so much as what is seen and heard. When TV first took hold, though its offerings already gave sure signs of what was to come, their content was less infantilizing and damaging than now.

To be sure, the continuing family and related dramas of the 1950s were shallow, sentimental, and unrealistic; but the news and sports programs were more straightforward and less inundated with ads and there were always a few reasonably worthy dramas to be seen (even if introduced, as with the GE Theater, by Ronald Reagan). But what is so common as to be unavoidable now was rare a few decades ago: some combination or another of prurience and puritanism, raw sex and violence, sentimentality and insipidity: 24 hours a day, 7 days a week enticements arousing the "seven deadly sins" and feckless hopes.

All this began in the United States; all of it, in one way or another and at varying speeds, now spreads over the globe, like an enormous oil spill. The costs to people, to society, and to the environment increase rapidly over time; as do the gains to those who control and pay for TV programs and their advertisements, whether for the selling of commodities, politicians, or ideas.

The group watching TV that grows most rapidly and ominously and that already watches it most are the young. In a 1999 survey of 3,000 children ages 2 through 18 in the United States these are some findings:

> children on average spend 5 hours, 29 minutes every day, seven days a week, with media for recreation. [For those] 8 years and older, the total is significantly higher, 6 hours 43 minutes a day, more than the equivalent of an adult work week. Much of that time is spent alone.

And elsewhere?

> A 1996 survey of teenagers in television-owning households in forty-one nations finds that they watch an average six hours of television per day, and nowhere in the survey is the figure under five hours.[41]

"Watching" is the key word. It is in the very nature of TV (and much of "online") that its audience is a passive consumer of its images. And what is diminishing as TV watching is expanding? Certainly reading, and, just as certainly, sustained interaction with other human beings. Reading (whether of philosophy or mysteries) *can* be merely a form of consumption, just as TV watchers *can* be reflective of what they are watching. But the probability lies elsewhere. As Neil Postman has put it:

> We are now well into a second generation of children for whom television has been their first and most accessible teacher and, for many, their most reliable companion and friend ... There is no audience so young that it is barred from television. There is no poverty so abject that it must forgo television. There is no education so exalted that it is not modified by television. And most important of all, there is no subject of public interest – politics, news, education, religion, science, sports – that does not find its way to television. Which means that all public understanding of these subjects is shaped by the biases of television.[42]

We are an emotional species, for better and for worse. As suggested earlier, the emotions that advertising brings out in us are quite the opposite of what may be seen as the best in us: our possibilities for compassion, for reflection and reason, for enlightened self-interest.

Whatever positive marvels science may have brought, techniques of persuasion have successfully acted to turn our lives as consumers to purposes that qualify as harmful, often to the point of social and self-destruction – as with the automobile, as with nuclear energy, as with TV itself, as with that large and growing bundle of goods and services the sale of which is useful to the sellers, but not to the buyers: we have come to want what we don't need, and not to want what we do. Long ago, Albert Einstein glimpsed what the past had already revealed and what was lying in wait over time:

> Our entire much-praised technological progress, and civilization generally, could be compared to an axe in the hand of a pathological criminal.[43]

That "axe" has been wielded by those in politics, the military, and in business. They have been given or have taken the power emerging from the interacting processes of capitalism, imperialism, industrialism, and nationalism, much aided now by the media, which "have become an increasingly important battleground for political debate and culture."[44]

How economics has or has not responded to the many foreboding developments signified by Monopoly Capitalism II will now come into focus.

FOR SHAME!

A major theme of this book has been the interaction of economics with capitalist development, and its evolution toward becoming what it is now, a branch of ideology. As noted, there have been and remain those economists who provided understanding, beginning with Adam Smith and including such diverse contributions as those of John Stuart Mill, Marx and Veblen and, among many others, those discussed in Chapter Four, such as Keynes, the post-Keynesians and Baran and Sweezy. The renewed dominance of neoclassical economists has been virtually unchallenged for about 20 years. Have they made a difference? And if so, for better or for worse? The answer here, unsurprisingly, is that they have made a big difference, and for the worse. The recent role of the media in "mind management" has been noted. But the media does not *produce ideas*, they *transmit* them. And what is transmitted regarding economic policy derives its authority directly or indirectly from the teachings of mainstream economists – in advertising, in governmental pronouncements in articles and in economics education with, it must be feared, enduring effect.

That there have been important exceptions has been noted; were it not for them, a book such as this could not be written (as its bibliography attests). But more than ever before, those exceptions must swim upstream against the powerful currents of ideology.

We have noted the manifold deterioration in many areas of existence since the 1970s: in the lives of billions of people who have been uprooted by globalization; in the quality of existence also in the richer countries; in the environment; in the general culture. Joan Robinson early on called that process a "right turn." A new text by the post-Keynesian economist Hugh Stretton has this to say about those years:

> The resort to deregulation, privatization and smaller government since the 1970s proves to have been a mistaken response to the new troubles, and an active cause of some of them. Economists share responsibility for that "right turn" in economic policy. Without their expert authority it is hard to believe that the various political and business groups who drive the new strategy could have persuaded majorities to support it, or tolerate it, for so long.[45]

As never before in history, recent decades have seen an always rising flow of publicized arguments by economists in journalistic essays, on TV shows, as governmental officials, and elsewhere. Here are some mainstream supporting arguments regarding certain public policies, along with some emphatic responses by Stretton (his emphases):

> 1) Monetary restraint alone will stop inflation and then revive employment – *in conditions in which it won't do either.*
> 2) Reducing public investment will increase private investment – *when in fact it will reduce private investment.*
> 3) Free trade exchange will make our manufacturing efficient – *when in our particular circumstances it will put too many of them out of business, increase long-term unemployment, and wreck our balance of payments.*
> 4) Cutting wages would increase employment – *when it would not.*
> 5) Shifting taxes off the rich onto the poor will induce the rich to employ more of the poor – *which it will not.*
> 6) A freer capital market will allow more people to buy their houses – *when in fact it allows fewer people to buy their houses.*
> 7) Rent controls always hurt tenants – *when in many circumstances they can greatly help tenants.*[46]

Recall the "methodological" discussions in the *Prologue*, and its argument that economics *should* be defined as answering the questions "What do we need to understand about the economy?" and "What must we do to improve its functioning for people, the society, and the environment?" Putting it thus allows us to see the behavior of today's mainstream economists as, quite simply, shameful. Far from adding to our understanding they have detracted from it; they have transformed economics into ideology supporting and strengthening business – not business as a whole, but the hard core of giant businesses.[47]

A dwindling number of economists continue to work at useful research and offer useful analyses, and in doing so provide much that is valuable for understanding the economy. Like the critics of capitalism, they have been relegated to the shadows, from whence they can have, at least at present, little effect.

Today economics is a profession utterly dominated by mathematical technicians. They have taken the always too lofty abstractions of neoclassical economics to a realm of symbols, which cannot be challenged by even the well-informed. As the priests of old performed their rituals in Latin, the economists of today work within a realm of obscurity, which they alone can decode.

We repeat, that to the degree that reality and appearance differ, understanding requires theory. That is especially complex for the world of socioeconomic processes. All the more reason, therefore, for socioeconomic theory to take great care in choosing what to abstract from, and when, and where; and when to return to ground level. Most especially is that so when the society is changing as rapidly as in the past century.

Notwithstanding, the mainstream economist continues to take *all* the main elements of those processes as "given," as outside the scope of analysis: political and social institutions and all realms of change, including those of technology, the structures and functions of business and individual income, wealth and power – and much more. It is the adherence to such procedures that has allowed economists to make the "mistakes" noted above by Stretton; such procedures may well have allowed many students (and their professors) to assume that "society," far from being the subject matter of the social sciences, is merely a synonym for "parameters."

The parade taking society on that "right turn" began in Britain in 1979 and became considerably more forceful in the United States in the 1980s. Sometimes leading, other times lagging, the economics profession began its compatible transmutation in the same years, and revivified the legacy of neoclassical economics – at its worst. E.K. Hunt summarizes this position as consisting of three "ideological arguments":

[1] ... that free market exchange harmonized all people's interests, created "rational prices," and resulted in an efficient allocation of resources [nationally and globally] ... [2] that the free market would automatically adjust to a full-employment equilibrium ... [3] that the distribution of income was determined by the marginal productivity of the different factors of production and that each individual received as income only that value created ... by his own factors.[48]

As that economics evolved into the twentieth century, it also moved within three categories, as we have seen: macro, micro, and trade. Its macro positions were temporarily undone by the depression of the 1930s and the work of Keynes and his associates; now his position is seen as "left-wing Keynesianism," and applied only in the forms of "bastard Keynesianism," of which Keynes surely would have disapproved.[49]

Neoclassical microeconomics has always depended squarely on the prevalence of small business. It was wrong-headed even as it was being constructed; now it is disgraceful. And today's much-touted principles of free global trade are an unchanged revival of Ricardo's treatise of 1817 (!): "free trade" is essential for the well-being of all, everywhere.

One can perhaps forgive *businesses* for advocating self-serving policies; after all, it is their business. It is more difficult to "forgive" economists as they provide protective coloration for big business. It will be remembered that Ricardo's "principle of comparative advantage," was propounded in a world in which his nation, Britain, stood alone as an industrializing nation, with a relatively primitive technology. Now there are a good dozen solidly industrialized capitalist nations, all endowed to one high degree or another with a set of advanced technologies that make Ricardo's Britain seem positively quaint.

Today's GATT, NAFTA, and WTO are modern codifications of Ricardo's "principle" – except that Ricardo argued only for "free trade," while the signatories of present trade agreements must submit to internal restrictions (regarding subsidies, copyrights, and much else). Also, instead of making for the utter domination of all nations by one, they allow for the domination of most of the people in the world by the giant TNCs of the strongest nations, the real architects of the agreements, themselves both part of and in turn dominated by financial markets – that is, by speculators.

In acquiescing or supporting all this, mainstream economics has become servant rather than analyst of the economic system.[50] The analysis of preceding chapters has never seen capitalism as a benign system; it has been portrayed as a social formation whose very nature has required it to damage almost all people and their cultures in its earlier developments and, in this century, the earth itself. Now, with the intensity and spread of globalization, the damages done up to the end of World War II, horrendous though they were, are in process of being outstripped – whether as measured by the dozens of societies that have been economically and culturally invaded, irreversibly; by the hundreds of millions of people over the world whose well-being and dignity have been crushed; by the similar, if less dramatic and obvious transformation of the lives of the peoples also of the richer countries, through the commercialization of virtually everything; and, not least, by the already serious and already growing threats to nature, which made ourselves and our achievements possible.

All this will be viewed summarily from another perspective in the Epilogue. It will center on what may be seen as another major change in policy and thought that now grips the entire world: economic growth, and let the devil take the hindmost – which the devil is doing.

We shall see that growth is now seen as the means – the only *acceptable* means – to resolve all wants and needs, whether those of business or consumers, or as regards social needs and problems: everything and anything. And it will also be indicated that there are other paths to follow, both safer and more desirable, for us humans, our societies, and Mother Nature.

6   The Unfolding Crises of the Twenty-first Century

INTRODUCTION

The contrasts between the euphoria of the last decade of the twentieth century and the opening years of the twenty-first are as worrisome as they are dramatic: *economically*, celebration has been replaced by attempts to cope, sugared with the recurring notion that all will be well soon enough, that "prosperity is just around the corner"; *politically*, the leaders of both the major and minor countries are faced at home with citizenries mixing apathy with outrage and uneasiness as seemingly intractable disputes in all realms persist; *militarily*, long-standing conflicts across the globe are coming to be overshadowed by what threatens to become an enlarging strife in the Middle East and Central Asia: even as the term "quagmire" has resurfaced, fears grow that matters could become much worse than that: although mortifyingly, the U.S. *did* finally manage to extricate itself from Quagmire #1, but as the bloodshed continues and worsens in Afghanistan, Iraq, and Israel/Palestine, apprehension is expressed that the United States can neither "win" *nor* leave, with who knows what related consequences.

Such troubling concerns are only the most prominent among many now demanding attention; none can be dealt with here more than summarily; some of the most pressing questions will be raised, which, in being so, will point to matters deserving continuing and serious investigation:

1. Do the collapse of "the new economy" of the U.S. and ongoing erratic developments of the world economy portend a replay of the 1930s? Put differently, whence the source(s) of healthy growth and stability for the predictable future?

2. Can the deepening and spreading socioeconomic stresses and struggles within and between nations be made manageable, or will the political extremes and conflicts of the interwar decades reappear, if also in different forms?

3. Are the numerous internecine and "small wars" and deepening tensions on all continents the prelude to one or more major

outbreaks between nuclear powers such as India and Pakistan, the U.S. and North Korea or, even, between the U.S. and China?

4. Asking essentially the same questions, but from a different standpoint, if the hegemonic position of the United States is now in decline, as now seems entirely possible, what then?

The complexities and their interactions of today's world preclude reliable answers to those questions; what can be said is that whatever happens over the next decade or two, its specific causes, nature, and resolutions will necessarily be different in both degree and kind from the past: possibly for better, probably for worse – "probably for worse" because of the heightened abilities of those both in and out of power around the globe to do harm, and the greater difficulties of restraining them from abusing those abilities; all that made more problematic if, as, and when the hegemonic power, as now, becomes unilateralist.

The ensuing and truncated responses to those questions will be mostly concerned with the ongoing U.S. and global political economies, and their similarities with and differences from the relevant past; after that, a brief comment on related global political and military troubles.

GLOBAL ECONOMIES: EASY COME, EASY GO

The framework within which the troubles of the nineteenth century moved toward crises and convulsions was imperialism; today's is that of globalization. Neither of those came to be in a vacuum; both were created by the existing *capitalist* powers, steered by *nationalism*, and energized by the *technologies* of their time; although there were many differences between the two eras, they had in common that in neither era could the weaker regions withstand the demands of the powerful.

Like imperialism, globalization has been a heedlessly destabilizing set of processes; both entailed the substantial and ubiquitous changes essential for the flourishing of capitalism:

> Constant revolutionizing of production, uninterrupted disturbance of all social conditions, ever-lasting uncertainty and agitation distinguish the /capitalist/ epoch from all earlier ones. All fixed, fast-frozen relations, with their train of ancient and venerable prejudices and opinions, are swept away, all new-formed ones become antiquated before they can ossify. All that is solid melts into air, all that is holy is profaned, and man is at last compelled to face with sober senses his real conditions of life and his relations with his kind.[1]

That was written more than 150 years ago; today's swift rates of change – and *what* is changed – make the earlier era seem like a stately waltz by comparison. Much of the recent acceleration can be explained by the extraordinary leaps of the technologies of communication, production, and transportation; but their way was paved for them by the institutional "clear cuts" of imperialist interventions; in both the imperialist nations and those they exploited, traditions of social cohesion and stability were all but dismantled before World War I; the interwar years and World War II sent them to the rubbish heap; the jazzy technologies of the past half century were free to do what they would, where they would, come what may.

The normal functioning of all social systems produces some who gain more than others; today's capitalist globalization does so spectacularly, producing winners and losers in ways such that the initial gaps between them widen irreversibly. The constituent and interacting elements of that gap are at once economic, political, and military, affecting all nations and all of their peoples.

Those presiding over these processes, whether past or present, do not concede that the game is one of winners and losers; their constant theme has been that "a rising tide lifts *all* boats" – some higher than others, to be sure; but to the benefit of all "in the long run." Never is it acknowledged that the "rising tide" has the destructive force of a tidal wave for all but a minority; never is it recognized that most of the people in the world have never had "boats" or, that when they have, that they have consisted of the land taken from them by that same "rising tide" – as with the enclosures in Britain during the industrial revolution; never is it understood that what the "long run" has brought has been socioeconomic upheaval weakening the already weak.

Nor is more than token attention paid to the already large and growing number of those in the globalizing countries who, having prospered in its earlier stages, have more recently seen their good jobs disappear in a less dramatic but steadily "rising tide" at home. As will be discussed more fully below, in being restructured to meet the needs and possibilities of capital, the socioeconomies of the rich nations have enfeebled the lives of many millions of their own people.

Consider the dynamic meanings of terms such as "downsizing" and "outsourcing" for the laid-off skilled workers of the richer nations: their dignity as well as their wages and benefits have gone down the drain. Try to imagine the plight of the masses of those in the "emerging economies" whose "agribusiness," "export platforms" and "modern-ization" have meant for most the irrevocable devastation of their villages, their cultures, their livelihood and, once more, their dignity – leaving them with a future of hard work at dirt wages in hostile cities in their own or other lands, with who knows what new dangers and horrors.

None of that – or the accompanying environmental damage – is or ever has been a matter for concern on the part of the giant companies that so enthusiastically bring them about; consider the factual experience of the crowning glory of globalization – NAFTA (North American Free Trade Agreement, 1993), where the possibilities for realizing globalization's favorable consequences were at their most promising for all concerned.

The *maquiladoras* on Mexico's northern border were a central product of the NAFTA accord. The following details are taken from the scholarly study of James Cypher, the leading student of Mexican–U.S. economic relations.[2]

NAFTA established policies between the U.S., Canada, and Mexico, but it began in 1993 as a bilateral *trade* agreement between the United States and Mexico, supported by four basic claims:

1. it would be a trade agreement, *not* a project to shift production to Mexico;

2. it was a binational search for efficiency, not a government/ corporate-led strategy to regain the steady loss of U.S. economic dominance from the 1980s on;

3. it would reduce consumer prices in the U.S.;

4. it would quickly create 170–200,000 jobs in the US, as a result of balanced trade.

In fact, as Cypher shows, barriers to *trade* had never been a problem between the two countries; barriers to *investment* had been. With NAFTA, U.S. capital managed to eliminate *all* constraints to the placing or practices of their factories in Mexico; indeed, Cypher declares, such unlimited investment was "the core of NAFTA." The eliminated barriers were those that might set floors to wages and working conditions or protect the environment: for U.S. companies, it was a free pass to recreate the "dark satanic mills" of the industrial revolution.

Item: U.S. auto workers' wages in the 1990s averaged $19/hour, plus benefits; in the Mexican *maquiladoras* they were well under $2/hour, usually with no benefits.

Item: already by 1996, as the U.S. car models produced in the *maquiladoras* amounted to half the models' total output, their prices in the United States *rose* by 20 percent.

Item: More *jobs*? "NAFTA was responsible for the loss of approximately 316,000 jobs by 1999, due to both trade and investment effects."

Still, at least it was beneficial for the landless and otherwise desperate Mexicans? Not quite: "... Mexico, far from developing its industrial base, has become an assembly site for /primarily/ U.S. corporations, which thrive on a workforce *whose worklife averages ten years*" – a workforce with ten hour-plus days, living in badly-overcrowded slum shelters, whose average life span has been shortened (like that noted for English workers in the early nineteenth century). But, surely the Mexican economy has grown more rapidly and will do so even more, and things will improve for all? Hardly: Before NAFTA, 1960–80, Mexico's GDP had grown at an average of 4 percent annually; since 1993 it has grown at just 1 percent.

And worse is on its way. In *"Maquiladora Bosses Play the China Card"* (*Dollars & Sense*, September 10, 2003) one learns that Mexican workers are told they must accept even *lower* wages and lose what meager benefits they may have had, lest their factories be moved to China or India – a repeat play of the threats issued to U.S. workers regarding a move to Mexico in earlier years; and, after unions caved in, factories continued to be shut down – most recently for several more U.S. auto plants. Significantly, the once powerful auto union (UAW) acquiesced, in order to keep benefits for continuing workers – at least for a while.

Like imperialism, globalization stems from the interaction of capital's opportunities *and* its needs. Contemporary opportunities arose from the extraordinary rise in the *mobility* of physical capital *plus* rapid transportation and instant communications *plus* the elimination of political barriers to the production in the weaker nations – all going well beyond the possibilities of the world presided over by Britain.

However, companies have become always more gigantic and always more "transnational" not only because they *can* but because they *must*; survival, as much as the lust for profits and power, is a driving force.

Be all that as it may, giant businesses now possess giant political as well as economic power; however, of the few hundred transnational companies that effectively control world production, trade, and services – and politics – it is those of the United States which generally prevail, imperiously. So far.

THERE IS NO FAILURE LIKE SUCCESS

As with Britain more than a century ago, the very source of what are seen as the triumphs of ongoing globalization are likely to be the cause of its breakdown in the looming future: the U.S. empire has probably "shot itself in the foot" in confronting the possibilities and the needs of its overweening power.

Earlier it was noted that history cannot repeat itself, least of all in specifics; but certain general patterns of change can occur, and have. Previous chapters have noted the ways in which the Dutch in the seventeenth and eighteenth centuries and the British in the nineteeth century "did themselves in." The reader is referred back to them and to the discussions of the reconstruction and emergence of "global economies II and III" since World War II. Here we treat of the destabilizing forces of the very recent past and the present, as they both compare and substantially contrast with their colonial and imperialist predecessors.

1. Just as the technology of the nineteenth century made it both possible and necessary for Britain to take a quantitative leap beyond the Dutch, that could and did happen also because of enormous qualitative changes: Britain brought more territories under control, penetrated them much more deeply geographically and economically, and was both able and required to gain explicit political control. But Britain and the other imperialists of that age exploited "their" territories almost exclusively for resources and, in a lesser way, for markets; that is still vital, but imperialism's hot core is now the global spread of *production*.

2. Although the politics of the post-World War II era did not allow the continuation of direct *political* control over imperialized societies, the political econony and the technology of the past half-century have enabled even further geographic and socioeconomic penetration *without* direct political control, facilitated by the always greater economic dependency of the poorer nations and by the susceptibility to corruption of their rulers.

But now, as earlier, something has gone awry. The main difficulties of nineteenth century imperialism arose from the conflicts between the major powers, all competing to gain control over the resources, markets, and strategic locations of the weaker societies. The latter, now *politically* independent, confront the ruling powers with numerous and always changing stresses and strains both in their own societies and at the same time as conflicts arise among and between contending transnational companies and, therefore, their nations.

In addition, the successes of globalization, in entailing the shoving aside of traditional cultures and their ways and means, have produced a wave of turbulence and anger that might easily accelerate out of control. That development will be examined further below; here it is pertinent to call the reader's attention to Benjamin Barber's *Jihad vs. McWorld*, which explores the explosive relationships between what is seen as economic progress by the richer nations but as a socioeconomic catastrophe by large numbers of those in the poorer societies.[3]

In what now follows, the prospects for sufficient rates of economic growth will be seen as dim; at least as important, and as will be discussed at some length in the Epilogue, the economic growth viewed as the cure-all for society's ills and needs not only is not, but is likely to be the very source of major problems.

Be that as it may, presently rising difficulties were potentially present from the beginnings of the postwar era, but were temporarily muffled or deflected by substantial global reconstruction and recovery from the 1950s on; 3–6 percent economic growth rates were then the rule; now 1–2 percent is seen as encouraging.

The first signs of enduring trouble emerged in 1991 in Japan, second largest national economy; it has yet to recover. Since 1991, Japan "has turned the corner" countless times; as I write in late 2003, once more its "economic growth is likely to exceed 1 percent this year." Such "growth" was once described as stagnation.

What has been true for Japan for more than a decade has taken hold since 2000 for the other six members of the "Group of 7" (the U.S., Germany, France, Italy, the U.K. and Canada): rates of unemployment for the Europeans hover just above or just below 10 percent; Canada's and Britain's, until recently fairly low, are now rising; the United States has lost about three million jobs since 2000, and its unemployment rate is stuck above 6 percent (which would be over 10 percent if measured in the European way). Such unemployment will continue until growth rates average 3.5 percent. As happened in the 1930s and again in the 1970s with the word "stagnation," the vocabulary of economics has altered to account for these phenomena, most recently in the United States: "jobless recovery" – or, more recently "job*loss* recovery." That process itself is the result of something else new, and is expected to persist: the relationship between increases in *productivity* and *unemployment*. Consider the following:

> Productivity is rising at the fastest rate in 30 years ..., more than twice the pace of the 1970s and 1980s and slightly faster than in the postwar era from 1947 to 1973 ..., /the/ golden age of productivity improvements ... Since the recovery began more than two years ago ..., the United States has still lost more than a million jobs.[4]

The "fault" is not that of productivity, as such, but that its increases take place in a period of persisting low growth. In turn, that is but one part of a larger development, first and foremost in the United States. Its constituent parts are (1) the now widespread adoption of the advanced technologies of the "new economy" of the 1990s by the "old companies" as a positive opportunity to enhance profitability *and* the need (2) to meet the general increase of global competition; meanwhile, (3) both blue and white collar jobs move from the richer to the poorer countries at an escalating rate. At the same time, especially in the United States, (4) there is a surge in income inequality within the labor force itself between the shrinking number who have been able to retain skilled jobs (and benefits) and the rising number of those who have become part of the always enlarging unskilled, low-pay, no benefits workforce – a transition already well underway in the United States in the name of "a flexible labor force" – while, at the same time, the Bush administration finds ways to widen the gap between the very rich and all others. Nor does it help that the West European powers are seeking to make their own workforces "more flexible."

To those developments, another must be added, again with special force in the United States (but spreading elsewhere) – never forgetting that it is "the consumer of last resort" for other nations' exports. The reference is to the already high levels of economic fragility brought about by vast increases in all realms of debt, which, along with exorbitant speculation, have been both cause and consequence of the financialization of the U.S. economy since the 1980s. The "realms of debt" comprehend households, financial and non-financial companies, federal and state governments, and U.S. foreign debt.

The fragility arises not just from the record-breaking levels of indebtedness, but from the necessity that all forms of it must continue to *rise* to keep the U.S. and the global economy "healthy." However, the U.S. population of "consumers of last resort" cannot function satisfactorily without a steady rise in *median* real incomes – not just merely those of the top 10 percent.

It is not only the "jobless recovery" which constitutes a problem in that respect, nor only the rising inequality of income; harmful though both are, there is a considerably deeper problem needing attention: If current globalization processes continue on their present track, the United States faces a continuous weakening of its manufacturing sector, the historic center of its economic strength – a process already well underway.

In recent decades, U.S. global dominance has trodden the path taken by the British more than a century ago, if with variations. Britain, utterly dominant in industrial production up through the 1880s, enhanced its wealth and strength by massive lending abroad, most especially to Germany and the United States; as they became more advanced technologically and stronger industrially, they emerged as Britain's devastating competitors. In his *Imperial Germany* ..., Veblen ironized this process as the "advantages of borrowing and the penalty of taking the lead": Britain had been "hoist by its own petard."

There are vital differences between Britain's devolution and what is likely to occur for the United States. We are the world's (and history's) largest borrower not, as Britain was, its greatest lender; Britain did very little of its manufacturing abroad; the U.S., combining the latest technology with very low wages, does a great deal and always more.

But the key difference between now and then is that while globalization has given the richer nations easy access to the cheap labor and abundant resources of the poorer countries, it has also made it possible for those countries (most notably China and India) to develop their *own* industry – while making ample room for outside investors they are also rapidly creating modern industries of their own – not only in the classic realms of textiles, clothing and non-durables, but of the entire gamut of industrial production, up to and including computer software.

The growth of manufacturing in previously non-industrial countries *can* become – as, for example, it has been in Malaysia, South Korea, and Taiwan – a beneficial development for the richer countries, if and *only* if the world economy is expanding at a goodly rate and their governments, not "the free market" shape their economic development.

The essential expansion is distinctly improbable for several reasons. It could occur only if stimulated by substantial increases in real investment (that is, productive capacities), and/or substantial increases in average levels of consumption. Neither is likely.

Item: "Overcapacity Stalls New Jobs" Much of the public outcry over America's failure to generate jobs has focused lately on a surge in the outsourcing of work to China and India. But another dynamic closer to home is weighing on job creation – the slow process of working through a glut of boom-era investment that continues to litter the economy with underused factories ...; U.S. manufacturers are using less than 73 percent of their capacity.[5]

China has been and remains the most rapidly growing economy in the world and the most tightly-controlled; and India is rapidly catching up. Taken together, their populations well exceed a third of the globe's; the largest percentage of both live in extreme poverty, and work under abysmal working conditions – and thus have the dynamism – of the British industrial revolution. Expanding at the rate of roughly 8 percent annually, China and India (expanding at 7 percent) may be expected to have a combined gross domestic product *at least* equal to that of Japan and Germany combined – or that of the United States?

Meanwhile, the "flexibility" of the U.S. workforce is gutting the ability of its own population to maintain consumption levels, with or without rising household debt – whose average monthly level is already higher than that of household income. Tellingly, a recent headline states that, "Necessities /education, health care, housing, prescription drugs/, not luxuries /durable consumer goods/, are driving Americans into debt."[6] It seems to have escaped the attention of business – not for the first time – that for modern industrial economies to prosper in the fabled "long run" it is essential that a goodly portion of their own population be sufficiently well off to purchase a goodly percentage of the domestic production of "non-necessities."

Alongside and connected to that ominous development, troubles have surfaced in the realms of foreign trade and foreign exchange. Since 2002, the dollar has weakened substantially against the yen and the euro. Initially, that sounds like good news for U.S. businesses: our goods are cheaper, so others will buy more of them; for the same reasons it is bad news for those "others." Question: on balance, *will* foreigners be buying more U.S. goods if their economies are weakened by reductions in our imports from them?

The cheapening of the dollar was preceded and has been accompanied by a rising wave of protection for both agriculture and industry by the United States, as it simultaneously preaches "free marketry" for others. The Europeans and the Japanese are furious at that, made all the more so by the sustained attempts of the U.S. to promote a weaker dollar (while President Bush publicly promises the opposite).

Significantly, China has wisely tied its yuan (or *renmindi*) to the dollar, no matter the appeals from the United States to "let it float": "China stands firm on keeping yuan at current rate,"[7] one of the policies enabling China to become a major player in the world economy:

Item: [In 2002,] for the first time, Japan's imports from China surpassed its imports from the United States. At the same time, Japan's exports to China surged ...; China has /also/ become South Korea's largest trading partner.[8]

Tremors are also being felt in the arena of global finance because of the trillions owed by the U.S. to foreigners, making us now also the world's "borrower of last resort." The U.S. started its journey to that position decades ago, when we were the Rock of Gibraltar in a relatively shaky world; in addition to becoming U.S. bondholders, foreigners became U.S. stockholders in vast quantities as part of the "irrational exuberance" of the "new economy" in the 1990s.

The economic slowdown and the corruption scandals of the U.S. in the past few years – and now its sky-rocketing deficits – have badly shaken foreigners' confidence in U.S. investments. In that more than one-third of all U.S. government bonds are held by foreigners, that is no small matter: any suspicion of a rise in interest rates creates a fall in bond prices; and/or, any sell-off of bonds leads to a rise in interest rates. And once such processes take hold, they threaten to become runaway. Probable? Not yet. But as recently as 1999, it would have been deemed impossible.

We have now arrived at the intersection of political economy and global politics.

ALTOGETHER NOW: QUARREL!

Like business strategies for companies, politics for nations is a matter of opportunity and need, with even higher stakes. The global structure of power and, to a significant extent, the structures of power within nations were able to be vitally shaped by the United States in the wake of World War II, which, as we have seen earlier, flattened virtually all other societies in all ways. In the ensuing half century of reconstruction and development, the relative power of all others set against that of the U.S. naturally increased substantially in the economic realm – leaving them, however, still effectively subservient both economically and politically.

In the past few years, most especially but not only in Europe, attempts have begun to surface for many of those nations to find ways of working together *in opposition* to the United States, instead of doing our bidding without protest. It is easy to see this as having been prompted by what they see as a combination of simple-minded, arrogant, selfish, and dangerous *military* policies in especially (but not only) the Middle East and Central Asia; but those policies have been the "last straws" of many in recent years.

The issues causing the Europeans, Asians, and Latin Americans to become increasingly disgruntled with the U.S. now include the economic, political, social *and* military realms: Our refusal to sign even the mild Kyoto Treaty for environmental constraints – even though, or because, we are the major culprit; our refusal to join the International Criminal Court unless it exempts our own citizens – most notably, Henry Kissinger – from prosecution; our piddling contributions to (or withdrawal from) global health programs, usually because of fundamentalist religious groups' pressures regarding abortion or sexual conduct; our continued substantial economic and military support of Israel in a conflict requiring even-handedness; and, of course, our resort to the policy of "preemption" in Iraq, and the fear that it is just a beginning.

The carrots and sticks of U.S. policy over the past half century have been used continuously. Now, we have fewer carrots to offer, and to kneel to our sticks is coming to be seen as more dangerous than to resist them.

There is no way any one nation can effectively resist us, unless it is a China (or, as a special case, a Malaysia); strong regional and inter-regional alliances are necessary. That path for both the rich and the poor nations is strewn with imposing obstacles.

Such can be no more than cold comfort for the United States; withal, the efforts are not only under discussion in Europe and in Asia and in Latin America, but have gone beyond mere grumbling to proposals: Romano Prodi, President of the European Union, rarely lets a week go by without making public comments on the need for Europe to lessen its dependence upon the U.S., by strengthening and reshaping the European Union – itself a product of U.S. pressures going back to 1950.

Even more striking is what is happening in Latin America and the Caribbean. In the eight nations of South America, only Chile can be a cause of merely minor concern for the United States (and even there, memories of the U.S. role in the fascist coup of 1973 remains a poisonous thorn in that relationship). The headline in the leading newspaper in Italy, *La Repubblica*, tells it all: "Challenge to the hegemony of the U.S.A., following the dream of Lula."[9] The day before, Bolivia's president had been forced to flee to Miami, lest a worse fate befall.

"Lula," president of that continent's largest and, in terms of resources, its richest nation, well aware of the ability of the United States to bring its economy down, is pursuing a slow but sure path to making Brazil's economy part of a regional alliance which would qualitatively reduce the economic dependence of the entire region on the U.S. Chavez, despite bitter opposition from the United States (very probably including its participation in some attempts to overthrow him) has wrested control over Venezuela's oil resources – as an important first step in the same direction.

The new president of Argentina, Kirchner, is at one with its population in seeking to rid the country of the IMF – that is, U.S. finance's – stranglehold, and to move also toward finding strength in regionalism. In one degree or another, long-suppressed anger with the northern behemoth has surfaced increasingly as well in Ecuador, Peru, Colombia and, now, Bolivia. In all those countries, significant percentages of the people have long been fed up with being used by the U.S., in whatever name: for free markets, against cocaine, you name it – ways and means always benefitting the United States at the expense of South America.

What happens now is not because the peoples of the South have all of a sudden become absolutely stronger; it is that the U.S. has become relatively weaker. It is likely to become always more so as its economic strengths decline and its military priorities rise. It does not help the United States that its attempts to get rid of Castro, in whatever form for whatever reasons, have not only failed but have, if anything, widened support for Cuba and deepened animosity toward itself, throughout the Caribbean but also in, for example, Europe.

The peoples of Central America are not likely ever to forget or to forgive the United States for its murderous activities in Guatemala, Nicaragua, El Salvador, Honduras, and Panama, whose effects do and will endure; nor, as Mexico's economy shrinks, are the Mexicans likely to support any government that supports NAFTA. The unfolding processes in Asia are in great flux; but it seems certain that Japan's economic domination in Asia is on its way out and that – and other forms of domination – by China on its way in. To what degree and in what ways that will emerge cannot be known, except to say that it will almost certainly leave the United States as a bystander concerning, potentially, the entire Asian continent, even of the world – dependent upon our preponderant military strength, not on our once great prestige and power.

Those are merely tendencies, signs of U.S. decline, rather than the emergence of a different "new world order." If the future will even roughly be similar to the past, unfortunately, *any* such new order will arise only from the ashes of the present order.

The Epilogue says more on that crucial matter; and it also goes on to suggest alternatives worth working toward.

Epilogue

INTRODUCTION: ECONOMIC GROWTH AS ICON

Economic growth was seen as one of many means to various ends until a generation or so ago. Now, growth sits as a dictator on the throne of economic policy: "growth regardless!" Or, as an American football coach once said, referring to winning, "It's not everything, it's the *only* thing."[1]

This may be confirmed in the daily news, where both the support for and the opposition to virtually all economic and many social policies take growth as *the* criterion – support because it will enhance growth, opposition because it will retard it, by labor and business, Democrats and Republicans in the United States, and both center-left and the center-right parties in Europe.[2]

In partial support of that broad generalization we examine a recent book by economist Jeffrey Madrick, *The End of Affluence: The Causes and Consequences of America's Economic Dilemma* (1995). His work is selected because it contains the rationale for growth not at its worst, but at its best. Madrick works in the mainstream, but at its useful edges; he is by no means among those disparaged as "shameless" in earlier discussions.[3]

His book contends that inadequate growth rates since 1973 are the source of the most important socioeconomic problems of the United States, and, symmetrically, that the achievement of more rapid growth is the means to resolve those problems.

Unusual among economists, Madrick is much concerned with what is wrong with our society from a laudable position; my criticism of his position is that the steps recently taken to insure "adequate" rates of economic growth in both the United States and, even more, globally, have worsened what Madrick sees as wrong and threaten to take an already alarming set of unfolding conditions into calamity. In contrast, this Epilogue will conclude with a skeletal argument proposing a set of desirable, necessary, and possible programs which, seeing the iconic status of growth in the realm of policy as both inadequate and dangerous, instead constitute qualitative and structural changes.

THE CASE FOR GROWTH

At the center of Madrick's argument is that in the century leading up to 1973 the U.S. economy grew at an average rate of 3.4 percent annually (over good times and bad); but that from 1973 to 1993 the rate flattened to a 2.3 percent annual average. He then calculates just how much that seemingly small percentage change has meant to the average family: "the accumulated losses in goods and services due to slow growth have come to ... more than $40,000 a person"[4] – enough to make the down payment on a good home, he could have added.

It could accurately be objected that growth rates since 1993 have been 4–5 percent, but Madrick is probably right that the average is at best likely to remain closer to 2.5 percent than 3.5 percent annually over the years to come – or considerably lower in the event of a global downturn.

Nor, at present, can one disagree with Madrick when, in his concluding pages, he describes emerging realities as follows:

> Slow economic growth may increasingly set old pensioners against young workers, homeowners against renters, suburbs against cities, natives against immigrants, light-skinned Americans against dark-skinned ones, debtors against creditors, and those with power, by virtue of their own wealth or their paid representation in Washington, against those who have none. We have seen too much of this already in the angry arguments over affirmative action, immigration, school curricula, capital punishment, the costs of welfare, Social Security, protecting the environment, and the government's role in health care. Once, equality meant that we could all get ahead. For too many of us, equality now means having to give something up. (Madrick, 163)

In his writings, Madrick has been considerably more conscious than most economists that from World War II to the present, rapid economic growth has depended on a mixture of undesirable stimuli (to be analyzed shortly). He thus claims no more for his position than that it could halt ongoing socioeconomic deterioration. However, a closer look at the nature and consequences of those stimuli (as well as the history described in our preceding chapters) raises grave questions for that hope.

Summing up some earlier discussions, the greatest overall socioeconomic improvements in the history of the richer nations were accomplished in the 30 years or so after World War II: among them, reduced poverty (especially among the old), more widespread and higher money and social wages than ever before, and the introduction of legislation on environmental matters. But the policies allowing those changes, valuable and beneficial though they may have been in all the major economies, were insufficient to sustain continuous well-being and improvement. In addition, when the focus was enlarged to include the poorer countries, we saw that the human costs and social destruction were not only severe but worsening, and likely to be irreversible.

More to the point, on average, that period saw the highest rates ever of growth, nationally and globally, but were followed by the first combination of stagnation *and* inflation, and a reversal of progress due the very institutions organizing the expansion.

Added to which, although the United States in the 1990s enjoyed its longest period ever of peacetime growth,[5] at the most only the top 20 percent of its people benefited. What is more, there is general agreement that the explanation for those years rested upon two worrisome bases: 1) robust consumption, fueled by always rising debt, a raging stock market, and flat prices, all those grounded in 2) the weaknesses in Europe and the crisis that began in Asia in 1997.

Given today's political economy, there is little reason to expect future periods of rapid growth to have a better outcome. If anything, a worse outcome must be expected as attempts are made to accelerate growth at the expense of an even larger majority of the world's people.

And then there is the environment. The enthusiasts of growth in all parts of the political spectrum, if for differing reasons, pay small if any heed to the already substantial and harmful "collateral damage" of continuous growth. They pay even less to what is implied by continuing down that road by the already industrialized nations *plus* the numerous "emerging-economies": the virtual certainty that the earth will lose its ability to support most species precisely because of the constituent elements making for growth.

THE *TOSSICODIPENDENTE* GLOBAL ECONOMY

Previously, we have used "addiction" to describe consumerism. The Italian term for drug addiction used above is more instructive: it means the dependence upon toxics – that is, poisons. What are the "poisons" on which in fact all contemporary economies *depend* for growth, and which have so many damaging consequences?

Here we shall look more closely at three of the bases for growth, to show that what are called "side-effects" are instead integral to the process of growth as now constituted: 1) consumerism, signifying what is bought and used (exemplified by automobiles); 2) the politics of globalization, and 3) the export-based dependence of the developing economies for their "health" – under the guidance of the giant TNCs and the financial system.

Taken together, the dynamic functioning of these developments has elevated growth to its present status; their interaction (and that with the other bases for growth) is moving economic, human, political, and social damage beyond that already inflicted and toward the point of devastation.

All these elements have been touched on earlier; as they are examined here it will be as regards their specific relationships to economic growth and their active interdependence. We return first to consumption.[6]

The theater of the absurd and the obscene

It is widely understood that most of the world's peoples are inadequately supplied with the basic necessities of food, clothing, shelter, education, and health care. Even in the very richest nation, the United States, that is true for a good third of the population. In the poorer countries, the World Bank reports, about a quarter of the world's population lives on *less* than $1 dollar a day, and their numbers are rising.[7]

Given that reality alone, today's feverish consumption by the top 10-15 percent of the world – what is purchased, plus its accompanying and often destructive wastes[8] – would be a cause for something more than concern. To be sure, a large percentage of consumption, whether in rich or poor nations, is for commodities serving some useful purpose; what is striking is how much of consumption is frivolous, irrational, or self-destructive – especially compared with the desperate lives of most in the world.

> *Item*: "Americans spend more than $8 billion a year on cosmetics – $2 billion more than the estimated actual total needed to provide basic education *for everyone in the world*."
>
> *Item*: "Americans and Europeans spend $17 billion a year on pet food – $4 billion more than the estimated annual additional total needed to provide basic health and nutrition *for everyone in the world*."
>
> *Item*: "Europeans spend $11 billion a year on ice cream – $2 billion more than the estimated annual total needed to provide clean water and safe sewers *for the world's population*."[9]

Such sorry data are grave enough, but much more is at stake. In earlier chapters we have seen some of the disturbing aspects of consumerism – whether concerned with debt or TV and advertising. Here the focus will be on the automobile, as we confront its most alarming dimension: the purchase, the debt involved, and the use of the automobile account for close to 10 percent of the average household's budget, and is directly responsible for much of the social and ecological damage.

The automobile's production and its use have already done so much harm, with worse veering around the corner, that automobiles can be seen as the most broadly destructive invention ever – although some might bestow that honor on TNT, nuclear energy, or TV. Whatever the case, they are in the same club.

The social damage has many dimensions. Among them are 1) the deliberate dismantling of public transportation systems (especially in the United States);[10] 2) the wholesale tearing down of substantial areas of urban housing (generally in poor neighborhoods) to make way for urban freeways;[11] the unmeasurable but surely substantial impact of the global oil giants on foreign policy – most obviously in the Middle East, and presently in areas of the former Soviet Union and the Balkans. There is more that could be added, including matters such as the impact of daily traffic jams on an always fragile civility. But the larger area of damage is to the environment.

Honk, if you need a gas mask

Many are the contributors to our threatened environment, whether as regards our air, water, soils, climate, the ozone layer, or disappearing forests. Joining them are the contributors to bodily ills deriving from what we eat and drink or smoke, whether because of their "natural" dangers (as with tobacco) or those arising from artificial products.

Some of those are being contained, some can be avoided; but we all must breathe the air around us, and whatever else pollutes and warms the air, the principal offender is emitted carbon dioxide and its largest source is automobile use.

In some parts of the world, steps have been taken to reduce that threat – with the consequence, however, of merely slowing the *rate of increase* of the problem, not eliminating it. In other parts of the world, little or nothing is being done.

Meanwhile, the industry has stated its need and its intention to increase car sales by 3 percent per annum. As if to confirm the anarchy of capitalism, despite the existence of global excess capacity of 20–25 percent the biggest auto-makers continue to build new and expand old plants at home and abroad – most recently in China, where the air is already lethal.[12]

Enough; except to add the latest news. The industry – with the United States in the lead – has recently discovered a new way to increase sales and, even more, profits: increased advertising and production of the so-called "sports utility vehicles" ("SUVs"): 1) they are far bigger than the smaller cars that began to be common in the 1970s (mostly from Japan), 2) their gasoline mileage is half or less than what recently was typical and they have increased air pollution, 3) they take up more space, are harder to park and to see around, 4) the death rate in their accidents, afflicting mostly those in the smaller cars, is higher, 5) they cost about twice as much and, oh yes, 6) SUVs produce 3–4 times the unit profit. By 1999, they accounted for *half* the sales of new private motor vehicles in the United States.[13]

GLOBAL ECONOMY III: TODAY, THE WORLD

Earlier noted was James Cypher's analysis of globalization's tendencies toward the deepening and strengthening of global production, trade, and finance, and their always tighter integration over the globe. Accompanying that has been the displacement of skilled labor in the rich countries and the steady impoverishment of large numbers of people elsewhere, and the "homogenization of dysfunctional movements such as crises." All this has been acquiesced in by all governments and most people. What has allowed that extraordinary mixture of developments?

It is not enough to answer: big business, surplus capital, weak labor. Crucial they have been, especially in that the major agents fueling these patently undesirable developments have done so with substantial ease within democratic societies; but it raises another question begging for an answer. What were the magic wands that permitted private trading, production, and financial interests to persuade their governments and most people to accept policies clearly beneficial to a few and just as clearly damaging to many? The answer lies in the overlapping worlds of ideology, media, and politics; and at its center lies the nature of contemporary democracy – as distinct both from its beginnings and its idealized form.

Democracy: the challenge met

In its modern form, democracy (when defined as universal adult suffrage) is generally viewed as having been implemented first in the Constitution and Bill of Rights of the United States. The "adult suffrage" was not of course universal until the abolition of slavery (and, in the South, the Civil Rights struggles), and until women won the vote *after* World War I. Democracy had taken firm root and, at one rate or another, was functioning in all the industrialized countries as the twentieth century opened. Since that time, it has come to be understood that industrial capitalism cannot function adequately *without* political democracy. Also understood, if usually left unsaid, is the need to guide that democracy from above. As democracy took hold and functioned, it was accompanied everywhere – in Europe, in North America and, as we have seen, in Japan – by workers' efforts to escape the brutal exploitation imposed on them by that industrial capitalism. Almost everywhere, those efforts moved in one way or another toward the achievement also of economic and social democracy – moved toward a brick wall, however, for full democracy is incompatible with capitalism's innate inequalities of income, wealth, and power, and of prestige and status.

But along with industrialization and political democracy, two other major developments that would "take the risk out of democracy" had also emerged in the early twentieth century – the growing predominance of the giant corporation and the "invention" of public relations. As with political democracy itself, both developments were accomplished first in the United States;[14] and public relations intertwined with politics and big business from the start.

That start was in World War I. Before the U.S. entered the war, Woodrow Wilson, running for President in 1916, had campaigned to keep his country *out* of the war. But immediately after being elected he hired Edward L. Bernays to assist in his efforts to persuade the people that the United States *should* enter the war. Thus public relations *began* with "political advertising," not with ads for commodities.[15]

In the 1920s the curtain rose on the first modern advertising campaign – on billboards, in periodicals, and then on radio. It was orchestrated by that same Bernays, this time for the American Tobacco Company: "Reach for a Lucky instead of a Sweet." His techniques of persuasion – "propaganda" would be a better term – swiftly spread for use in other commodities, and thence back into politics, in the same years that saw the rise of radio.[16] Those techniques came to be much refined in the 1930s, both for business and politics, and were carried to their special heights in Germany.

After World War II the heights of persuasion found new variations in the United States, with its combination of consumerism, the Cold War and McCarthyism, and the special powers of television.[17] Advertising and public relations became indistinguishable in their techniques; with the latter much assisted by the employment of social psychologists, and the transformation of all programs into entertainment. A further look at the intertwining within that combination is in order.

Orwell revisited

In *1984* (written in 1948), George Orwell sought to show the dangers of a "Big Brother" presiding over a totalitarian society, for which there were of course historical counterparts in the totalitarian states of the twentieth century. The rulers of all those societies used force and violence at least as much as persuasion to gain and hold power. Within none of the major capitalist powers are force and violence used, nor does any have its "Big Brother."[18] He is no longer needed.

It is many years since Orwell wrote his novel, and not many will remember his work. Even fewer will know of a much earlier warning of what was on its way, and that had arrived by the 1980s: Aldous Huxley's *Brave New World* (1931). Neil Postman, cited earlier, captures the difference between Orwell and Huxley:

> in Huxley's vision, no Big Brother is required to deprive people of their autonomy, maturity, and history. As he saw it, people will come to love their oppression, to adore the technologies that undo their capacity to think. ... What afflicted people in *Brave New World* was not that they were laughing instead of thinking, but that they did not know what they were laughing about and why they had stopped thinking.[19]

The members of our trio, consumerism, et al., came into existence essentially independently; the strength all ultimately achieved was due to the ways in which they nourished each other. Consumerism obviously depended on a strongly expanding economy and rising real wages; the connections between that and the Cold War's military expenditures are undoubted – as is the related support of the Cold War by virtually all of organized labor. But that support went well beyond organized labor and – especially considering the strong wish for peace after 1945 – must be seen as having been created.

The Brave New World created after World War II had many elements, vital among which was McCarthyism. Those who did not live through the 1950s must now find its realities hard to comprehend; yet those realities permeated the entire society, and in the process accomplished a process of thought control that any "Big Brother" would have envied: whether in unions, in the entertainment world, in politics, or in education, McCarthyism had the same "cleansing" effect.

Communists were a small minority of those "cleaned out," and not only because there were only a few thousand members of the Communist Party in the United States at any time.[20] Within a decade or so of McCarthy anyone who was critical of the Cold War, of capitalism, of racism even, whether that criticism emerged in class-rooms, books, films, political speeches, union meetings, was put under pressure, or fired, or even jailed (as with the "Hollywood Ten"). More important and considerably more numerous were those who learned to keep quiet, even *not* to read certain books;[21] and, most important of all are those many millions of students who since have had a seriously amputated education and who will never know what they missed.

In the United States, much more than elsewhere of course, social and cultural discourse was simply flattened. And those who came to be the "leaders" in all areas – including, of course, economics – would surely not have become so without the enforced silence of many deserving others. Now, in the United States, that natural progress of such repression is in place: "liberal" has joined "Communist" beyond the political Pale.

Whatever else that has meant, it has eased the birth of the newest member of the ancient family of political corruption, the openly bought and paid for corrupt politicians of the past 20 years or so.

The political economy of corruption

Corruption now prevails in the United States and it has two dimensions. First, and well known, is the domination of election campaigns by raw money; second, at least equally important, is the less publicized importance of lobbying. The latter deserves a moment's attention.

The old expression has it that "money talks"; it always has, but in U.S. politics it now yells and stamps its feet – and allows business to get its way. In Washington, D.C., a decade ago, there were 90,000 registered lobbyists; and who knows how many more at work on local and state governments.[22] When, at the abrupt end of an honorable career, Senator Dale Bumpers (Dem., Ark.) retired, he did so with this comment:

> My office was next to the Finance Committee's hearing room. It would be instructive for all Americans to see that room and the hallways – cynically called Gucci Gulch – packed with lobbyists when the committee considers tax bills. Money does indeed buy access, and that is when access pays off.[23]

"Access" signifies more than getting an audience with legislators; it has come to mean participation in writing legislation – for tax cuts and "pork barrel" expenditures, among many other items; against environmental rules and adequate health care, also among many other items.

But let's move on to the third major area of damage associated with the dogma of growth. We have seen that in the years after World War II there was a growing consensus for an expanding world economy; as part of that, there was a specific set of programs concerned with "the economic development of backward areas."[24]

Always present among those programs, at least from the 1960s on, was the argument that the hopes of the non-industrial societies lay in their economic growth, which in turn depended upon their developing "export-based economies." On which they now depend. And how have they fared?

FROM BAD TO WORSE

For some of the developing countries that have pursued the "export-based strategy" there have been much-publicized success stories, most prominently the "Asian tigers" – Hong Kong, Singapore, South Korea, Taiwan; and the success is attributed to their having adopted the ways and means of the "free market." To the degree that there has been success, it has not been owed to free marketry; and recently the success has been muddied for them and, as well, many other developing economies – whether Mexico and Brazil in Latin America, Thailand, India or China in Asia, or any country in Africa, to say nothing of Russia.

To the degree that the record of the "Tigers" after the 1970s *can* be seen as a success story, it has depended upon either a closely controlled economy, special ties with a major power, or both; for all four, success was sidetracked by the Asian crisis.

Hong Kong

Long an outpost of the British Empire, Hong Kong specialized in cheap labor and dreadful living conditions for most of its inhabitants, whilst becoming a financial center for the British (along with Singapore). As such it was cosseted by the British until its return to China; now it is used and sheltered by the Chinese. Notwithstanding, in the Asian crisis of 1997–98, Hong Kong was unable to withstand the pressures, and its market took a nose-dive. Its "free market" reputation was earned from inside a cocoon, in both cases.[25]

Singapore

Its per capita income exceeds that of Great Britain, but far from being a free market economy its classification is "state-capitalist," like China – except that (*inter alia*) China is vast and Singapore a city-state. That unique characteristic among "economies" very much eased its way, along with two other features – when it regained its independence from

Britain, it was after a long period in which its social and physical structure had been constructed, so to speak, by the British, and its subsequent development was and remains very tightly controlled – as regards human rights and those of labor.

South Korea

The industrialization of South Korea cannot be separated from its decades-long relationship with the United States, in effect its master from the outbreak of the Korean War until the late 1970s. That relationship had three key features of relevance here: 1) Korea's economy developed importantly under the supervision of the United States, 2) that supervision allowed, some would say encouraged, the emergence of a fascist society and, among other things, cheap labor, and 3) the "presence" of the United States also meant much in the way of subsidization and protection.

When, in the 1980s, democratic efforts began to stir and then to succeed, that led to unions and higher wages and pressure for South Korea, too, to "outsource and downsize," as it too, came into the gun sights of the TNCs and global finance.

Taiwan

Controlled by the Japanese for about half a century (when it was known as Formosa), it came into being as Taiwan as the defeated nationalist forces led by Chiang Kai-shek fled there. In doing so – given the Cold War and the Korean War – they immediately came under the economic and military umbrella of the United States. As with Japan and Korea (and Italy and Germany, et al.) this meant much in the way of military expenditures and subsidization, along with an effective guarantee against national economic hardship. In such a context, Taiwan was able to utilize the long-standing business abilities of the Chinese to maximum economic effect; even to the point of being the only Asian nation to keep from being badly battered by the crisis of 1997–98.

Summarizing, the "Tigers" may be seen as successful economies in the same way that tigers in a zoo may be seen as sustaining themselves. As for the rest of the developing economies, they were at best cats, with many unhealthy throughout the postwar years and others, in the old expression, sick as a dog. Whether for the tigers or the others, in all cases, the non-leading economies have bowed to the command of being export-based, and thus to join the race of economic growth – and to take the consequences.

The eleventh commandment: export!

The World Bank reports that since 1987, East Asian and Pacific economies have increased the ratio of their exports to their GDPs from an average of 25 percent to (1997) just under 35 percent; the numbers for Latin American and Caribbean countries are about 14 percent over the whole period. That is a high figure; even in the exporting heydays of the 1950s–60s the United States was exporting only about 5–7 percent of its GDP.[26]

More important than the numbers is that the United States was controlling its own economy, in the small and in the large. For almost all the developing countries, and to the extent that their resources and factories are indebted to, and/or owned and directed by outsiders – an extent which is almost always substantial – both their natural resources and their labor forces are directly or indirectly under the control of foreigners, and exploited with little or no consideration of their harmful effects.

The developing economies of today were the colonized and imperialized societies of the past; now, under neocolonialism, they are once more under the thumb of policies that recall too well their pasts – whether as the "white man's burden" of the British, *la mission civilisatrice* of the French, or the "manifest destiny" of the United States, but with one big difference. Now the thumb is not so much another nation as it is a complex of giant agricultural, industrial, and financial companies.[27]

That thumb pressed down very hard during and after the Asian crisis of 1997–98, and not only in Asia. It is now coming to be accepted that the policies of intervention by the IMF were made for the benefit of the creditors outside the afflicted countries and to the great damage of those inside.[28] And, as a broad range of companies in those same afflicted countries find the values of their assets plunging and their debts unpayable, they also find themselves at the mercy of roving "vulture capitalists" (whose more polite designation is "distressed securities investors").[29]

*

A reasonable response to the foregoing critique of economic growth might well assert (in a variation on Madrick's earlier cited view) that even if all of what has been said is valid, wouldn't we be worse off with low or no growth? Other things being equal, to use the economists' favorite phrase, that is probably (not certainly) so. To which it may added that if by "we" one includes the peoples of the non-rich countries, that position in favor of growth would seem to gain considerable strength. After all, if (say) 4 billion people are already without even the bare necessities of life ...? Stuck on a desert island, the same position would recommend that the strong eat the weak – and then, a battle amongst the strong, and starvation for the big winner.

In the real world, and even though hundreds of millions are *already* starving to death, the underlying threat is not starvation but ecological disaster for all – preceded and accompanied by what has been seen here as an ongoing set of social disasters, including in the richest countries. And the real tragedy is that there are not only possible but also very desirable alternatives. To those we now turn – in a form something like an annotated and very general outline.[30]

NEEDS AND POSSIBILITIES AND NEW DIRECTIONS

In the Prologue it was argued that economics should seek to answer the questions "What do we need to know about the economy?" and "What can and must we do to have the economy better serve human, social, and environmental needs?"

In the entire literature of mainstream economic theory you will never find the word "need" – it's almost as though it were a "dirty word." In any case, it is not a simple matter to answer those and related questions, such as *whose* needs and *which* needs. And in the exploration and the resolution of such questions it would be found that still other questions are thus raised, among them: What structures of production, consumption and foreign trade, and of income, wealth and power are required to allow the economy to meet those needs? What is it in *existing* structures that prevents those needs from being met and in what ways must such structures be modified? By and for whom? In what patterns and at what pace? It's a puzzle.

So has been and is much else. But it is useful to recall the sensible (if also penetrating) observation of Marx:

> mankind always sets itself only such tasks as it can solve; since, looking at the matter more closely, it will always be found that the task itself arises only when the material conditions for its solution already exist or are at least in the process of formation.[31]

It is essential to add that the mere existence of the "material conditions" for the solution of any given "task" assures only the *possibility* of their appropriate use. What is required to transform possibility into reality is human action. To implement the kinds of changes to be noted now, the human action needed is that of a political movement substantial enough to surmount the great power of those who have constructed the status quo out of those same possibilities. With that in mind, we now seek to answer the questions put forth above. We begin with some remarks about the necessary political movement.

Politics and understanding

The starting-point for the required politics is to understand that, as Lincoln put it when facing the Civil War, "We must disenthrall ourselves." In our day, there is much to *unlearn* as we undertake to *learn* what we do not know. One part of the "unlearning" has to do with what now constitutes economic wisdom, to know why it is that what is now taken as "common sense" – about free markets, world trade – is not *good* sense. To unlearn means to take thought, to be skeptical, and to find ways of learning anew.

At its very best, this book can be seen as a few steps in that direction, constituted mostly of history. It is also necessary to learn "what we need to know about the economy" – that is to study the economy. Fortunately, for that purpose, the new introductory text by Hugh Stretton (noted earlier) is just right. It is written clearly and, when appropriate, in a conversational tone; although it would be good if it were taught in university classes, it is "accessible" to any serious person (and those who might form their own "classes"). It is usefully suggestive as regards history, and usually adequately comprehensive as regards theory and policy and social values and data – and so on. And, among other virtues, its perspective is global.

Stretton's book has only one seeming defect: it requires the reader to work – to persevere, to think, to reflect. But there is no way for a serious person to think usefully and with confidence about appropriate economic policies without an adequate grasp of how economies work. As they say in the world of sports, "no pain, no gain."

But even if we and multitudes of others were to know *everything* the world would stay the same, unless our values and our understanding are put into political practice. That requires more than understanding the economy, and more than understanding as such.

It surely requires knowing how the economy works. Just as surely, it requires understanding what we have been socialized to perceive – and what *not* to perceive – and how to evaluate it; understanding, that is, the ways we have learned to think and to feel and to "learn" and *what* to think about – 'or not to think or feel about. It is this that Antonio Gramsci understood so well, and concerning which he wrote in his *Prison Notebooks*.

We referred earlier to his notion of "the ideological hegemony of the bourgeoisie" (using such language because his words had to go through a prison censor). He meant that our entire vision of what constitutes the good society – in its economic, political, social, and cultural dimensions has of course been *learned*; that it is not enough, say, to be against environmental deterioration, or for higher wages and public health care. If we are to make substantial and enduring progress toward a better society, we must combat what we have been taught with our own *social* vision, not just fragments of such a vision. To repeat: we must think anew.

If that sounds like too much, consider how *existing* realities, to say nothing of those on their way, "sound." The peoples of the rich societies have allowed all traditions, good and bad, to be shunted aside, to be replaced by rampant commercialism and heedlessness; and the peoples of the poorer societies have had their lives pulled out from under them by the voracious giant companies, and acquiesced in by their often corrupted rulers. It is *worth* a lot of work to reverse those processes; especially if one understands what can be put in their place.

What will be put forth now will be objected to not only by today's conservatives and many liberals, but also by most radicals: too much for the former, too little for the latter. In answer, the themes of this book say that it is what we live with now that is too much, and that what might constitute "enough" is out of reach without a popular political movement that simply does not now exist. But such a movement can grow and strengthen if there is a meaningful program for which it might be expected to work. What follows is a skeletal version of the nature of such a program.

Structural changes

The structures noted earlier – of production, consumption, and foreign trade, and of income, wealth, and power – are such that a change in one leads to and/or requires changes in the others. Thus, a change in the structure of production away from private and toward public transportation, or away from privately to publicly financed health care, automatically affects the structure of consumption and production and also depends upon there having been a change in the structure of decision-making – that is, of power.

Even more clearly, the desirable changes in the structure of *world* production, trade, and consumption (and so on) require not just changes in the structures of global power, but would also bring with them changes in income and wealth in both the rich and the poorer countries. In addition, in that we are referring to qualitative changes, it is important to note that the emphasis on quantitative change (that is, growth) both could and would have to be altered. But that leads to another and important point.

Clearly the peoples of the poorer countries need a considerable increase in at least their levels of consumption of necessaries. Such changes are likely to be accompanied by sustainable economic growth in those countries, as an accompaniment of sustainable economic *development.*

That need not depend on high rates of growth in the already industrialized countries. It is entirely possible (as well as desirable) that the richer countries, in changing the structures we have been discussing, could do so along with a new version of well-being based on qualitative/structural changes, including a reduction of the now severe inequalities of income and wealth. It may be asserted that the lessening of those inequalities also lessens the need for rapid growth – a difference that may be seen as something like that between a falcon and a humming bird.

In essence, what we can and must work for if life is to become better for all and cease to become worse for most are changes in the structures of production that yield less in the way of frivolous goods and services and more in the way of those needed – and enjoyable – by all, in the realms of goods and services, within and between all nations. That could not happen without a substantial lessening of national and global inequalities of income, wealth and power; as it happened it would constitute a movement toward economic, political and social democracy.

All this can be put another way. Most of the people of all the rich countries now work very hard – even harder – to pay for things that add little to the meaning or satisfaction of their lives. In doing so they contribute to a socioeconomic global system that has already ruined countless lives and that threatens to end all life. Many thoughtful and decent people think there is no reasonable alternative. But there is. And if not now, when?

Notes

PROLOGUE

1. Braudel puts the highest figure at 915 million, an estimate only, but the best to be had. The first reliable census was done in England in 1801 (whose population was then 21 million); China had taken censuses much earlier, but based on fiscal collections as they were – which varied in rubric from time to time – they are not fully reliable. For the rest of the world the numbers are based on indirect evidence. All this is discussed in the opening chapter of Fernand Braudel's marvelous historical study, *The Structures of Everyday Life: The Limits of the Possible*, Vol. I (of three) of *Civilization and Capitalism: 15th–18th Century*, where a table of estimates is found (1979, 42).

2. An idea of contemporary magnitudes for those at the bottom is provided by UNICEF in its annual reports. In 1986, for example, they reported that every *day* 40,000 children were dying from malnutrition-related causes: that's 14.6 million a year. Then, in 1993, UNICEF noted that 700 million suffered from famine, and 2 billion were malnourished. As for famine, probably the most profound student of that matter in recent years has been Amartya Sen (awarded the Nobel Prize for Economics in 1998). In his book *Poverty and Famine: An Essay on Entitlement and Deprivation* (1981), he pointed out that "Starvation is the characteristic of some people not *having* enough food to eat. It is not the characteristic of there not *being* enough food to eat" (p. 1) despite the enduring Malthusian view, from the eighteenth century to the present per capita food production has *always* outstripped population growth – a fact recognized by the scientific community. That the powerful societies continue on paths that worsen rather than eliminate such tragedies cannot be called a crime, if crime requires conscious deliberation. But it can be condemned, especially from the seats of learning. Professor Sen is one of a very small handful of economists who has responded appropriately.

3. For an extensive and thoroughly supported examination of this increasingly vital matter, see the excellent book of Robert W. McChesney, *Rich Media, Poor Democracy: Communication Politics in Dubious Times* (1999), to which further reference will be made in Part II.

4. Or, it may be added, of all life: as in psychology, biology, the arts. It would surprise any mainstream economist who might read this that I am in agreement with one of their greats, Joseph A. Schumpeter – also

an eminent conservative, which I am not. Thus, in his worthy *History of Economic Analysis*, he stated: "if starting my work in economics afresh, I were told that I could study only one [field in economics] but could have my choice, it would be economic history that I should choose" (1954, 12). In his day, and through the 1950s, there were three "field" (subject area) requirements: economic theory, economic history, and the history of economic thought (plus two or three others of one's own choice). Now? Theory still, plus some math; the two historical fields are rarely required, and rarely offered.

5. Keynes put it this way: "The ideas of economists and political philosophers, both when they are right and when they are wrong, are more powerful than is commonly understood ... Practical men, who believe themselves to be quite exempt from any intellectual influences, are usually the slaves of some defunct economist. Madmen in authority, who hear voices in the air, are distilling their frenzy from some academic scribbler of a few years back" (1936, 383). My critique of most economists' ideas takes Keynes seriously; it also differs with him, in arguing that those ideas usually come to be accepted because they serve an existing or evolving structure of power.

6. Their respective titles, *Birth*, *Maturation*, and *Death Throes*, will recall for some readers the unforgettable verse from T.S. Eliot's "Sweeney Agonistes, Fragment of an Agon" (1937):

> Birth, copulation, and death.
> That's all the facts when you come to brass tacks.
> Birth, copulation, and death.
> I've been born, and once is enough.

But Eliot's gloom will here be replaced by outrage and hope.

7. That the groundwork had been laid for industrial capitalism in Britain by 1800 is thoroughly established in the classic study of Paul Mantoux, *The Industrial Revolution in the Eighteenth Century* (1906). Mantoux is concerned solely with Britain, and with the achievement of all the conditions for capitalism (social, political, economic) in all sectors (agriculture, industry, finance, trade). His treatment of the "enclosures" of that century is especially vivid, as it was especially vital. It was that "modernization" of agriculture that pushed hundreds of thousands of families off the land, instantly creating a powerless labor force for the nascent factory system. By the time the first (then "modern") factory arrived in 1815, there existed a completely demoralized pool of desperate men, women, and children. See his Chapter 3. In our Chapter 1, more will be said of that and related matters, and Oliver Goldsmith's famous and epic poem concerning the process – "The Deserted Village" – will find its voice.

8. "External" here refers to war with one or a group of other nations. The only conceivable contenders would have been France, Spain, or Austria,

singly or – quite unlikely – in combination. In the event, of course, France and Britain fought long and hard, at great cost to France and great benefit to Britain in both the short and the long term.

9. And as will be discussed at some length in the appropriate chapters, the depth and penetration and consequences of these developments in the societies thus penetrated have multiplied and increased logarithmically.

10. Subsequently, Marx would refer to "the bourgeoisie" as capitalists; and it was he who began the use of that term. He also coined the phrase "industrial revolution" and gave its name to "classical political economy." The *Communist Manifesto* is found in many editions. My pagination is from the very valuable compendium, *Karl Marx and Friedrich Engels: Selected Works in One Volume* (1967c). A few extra words seem appropriate here: Marx began to study economic processes only in 1843, urged to do so by Engels. His first relevant writings were those of what came to be called *The Economic and Philosophic Manuscripts* (1844), available in many forms including *Early Writings* (1963) which I use here. In that work, under the influence (as well as very critical) of Hegel, Marx developed his theory of "alienation." In modernized and broadened terms, that theory remains of great importance for understanding contemporary socio-psychological phenomena. See Bertell Ollman, *Alienation: Marx's Conception of Man in Capitalist Society* (1976). And an additional note: Marx's works remain the indispensable basis for understanding capitalism – necessary, but not, of course, sufficient. It is important to add that in these days of triumphant capitalism and free marketry the strident claim that "Marxism is dead" usually refers to what many (but that Marx would not) call "Marxist societies" (the ex-USSR, for example). Marx, though working for socialism, never described what might be "his" society: indeed he is famous for having derided programmatic utterings, classifying them as "kitchen recipes for the future." When, however, the Marxism that is "dead" is meant to refer to his analysis of capitalism, that would be seen as laughable by very few except U.S. economists, who seldom if ever have read Marx – or for that matter, Smith or Keynes. That intellectually scandalous ignorance inspired the late and great U.S. historian, William Appleman Williams, himself far from being a Marxist, to devote a book to it: *The Great Evasion* (1964).

11. Here I am borrowing from my *U.S. Capitalist Development Since 1776* (1993), Chapter 2: "Capitalism."

12. See the discussion of Marxian analysis in Chapter 2.

13. And a few pages later (652) Marx goes on to say in a famous passage, "Accumulate, accumulate! That is Moses and the prophets! ... Accumulation for accumulation's sake, production for production's sake: by this formula classical economy expressed the historical mission of the

bourgeoisie, and did not for a single instant deceive itself over the birth-throes of its wealth." And in note 3 to that statement he quotes J.C. Sismondi (1773–1842), Swiss historian and economist, who, in comparing Imperial Rome with then emerging capitalism, observed that "The Roman proletarian lived almost entirely at the expense of society ... It can almost be said that modern society lives at the expense of the proletarians, on what it keeps out of the remuneration of labour."

14.   The phrase is Richard Du Boff's, in his *Accumulation and Power* (1989). Its meaning will be examined in Part II.

15.   Why that has been so is usually explained by mainstream economists by the fact that the United States is the most "businesslike" of all nations. That reverses the causality: the question should be, how has it been possible for *that* to be so? That is also discussed in my *U.S. Capitalist Development*, under the heading "Capitalist Paradise, U.S.A.," pp. 73ff.

16.   In Chapter 2 the components of what may be seen as the "theory of profits" of mainstream economics will be examined. They are two: 1) that which sees profits as a reward for undertaking risk and uncertainty in investment; 2) that which sees profits as equaling "the marginal productivity of capital." Both arguments are ideological, both lack a basis in fact or logic, though both can be persuasive if not thought about seriously. For example: it sounds reasonable that high risks should be rewarded with high returns (at least some of the time). The problem is that the firms that have the greatest market power and thus the least risk are also those that have the highest profits, most of the time; and those who suffer the greatest risks – small businesses, including small farmers – have considerably lower incomes, and it is they, not big business, that fill the bankruptcy rolls. To say nothing here of workers in general and low-wage workers in particular – especially those who risk not only income but their lives in dangerous jobs (for example, coal miners).

17.   Smith called it "the mercantile system." The literature on the period is immense (and fascinating). Perhaps two studies most efficiently capture the period: G.N. Clark, *The Seventeenth Century* (1950), and the massive and authoritative two-volume work of Eli Heckscher, *Mercantilism* (1950). Heckscher has also written the (much shorter) entry of that name in the always useful *Encylopedia of the Social Sciences*. Although – or perhaps because – it was published in the 1930s, it remains useful on a broad variety of topics and individuals (for example, Adam Smith, Karl Marx, et al.). See the entry "Colonialism," by M.M. Knight, an expert on that subject – and one of the three to whom I have dedicated this book. I took his graduate seminars in economic history for two years and continued to do so after I had joined the faculty (at Berkeley) for another three. In that capacity I was one of 30 or so faculty members with a desk (for student consultations) in what was called "the bullpen." More than once one of the visitors to that room was M.M.'s more

famous brother, F.H., who may be seen as a main founder of the Chicago School of Economics (Milton Friedman's theoretical birthplace) – and the author of the key book for neoclassical economics that presumes to explain profits: *Risk, Uncertainty, and Profit* (1926).

18. That phrase was given its clear meaning in the seventeenth century by Colbert (first minister of King Louis XIV):

> Commerce is carried on by 20,000 vessels and that number cannot be increased. Each nation strives to have its fair share and to get ahead of the others. The Dutch now fight this war [of trade] with 15,000 to 16,000 vessels, the English with 3,000 to 4,000 and the French with 500 to 600. The last two countries can improve their commerce only by increasing the number of their vessels and can increase the number only by paring away from the 15,000 to 16,000 Dutch ships ... It must be added that trade causes perpetual strife both in time of war and in time of peace between all the nations of Europe to decide which of them shall have the major share. (Heckscher, vol. 2, 26–7)

19. And it is interesting to note that both Ricardo and Keynes were successful financial speculators: Ricardo for himself, Keynes for Cambridge University (as its Bursar) as well as for himself.

20. Which, taken together, bring about a redistribution of real (as distinct from money) income downwards – a restructuring of purchasing power – and a restructuring of production and services.

21. The first has been termed "investment for further investment," in which one has to envisage industries keeping each other alive by engaging in mutual expansion – with some secondary effects on consumption (because of maintained jobs): a kind of merry-go-round of perpetual motion – not the first time vain hopes of that sort have been raised. The second means, increased exports, is of course unrealistic unless there are also offsetting imports – a global process that eventually runs into the same set of obstacles as one nation's expansion – unless, as has happened since 1950, there is global expansion. When government is allowed to enter this process, the possibility of changing structures – of production, consumption, and income distribution, and world trade – also changes the rules of the game. As indeed it has, in the past half-century. The largest structural change in the United States has been the adaptation called "military Keynesianism" – which Keynes noted as possible and derided as absurd. Of which, and related matters, more in Part II. Suffice it to note here that the capitalist class, most especially in the United States, has for the most part done whatever it could to weaken or prevent the very kinds of steps that might allow for the expansion they seek and need.

22. Others will have their own favorite recommendations in this vital and complex area; mine is the comprehensive study of Karl Mannheim, *Ideology and Utopia: An Introduction to the Sociology of Knowledge*

(1936). Louis Wirth, who wrote the Preface for the work, joins me in my deep respect for this book: "He [Mannheim] has succeeded in showing that ideologies, i.e., those complexes of ideas which direct activity toward the maintenance of the existing order ... do not merely deflect thought from the object of observation, but also serve to fix attention upon aspects of the situation which otherwise would be obscured or pass unnoticed" (xxiii). And a tidbit from Mannheim himself: "The concept ideology reflects ... that ruling groups can in their thinking become so intensively interest-bound to a situation that they are simply no longer able to see certain facts which would undermine their sense of domination" (36).

23. The professor was Robert A. Brady, one of those to whom I have dedicated this book. His teaching was by no means confined to the classroom. A discussion of his writings and connected matters are set out in my article, "Against Decadence: The Work of Robert A. Brady (1901–63)" (1994).

24. R.H. Tawney, *Religion and the Rise of Capitalism* (1926, 35). Tawney is seen by many, myself included, as perhaps the clearest thinker on the social philosophy of capitalism. Others of his works will be cited as we proceed.

25. Probably the best analysis of how and why economists have developed their theories is that of Leo Rogin (1893–1947), *The Meaning and Validity of Economic Theory* (1956) (one of those to whom this book is dedicated). But see also the several methodological essays by Thorstein Veblen (1857–1929) in his *Place of Science* (1919). A book of broader scope with the same qualities, is that of C. Wright Mills, *The Sociological Imagination* (1967). This is also a good time to mention two fine books of essays in this area: 1) E.K. Hunt and Jesse Schwartz (eds), *A Critique of Economic Theory* (1972), and 2) Robin Blackburn (ed.), *Ideology in Social Science: Readings in Critical Social Theory* (1973).

26. When I was an economics major and then took a Ph.D. in it at U.C. Berkeley (in 1950), I studied neoclassical economics thoroughly and well (well enough to be graded as "distinguished" in that field). But at no time did it ever strike me that the *economics* had anything to do with the *economy*. I do not overstate when I say that I learned not one thing about the economy in studying standard theory; what I did learn about the economy was through studying economic history, the *evolution* of economic theories, industrial organization, the functioning of "labor markets," and the like. *Why* did I learn the theory so well? Because it was the only way one could become an economist (and teach against it).

27. That generalization, and many others related to it will be supported in later chapters, when the focus is on the rise of the giant corporation and the beginnings of consumerism in the United States in the 1920s

and the spread and deepening of consumerism – the process of *making* wants unlimited – after World War II. Suffice it to point out here that what is touted as the most precious and scarcest resource of all – petroleum – began to receive that treatment in the 1920s and it recurs regularly. The reality is that what frightens oil producers most is their inability to keep abundant supplies restricted to market tightness in order to keep prices up. *Of course* one day oil resources will be exhausted. (Quite apart from which, we should use less and less oil for environmental reasons.) But ever since the 1920s – and except for periods of war – oil supplies have always risen more rapidly than always rapidly increasing demand. As for wants: the advertising sector's main function is to stimulate people to want and buy things they do not need; and it does its job all too well. Of which, more later.

CHAPTER 1

1. Later discussions of Germany will elaborate on that point. Formally, Germany did not become a nation until the 1860s.
2. The most comprehensive (and readable) study of background and consequences of this turning-point in British history is that of Christopher Hill, *Reformation to Industrial Revolution* (1967).
3. The process began in the late medieval period, very slowly. It accelerated in the sixteenth century, and even more so in the seventeenth. Those developments provided an important socioeconomic basis for the onslaught of the eighteenth century. See the classic study of R.H. Tawney, *The Agrarian Problem in the Sixteenth Century* (1912).
4. See Mantoux (1928), Chapter III, "The Redistribution of the Land." See also Karl Polanyi, *The Great Transformation* (1944), Chapter 3, "Habitation Versus Improvement," and J.L. and Barbara Hammond, *The Village Labourer*, Vol. I, Chapters I–IV (1911), which treat of the "village" before, during, and after enclosures. As most will know, the pattern of holdings in England (as well as much of Western Europe) established in the medieval era was such that an area of, say, 1,000 acres would typically have many criss-crossed and scattered holdings cultivated by many families. Enclosing was a process that set a fence or wall around the whole area, to be controlled by one owner (whose ownership was achieved by foul as well as fair means). This meant a more efficient agriculture; just as much, it meant a devastated agrarian population, as famously decried in the Irish poet Oliver Goldsmith's epic poem "The Deserted Village" (1770), and that begins

    > Ill fares the land, to hastening ills a prey,
    > Where wealth accumulates, and men decay.

    The most comprehensive, as well as excellent discussion of this period (and subsequently) is E.J. Hobsbawm, *Industry and Empire*, Vol. II (1750 to the Present Day) of the series *The Making of Modern English Society* (1968). See his Chapter 5 for the transformation of agriculture.

5. "State" is capitalized throughout this book, to distinguish it from the U.S. usage, where it almost always refers to the separate "states"; and, it may be added, to signify that something different from – and more than – "government" is the reference. Much of what follows immediately was argued in my monograph, *The State, Power and the Industrial Revolution: 1750–1914* (1971).

6. W.O. Henderson, *The State and the Industrial Revolution in Prussia, 1740–1870* (1958, xiii–xiv).

7. I perhaps need to add that the sources of mountains of other information concerning working conditions are the government inquiries of the first half of the nineteenth century. They were the basis of much of what Marx and Engels wrote concerning "the condition of the working class."

8. It is telling that the life-span of the average working person in Britain in this period was very low, and that it *fell* between 1821 and 1851: in 1821, 37 per cent died by age 19, and 70 per cent by age 44; in 1851, 46 per cent by age 19, 78 per cent by age 44. By comparison, Smith and Malthus died in their late sixties, Bentham in his eighties. Thus what might be meant by the usual "subsistence" wage of that period has a somewhat euphemistic definition. See Hobsbawm (1968, 277).

9. As will be discussed at greater length in Chapters 5 and the Epilogue the working conditions – and the disappearance of work – in today's "developing" societies are considerably worse than those of the industrial revolution in Britain, viewed either quantitatively or qualitatively. Thus, as regards India, seen as one of the major successes of the global economy, "While the total number of unemployed persons registered with employment exchanges stood at 336 million in 1993, the number of employed persons in the same year according to the Planning Commission stood at only 307.6 million. ..." (Meszaros, 1998). It is a simple and uncontestable fact that the *average* Indian of the seventeenth century was better off in that distant past than now, by any meaningful measure.

10. "Working" never less than 10 and often as much as 14 hours a day, 6 or 7 days a week, with perhaps 30 minutes off during that day – to eat what was of course a meager "lunch."

11. J.L. and Barbara Hammond, *The Rise of Modern Industry* (1926, 196). This is an excellent survey and analysis of the background, nature, and consequences of that "rise," as may be seen in the three Parts of the book: "Commerce Before the Industrial Revolution," "The English Industrial Revolution," and "The Social Consequences."

12. In her magnificent study *The Wool Trade in English Medieval History* Eileen Power suggests wool's dominance of both the economic and the

political life of England:

> The very Lord Chancellor plumped himself down on a woolsack, and the kingdom might have set on its great seal the motto which a wealthy wool merchant engraved on the windows of his new house: "I praise God and ever shall / It is the sheep hath paid for all" (1941, 17).

(It was spelled as "shepe" on the woolsack.)

13.   And, as a foretaste of what was to come, what may be seen as the Indian economy began to descend from what was its most stable and prosperous era to its ultimate complete subjection as a colony of Britain. What this meant, among many other things (such as over-population), was that as the cotton industry took the place of wool as prime mover for Britain, India as a colony (in the nineteenth century) was forced to follow the principles of "free trade," which meant the utter destruction of Indian industry and the impoverishment of the agriculture joined to it and requiring that balance for its vitality.

14.   Including the vast space within what became the United States: between 1830 and 1900, more than 200,000 miles of track had been laid there.

15.   For a penetrating overview, see Chapter 4 of Hobsbawm (1968). A broader survey for Britain is that of G.D.H. Cole and Raymond Postgate, *The Common People* (1956). But it is well worth the time it takes to take a closer look, at the cotton industry and its main center, Manchester: see Friedrich Engels, *The Condition of the Working Class in 1844* (1950). In that his family owned one of the mills, Engels knew whereof he spoke. But it is also useful to consult works of fiction – Dickens, of course, but also lesser-known writers such as Alexander Cordell's *Rape of the Fair Country* (1960).

16.   The deservedly classic study is E.P. Thompson, *The Making of the English Working Class* (1968), worth reading not only for what it tells of the destructive processes of burgeoning capitalism but for the thought it provokes about attitudes and behavior at least some of which might usefully be brought back to life.

17.   E.J. Hobsbawm, *Labouring Men: Studies in the History of Labour* (1964, 88). This quote is taken from the chapter entitled "The British Standard of Living, 1789–1850," a detailed argument against a growing group of economic historians in the 1950s who had seen fit to argue against the prevailing view that the industrial revolution had meant hard – and harder – times for most people; among them W.H. Henderson, quoted earlier in this chapter. These historians had come to be called, at least by Hobsbawm, "cheerful," as contrasted with those like himself and, among many others, those such as Malthus, Ricardo, Mill, and Marx who had been able to see much of what had happened at first hand. Those are termed "pessimists." It is worth noting, though not an important issue, that in this book I have gone along with the customary dating of the industrial revolution as

1750–1850. Hobsbawm puts it as 1790–1850. And a further note: in the United States in the 1950s there was born a group of economists/economic historians who termed themselves "cliometricians," seeing themselves as adapting statistical *theory* (statistics had long been used) and its abstractions to the understanding of history ("Clio" being the Muse of history). What they were also – or only – doing was to transform historical understanding to a tool usable for neoclassical economics and, in doing so, also to "show" not only the presumed manner in which the magic of markets has always worked well when allowed to work but also, in the process, to render fuzzy or obliterate its obvious damages to human beings. The first work in that process was concerned with U.S. slavery, which emerges as rational and, surprisingly, not as bad a system as you thought it was. Subsequently the reasoning and the procedures of that work – which won for its author the Nobel Prize in Economics – was shown to be at best dubious with respect to both fact and procedures. And the critics were themselves "cliometricians."

18. That French term supporting economic individualism (along with *laissez-passer*, freedom of movement), did not become applicable to the French economy until late in the nineteenth century – if then. Thus, when de Gaulle presided over France after World War II, he was often described as the Colbert of this century.

19. And that Smith, it may be believed, would have rejected. See the useful treatment of Smith's concerns with the population as a whole provided by Eli Ginzberg in his *The House of Adam Smith* (1964).

20. As will be discussed shortly (and briefly) when Bentham's utilitarianism is discussed, this sees us as rational creatures, where "rational" does not signify "reasoning" or "reasonable" but as perpetual *calculators* of what gives us "pleasure and pain," or, in the later versions of neoclassical economists, "utility and disutility." That such a view of human beings makes inexplicable most – and much of the most important – human behavior (exemplified, for example, in parenting, sports, creative activities, much of work, almost all warfare, etc.) has escaped the perspective of economists. Also interesting is that their absurd encapsulation of human nature leaves most economists' own behavior unexplained insofar as it is prompted by, for example, status. Or one or another of the "seven deadly sins" shortly to be noted.

21. You may have forgotten what they are: anger, envy, gluttony, avarice, lust, pride, and sloth. Does a day pass when most of us do not respond to at least one of those – whether with guilt, pain, pleasure, or shame? The advertising world would disappear without them; and where then would consumerism and contemporary capitalism be?

22. By Milton Friedman, as we shall see, and his numerous followers: where "everything" means not just TVs, cars, cornflakes, apples, and the like, but health, education, the roads, parks, the military, prisons

... *every*thing.

23. To which it must be added that unfettered competition when it did occur had more baneful than beneficial effects. One has to study only the experience of the most competitive experiences of the U.S. economy – in bituminous coal mining, cotton textiles, and the staple agriculture of the Plains to see the destructive consequences for labor and natural resources, on the one hand, and small business enterprise (and farmers), on the other. Of which, more later.

24. Although it must be added that the impact of the free market for land was quite evident in the ongoing enclosure movement as Smith was writing his *Wealth of Nations*; and Goldsmith's "Deserted Village" which was published in 1770, six years before *Wealth*. But it is "natural" for those who push hard along new lines to overlook the negative possibilities that might well accompany their realized hopes. Be warned.

25. The nature and functions of "big business" will be given due attention in later chapters; suffice it to note here that *Fortune* magazine has for many years devoted some of its spring issues to (what began as) "The Fortune 500" – the 500 largest U.S. industrial corporations. The data provide comprise sales, assets, employees, etc. An example from the issue of April 29, 1996: The Top 500 U.S. corporations had revenues of $4.7 *trillion*, assets of $10.5 trillion, profits of $244 billion, and collected *two-thirds* of all business profits. The Top 10 alone took 30 percent of that; roughly 15 million other businesses divided up the rest. We shall look once more at some later data, in Part II.

26. See George Gilder, and his influential book *Wealth and Poverty* (1981). Gilder is a highly paid and a most appreciated speaker for the business world, and why not? He portrays the latter as engaged in "conscious philanthropy" – referring to their business, not to their charitable contributions – and compares their activities with the potlatch feasts of certain tribes in the Northwest United States who vie with each other in generous giving. He also warns against taking Adam Smith too seriously.

27. "Presumably" because, as will soon be noted, Say's "theory" – in a phrase, "supply creates its own demand" – served to deny the *need* for macroeconomic theory. That need became tragically evident in the 1930s, when Keynes rose to the occasion.

28. "Barely" because that portion of his major work that deals with reality is not only minimal but by no means central to what became his legacy – abstract theory and the principles of free trade.

29. As Hobsbawm (1968, 82) points out, "the concentration and consolidation of farms ... made what passed for a 'small farm' in the England of 1830 as big as a small estate on the continent." When the U.S. government began (in 1928) to interfere with farm prices (and, later, output), the policies were sold in the name of preserving the small family farm. With the passage of more than half a century, the slogan remains the same, although the small family farm has virtually disappeared, and

now a good 90 percent of the government payments go to less than 10 per cent of the "farmers" – which are, in fact, corporations.

30. In Chapter 2 it will be shown that Marx, using the same reasoning as Ricardo, showed that what was true for agricultural "rents" applied equally to industrial profits: one reason why economists jettisoned the reasoning of classical political economy and its emphasis on production, and developed a theory whose center was "the market," with its emphasis on "demand."

31. An example of such "validity" is found in Newton's "law of gravity." Newton assumed away the friction that every falling body generates, and that slows its fall. When appropriate adjustments are made, the "law" still holds. The same does *not* hold when the assumptions of microeconomic and trade theory are "relaxed," as will be discussed in later chapters.

32. The U.S. experience of the early nineteenth century was used as a model for Prussian-led German industrialization in the second quarter of the century, guided to an important extent by Friedrich List and his *National System of Political Economy* (1841). List had studied the relevant institutions while in the United States (prior to 1832, when he returned to Germany). See the discussion of List in Eric Roll, *A History of Economic Thought* (1946, 244–8).

33. Most importantly in seeking to substitute a "utility theory of value" for the labor theory of Smith (and Ricardo). His effort, along with Bentham's, constituted a major part of the foundation for neoclassical economics. But it may be said that what Say put forth in that regard was likely to have come forth in any case. The same cannot be said for his famous "law of markets," now to be commented upon. For an excellent discussion of this and all other developments in the evolution of economic theory, see E.K. Hunt, *History of Economic Thought: A Critical Perspective* (1979). I have found Hunt's presentations among the most useful.

34. For those wishing to check out the "business cycles" before World War I, and the contrasting descent into "depression" of later years "ahead of time," see William Ashworth, *A Short History of the World Economy Since 1850* (1987) and the exellent and succinct analysis by W. Arthur Lewis, *Economic Survey: 1919–1939* (1949). It may be useful to add here that toward the end of the nineteenth century there was what was called a "great depression." Its nature and causes and gravity were quite substantially different from *the* Great Depression, of the 1930s – most significantly in that large-scale unemployment was not a main characteristic of the earlier instance.

35. There was a "first" in 1798 and then a "second" much revised and two-volume edition in 1803. The long quote soon to follow is taken from the latter, noted here and in the bibliography as 1970.

36. In that this has become an obsolete word – not least because it was

biblical in origin and, at that time, in usage – it is germane to define it here. From *Webster's International Dictionary* (1909 edition): "Reprobate: Condemned or rejected by God's decree. Hence morally abandoned; depraved. ..." That is, specific remedies for diseases afflicting the poor should be seen as immoral. Thus spake Parson Malthus.

37. It is pertinent to repeat here the quotation earlier (in the *Prologue*) from Amartya Sen: "Starvation is the characteristic of some people not *having* enough food to eat. It is not the characteristic of there *being* not enough food to eat." Decades ago, the Brazilian biologist Josué de Castro provided a study showing that the relationship between population growth and poverty is such that the main means to slow population growth is to reduce poverty: *The Geography of Hunger* (1952). Demographers are in general agreement. Quite apart from that, a question to ponder – and which will be touched upon more than once in more ways than one in what follows, is this: Why is it that there is enough food to feed all, but that hundreds of millions are at or over the edge of starvation?

38. For an excellent journalistic treatment of this matter, see John Hess, "Malthus Then and Now," *The Nation*, April 18, 1987.

39. In this respect, the treatment of cholera in England is revealing. With industrialization, cities grew rapidly, and festered in their crowdedness and filth. Open sewers were common, making not only for foul air, but the ongoing threat (and reality) of cholera – and of an epidemic. The realization slowly grew that an epidemic would be unlikely to select its victims by class. A Public Health Act was passed in 1848 but, like the U.S. Clean Water Act (and similar legislation), was gradually worn away to dangerous meaninglessness. It was not until the 1870s (really, for all of England, until 1888) that Great Britain took lastingly effective action. Better late than never, for them; for us, and *our* planetary "cholera," let us hope that those in power will realize that they are on the same planet as the rest of us. Hope, and, on the assumption that "they" will not wake up in time, organize to make it be. See G.D. Cole (1952, 62 ff.) for the relevant discussion of England.

40. What has become the classic study of the calculated inadequacies of such programs is Frances Fox Piven and Richard Cloward, *Regulating the Poor: The Functions of Public Welfare* (1971). The "steps" that could be taken to end poverty will be discussed in our concluding chapter.

41. The M.I.T. sociologist Herbert J. Gans has developed the notion of "the uses of poverty." See his *The War against the Poor: The Underclass and Antipoverty Policy* (1995).

42. It is also of some interest that Bentham's notions of "utility," put forth in 1780 had by 1801 undergone a significant change: by then he had begun to anticipate Malthus in believing that in the absence of "Keynesian" governmental intervention on the macro level, there was a high probability of economic trouble; and he had also come to advocate

governmental actions effectively to redistribute income downwards (also "Keynesian") – on the plausible grounds that *overall* (as distinct from individual) "utility" would thus be maximized: an additional dollar of spending power means much more to a poor than to a rich person – the notion of "diminishing marginal utility" that so much delights economists, if not in this particular application. See Bentham in Stark (1954, 3: 124, 411). As will be seen shortly, John Stuart Mill, who began as a staunch advocate of *"laissez-faire"* capitalism had begun to express deep reservations in the later editions of his *Principles of Political Economy*, and was seen by most as having taken a socialist stance by the time of his death. See also J.B. Brebner, "Laissez-faire and State Intervention in Nineteenth Century Britain" (1948).

43. "Tautologically," as used here means "by definition." So, if we say that a woman, though she may suffer greatly (even, in some cases, die) in childbirth, and go on to say that the pain is really pleasure, because it is immersed in a larger anticipation of pleasure, we are speaking tautologically. And there are some pains – orgasmic being only one of such – much sought after. Such pains can of course be classified as pleasurable (even though for others they happen only involuntarily), but once that word game begins we are in the land of tautology, departing rapidly from anything approaching scientific reasoning. We shall see that this is one of the games played most frequently in contemporary economics.

44. *Principles of Political Economy and Taxation* (1921, 1).

45. The edition used here is that of 1872, and will be cited accordingly.

46. *Principles of Political Economy* (1872, 128). The "difficulties great or small" of "communism" (in his day, meaning "socialism") referred to economic processes; as the author of *On Liberty*, he would of course have seen modern totalitarianism as something going well beyond a "great difficulty." By the time Mill died (1873), it is widely believed that his long and deep relationship with the socialist Harriet Taylor, along with his persisting concerns about capitalism, had made a socialist of him.

47. In 1999, there emerged a discussion of the size and convolutions of Einstein's brain: larger and more convoluted than yours and mine. All right. Somewhat earlier, the deservedly eminent U.S. biologist, Stephen Jay Gould, had commented that he was "somehow less interested in the weight and convolutions of Einstein's brain than in the near certainty that people of equal talent have lived and died in cotton fields and sweatshops." Einstein would probably have agreed. To assume anything else, for those who see themselves as "naturally superior," is arrogance; for those who see themselves as "naturally inferior" it is a form of obedience.

48. Its leaders may be seen as Beatrice and Sydney Webb, and their "Fabian socialism." "Fabian" because gradualist rather than revolutionary, after the Roman general Fabius, a strategist known for playing the patient

game. There was also a Marxian socialist group (led by Keir Hardie), but to this day (and quite apart from the non-socialist leadership of today's Labour Party) British socialist politics have been considerably less Marxian than on the Continent.

49.   And what he did, in that preparation for Volume I of *Capital* (1867) was quite simply phenomenal. The general belief is that *Capital* had three volumes – as in some sense is true. But *Capital* also had, as Marx saw it, a fourth volume. That in turn, in fact not one but also three volumes, was entitled *Theories of Surplus Value*. It was completed *before* and as a basis for Volume I and may be seen as Marx's "history of economic thought." Essentially, it is the ideas of those who preceded him in time, with the focus on classical political economy. Nor should the *Grundrisse* (1859) be forgotten. It was a collection of "notes" (making a book of close to 1,000 pages) also in preparation for *Capital*, not made available until after World War II. Marx's first works in the 1840s have been published in many versions (the one used here is *Karl Marx: Early Writings* [1963], also published as *Economic and Philosophic Manuscripts*). It was concerned most interestingly with "alienation," now to be discussed in the text. And then (with Engels, of course) the *Communist Manifesto* (1848). On alienation, see the excellent study of Bertell Ollman, *Alienation* (1971). It is worth adding, in these days of economics "scholarship" when mathematical diddling by economists all too often passes as knowledge, that Marx saw many years of arduous work for *Capital* as "only one of four brochures [!]." That "one" was to be concerned with "political economy"; the other three with "sociology, the State, and foreign trade." Not only was he unable to get to the other three "brochures," but he finished only the first volume of *Capital*; the other two were put together for publication by Engels and Karl Kautsky after Marx's death in 1883.

50.   For a thorough examination of the long history of and distinctions between the words "labor" and "work" see Hannah Arendt, *The Human Condition* (1958), Chapters III, IV and VI. She shows that in all the major European languages there is a sharp difference made between the two words: thus, going back to Latin there is *laborare/facere*, in French, *travailler/ouvrier*, in German, *arbeiten/ werken*; although it must be added that in our time, as language tends to lose its edges, the distinction is being lost. Arendt, incidentally, to emphasize the difference, goes back to the ancient world, where "... the institution of slavery was defended and justified [... for] to labor meant to be enslaved by necessity ..." (p. 85).

51.   *Karl Marx: Early Writings* (1963, 124–5) (emphasis in original). He goes on to add that "eating, drinking and procreating are of course also genuine human functions," with some "buts." The latter connect with Marx's vision of human needs and possibilities (expressed in the *Grundrisse*), which have a soaring quality to them – and to which we

shall return in a later chapter.

52. Whose "real title" was *Manifesto of the Communist Party*. Here, as in all his early writings, Marx uses "bourgeoisie" to signify what he later came to call "the capitalist class." Here we follow the early usage (and also British spelling).

53. The *Manifesto* has been published in countless editions. This quotation is taken from its appearance in perhaps the single most useful compilation of Marxian literature: *Karl Marx and Friedrich Engels: Selected Works* (1968, 34–63).

CHAPTER 2

1. Witt Bowden, Michael Karpovitch, and Abbott Payson Usher, *An Economic History of Europe since 1750* (1937, 406). This comprehensive study (of almost 1,000 pages, hereafter cited as BKU) has deservedly become a classic. It was reprinted in 1970, without modification. After its initial publication, and even more since its reprinting, there have been numerous specialized and general works covering the same ground; BKU's main generalizations and conclusions need very little in the way of retouching.

2. Quite apart the "kindness" of both world wars to the U.S. economy – and our much lesser casualties – there is the difficult to calculate but nonetheless vital difference in the political differences of both wars as between the United States and the other industrial powers: in all cases the latter (excepting Japan after World War I) began to undergo significant to severe stresses in their sociopolitical processes. And quite the opposite was true in the United States. Putting that together with the economic blessings of war allows one to understand why – excepting for our Civil War – Americans took what might be seen as a "sporting" view of war: until Vietnam.

3. Hobsbawm (1968, 91), where he refers to "the pressure of the increasingly vast accumulation of capital for profitable investment" in Britain by 1830, which went most critically into the construction of railways (soon to be discussed).

4. The most compact as well as thorough history is C.R. Boxer, *The Dutch Seaborne Empire* (1965). Their way had been partially cleared by the Spanish, concerning which see J.H. Parry, *The Spanish Seaborne Empire* (1966).

5. BKU, 75–6.

6. Perhaps it should be interjected here that when Adam Smith assailed the mercantile system (including the Navigation Acts and colonies among his targets) he acknowledged that before the late eighteenth century that system of governmental–private "intrusions" into markets was not only useful but essential. His point was that they had done their work; they should be retired.

7. Or, we may add here, industrial in the modern sense. It was the main

thesis of Nef's *Industry and Government in France and England, 1540–1640* (cited earlier) that although industry in France in that century (in textiles and metallurgy, for example) was more advanced than that in England, the products were aimed at what today would be called the luxury market; that is, industry was specialized to produce elegant and expensive products (such as lace and intricate iron grillwork) for the Crown and its circle not, as would be true for Britain, a relatively mass market.

8. What came to be true for both the Dutch and the British also came to be the tendency for the U.S. economy as the twentieth century ended. But the many similarities between the three nations in these respects stand in sharp contrast with many crucial differences (to be noted in due time).

9. Called "turnpikes," and requiring a fee for passage.

10. Maurice Dobb, *Political Economy and Capitalism* (1937, 239–40). What Dobb could not anticipate was the next stage of domination of the weak by the powerful nations that took hold after World War II, with its own (self-given) classifications, shifting over time: the development of "backward nations," of "underdeveloped nations," of "developing nations" and, most recently, of "emerging economies." As will be seen in Part II, each successive stage, like that from colonialism to imperialism, has entailed a deeper, broader, and more irreversible set of "penetrations."

11. The importance of what imperialism meant to the imperialized will be examined later and separately. A most useful study of the nature and meanings of imperialism, which summarizes and compares the most relevant theoretical approaches, is Tom Kemp, *Theories of Imperialism* (1967).

12. The period 1815–1914 was called "the century of peace." Like so many such characterizations, their source and their definitions are found in the halls of power. There tended to be peace among and between the major powers in that century – on the Continent itself, that is (and excepting the Franco-Prussian War); elsewhere, there was what seemed very much to be war, between a major power and a lesser society – in the Middle East, in Latin America, in Africa, in Asia ... Similarly, in the next chapter it will be seen that the 1920s in the United States were dubbed "the Prosperity Decade." So it was, for opinion-makers; it was not for the bottom three-quarters of the population, whose incomes were stagnant or falling in the 1920s.

13. By the end of the nineteenth century there were, of course, other industrial nations: France and Italy, the Scandinavians and the Low Countries. But none of them had the strength of the quartet examined in this chapter; and for analytical purposes, all may be seen as variations to one degree or another on the latter.

14. A fact noted by many economic historians, but rarely by other economists.

15. Forty percent of which was for railroads. The pound was then equal to five dollars, nor should it be necessary to say that in today's terms £4 billion would translate to a great multiple of that amount. As would the £200 million sterling of net annual income from those investments. Britain's total exports at this time were roughly £500 million, its imports about £600 million – thus allowing an import surplus and the basis for continuing investment abroad. See Peter Mathias, *The First Industrial Nation: The Economic History of Britain, 1700–1914* (1987, 229), as well as for closely related data.

16. That is, far from paying for the imports with the gains from foreign investment, we are always going further into debt. That phenomenon, as will be detailed at the appropriate time, came into being as Reagan became President: we began the 1980s as the largest *creditor* in the world; we ended it as what we remain now, *history's* largest debtor, owing over $2 trillion to others (principally the Japanese). That huge debt in 1998 alone was increased by over $200 billion and in 1999 increased at annual rate of $300 billion.

17. For most of the years after Independence, the southern states were able to control Congress and the Supreme Court; and of the twelve presidents from 1789 through 1850, eight were from the South.

18. Thorstein Veblen, *Absentee Ownership and Business Enterprise in Recent Times* (1923, 171n).

19. As will be seen when Germany is discussed, their developmental policies were inspired by the works of Friedrich List, and what was called "Smithianismus" was from the beginning never more than a dissenting voice. List developed his ideas after a lengthy period of studying Hamiltonian policies in the United States. Included among the policies put into place in the new United States were the foundation of a national bank, national responsibility for state debts, creation of a national debt, protection of new industries by a wall of tariffs, and a national excise tax: sounds pretty un-American, but it worked. France never deviated from the mercantilist principles of Colbert. Indeed, in the long administration of Charles de Gaulle after World War II, economic policy was undisguisedly based upon a regeneration of such principles. Italy's development was an explicit modification of Germany's, as was Japan's – except that Japan was "more German than Germany." And still is.

20. As for the war against fascism: In all three of the leading fascist nations against whom we fought, U.S. relationships had been amiable through many years of fascism, and it may be noted that we did not enter the war that began in 1939 until we were ourselves bombed in 1941. At least as revealing is that postwar political resolutions alone leave one to wonder if it was the expansionist aims of the fascist nations or the fact of their being fascist that drew our fire; for in all three, in one variation or another, leading personnel in business, in the military, in the judiciary, even in the political hierarchy, found

their way back into the seats of their previous power – presumably to help capitalism back to its feet while, at the same time, finding reliable anti-communists to watch the store. And then there is what should be a national embarrassment that those in the United States who raised the cry against fascism in Italy, Germany, and Japan (or who fought in Spain as volunteers against its fascist coup from 1936 through 1938) were rewarded by the classification "premature anti-fascist" in their FBI and military files – which has its rough counterpart in what happened in the South after the Civil War.

21. The "external" or "overseas" path, that is. The processes of what we called "westward expansion" which transformed the 13 colonies of 1776 into the 48 states of 1912 were what all but Americans saw as "imperialist." As William Appleman Williams has pointed out in his writings – most pointedly in *The Roots of the Modern American Empire* (1969a) – the United States was simultaneously "anti-colonial" (most especially for lands in the western hemisphere) at the same time that it was assembling the most fruitful of all empires – an instance of policies occurring in that "moral penumbra" noted by Veblen, where "the right hand does not know what the left hand is doing." Or chooses not to.

22. "Need" was in some sense relevant to our participation in the Spanish–American–Cuban–Philippine war. U.S. farmers, faced with protective tariffs against agricultural imports in Europe and rising productivity in their own lands, were anxious to find additional and relatively secure markets. As Williams puts it, "The farmers who were quasi-colonials in the domestic economy thus became anti-colonial imperialists in foreign affairs ..." (1969a, 25). Thus did "westward expansion" become "manifest destiny."

23. Nor were the characteristics of the immigrant population trivial: the highest percentage of them were over 15 years old upon arrival, their childhood needs having been "subsidized" in their native countries; and they were ready, willing, and able to work hard, at low pay, and consider themselves lucky. At least for a while. The history is most conveniently told in Oscar Handlin, *The Uprooted* (1951).

24. It is relevant to add that many basic inventions, most especially in the critical machine tool industry, were made in France, or elsewhere on the Continent. But "economics" allowed those inventions to become "innovations" only where the appropriate economy existed: the United States. As will be seen, Germany soon joined and, in with its own technological advances, went beyond the United States.

25. Thus, the United States did not have a meaningful chemical industry until after World War I – and then the industry (largely to the advantage of Du Pont) was forcibly "imported" from Germany as the U.S. part of the spoils of war provided by the Treaty of Versailles.

26. Veblen's argument along these lines, along with much else that is valuable, was put forth in his *Imperial Germany and the Industrial*

Revolution (1915).

27. Mass production also characterized German industrialization. But, as will be seen, it came later and was an outcome of its unique ability and need to combine science and technology and early forms of economic planning – the *sine qua non* of its economic development.

28. There have been several "merger movements" subsequently, that of the 1920s, again in the 1930s and 1960s and, the most rapacious of all, that which spurted in the 1980s and was seen as the ultimate in spectacular-ity. Until the 1990s, most especially its last two years, whether in the United States or elsewhere. The data for mergers and acquisitions ("M&As") between the two world wars will be examined in the next chapter, and those since World War II in Part II. For the M&As of the period here under discussion there is an abundant literature, combining facts with analysis and comment. Among the most readable and most passionate is Matthew Josephson's *The Robber Barons* (1934). For a relatively dispassionate discussion and analysis and much in the way of factual detail, see Chapters 3 and 4 of Richard B. Du Boff's excellent *Accumulation and Power: An Economic History of the United States* (1989).

29. Thorstein Veblen, *Absentee Ownership and Business Enterprise in Recent Times* (1923, 78). Veblen first noted this "decay" in his *The Theory of Business Enterprise* (1904).

30. The rivalry is real. GM and Ford really do seek to take customers from each other, as do USS (now called USX, for it is now a transnational and multi-industry company) and Bethlehem Steel. I know about the latter because I once worked for USS, and the attitudes toward Bethlehem (I worked in the office of a vice-president) were not much different from the attitudes of the United States toward the Soviet Union during the Cold War. But there was *never* a hot war between the two companies – their prices were always in agreement down to three decimal points, etc. – and thank goodness there was not between the two countries. And it may be added that just as the Cold War severely damaged both countries, so does oligopolistic rivalry damage the economy.

31. To one degree or another, something like that or fascism or sheer chaos took hold in Europe in the interwar period. In the years since World War II the U.S. model ("oligopoly," a few dominant giants in each industry) has become universal, with variations to be noted in the country discussions to follow.

32. In this respect it was very much the model for the European Common Market, created in 1956 (a critical comment concerning which and the *Zollverein* I put forth in my "Some Second Thoughts on the Common Market," *Yale Review* (1964).

33. List's thinking, as noted earlier, was influenced by the Hamiltonian projects he had observed in his visit to the new United States. But his analysis and program were considerably more coherent and self-

conscious than Hamilton's; they have rightly been called "economics for the backward areas." He was Germany's Adam Smith *cum* Ricardo – but, because Britain was first, he saw the need to turn the free market and free trade arguments inside out.

34. "Feudalistic" up to a point: they were producing for the market. With some resemblances to the planters of the U.S. South, they believed in free trade (they were exporters of foodstuffs and importers of other goods) – again, up to a point. That point was reached in the 1870s, when worldwide depression and intense competition ensued (for the East Prussians, with the grains coming mostly from the United States, Argentina, and Russia; for the West, in capital goods). This led Otto von Bismarck (of East Prussia) to create the "Solidarity Bloc" in the Reichstag – a complex of compromises first *between* industry and agriculture, and then *within* industry and agriculture: "iron and rye" first, "rye and pigs, and iron and machinery" later. This yielded the protective Tariff of 1879, and later those of 1885 and 1887, the rates always rising and spreading. (And at the same time France, Italy, the United States and others were moving in the same direction.)

35. Robert A. Brady, in his succinct and penetrating explanation of German economic development, "The Economic Impact of Imperial Germany" (1943a, 109). The achievements, and even more, the disasters that Germany's socioeconomic and political tensions would lead to were earlier examined and explained in two books by Brady, his monumental *The Rationalization Movement in German Industry* (1933) and – in what was both the first and remains the most acute analysis in English of Nazism – *The Spirit and Structure of German Fascism* (1937). The latter work earned for Brady the honor of having to appear before the House Un-American Activities Committee in 1938; subsequently he was awarded the uniquely American classification of "prematurely anti-fascist."

36. The conscious design of the system had Berlin at its hub with the major lines moving outward as spokes toward all their borders – borders marked by enemies, but also within which lay the best of their limited resources. See, for example, W.O. Henderson, *The State and the Industrial Revolution in Prussia, 1740–1870* , his *The Zollverein* (1959), Thorstein Veblen, *Imperial Germany and the Industrial Revolution* (1915), and A.J.P. Taylor, *The Course of German History* (1961).

37. Brady (1943a, 116).

38. But when they became so, Germany either made substitute supplies via "science" (as with rubber) or took them by war (as with oil), as will be seen.

39. Whatever else the Soviet Union got wrong, when it came to their economic organization what they got right they borrowed from the Germans: most notably what they called "the combinat," their version of

the German "agglutination" soon to be examined.

40. There was a small group of German economists (largely in the Rhineland) that sought to apply "Smithianismus" in Germany in the mid-quarters of the nineteenth century. They are remembered almost entirely for their failure to have effect.

41. Brady, (1943a, 115–16).

42. As will be seen later, when socialist movements are discussed, Germany produced the strongest pre-World War I socialist movement. Among the several reasons for this, probably most important was that the German working class was simultaneously the most highly-skilled, the lowest-paid, and – of necessity, therefore – the most repressed of all the leading industrial nations. Which is saying a lot. Reference to all the foregoing generalizations will be made later in this chapter.

43. Germany had by then created what may be seen as the world's first "military-industrial complex," soon followed by Britain. It is interesting to note that the legislation funding the modernization of the British navy simultaneously took the first step in creating something like what is called public education in the United States. See Ross J.S. Hoffman, *Great Britain and the German Trade Rivalry, 1875–1914* (1933) for this and related matters. The children of the urban working class were granted the right to primary education in 1870; the education acts of the 1890s and that of 1902 allowed "the less privileged sectors of the new middle class to construct a new system of secondary education ... whose main object was to exclude from higher education the working class ... knowledge, especially scientific knowledge ... took second place in the new British educational system to the maintenance of a rigid division between the classes. In 1897 less than seven per cent of grammar school pupils came from the working class. The British therefore entered the twentieth century and the age of modern science and technology as a spectacularly ill-educated people" (Hobsbawm, 1968, 141). Most will know that the resulting "public school system" of Britain became what would be called "private schools" in the United States.

44. From *Saturday Review*, September 11, 1897, quoted in Hoffman (1933, 281).

45. It is relevant to note that the U.S. chemical giant Du Pont was much assisted in becoming so by that part of the peace settlement that required I.G. Farben (and other German firms) to share their "patents" with us.

46. It has been conservatively estimated that some 20 million Africans were enslaved for transportation to the western hemisphere, but that only 4 million arrived. Not all of those were destined for subjection in North America, of course. There is no knowing how many "Indians" lost their lives in the wars and displacements; but like the African-Americans who survived the historical process to this day, some unaccountably high percentage has in some real sense "lost its

life." Inexcusably, in this, the proudest democracy in the world. An excellent treatment of the slave trade from its beginnings is W. Schulte Nordholdt, *The People that Walk in Darkness* (1970), which also provides a comprehensive bibliography.

47. Among whom, most succinctly, Noam Chomsky, in his *Year 501: The Conquest Continues* (1993). The book came out in 1993, which, minus 501, of course, equals 1492. And Ronald Wright's *Stolen Continents* is of great value for understanding these processes in the entire Western Hemisphere.

48. Some of what follows is drawn from my essay "Technology and Social Change: Japan and the Soviet Union," in Douglas F. Dowd (ed.), *Thorstein Veblen: A Critical Reappraisal* (1958). The main themes of that analysis depend on Veblen's essay "The Opportunity for Japan," first published in 1915 and reprinted in Leon Ardzrooni (ed.), (Veblen's) *Essays in Our Changing Order* (1943), Brady's *Business as a System of Power* (1943b), and G.C. Allen, *A Short Economic History of Modern Japan, 1867–1937* (1946). A useful and more recent work, a collection of essays by a large number of authorities, broad in scope and time, is Jon Livingston, Joe Moore and Felicia Oldfather (eds.), *Imperial Japan: 1800–1945* (1973), to which reference will also be made.

49. Peter Duus, *The Rise of Modern Japan* (1976, 56, 61). In the several pages separating those two sentences Duus has described the rising waves of intrusion into Japan itself as the nineteenth century began and then, from mid-century on, the constant efforts of westerners to have their way in China, most vividly in the Opium Wars of Britain against China, 1839–42 – themselves worth a comment. Although conventional opinion holds that the Chinese are somehow prone to use and become addicted to opium, and have spread that habit to others, their historical connection to opium is quite the opposite: the British, with a growing unfavorable balance of trade with Asia, sought to even that balance by selling opium (grown in their Indian colonies) for gold in China; when the Chinese prohibited its importation, Amoy and Ningpo were blockaded, Canton bombarded, and finally the Chinese "fleet" was defeated by British gunboats. And the Treaty of Nanking gave Britain free sway in China (to be followed shortly by other westerners and the institution of "the open city" and history's first instance of "most favored nation" clauses). All this was noted with growing horror by the Japanese, already in the 1840s, as Duus notes.

50. Duus (1976, 61). It is not inconceivable that the Japanese had that occasion in mind (among other matters, of course) when they laid their plans to strike Pearl Harbor.

51. Japan was thus the location of the second application of the "most-favored nation" clause, granted first to the United States, then to England, Russia, Holland ... It is worth adding here that in a

representative view of the relevant history, the widely-read historian of Japan – Kenneth Scott Latourette – after noting that Americans were granted not just trading rights but the privilege of residing in Japanese "open ports" under U.S. – not Japanese jurisdiction – comments that all this was negotiated by our consul-general Townsend Harris "not by any display of force, but mainly by his sympathy, tact, and persistence." *The Development of Japan* (1918, 109).

52. E.H. Norman, *Japan's Emergence as a Modern State* (1940) reproduced as one of the essays in Jon Livingston, et al. (1973, 118).

53. Formally undone by the U.S. occupation of Japan after 1945, the *zaibatsu* came back to life – were allowed to come back to life – with a different name and in a different setting: they are today's *keiretsu*, and they are to Japan's power structure what the top industrial/financial corporations of the United States are to ours.

54. For a compact and lucid discussion of the *zaibatsu*, see William Lockwood, "The Great Combines," as contained in Jon Livingston, et al. (1973, 285–91).

55. In Ardzrooni (1934, 250–1).

56. Prescient in 1915; nowadays his viewpoint – that industrialization develops intrinsic pressures for democratization – has become commonplace. A recent confirmation of it has been in South Korea. It began to industrialize under a (U.S.-sponsored) fascist State after the Korean War; the industrialization that became substantial in the 1970s and strong by the 1980s also produced a democratic workers' movement, and today's relatively democratic polity – more than symbolically headed by Kim Dae Jung, elected President in 1998, but who was imprisoned during the fascist period.

57. "Opportunity for Japan," Ardzrooni (1934, 255 ff).

58. Those "other industrializing societies" are not without interest of course, for a variety of reasons. This is not the place to provide anything like a comprehensive reading list for such purposes; but we may suggest a few useful works to start with. Bowden, Karpovich and Usher has already been noted; it has the broadest coverage of any such book, and it also provides a sweeping bibliography. Two useful studies of global economic developments are William Ashworth, *A Short History of the International Economy, Since 1850* (noted earlier) and Herbert Feis, *Europe, the World's Banker, 1870–1914* (1930).

59. This is of course from "The Internationale," the song it was hoped would accompany global revolution. In full, it reads as follows:

Arise, ye prisoners of starvation,
Arise, ye wretched of the earth,
For justice thunders condemnation –
A better world's in birth.

When in 1968, Frantz Fanon wrote his *Wretched of the Earth* with its focus on the rising number of "prisoners of starvation" in the Third World, he was of course borrowing from this (anonymous) song.

60.   These words were uttered by Joe Hill, moments before he was executed by a firing squad in Utah, in 1915. He was a principal organizer for the Industrial Workers of the World ("Wobblies"), active among miners, agricultural workers, and merchant seamen.

61.   It was the Reports from these inquiries that provided Marx with his many pages of gruesome details in Vol. I of *Capital*.

62.   The British Labour Party was officially founded in 1906; not even in theory did it proclaim itself in favor of even moderate socialism until 1918. Robert Owen was himself a textile factory owner, but one whose reformist hopes and plans typify the "enlightened capitalist" at his best: he was the early inspiration for what became the British cooperative movement, for moderate socialist living arrangements (one of them in Harmony, Indiana!), and the like. There is a biographical sketch of Owen in recent editions of the *Encylopaedia Britannica* – written, you will be surprised to learn (but not as much I was surprised when asked to write it) by yours truly.

63.   Remember that the pre-industrial family typically was one in which all lived and worked together, usually combining agricultural with cottage industrial work of some sort, working in *relatively* pleasant surroundings to "the rhythm of the seasons" rather than to a factory clock under the harsh supervision of some Dickensian brute.

64.   In his first book, *The Theory of the Leisure Class* (1899).

65.   Concerning whom there is something close to total confusion, even among historians – concerning when and where such labor protests occurred, by whom, and why. Suffice it here to say that such activities began as early as 1675 (weavers in Spitalfield) and went on intermittently until the 1830s. Those who became best known were the so-called Luddites of 1811–13, in the textile mills, but such activities also took place by coal miners, in the silk industry, and elsewhere. As to their motives, Hobsbawm makes clear that they were diverse over time and place; but seldom if ever were they simply a matter of rage against new machinery – the notion that is most popular among most historians (and industrialists). If one main motive is to be singled out it is that in these early days of industrialization – workers' protective organizations, gilds, and protective laws having been done in – the workers had few means with which to struggle against capital: crippling or breaking costly machinery was in fact a shrewd means to a very necessary end. See Hobsbawm, *Labouring Men* (1964, 5–22).

66.   Just how hard may be understood by reading the fine book of J.L. and Barbara Hammond, *The Age of the Chartists, 1832–1854: A Study of Discontent* (1930). And, in addition to many of the essays in Hobsbawm's *Labouring Men*, see what is in effect the second volume of those studies, *Worlds of Labour: Further Studies in the History of Labour* (1984).

67. Hobsbawm (1968, 137). And when for the first time the British people were *en masse* examined medically with military service in mind – in 1917 – 10 percent were found to be totally unfit, over 40 percent with "marked disabilities" (48–9 percent in London), and only a third in satisfactory medical condition. Hobsbawm goes on to say that "By the standards of 1965, or even of 1939, the rise of the working-class standard to a modest human level had barely begun." As will be seen in Part II, the conditions now for many hundreds of millions in the "emerging economies" is worse than for their counterparts in the nineteenth century, and getting worse.

68. This desperately brief summary needs considerable amplification. It may be found in many works, one of the best of which is the classic of G.D.H. Cole, *A Short History of the British Working Class Movement* (1927): in three volumes; not quite short. And see also R.H. Tawney, *The British Labour Movement* (1925). Tawney is generally seen as having provided the analytical and ethical core for the post-World War II British "New Left."

69. For present purposes, Belgium and Holland and the Scandinavian countries will be left out of the discussion. The first two industrialized before France, Germany, and Italy, and more fully than France and Italy. Their labor and socialist movements were different from each other: those of Belgium closer to the French and those of Holland a mixture of Germany's and Britain's. The Scandinavians – Denmark, Norway, and Sweden – all moved toward what has become social democracy initially by way of their cooperative movements. The latter took hold in the nineteenth century in the face of difficult economic and social conditions both in agriculture and for seafarers. An excellent Swedish film of some years past, "The Emigrants," shows just how difficult those conditions were.

70. And another similarity: between the two world wars, all three became fascist – in name, as with Italy and Germany, or in fact as with Vichy France. The assertion concerning France will come not only as a surprise to most, but as quite wrong. See, however, Robert A. Brady, *Business as a System of Power*, Chapter IV, "France: Through Double Defeat to Vichy's 'New Order'" (1943). The evolution toward fascism, as will be seen in our next chapter, was a consequence of the greater intensity of class struggle in those three countries than in Britain (or as will be seen), in the United States. Japan became fascist in the same years, in a largely though not entirely different context.

71. And/or Holland, also relatively advanced, comfortable (not least because of its enduring empire), and democratic.

72. For many reasons. Paul Baran, along with Paul Sweezy the leading Marxist thinker in the United States in the 1940s through the 1960s, once said that it was the *world's* great tragedy that socialism had come first in Russia, the most backward and oppressive of all major nations,

rather than in the advanced societies.

73. Emphasis in original. From his essay "The Decline of American Radicalism in the Twentieth Century," in James Weinstein and David W. Eakins (eds.), *Toward a New America* (1970, 208). Kolko's point overlaps very much with Antonio Gramsci's notion of "bourgeois ideological hegemony," an analytical framework that helps greatly to explain the universal failure of socialist movements in *all* the industrial countries in this century (to be examined in the next chapter). Gramsci (1891–1937) was the founder of the Italian Communist Party in 1921. He was imprisoned in 1926 by the Fascists. After ten years in prison he became fatally ill, was released, and died shortly thereafter.

74. William Lockwood, "The Great Combines," in Jon Livingston, et al. (1973, 290). See also the useful essay in the same book by George O. Totten, III, "The Early Socialist Movement," pp. 298 ff. It was a movement stifled from the beginning, and which met a tragic end in 1910–11. Then a dozen socialists "were condemned to death for allegedly plotting against the life of the emperor. This trial now appears to have been a conscious frame-up by the Katsura government." (p. 304). Totten's essay in this book is an excerpt from his book *The Social Democratic Movement in Prewar Japan* (1966).

75. From his essay "The Socialist Economics of Karl Marx," one of his many essays collected in *The Place of Science in Modern Civilization* (1919, 453–4). For purposes of clarification, the German Social Democrats were Marxian socialists (if with many internal divisions); today's "social democrats" (throughout Europe) quite explicitly *do not* advocate socialism; rather, they propose one set of reforms or another to "tame" capitalism, whether that means to make it less inhumane or less dangerous.

76. It may be noted that of the "Big Four" of institutions and processes that serve as the unifying theme of this study, little explicit attention has been paid to nationalism; nor will there be. Nationalism infiltrates all social activities in this era, has done so, continues to do so. It is, to paraphrase Veblen, "the parchment on which the social process is written." The original of that phrase appeared in an essay of his which is by no means irrelevant to what is presently under discussion. It was entitled "The Economic Consequences of the Peace," and was a review of Keynes's book of the same title, concerned with the Versailles Treaty. Veblen's contention was that the "Great Powers are banded together for the suppression of Soviet Russia." "Of course," he adds, "this compact was not written into the text of the Treaty; it may rather be said to have been the parchment upon which the text was written." The essay is reproduced in Ardzrooni (1934); the quote is from p. 464. A lucid, compact, and comprehensive elucidation of the broad range of confusions surrounding that dangerous and complex question we call nationalism is E.J. Hobsbawm, *Nations and Nationalism Since 1780:*

Programme, Myth, Reality (1990).

77. Fortunately there is a fine book examining those differences, and clarifying the matter as well as might be: Tom Kemp, *Theories of Imperialism* (1967), from which much of what now follows has been drawn.

78. Whether or not as a matter of "imperialism," the combination of high unemployment, an unequal distribution of income, and dependence upon foreign investment and exports exactly fits the situation in Western Europe today, as it has now for many years. As will be seen in Part II, unemployment rates in the 15 countries of the European Union average over 10 percent. And the conventional "market" solution is for each country to become "more competitive" by the "downsizing and outsourcing" that is usually seen to have made or kept the U.S. economy so "successful" – the latter term finding its definition from on high, not least those in the economics profession. And as the reality behind the terms renders the distribution of income always more unequal.

79. It is not too much to say that Schumpeter was the only mainstream economist who took capitalism seriously, who did the work essential for understanding it – from any viewpoint – and managed to write of it in both historical and theoretical terms. Here it is pertinent to note that his *The Sociology of Imperialisms* (1919) (note the plural), a critical response to the Marxian position, when first published in the United States (as *Imperialism and Social Classes* [1951]), was edited and introduced by Paul Sweezy, then the leading Marxist in the United States. Sweezy has said of Schumpeter that he was the best professor he ever had (at Harvard); and Schumpeter has said that Sweezy was his best student.

80. My emphasis. The first part of the quotation is Kemp's summary of Schumpeter; the internal quote is from Schumpeter himself: Kemp (1967, 88), Schumpeter (1951, 7).

81. A horrendous story in itself, centering on Belgium's megalomaniacal King Leopold. Stimulated by the publicity surrounding the explorers Stanley and Livingstone, he founded the modern-sounding "International Association for Exploration and Civilization of Central Africa" in 1876; by 1885, the Congo was *his* – called the Congo Free State – held by *him*, not Belgium, as though a medieval fief, for over 20 years – throughout which slaughter and destruction were both massive and commonplace. Schumpeter's analysis of imperialism might well hold, were that conquest typical of the larger process. It was not; indeed, when Leopold's Congo became Belgium's Congo in 1908, it was principally because the capitalists of Belgium had simply had enough of his foul games. They cost too much to Belgium and yielded too little for its economy. See BKU (1937, 629–50) for this story and related matters. Joseph Conrad's *Heart of Darkness* is based on Leopold's Congo in 1890 (when the author himself was a sailor on the

river). It is as good a way as any, and better than most, for gaining a glimpse of the horrors of imperialism, past and present. Thus Kurtz, the legendary head of an upriver post: He had begun his career in that post with the exalted notion that "with the simple exercise of our will we can exert a power for good practically unbounded ..." As he dies, he exclaims "Exterminate the brutes!" The U.S. variation on that theme was found in Vietnam where, famously, a commander explained that he had "destroyed a village in order to save it."

82. A current egregious but not exceptional instance is that of the Sudan. It was organized by the British into the largest piece of geography in Africa, putting togther under one rule peoples of extraordinarily diverse ethnicity: about 600 groups speaking about 400 languages. Since 1956, the non-Muslim South has been in rebellion against the fiercely Muslim (and ruling) North. It is estimated that over 2 million "Sudanese" have died in that civil war, in a "State" created by the British a century ago, as a product of their conflicts with the French, Egyptians, and Italians related to strategic concerns centering on the Suez Canal and water supplies for Egypt. Such noble desires are the source of the tragedies of today's "free ex-colonies", not only in the Sudan, but in Angola, the Congo, et al., throughout Africa (as well as in the Middle East and Southeast Asia ad infinitum). An excellent idea of all this, centered on the Sudan, may be found in an essay by the superb journalist William Finnegan – "The Invisible War" – in New Yorker (February 25, 1999). The French are known to believe that "to understand all is to forgive all." Maybe that's true of personal deviance; with imperialism, enhanced understanding leads to enhanced outrage.

83. A few representative "interventions": 1873: Columbia, Bay of Panama (it was still Colombia's), five weeks spent protecting Americans during hostilities over possession of the State of Panama; and so it went many times until 1903, when the Marines landed to stay for good to support "the independence movement" from Colombian disturbances and, at the same time, to protect the construction of the Canal, which went on from 1904 to 1914. Beginning in 1904 and up through World War I and beyond, Nicaragua was receiving the same treatment (partially because there was a strong push for a Nicaraguan canal, also or instead); and then there was Honduras, and Guatemala, and ... in Central America, and in Mexico, to protect (or advance) U.S. interests. Plus much of the rest of the world – 1882, Egypt; 1888, Korea; 1889, Hawaii; 1893, Hawaii again (to promote a provisional government under the head of Dole pineapple); 1894–95, China; 1900, China again; 1904, Dominican Republic; 1904, Tangier, Morocco; 1912, Turkey; 1914, Mexico; 1914–17, Mexico still ... And so it went. Some of them (and others) were wars, some not: none declared. See William Appleman Williams, Empire as a Way of Life (1980, 73–6, 102–10).

84. Two excellent books covering not only the past five centuries but the considerably longer background, are those of the unjustly little-known L.S. Stavrianos, *Global Rift: The Third World Comes of Age* (1981) and *Lifelines From Our Past: A New World History* (1989, republished 1992). Among his many good qualities is that of brevity. Prof. Stavrianos teaches at the University of California, San Diego.

85. See BKU (1937, 644–9) for details and locations concerning these processes.

86. Keynes (1921, 6–7). I have noted earlier that Keynes was unusually well-informed for an economist; nor was he innocent concerning either imperialism or the functions of the State – having served at high levels for Britain as an economist both in India and in the Exchequer (our "Treasury Department"). He was known for his irony as well as his other talents; thus my question about his being sardonic.

87. Included in the exceptions were Canada, Switzerland and a few others; but the generalization holds.

88. They are of course those of Lewis Carroll's *Through the Looking-Glass*. He called that poem "Jabberwocky" (187, 134–6), a term which almost perfectly fits mainstream economics. Only "almost," for the sinister consequences of mainstream economics drown out the chuckles it might otherwise provide. His real name was Charles Lutwidge Dodgson (1832–98), and he was a math professor at Oxford. "Jabberwocky" was written as neoclassical economics was taking shape. It would be nice to learn that Professor Dodgson had its absurdities in mind as he wrote.

89. Which once led Marx to note that "If appearance and reality were identical, there would be no need for theory." *Capital*, Vol. III.

90. Alfred Marshall (1842–1924) published his masterwork, *Principles of Economics* in 1890. (It went into eight editions, the last of which was 1928.) What he synthesized and, in doing so, went beyond, was the work of a number of diverse theorists. They included, most importantly, Leon Walras (1834–1910), William Stanley Jevons (1835–82), and Carl Menger (1840–1921) – from France, England, and Austria, respectively. All three centered their arguments on the concept of "utility," and laid the basis for the basic role of "marginal utility" of neoclassical economics. Walras, with his theory of "general equilibrium," was the most abstract of all. Jevons was most relevant in establishing the links between exchange and capitalization; Menger's arguments on the "subjective basis" for value (in sharp contrast with the objectively-based labor theory of value), have endured to this day. Given those contributions, it may be said that Marshall was decisive in solidifying the place of those abstract theories for economic thought, most especially because – although he himself was an accomplished mathematician – he made the theory understandable, formulating it in accessible language (with all math relegated to appendices). The very best way in which to comprehend what all the foregoing (along with Smith, Ricardo, Marx and

Keynes) were up to is through a reading of Leo Rogin's *Meaning and Validity of Economic Theory*, cited earlier.

91. That theory was itself brushed away by the depression; only to come back in the Reagan years dressed as "supply-side economics," the rationale for cutting the taxes of the high brackets. Such "brackets" had no taxes in Say's day.

92. In his massive two-volume work, *Business Cycles* (1939).

93. The abstract and unreal theory of income distribution that has endured was, like Marshall's work, a synthesis of what had preceded. It was done by John Bates Clark (of the United States) in his *The Distribution of Wealth: a Theory of Wages, Interest and Profits* (1899/1965). Of some interest is that his son, J.M. Clark, researched and generalized from the realities of his time and, in doing so, effectively demolished the main elements of neoclassical theory in his *Studies in the Economics of Overhead Costs* (1923) – while, at the same time, providing a still useful (but not used) integration of micro and macro analysis. Also of interest is that Veblen was a student of John Bates Clark and, as well, a teacher of J.M. Clark. There's some kind of justice there.

94. In his *The Nature and Significance of Economic Science* (1932, 16; my emphasis).

95. Thus in a widely used introductory text by Joseph E. Stiglitz, *Principles of Microeconomics*, we find that economics is defined "as the science that studies how individuals, firms, governments, and other organiza- tions make choices, and how those choices determine how the resources of society are used ... in a situation where they are faced with *scarcity*." And a bit later: "The fact of *scarcity* ... implies that individuals and firms must make choices ..." (1993, 27, 29; my emphasis). It is worth remarking that Stiglitz, one of today's top economists, left his position at Stanford to become the chief economist of the World Bank. Since there, he has intermittently issued statements combining good sense and decency – including the supervision of a report in 1998 noted in the *NYT* (December 3, 1998) as follows: "IMF and U.S. Mishandled Asia Crisis, World Bank Charges" – despite, one may say, his view of economics. He now sees his main focus at the Bank as being on the needs of the poorest countries in the world, where not choice but survival is the problem: survival in the face of the destruction of their societies by businesses (and governments) that have made their choices for them. In January 2000, Stiglitz resigned from his World Bank post – or was pushed to leave.

96. The main theme of my *The Waste of Nations*, cited earlier.

97. It might be of interest to some that in the years 1894–98, as he was constructing his *Theory of the Leisure Class* (1899), Veblen wrote three articles in which women were the analytical focus, and capitalism and male domination its targets: "The Beginnings of Ownership," "The Barbarian Status of Women," and "The Economic Theory of Women's

Dress." There is much of importance and interest contained in all three essays; here it is worth highlighting three of his findings: 1) Women, taken as slaves in warfare in primitive times, were the first form of private property. 2) In the barbarian era (that is, when settled agricultural production began), the most honorific functions were those of fighting and hunting, conducted by men; the most enduringly useful and "progressive" were those of agriculture, performed by women. But typically the women were "owned" by men, with an accordingly lower status. 3) Women's clothing (he is speaking of the clothing of those *not* in the working class – which he always called "the underlying population") serve two purposes, one of comfort, the other of appearance. And the clothing that is seen as "fashionable" serves the purpose almost entirely of appearance, an "appearance" meant to enhance the status of the man who paid for the clothing. And the more "conspicuously" useless the woman appears *because* of her clothing – high heels, tight corsets, and so on – clearly the more standing in the community for the man who can afford to waste his money so. These generalizations appear in the articles in the same order. For those who like novels, Edith Wharton's novels about turn of the century New York society are very much in accord with Veblen's observations; so much so that it is not too much to think that some of her insights were enhanced by some of Veblen's. See her *House of Mirth*.

98. In his essay "Theses on Advertising," reprinted in *The Longer View* (1971).

99. Depending on time and place, a "small business" in the United States is defined as one having fewer than 500 employees. For almost *all* businesses, having even 100 employees would seem very *big*.

100. Although it may be said in defense of the *British* neoclassicists that their economy was the last and the least to become monopolistic in its structures. But even that is not good enough, for as Marshall was writing, the processes of merger and combination were rendering "ingredient No. 3" anachronistic.

101. As noted earlier, Marx was a radical from his youth, and a critic of capitalist *society* by 1843 (the time of the "early manuscripts"). It was Engels who pushed him toward the study of the political *economy* of capitalism – a push which ultimately led Marx to produce what may be counted as ten volumes of studies of "the economics" of capitalism, of which the three volumes of *Capital* were the last.

102. See note 48 in the preceding chapter, where *Capital* was seen by Marx as one of four "brochures." The other three – concerned with what we might call the State, sociology, and imperialism – even his followers never did more than begin until much later, leaving much to be done to this day. Of course Marx composed many relevant and striking epigrams relevant to those three areas noted above, and that still resonate: thus, as regards the State "as but the executive committee for managing the common affairs

of the bourgeoisie"; or as regards "sociology," where he argued that "the ruling ideas of any era are the ideas of its ruling class." And so on. But epigrams, even those as suggestive as Marx's, are not analysis.

103. Published in English originally as a pamphlet (1904), it became the introduction to the *Grundrisse*. The latter was completed in 1858 and published in 1859 in German; its first publication in English was in 1973.

104. This is part of the opening statement of *The Eighteenth Brumaire of Louis Bonaparte*, available as a separate pamphlet, also contained in *Selected Works* (1967).

105. The foregoing is what might be seen (at best) as a thumbnail/poetic version of Marx; of which I am conscious. I shall dip into his economic theory in just a moment. For a clear and concise and more detailed presentation of that theory, see E.K. Hunt (1979, Chapter 9); or, less technically, Chapter 3 of John Gurley's excellent *Challengers to Capitalism: Marx, Lenin, Stalin, and Mao* (1979). For a comprehensive treatment that integrates the analyses of all three volumes, see Paul M. Sweezy, *The Theory of Capitalist Development* (1942), still the best overall statement of Marxian economic theory, despite that some of its observations on the then contemporary world (1940s) are now dated. But Marx is never just economic theory. See the fine work by Bertell Ollman, *Alienation: Marx's Conception of Man in Capitalist Society* (1976), noted earlier, for the ethical, social, and philosophical Marx. And I cannot refrain from noting the sham nature of the innumerable criticisms of societies – dubbed "Marxist" by the critics – that have sought to free themselves from the domination of capital (whether Russia, China, Cuba, Chile, Vietnam or elsewhere). It would be more accurate to see them as failed socialist societies, and to understand *why* they have failed, which would entail a criticism also of the "successful" capitalist societies' economic and military assaults against them. As actual readers of Marx know, he laid out no plan, program, or blueprint for a post-capitalist society. He did put forth some epigrams, including the most famous: successful revolution would lead first to a society whose slogan would be "from each according to ability, to each according to work," which would enable progress to a society in which the slogan could change to "from each according to ability, to each according to *need*." Other than that, he made it clear that his work was to understand, not, as he put it, "to concoct kitchen recipes for the future." For those whose model of the good society begins and ends with capitalism, all that is, of course, hot air.

106. Thus begins the Preface to his *Principles of Political Economy and Taxation* (1817, I).

107. The main works of Veblen in this respect were his *The Theory of Business Enterprise* (1904), *The Instinct of Workmanship* (1914), *An Inquiry into the Nature of Peace and the Terms of its Perpetuation*

(1917) (regarding foreign trade and imperialism), his methodological essays in *The Place of Science in Modern Civilization* (1919a), and *Absentee Ownership and Business Enterprise in Recent Times* (1923).

108. *Place of Science ...* (1919a, 410–11).

109. Although I tried to do something of the sort. Some of the remarks on Veblen have been borrowed from a small book on him which sought to bring together into "a coherent whole" the largest part of his works, *Thorstein Veblen* (Dowd, 1964a/1999). I have also relied somewhat on an article in which I compared him with C. Wright Mills, "On Veblen, Mills ... and The Decline of Criticism" (1964b). It is worth adding that although Veblen did not seek followers, he has had many – and a diverse crew they have been, varying from radical to conservative, from theoretical to anti-theoretical, and so on. And there is a journal that seeks to extend his tradition in one way or another: *The Journal of Economic Issues*. The tradition is called "institutionalism," or "institutional economics."

110. From his essay, "The Limitations of Marginal Utility," in his *The Place of Science ...* (1919a, 73–4).

111. In *The Vested Interests and the Common Man* (1919b, 141).

112. In *The Higher Learning in America: A Memorandum on the Conduct of Universities by Businessmen* (1918). It was written in 1908 (soon after Veblen had been ushered out of Stanford), and had trouble getting published for a decade – one reason for which was its original subtitle: *A Study in Total Depravity*. The more polite subtitle would seem to be pretty off-putting in itself, except for those – now almost a majority – who see nothing wrong in having universities "conducted by businessmen."

113. *Theory of Business Enterprise* (1904, 391–3). I did not read those words until about 1950; in the four years I was in the military for World War II, I was brought up to be court-martialed four times for the insubordination Veblen notes: clearly a potential fan of Veblen's.

114. Veblen makes it clear that "instinct" does not connote "tropismatic action" (the sort of thing that happens when a sunflower turns with the sun) but that "instinct involves consciousness adaptation to an end aimed at" (1914, 4).

CHAPTER 3

1. The fancy term for which is *ceteris paribus*, used with great frequency by economists whose possession of Latin is confined to that and *et cetera*. But who's counting?

2. The Keynesian macroeconomic "model" will be discussed later in this chapter. It will be judged as having been useful, even though its method is subject to at least some of the criticisms leveled in the text. At least two points may be made in that regard: 1) The arguments made by Keynes with his model could have been made just as

forcefully had they been on a considerably lower level of abstraction; indeed, as has been suggested earlier, the gist of his argument regarding "excess capacity" (by whatever name) was made at least by Malthus, Marx, Hobson, and Veblen. 2) The defects of the Keynesian argument are found precisely in what *he* abstracted from – not least those concerned with power, as it relates to policy formation. It may be added, as well, that Keynes made his own argument best (in *The General Theory*) in normal language: his "model" was inessential even for him. But, as with so many economists, Keynes wrote with other economists in mind, and presumably felt he had "to speak their language." I hope the foregoing points will be clarified in the section on Keynes below.

3. Which Adam Smith took; but those economists who came after did so in always dwindling numbers. In recent years, the convictions of the economists give the impression that any set of social relationships other than those of capitalism (that is, of "the free market") were, in some sense, artificial, unnatural, only waiting, so to speak, to *become* capitalist. In other words, what is "natural" (in the sense of corresponding to human nature and/or God's will) are those institutions corresponding with the social relationships of capitalism. Already in Marx's day that was coming to be a common conviction, leading to his comment "Thus, there has been history, but there is no longer any." And wasn't there a book in the 1980s called *The End of History*? History repeats itself, over and over again. (But then, to quote Marx again, does so "the first time as tragedy, the second [and third and fourth ...] as farce" from *The Eighteenth Brumaire*, cited earlier).

4. One way of understanding both how awful and how shocking the war was as seen by those who lived through it *at home*, as well as in the trenches may be found in Paul Fussell, *The Great War and Modern Memory* (1975). But see also the great antiwar novel of Erich Maria Remarque, *All Quiet on the Western Front* (1928, 1996).

5. Let us assume that to be so. Where that *might* be said to be the case, it occurred in those societies *least* modern – least industrialized, least "capitalistic" – but by no means untouched by colonialism and imperialism before and after 1914: for example, Hungary, China, Turkey, Vietnam, Cuba.

6. Of which a fuller discussion soon. Here it may be noted that fascists also came to power in a number of other countries, most notably in Hungary, Portugal, and Spain. In Hungary – one of the pieces of the former Austro-Hungarian empire – in a period of three years there was social democratic (1918), then communist (1919), then fascist rule (from 1920 into World War II). Portugal, an economic colony of the British after the eighteenth century, became turbulent with the end of the war, and became fascist through a *coup d'état* led by Antonio Salazar in 1925 (a regime that lasted into the 1970s). Spain, also very

much an economic colony of the British, was ruled by an unstable monarchy in the 1920s that became effectively fascist under Miguel Primo de Rivera in 1923; then, in the democratic election of 1931, a mildly social democratic government came to power. It was overthrown by Generalissimo Franco in the civil war of 1936–39 – much aided and abetted by German planes and Italian troops and by military supplies indirectly supplied by (among others) the United States. The Spanish Civil War was most prominent among all the foregoing, and it has been much written about. Unquestionably the most comprehensive and incisive history is Gerald Brenan, *The Spanish Labyrinth: An Account of the Social and Political Background of the Spanish Civil War* (1943), George Orwell's *Homage to Catalonia* (based on Orwell's observations when a volunteer for the Republican forces) catches some of the tragedy and the controversial politics. Good novels often illuminate the horrors of war better than history; here are two for Spain. André Malraux flew for the Republic, and his *Man's Hope* (1939) has become a classic. A piercing portrait of the terrors of the struggle is that of Ramon J. Sender, *Seven Red Sundays* (1961).

7. In the country surveys to follow, I have depended mostly on the excellent book of W. Arthur Lewis, *Economic Survey: 1919-1939* (1949), unless otherwise indicated.

8. Lewis (1949, 16). But that damage was severe, as he points out: half a million houses destroyed or badly damaged, over 20,000 factories, 6,000 kilometers of railways and canals, and 60,000 of roads, along with more than 5 million acres of arable land, rendered useless. But, by comparison with the effects of World War II, "the destruction was small." But it didn't seem so, that first time around.

9. M.M. Knight, one of the three to whom this book is dedicated, was a pilot in the "Lafayette Escadrille" during the war, and after the war worked with the Red Cross relief effort in Hungary.

10. The postwar inflation was on top of an often serious inflation begun *during* the war: Already by 1918 prices (since 1913) had more than doubled in the United States, tripled in Britain, had risen more than 5-fold in France and 15-fold in Germany.

11. This had more than one quantitative meaning: incomes not only did not shrink, they expanded. Thus the customary expansion/contraction phases became instead a very substantial expansion. That, taken together with the ultimate shortages of goods during our own participation, meant a very strong level of "pent-up demand" for consumer goods and sustained or expanded productive capacity for the new consumer *durable* goods, at just the right time – and *only* in the United States did this occur in that way.

12. Lewis (1949, 24) has a table showing that, taking wholesale prices of 1913 as 100, the index moved from 245 in December 1918 to

126,000,000,000,000 (that's trillions) in December, 1923. The inflation's initial push came from deficits incurred for military expenditures during the war; that creation of money continued after the war, and was added to because Germany (critically because of Versailles) could not pay for its imports, and its horrendous price increase led to continuous wage demands, and round and round it went. Although Germany broke all records, inflation was stunning elsewhere: at the end of their respective inflations, prices in Austria had risen 14,000 times, in Hungary 23,000 times, in Poland 2,500,000 times, in Russia 4,000,000,000 (that's billion) times.

13. The inflation was brought under control by U.S. intervention in 1923 (the so-called "Dawes Plan"), with an early version of IMF intervention. The U.S. in effect loaned a new money supply to Germany, which meant retiring the existing currency. This required trading in old Marks for new with, as one can imagine, ongoing mountainous consternation, fears, and confusion. The surgery worked that time: by 1925 the German economy had begun to prosper. For only for four years.

14. It was this, of course, that occupied much of Keynes's scorn in his *Economic Consequences of the Peace*. It was reasonable, of course, for Germany to have to return Alsace-Lorraine to its "rightful owner." It was unreasonable to the point of economic insanity (as Versailles provided) to load Germany down with unpayable (and, ultimately, largely unpaid) war "reparations" while, at the same time, depriving it of much of its shipping, territories, and other crippling penalties. One doesn't have to be a friend of Germany to realize that these and other provisions had vindictiveness and greed as their motives, not something more sensible – and less dangerous.

15. See the excellent study by economic historian Alexander Gerschenkron, *Bread and Democracy in Germany* (1943). In addition to later references, for a grimly entertaining, almost "pointillist," portrait of that moment in time, see Christopher Isherwood's *Berlin Stories*. One of those stories was made into the play "I Am A Camera," in turn made into the musical comedy "Cabaret," in turn made into a film of the same name. Recently in New York "Cabaret" has gone back to the stage again, in a new and harsher version. The time of that story is the year 1930, and Nazism's face is leering behind almost every scene.

16. Robert A. Brady, *Business as a System of Power* (1943b, 86–7). The quoted phrases at the end are credited to Veblen.

17. Ibid. Those familiar with the Pacific war will remember that in its last stages, suddenly, Japanese planes began to attack naval ships as though the planes were merely directed bombs – as, in a real sense, they were. These were the *kamikaze* suicide pilots.

18. Their serfs were "freed" about the same time as our slaves. And though the subsequent fates of both were quite dissimilar, both were a very tortured kind of "freedom." See BKU (1937, Chapter 29).

19. BKU (1937, 697).

20. John Reed's *Ten Days that Shook the World*, written immediately after 1917, is very much worth reading for its vivid portrayal of just how chaotic the politics of the transformation from Kerensky to Lenin were, and how much up in the air the outcome was, moment to moment.

21. For an excellent examination and analysis of the years immediately preceding 1917 and up through the 1930s, see Maurice Dobb, *Soviet Economic Development since 1917* (1966).

22. The "war" was that of the attempts to overthrow the Soviet regime both from within and outside. The attempts were those of the "White Army," financed and supplied and augmented by the armed forces of Britain and the United States (among others).

> Kolchak [head of the White forces] received half a billion dollars of support from Britain. By March 1919, the French, British, Italians, Romanians, Serbs, and Greeks had poured 850,000 counter-revolutionary troops into south Russia. From April 1920 to March 1921, the Poles were battling in the Ukraine ... In the Baltic, British commanders and tanks and American gasoline nearly made a success of the White campaign ... In north Russia, a total of 5,500 American and 37,000 British troops supported the White regime ... Throughout this time, the Allied Supreme War Council's naval blockade deprived the Red government of the use of all seaports.

> That quotation is from Carl Oglesby and Richard Shaull, *Containment and Change* (1967, 34), which has two parts. The quote is from Oglesby's "part," where he is trying to make the point that the Cold War, and the war in Vietnam, began in 1917.

23. Below the Spanish Civil War and the "'Allies'" behavior with regard to it will be discussed; here let it be recalled that as late as the fall of 1938 representatives from the United States, Britain, France and Germany met *in* Germany to arrange an international steel cartel (as a means of fixing prices and geographic quotas).

24. And favorably – and famously – commented on by Winston Churchill at the time.

25. In 1938, Roosevelt prohibited the Spanish Republican ("Loyalist") government's freighter *Mar Cantabrico* from leaving New York harbor with its cargo of military supplies purchased in the United States. At the very same time the U.S. government looked the other way when oil was shipped to Japan and Germany (1938!) and Italy – all fascist, all engaged in military expansion – while Germany was providing virtually the entirety of Franco's airpower (mostly Stuka bombers, later to be used to bomb and strafe the roads of Belgium, Holland, and France) as Italy sent 50,000 of its (drafted) infantrymen.

26. It was in 1943 that allied forces landed in Italy; soon after, Mussolini was captured in the North, shot, and hung up in a public square.

German troops had begun their retreat northward to Central Europe to shape their own defense, their northern armies having been badly depleted by the disastrous and failed offensive against the Soviet Union.

27. By Harold Laski in his *The Rise of European Liberalism* (1936).

28. The numbers of workers organized by 1912 show both the unusually high number of agricultural workers (compared with other nations) and their virtual equality with industrial workers: 408,000 in agriculture, 450,000 in industry (Brady, 1943b, 67). There is an abundant literature for this history, and some of it will be noted along the way. Here mention will be made of two marvelous films, one dealing with farm workers, the other with textile workers. The first is *Bitter Rice*, which deals with struggles in the rice farms; the other is *The Organizer*. The man of the title is an impoverished and dedicated organizer (Marcello Mastroianni, in perhaps his best performance, in the 1960s). The setting is a turn of the century cotton textile factory, replete with dangerous and ear-splitting machinery worked by men, women, and children, with daily accidents, all occurring in the conditions of the early industrial revolution. (The factory itself was "borrowed" from Yugoslavia, where it was still operating at the time.) The film is worth many a book for giving one the sense of just how cruel (and forceful and violent) that industrial revolution was.

29. See Gaetano Salvemini's *Under the Axe of Fascism* (1936) and *The Origins of Fascism in Italy* (1973), Carl T. Schmidt, *The Plough and the Sword* (1938) and *The Corporate State in Action* (1939). A note concerning the Catholic Church and Italian Fascism. Beginning with Pope Leo XIII and his 1891 encyclical *Rerum Novarum* (in effect "new developments"), the Church showed its awareness of the dangers of capitalism to its own stability (as revealed not least in agricultural workers' struggles). The message of Leo XIII was that raw capitalism had to be tamed, because of its threats to the family and of inciting social conflict and skepticism. Out of that came the Catholic notion of a "corporative order": a throwback to the medieval social structure in which all elements of society are seen as working together harmoniously for the larger good – and overlooking that the medieval world at its most "harmonious" depended upon the servility of the many to the power of the few. After that encyclical, while capitalism was stimulating the growth of "red" unions the Church was doing the same for Catholic unions. Between then and Mussolini's triumph, the Church was politically active through such labor organizations. But Mussolini had originally been a Socialist (until expelled for his militarism in 1914), and anti-Church. So, the first few years of fascist rule were uncomfortable for the Church. That was changed with the Lateran Accord of 1929, whose deals achieved, at last, harmony – although not quite the sort Pope Leo XIII had in mind. See Brady (1943b, 58 ff), and Salvemini (1973, Chapter 27).

30. 500,000 battle deaths, 500,000 maimed, and 1,000,000 dead from wartime epidemics. Salvemini (1973, 7). For a sense of the meaning of those figures, compare with the United States: with a population four times as large, in those same years the United States had half as many killed and wounded, and only a few thousand deaths from the flu: all too many, of course, but not even one-eighth the human cost paid by Italians.

31. Again, reference to a film. This one – "The Great War" – made in Italy in the 1960s and enormously popular, tells the story of two Italian soldiers in the Alpine fighting around the Piave River, which became an Italian and Austrian graveyard. These hapless draftees get lost behind the enemy lines, are captured, (wrongly) accused of being spies and, after a deeply poignant set of experiences, executed: all for nothing. Like the war itself as most Italians had seen it. Significantly, the two "heroes" were also two of the most popular stars in Italy in the years in which the film was made: Alberto Sordi and Vittorio Gassmann, the one usually a comedian, the other a romantic hero.

32. See Salvemini (1973, Chapter 2).

33. See Quintin Hoare and G.N. Smith (eds), *Selections from the Prison Notebooks of Antonio Gramsci* (1971) and Gramsci, *The Modern Prince and Other Writings* (1967). There are many books about and deriving from Gramsci; among those I have found most useful are Carl Boggs, *Gramsci's Marxism* (1976) and John M. Cammett, *Antonio Gramsci and the Origins of Italian Communism* (1967).

34. Cammett (1967, 204). He is quoting Gwynn Williams. The germ of the idea of hegemony Gramsci doubtless found in Marx:

    The ideas of the ruling class are in every epoch the ruling ideas: i.e., the class which is the ruling *material* force of society, is at the same time its ruling *intellectual* force. The class which has the means of material production at its disposal, has control at the same time over the means of mental production, so that thereby, generally speaking, the ideas of those who lack the means of mental production are subject to it.

    This is from Part I of *The German Ideology*, as reproduced in the very useful collection by Robert C. Tucker (ed.), *The Marx-Engels Reader* (1978, 172; emphasis in original).

35. *Prison Notebooks* (1971, 238).

36. It may be added here that because Gramsci was writing from a fascist prison, and all his writings were censored, he used many circumlocutions. Thus he (like Veblen) never used terms like "ruling class" (among other such); rather he spoke of the "ideological hegemony of the bourgeoisie," and so on. And this may be as good a place as any to remark that U.S. capitalism walks away with first prize for the strength of its "ideological hegemony."

37. As would be true also in Nazi Germany by 1938. See below.
38. There is no way to make Italian fascism appear as benign. It was not. It was a harsh, totally irrational, militarized, deadly society. Despite the high dangers of doing so, many thousands of Italians risked their lives to fight against it throughout its 20 years of rule (notably, but not only, the deservedly lauded *partigiani* of World War II). A fine novel that shows some of this, and does so simply, is Ignazio Silone's *Fontamara* (1934), still available. Although the word *ghetto* is Italian, and Jews were anything but lionized in Italian history, it is nonetheless true that not until 1938, under strong German pressure, did the Italians begin to participate in the Holocaust, and then reluctantly. Primo Levi's stunning novel *If Not Now, When?*, which centers on a Russian Jewish soldier stuck behind Nazi lines who finally ends up in Italy as the war ends, gives some sense of this when the Russian Jew is stupefied to learn that in Italy "the Jews don't even dress differently." And then there is the lovely novel of Carlo Levi (no relation), arrested for his anti-fascism: *Christ Stopped at Eboli*. If he had been in Germany he would have been gassed or beheaded; he was in Italy, and was instead exiled to a small village in the South. All that being said, Italian fascism was *fascist*; that is, cruel and deadly – insane – and especially so to the Italians persecuted by it and who died for it and against it in its several wars.
39. The most dramatic instance of that was in "the pearl" of the British Empire, India. India demanded its independence as the war ended; and without a shot being fired, was granted it in 1947 (under pressure from the United States, then arranging a $3-5 billion badly needed loan to Britain). The general process of loosening as brought about by crisis in the powerful countries was first analyzed carefully by André Gunder Frank in his "dependency theory." See Chapter 1 in James D. Cockroft, André Gunder Frank and Dale L. Johnson, *Dependence and Under-development* (1912).
40. The "viciousness" of the fighting became proverbial; it was immortalized in the first novel of André Malraux, *Man's Fate* (1927). One scene cannot be forgotten: when one of the Red soldiers is thrown alive into the roaring furnace of a locomotive. As later in Spain, Malraux served in *that* war. (Yet – or and? – he subsequently became a minister in de Gaulle's government after World War II: President de Gaulle's "left-hand man," the joke went.)
41. In fact, industrial production had already been softening before he spoke. More importantly (as will be explained soon), the "prosperity decade" in the United States was not that at all for most of the population. (All this talk of "globalization" and the "prosperity" in the 1920s might make some nervous, given the same chatter – and all too similar realities – today. See Part II for a fuller discussion.)
42. Lewis (1949, 50).
43. It is probably useful here to pause for a thumbnail discussion of a very few

of the many differences between now and then. By the 1920s the United States was already the strongest economy in the world (and a creditor nation), but by no means as strong (absolutely or relatively) as now (when it is a debtor nation), nor did it have the military strength or political clout of today. Be that as it may, during those years the United States did pretty much the opposite of what was required of its strength if the looming collapse was to be mitigated, to slow down, to be somewhat contained. (It is unlikely that it could have been *averted*.) The United States is still the most powerful economy; unlike the 1920s, today there is another power-house, Japan: No. 2 in the world, but No.1 for Asia – its biggest creditor, importer, exporter and investor. But Japan has been in a prolonged contraction since 1991. With many differences (the United States was "prosperous" in the 1920s). Japan, like the United States in the 1920s, has not handled its own economy well and, at least as often as not, has behaved counter-productively towards those for which it is vital. Japan is *the* economy in all of Asia (its economy has a GDP greater than all the others combined): an Asia that holds more than half the world's popula-tion. There is much more involved: to be discussed later.

44. In addition to Lewis, dependence will be on George Soule, *Prosperity Decade* (1947) and Broadus Mitchell, *Depression Decade* (1947). Both books are useful for analysis as well as data, and Mitchell presents a comprehensive account of the evolution of New Deal policies.

45. The margin of economic "fat" in the U.S. economy was thicker than in Germany, where average consumption was always much lower – except for those on the top. For an idea of the latter, see Thomas Mann's *Buddenbrooks*, which tells the tale of a turn-of-the-century North German mercantile family of that name, whose margin of body fat was substantial. A prolonged eating scene is enough to turn the stomach.

46. See Du Boff, *Accumulation & Power* (1989, Chapter 5) for a tracing-out of the processes creating that "duality."

47. My emphasis on "cash," Soule (1947, 288). That whole discussion and much to follow (and documentation) is found in slightly different form in my *U.S. Capitalist Development* (1993, Chapter 4).

48. Robert A. Gordon, *Economic Instability and Growth: The American Record* (1974, 49–52).

49. The data are taken from Baran and Sweezy, *Monopoly Capital* (1966, 242). Note the fall from 1937 to 1938. Because of the stimulative fiscal policy of the years after 1935, the economy had slowly begun to recover. The Fed, ever on the alert to quell the monster of inflation, tightened the money supply, sent interest rates up, and the economy went into what pilots call a secondary spin. (Note the unemployment figures, soon to follow, for the same years.)

50. *Economic Report of the President* (1991, 323). As will be commented upon in a later chapter, the official measure of unemployment is systematically understated: the "hard-core" jobless (those who have

sought work unsuccessfully so long as to have given up), are not counted at all; those who have lost full-time jobs and need to have another one, but who are working part-time, are counted as employed (even if they work only one hour a week). The U.S. rate, if tabulated in the German way, for example, would be about 50 percent higher. (The Japanese rate would be three times higher.) And, in different ways, the same applies also to poverty rates, as defined here in comparison with Europe.

51. Today Creditanstalt is still Austria's biggest bank.

52. Lewis (1949, 63–4).

53. By 1929 U.S. industrial production was over 40 percent of the world's, and its consumption of the nine principal foodstuffs and raw materials was almost 40 percent of the 15 largest economies. See Lewis (1949, 57–8).

54. See Mitchell (1947, Chapter VII) for the details and the workings-out of the NRA; and the entire book for much else.

55. Mitchell (1947, 231).

56. The "best reasons" for ending the NRA would have included that it both increased and gave governmental legal backing to the powers of big business at the expense of small business and the general public. The Court's almost foolish reasoning was that the live poultry business around New York City did not come under interstate commerce and was not subject to federal jurisdiction. But at least the NRA was ended. See Mitchell (1947, 238).

57. Without question FDR was most influenced to become so by his closest advisor, Harry Hopkins. Eleanor Roosevelt, from her youth forward, was deeply involved in "liberal" causes, and surely had FDR's ear. But it appears that he heard more clearly when it came from the politicians. Be that as it may, what he "heard" made him the most popular president in our history: he was elected president four times – the reason for the subsequent ban on more than two terms. The sweet irony of that law, introduced by the GOP when they controlled Congress in the 1950s, is that Ronald Reagan was thus prevented from having a third (fourth, fifth ...) term.

58. See Gary Knox, "Slums and Poverty," in John E. Ullmann (ed.), *Social Costs in Modern Society* (1983) for those and related data for those years; by the late 1990s (as will be discussed more fully in Part II), matters had deteriorated considerably more – despite (or because of?) the exuberant economy: for example, in 1995 the all-time high in the "deficiency of rental units" was reached (4.4 million units), with poor families paying more than 60 percent of their incomes in rent; "from 1995 to 1997 the number of 'struggling renter households' increased by 3 percent" with (in New York City) "116,000 on waiting lists for public housing ... [and] 203,000 on lists to get rental assistance vouchers." All figures are from U.S. Census data. (A "struggling household" refers to a family of four with a maximum income of $16,000, which is only 30 percent of the

median income for a New York City family of four.) When we discuss contemporary poverty rates in the United States in the next chapter, we shall see that however dismal all this sounds, it amounts to a serious understatement of the realities.

59. From "King Lear," of course, placed by Brady on the title page of his *Spirit and Structure of German Fascism* (1937). Much of what follows depends upon that book; some is borrowed from my memoir of Brady: "Against Decadence: the Work of Robert A. Brady (1901–63)" (1994).

60. Brecht and Weill collaborated in "The Threepenny Opera." It was at the same time satire, biting critique, and a scream for help prompted by the then evolving Germany. One song – "What Keeps Mankind Alive?" – answers that question as Hitler soon would: "For once you must try to face the facts: Mankind is kept alive by bestial acts." For those unacquainted with their work – as well as for those who are – it is worth noting that recently a documentary film has appeared – "September Song" – recounting Weill's (and, and to a lesser extent, Brecht's) musical works, and doing so splendidly. William Burroughs sings the song quoted in the text, and Weill, Lotte Lenya and Brecht are also heard from old recordings. Not to be missed; and perhaps available in video. There are some, among them myself, who find all too many similarities between the decadence of that Germany and today's United States.

61. Item: Rosa Luxemburg, a gifted social analyst and wondrous human being, was murdered and her corpse thrown into a canal in 1919, when there was continuous fighting in the streets led by the *Frei Korps*, which would become the core of the *Schutz Staffel* (the *S.S.*: Hitler's "special guard") and the storm troopers. Hitler took on heroic status when he led the "Munich Putsch" of 1923, for which he was imprisoned. There is an excellent German film (available in video) on Luxemburg and her times: "Rosa."

62. Plus, of course, the previously noted mixture of cruelty, greed and recklessness of Versailles. Shortly after writing this section on Germany, I was pleased, though not completely surprised to see these words of George Kennan:

> I have never shared the tendency of so many in Europe and elsewhere to regard the modern Germans as by nature an aggressive and dangerous country. I have seen the Germans, en masse, as no better and no worse than the other European peoples ... I see their part in the origins of the First World War as certainly no greater, and perhaps even smaller, than that of the French and the Russians. And I see the entire terrible period of Nazi ascendancy as the product of the coming together of a whole series of quite abnormal factors.

"A Letter on Germany," in *New York Review*, December 3, 1998. Lest Kennan be seen as an innocent or as sentimental regarding Germany, note that he was a graduate student in Germany (1929–31) as the Nazis rose, served as an officer of the U.S. Embassy in Berlin for two and a half years after 1939, and then spent six months in a German prison. His famous "telegram" of 1946 from Moscow is widely seen as a key moment in what became the Cold War. But he was opposed to the militarized policies of the Cold War, as he often insisted after 1946; as he was also opposed when (as part of the State Department Planning group for Germany) he opposed partition and occupation in Germany (as did the Soviet Union). Kennan left the Department shortly after. As he wryly points out in the "Letter ...," "It took me longer than it should have taken to recognize that in governmental service one is routinely forgiven for saying the wrong thing at the right time, but for saying the right thing at the wrong time – never."

63. There are important resemblances (and differences) between the early Nazis and the "skinheads" of today. Today's skinheads are less "political" and more "cultural" than their predecessors; but one relevant similarity is that then as now they were divided as between those who were "anti-capitalist" and those whose focus was dominated by nationalism, militarism, racism, etc. It was the anti-capitalist (and generally more left in other terms) group of the Nazis that was slaughtered at a party conference on "The Night of the Long Knives" by the S.S. in 1934: at least 10,000 men (including their leader Gustav Roehm).

The differences among today's "skinheads" in the United States are noted in the excellent book of William Finnegan, *Cold New World: Growing Up in a Harder Country* (1998). Also see the intriguing article "A Politics for Generation X" by Ted Halstead on the "twenty-somethings" of the United States (often seen as "slackers, cynics, whiners, drifters, and malcontents"). Basing his essay on academic research, Halstead draws a considerably more complicated and by no means entirely depressing picture of young people – and reminds one at least somewhat of the situation in Germany described above. *Atlantic Monthly* (August 1999).

64. The enormously entertaining film "Cabaret" (mentioned earlier) is also instructive in these regards. It is set in the year 1930, and depicts several scenes of the sort just noted.

65. Which had for years been split between the Social Democrats and the Communists. They fought each other with considerably more efficacy than they fought the Nazis.

66. And millions were enslaved as forced laborers in German industry. In 1944 alone, 750,000 of those laborers were Jews taken from the concentration camps, to be worked – literally – to death in factories. But there were also 7 million *non*-Jewish workers brought in from other countries – France, Italy, Belgium, Holland – and held against their will under deadly conditions. See "Germany Seeks Plan on Nazi-Era Labor," *New York Times*, December 15, 1998. (Primo Levi, author of *If Not Now, When?*, was one such.)

In addition to the millions of Jews murdered in the camps were untold millions of others: Catholics, Gypsies, homosexuals, and others who just simply upset some Nazi. And who knows how many whose lives continued, but did so as cripples, figuratively and/or literally?

67.   Although, as we have noted, Versailles provided abundant reason for deep anger. Herewith a factual summary of some of its provisions:

> The Treaty of Versailles deprived Germany of 13 percent of her [German] territory, 13 percent of her population, and 14.3 percent of her arable land. In terms of her 1913 production, Germany surrendered 19 percent of her coke, 74.5 percent of her iron ore, 26.6 percent of her blast furnaces, 19.2 percent of her raw iron and steel, 15.8 percent of her rolling mills, 68.5 percent of her zinc foundries, 12 percent of her livestock, her entire ocean-going merchant marine, 5,000 locomotives, 40,000 boxcars, and other miscellaneous equipment. More serious still ...

It couldn't get *much* more serious. (From Brady, *The Rationalization Movement in German Industry* [1933, xiv].)

68.   See Brady, *Spirit and Structure* (1937, Chapters V and VI).

69.   Thus, the Selective Service Act of 1940 revived the military draft of World War I (and of the Civil War), but when it had to be renewed in October 1941 it was facing substantial popular resistance, as signified by the anti-draft group "OHIO" – "over the hill in October." On the other hand, FDR earlier had become convinced that the United States should become part of the resistance to Hitler. In 1941 he had pushed through the "Lend-Lease Act," whose title referred to military equipment (including naval craft). And there is some reason to believe that FDR encouraged the State Department to be deliberately "sticky" with the Japanese at the same time.

70.   See Paul Kennedy, *The Rise and Fall of the Great Powers* (1989, 361–2) for such figures and a useful discussion of the war. His figures, monstrous though they are, may well be an understatement. See Gregory Frumkin, *Population Changes in Europe since 1939* (1951). His study for the United Nations estimated losses of 28 million in the Soviet Union during the war.

71.   It will be seen in the next chapter that in the fifty years *after* 1946 the United States expended over $11 *trillion* for the military, using official data (and 1992 dollars). And continues to spend $250–$300 billion annually. And the military asked for and got more, for fiscal year 2000. Oh! Cold War, wilt thou never lose thy sting?

72.   As we also have the possibility of producing repressive societies that do not take the particular forms of Italy and Germany. See the important book of Bertram Gross, *Friendly Fascism: The New Face of Power in America* (1980), written just before Reagan occupied the White House for the first time.

73.   Not to mention that where anything like perfectly competitive market

structures have existed, they were disastrous in effect. In the United States, for example, such structures existed in staple agriculture and in bituminous coal mining – in both of which there were literally thousands of "companies," selling an identical product – if also without that third assumption for such a market structure, "ease of entry and exit." This left economists with the decidedly unsettling task of deciding either that there were *no* perfectly competitive market structures (except, for a while, in *some* financial markets), or that there were (those just noted), and that they were disasters to all concerned: owners, workers, and nature. Better to dance around the question than answer it.

74. See "Joan Robinson's 'Wrong Turning'," by Brian J. Loasby in Ingrid H. Rima (ed.), *The Joan Robinson Legacy* (1991). The phrase was Robinson's in an essay of 1951, reproduced in *Collected Economic Papers* (1957, vol. 1, vii–viii). The Rima book is quite valuable in many ways, not least in its several discussions of Robinson in the light of what has come to be called "post-Keynesian economics." The two 1933 books noted here are Chamberlin's *The Theory of Monopolistic Competition* and Robinson's *The Economics of Imperfect Competition*.

75. As will be seen, this included Keynes (except for his treatment of savings, investment, and the rate of interest). In his *General Theory*, Keynes assumed (among other things) perfectly competitive markets and the neoclassical determinants of income distribution. This did not detract from the strength of his main theoretical argument. But, earlier noted and later to be elaborated, the whole range of neoclassical assumptions needed not just "relaxation" but pretty much abandonment if the *policy* implications and intentions of his theory were to become feasible.

76. For a fuller discussion and critique of those "developments," see E.H. Hunt's *History of Economic Thought* (1979, Chapters 11–12) and his and Jesse Schwartz's (eds.) *A Critique of Economic Theory* (1972).

77. "Obfuscation" because there is quite simply no way to measure what needs to be measured, namely, the "marginal" contribution of *any* "participant" in production. There are many reasons for this, not the least of which is that the theory assumes our old pal perfect competition – which in turn assumes, among many other things noted earlier, that each firm produces only one product: only (one model of) shoes, or ships, or sealing wax, etc. But among the many identifying marks of modern industry is that most firms produce *many* products in the same or in many other plants: GM, for example (at last count), 50,000 separate products.

78. For a considerably more sympathetic, indeed laudatory, treatment of Fisher, see Schumpeter's lengthy discussion of his work in *Ten Great Economists* (1951, Chapter 8).

79. Robinson (1933, 2). She is quoting from a 1926 article by Piero Sraffa

in the *Economic Journal*, very much *the* professional journal of economists at that time – as Piero Sraffa (1898–1983) was very much "the economists' economist." Like so many important economists both preceding and following Marshall, Sraffa (and Keynes and Robinson) taught at Cambridge; and Sraffa, Italian by birth, had a range of knowledge and insight that was equally at home in the mainstream or on the cliffs overlooking them (for example, Marxism). Joan Robinson was, of course, a woman and "As a woman, she was not a full member of the University and was not admitted to the degree she had earned in 1925 until 1948." From "Joan Robinson (1903–1983): A Biographical Memoir," by Phyllis Deane, in Rima, *The Joan Robinson Legacy* (1991, 15).

80. The testing, it may be added, of an aspiring by an established alchemist. When I took my Ph.D. orals at Berkeley (in 1949, then one of the top one or two economics departments in the States), the first – and very important (everyone's eyebrows raised) – question required that I draw one of Chamberlin's (unrealistic) diagrams on a chalk board. When I did so correctly, the questioner slapped his knee and exclaimed "Fantastic!" and settled back, satisfied that I was one of them. The next questioner (of five) then began by asking me to state "the law of diminishing returns." By then, almost half-dazed, I did so (it was what one learned in *introductory* econ), and asked "Is *that* what you wanted?" "Exactly," he replied, smiling with satisfaction. True stories, heaven help us.

81. Joan Robinson, *Collected Economic Papers* (1979, vol. 5, 58). If Chamberlin ever changed his mind, it has not come to my attention.

82. Except for a few passing remarks, Veblen will not be discussed, because he already has been, and will be again in another context; but also because after World War I ended, Veblen began to "close." The war and its aftermath confirmed Veblen's darkest fears; the continuing descent into patriotism, "red scares," and other irrationalities seemed to sap him of his intellectual energy. He wrote many essays after the war, but only one book. The essays – perhaps best represented by "Dementia Praecox" (in *Essays in Our Changing Order* [1934, 423–36]) – are despairing. One sentence tells the tale: "The current [1922] situation in America is by way of being something like a psychiatrical clinic" (429). His last book, *Absentee Ownership* (1923), although valuable in its substantial updating of the *Theory of Business Enterprise* (1904), is clothed in gloom. Even so, it remains one of his most informative (and entertaining) books.

83. *Economic Consequences of the Peace* (1920, 16). On an earlier page, waxing ironically on the "paradise" that was lost when war erupted in 1914, he wrote of the "projects and politics of militarism and imperialism, of racial and cultural rivalries, of monopolies, restriction, and exclusion, which were to play the serpent to this paradise ..." (ibid., 7).

Not quite the view of his fellow neoclassicists, that.

84. From "The End of Laissez-faire," in *Essays in Persuasion* (1931, 284–5), written in 1926. In that same volume is found "The Economic Consequences of Mr. Churchill," as critical as it was insightful. (Yes, *that* Churchill.) As Chancellor of the Exchequer that year, he advocated supporting (even strengthening) the pound, even though that would reduce exports and, not so incidentally, increase already high unemployment (and struggling businesses). He won the day, and Britain's economy managed to write the first chapter of what became the depression of the 1930s.

85. Op. cit., 287–8. Emphasis and capitalization his.

86. Op. cit., 291–2. A few quotations from the *General Theory*, both to corroborate the continuity of Keynes's thought, and its increasing vigor:

> There is no clear evidence from experience that the investment policy which is socially advantageous coincides with that which is most profitable. (157)

> Speculators may do no harm as bubbles on a steady stream of enterprise. But the position is serious when enterprise becomes the bubble on a whirlpool of speculation. When the capital development of a country becomes a by-product of the activities of a casino, the job is likely to be ill-done. (259)

> Thus our argument leads towards the conclusion that in contemporary conditions the growth of wealth, so far from being dependent on the abstinence of the rich, as is commonly supposed, is more likely to be impeded by it. One of the chief social justifications of the great inequality of wealth is, therefore, removed. (373)

87. Many readers will wish to know more than the "major outlines." There are many books concerning Keynes and his work. An excellent beginning that covers both is Robert Lekachman, *The Age of Keynes* (1966). The first attempt by a U.S. economist to put together and explicate Keynesian theory for the non-specialist – aside from the quite different works of Alvin Hansen, soon to be discussed – was Dudley Dillard, *The Economics of John Maynard Keynes* (1948); it seems to me still the best of many such efforts. By the 1970s, Keynesian analysis had developed two major problems: it had been diluted by its followers, and it was under increasingly severe attacks from its opponents. A probing examination of both these developments is found in Hyman Minsky, *John Maynard Keynes* (1975). We shall have more to say of Minsky (who died in 1997) in Part II.

88. This work is not meant to be a course in economic theory. But a brief delineation of the abstract *theoretical* nature of Keynes's theory may be useful for some readers. First, Keynes sought to understand the behavior of a *laissez-faire* (now called "a free market") capitalist economy; and his

understanding would show that it could no longer function safely as such. His model thus sets aside governmental economic activity; and his analysis shows why it must be brought into the picture as remedy.

His model at its most abstract is $Y = C + I$, where $Y =$ the net national income which in turn $= C$ (total consumer expenditures) $+ I$ (total net "real" [non-financial] investment, which adds to productive capacity). That is, national (aggregate) *income* equals national consumer and net business *expenditures*. "Net" there is meant to exclude business expenditures for capital depreciation (that is for keeping capital intact), as it also excludes expenditures on "working capital."

So: $Y - C = S$ (savings). And if $Y = C + I$, then $Y - C = S$. Thus, $S = I$. Less abstractly, if I rises, so will S; more to Keynes's point, when S rises, so *must* I. Say thought that an intended increase of I would bring about a rise in interest rates (the reward for *not* consuming) and thus in S (and would explain a fall in C). The relationship between C and Y – C/Y – Keynes called "the propensity to consume." ("Normally" that is about 2/3 in the United States.) When Keynes argued that S rises as Y rises, and increasingly so as a percentage, he was also arguing that I *must* rise as Y rises; and he well knew that the primary reason for a rise in Y was a prior/ongoing rise in I. But with the inequality of incomes intrinsic to capitalism, an increase in Y means that C/Y will decline, and that to sustain Y, I must then *continue* to rise. The contradiction lies in the fact that the increases in productive capacity at some point will *not* be matched by increases in C, and therefore pervasive excess capacity appears, causing economic contraction, falling profits and rising unemployment.

Finally: the more advanced a capitalist economy, the more likely that such excessive capacities will be chronic, around the corner, and getting closer. And to resolve that problem it is necessary for G (governmental fiscal policy: expenditures and taxes), along with monetary policies to lower interest rates (the cost of borrowing) in order to stimulate both C and I so that unemployment and unprofitability may be contained or eliminated.

Get it?

89.   Bourgeois though he was – by his own estimation – Keynes was by no mean conventional. One aspect of his character led him to become a central figure in the so-called Bloomsbury Group, not the usual setting for an economist (or anyone else, for that matter), made up of the likes of Virginia Woolf (and her relatively radical economic historian husband, Leonard Woolf), Roger Fry, et al. Through them he met and married the Russian ballerina Lydia Lopokova. That in turn took him to Moscow (though on an official mission) in 1925, which prompted a thoughtfully critical (or critically thoughtful) set of reflections: "A Short View of Russia." His disapproval of and distaste for what he observed there is unmistakable. But it is a measure of Keynes's oft-remarked generosity of

spirit that he concluded that "short view" in this way:

> So, now the deeds are done and there is no going back, I should like to give Russia her chance; to help and not to hinder. For how much rather, even after allowing for everything, if I were a Russian, would I contribute my quota of activity to Soviet Russia than to Tsarist Russia! I could not subscribe to the new official faith any more than to the old. I should detest the actions of the new tyrants not less than those of the old. But I should feel that my eyes were turned towards, and no longer away from, the possibilities of things; that out of the cruelty and stupidity of Old Russia nothing ever could emerge, but beneath the cruelty and stupidity of New Russia some speck of the ideal may lie hid. (*Essays in Persuasion*, 1931, 270–1)

Bravo, Keynes.

90. They didn't have to be smart at all to appreciate that when it came to military spending. They're all (military-) Keynesians now.

91. *Full Recovery* was written in 1938. Among the books to follow, the most important were *Fiscal Policy and Business Cycles* (1941) and (his "final" version), *Monetary Theory and Fiscal Policy* (1949). And see also his very useful *Guide to Keynes* (1953), which accompanies the reader through the *General Theory* chapter by chapter. Dillard's *Economic ... of Keynes*, is quite a different work: it takes the entire work and *re*-works it, explicating it and applying it, so the reader is participating in a lengthy seminar.

92. In the nineteenth century it was the railroad and its numerous relationships with other industries, the growth of cities, and so on (as discussed in Chapter 2) that were the prime technological stimuli. And it combined with "westward expansion" and urban development, in conjunction with ever-rising population growth, itself dependent in turn on rising immigration. The automobile (and other consumer durables) served that role into the mid-twenties. And then the slack began. Critics of the stagnation thesis after World War II have pointed to the expansion that ensued then (see Chapter 4) *without* all those elements. But they were still there, but in different clothing: military expenditures combined with the growth of a U.S.-dominated world economy along with consumerism (and debt) to turn the trick. The question conventional economists and opinion makers never even consider is this: what would have happened to the U.S. and the capitalist world economy without the Cold War?

93. See the extraordinary "Bibliography: The Writings of Joan Robinson," by Maria Cristina Marcuzzo, in Ingrid H. Rima (ed.) (1991, 250–76). If you are wondering why she was not awarded the Nobel Prize in Economics (begun in 1969), you might wish to read the essay in that same book, by Marjorie S. Turner, "Joan Robinson: Why Not a Nobel Laureate?" (242–9). On the basis of interviews with laureates, committee members,

and relevant materials, Turner answers her own question with this conclusion:

> [Robinson] disowned the method [of] her early contributory work *The Economics of Imperfect Competition*; she worked diligently to undermine the hegemony of the central core of general equilibrium theory in all her later work; she proposed another path in *The Accumulation of Capital*, but this path led nowhere as far as *mainstream* research programs are concerned ... she engaged in the capital controversy, which was also destructive of the central core of general equilibrium analysis, its complacency, and its methodology; she failed to use the latest mathematical techniques. Being a leftist ... did not help. Being a nonconventional woman did not ingratiate her. The committee is all-male. (248)

No surprises there. Although it reveals a certain lack of objectivity on my part to admit it, I have been an admirer of Robinson from the beginnings of my studies; nor did my admiration for her lessen when I received a letter from her (in the mid-1970s) concerning a book of mine in which she wrote "Your book seems to be just the sort of thing there ought to be more of." Give that woman a PRIZE!

94. Whose other members were Roy Harrod, R.F. Kahn, James Meade, Austin Robinson (her husband), Piero Sraffa, Nicholas Kaldor, and Michal Kalecki (1899–1970). Kalecki was a Polish emigré and a Marxist, and very much the protagonist of what became "Left Keynesianism." The most accessible of his works may be found in the collection of his essays, *The Last Phase in the Transformation of Capitalism* (1972). Working along similar lines was Joseph Steindl, in his *Maturity and Stagnation in American Capitalism* (1952). Taken together these two were most influential for the ideas put forth in Baran and Sweezy's *Monopoly Capital* (1966), to be discussed in detail in Chapter 4.

95. From the Preface to *The Rate of Interest and Other Essays* (1952). Her argument here concerning "equilibrium" was central to the development of "Post-Keynesian economics," to be discussed in the next chapter.

96. Phyllis Deane quotes her as later saying, "For me, the main message of Marx was the need to think in terms of history, not of equilibrium." In her "Biographical Memoir," in Rima (1991, 17).

97. In the foreword to his *Ten Great Economists* (1951, xii, edited and put together by his widow. Like Schumpeter, she taught at Harvard. This book (of 13, not 10, essays) was never planned as a book by Schumpeter; it is composed entirely of articles and reviews (many of them memorials), except for the long essay on Marx. That was originally Part I of his *Capitalism, Socialism and Democracy* (1943). Elizabeth Boody Schumpeter also did the considerably more daunting work of getting Schumpeter's 1,000 + page *History of Economic Analysis* (1954) into

book form. It was daunting in many ways, not least that it was handwritten (in German), much of it in fragments, and left by him in something other than good order. It is a mark of Schumpeter's and Paul Sweezy's admirable and remarkable relationship that he is acknowledged in Elizabeth Boody Schumpeter's introduction as having "read all the proofs, made many valuable suggestions, and caught several errors which had escaped me."

98. *Ten Great Economists* (1951, 266). To my knowledge Schumpeter was the *only* one voicing such notions, at the time or later. There was, however, a great deal of criticism of Keynes for having betrayed his trust, and so on.

99. Having earlier denigrated the entirety of Keynes's "conceptual arrangements" as "a novelty of some importance," goes on to say of them:

> What I admire most [about them] is their *adequacy*; they fit his purpose as a well-tailored coat fits the customer's body. Of course, precisely because of this, they possess but limited usefulness irrespective of Keynes's particular aims. A fruit knife is an excellent instrument for peeling a pear. He who uses it in order to attack a steak has only himself to blame for unsatisfactory results. (287; his emphasis)

Touché?

100. Considerably more "sustained" in the *Ten Great Economists* than in his *History of Economic Analysis*. In the latter, Marx and Marxism are referred to frequently (when appropriate); but for Schumpeter's coherent statement concerning Marx one must read the essay. As noted, it was taken from *Capitalism, Socialism, Democracy*, where Marxism is a sensible, almost unavoidable point of departure for Schumpeter's main thesis about capitalist development.

101. *Ten Great Economists* (1951, 73); *Capitalism, Socialism and Democracy* (1943, 58).

102. *Business Cycles: A Theoretical, Historical, and Statistical Analysis of the Capitalist Process* (1939).

103. One of his books, which I struggled through as a beginning graduate student, was *Mathematics for Economists* (1946). It was a labor of loathing for me.

104. The emphasis of my discussion of economics in the interwar period has been almost entirely on its "theoretical" developments. There was much useful work connecting less abstract analyses with data in those years. Here a few representative studies worth examining (some published a bit after 1945) which were stimuli for a proliferation of such work for a whole generation after the war:

> A.A. Berle and Gardner Means, *The Modern Corporation and Private Property* (1932).

Robert A. Brady, *Business as a System of Power* (1943b).

J.M. Clark, *Studies in the Economics of Overheat Costs* (1923).

Wassily Leontief, *The Structure of the American Economy, 1919–1939* (1951).

Maurice Leven, H.G. Moulton, and C. Warburton, *America's Capacity to Consume* (1934).

Cleona Lewis, *America's Stake in Foreign Investments* (1938).

George W. Stocking and Myron Watkins, *Monopoly and Free Enterprise* (1951).

Keith Sward, *The Legend of Henry Ford* (1948).

CHAPTER 4

1. The term "monopoly capital" – along with "finance capital" – was first used in the late nineteenth century, and often in the years *before* World War II. When thus used it had – and could not but have – a different meaning than the term as it is now used. The earlier mentioned and path-breaking book of Paul Baran (1901–64) and Paul Sweezy (1910–2004), *Monopoly Capital* (1966), is the point of departure for what here is treated as "Monopoly Capitalism I," with the discussion of "Monopoly Capitalism II" to be taken up in the following chapter.

2. See, for example, Paul M. Sweezy, *Monopoly and Competition in the English Coal Trade: 1550–1850* (1938). Sweezy wrote this as his Ph.D. dissertation. It involved studies in England in the early 1930s; that in turn (accompanied by visits to Germany as Nazism was emerging) was influential in his becoming a Marxist. Subsequently, as he has written, when he returned to the United States (and taught at Harvard) it was his intention to assist in the adaptation of Marxian analysis to the United States. *Monopoly Capital*, to be much discussed in these pages, was one important result.

3. The general developments in the United States strengthening or creating the "Big Six" in this period are given a comprehensive and readable description and analysis by Morton Mintz and Jerry S. Cohen in their *Power, Inc.* (1976).

4. The "stains" refer to matters noted earlier, such as the trade in oil and weapons with Germany and Italy that were used for supporting the fascist forces in Spain (while preventing shipments to the Loyalist forces). But there was something else even more difficult to accept, that which had to do with the efforts *not* made to lessen the cruelties and mass murder of Jews by the Nazis. That has been fully documented recently by the U.S. historian Richard Breitman, in his *Official Secrets: What the Nazis Planned, What the British and Americans Knew* (1998).

5. For almost all people in the United States (and many elsewhere), this

way of putting things will appear as wrong-headed, for whatever else the Cold War was it was a successful (and lasting) socialization process. I have discussed this at some length in my *Blues for America* (1997), most specifically in its Chapter 3, "Creating a Cold War and a Global Economy: 1945–1960." As we go along, some of the socialization processes, along with references furnishing documentation and analyses, will be brought to bear.

6. Of the several international agreements and institutions to be noted in what follows – financial, trade, production, or other – the Soviet Union was often a participant in discussions, but only in the case of the United Nations did it become an active "member." Even at the height of the war (1942–43), when the Soviet Union was carrying more than its share of the fighting, it was seen – especially by U.S. representatives involved – as a past and future problem rather than as a partner in international relations. While FDR lived there were proposals for extending substantial assistance to the Soviet Union after the war; when FDR died (April 12, 1945), his place was taken by Truman, his spirit replaced by the Cold War, and all such proposals (including those for an independent Indochina, not so incidentally) abandoned.

7. For both the economics and politics, see the excellent and comprehensive analytical history by Fred Block, *The Origins of International Economic Disorder* (1977), especially Chapters 3 and 4. Block's analysis is, one may say, academically critical; there have been other critiques going beyond academic strictures. Among the best of them are the several books of Susan George, who emphasizes the consequences of these (especially financial) institutions for the weaker societies. See her *How the Other Half Dies* (1976, especially Chapter 3, on the IMF), and her later *A Fate Worse than Debt: The World Financial Crisis and the Poor* (1988). On the Marshall Plan, Block's Chapter 4 is revealing. That program was proposed by General Marshall (as Secretary of State) in 1947, and enacted as the European Cooperation Act (ECA) in 1948. Put forth to the people of the United States as humanitarian, it was sold to Congress as being in the direct economic and strategic interests of the United States. Among its most revealing provisions were those having to do with oil: "[The] head of the Marshall Plan's oil division, and previously an economist for Mobil, noted in 1949 that 'without the ECA American oil business in Europe would already have been shot to pieces ...; the ECA does not believe that Europe should save dollars or even foreign exchange by driving American oil from the European Market.' Some $2 billion of total Marshall Plan assistance of $13 billion was for oil imports ..." Michael Tanzer, *The Energy Crisis: World Struggle for Power and Wealth* (1974, 236). The Soviet Union and the countries in its bloc – most notably, Czechoslovakia – were invited to join, but on terms that the Soviet Union saw as threatening more than

helping. It is generally agreed that the takeover of Czechoslovakia in 1948 was in important part provoked by the controversy over the Marshall Plan. NATO, very much an institution of and for the Cold War, was the military "flipside" of the ECA – all nations part of one becoming also part of the other.

8. The expenditures were lower, but their relative impact was as substantial for smaller countries such as Taiwan and South Korea in Asia, and for Spain and Turkey in Europe. And there were other kinds of "subsidization": the decades-long single-party rule in Italy and Japan, for example (with variations in Greece and diverse nations in Latin America). There the United States overtly or, more usually, covertly assisted – it would be called *interfering* if done by others in the United States – overground and underground elements to stifle opposition, with money and who knows what else.

9. Of the almost $2 trillion we owed to the rest of the world in 1998, about $300 billion was held by Japan, in the form of U.S. Treasury securities. That number has risen since then, as the U.S. trade deficit with Japan (and generally) has continued to rise and now surpasses $2.5 trillion.

10. William Ashworth, *A Short History of the International Economy Since 1850* (1975, 287).

11. Richard B. Du Boff, *Accumulation and Power: An Economic History of the United States* (1989, 111–12).

12. The "others" include George F. Kennan, often seen as providing a key reason for the Cold War with his 1946 cable to the State Department from Moscow. But there he wrote of the need to come to grips with the Soviet Union *politically*, while explicitly against the militarization of our policies as being both unnecessary and harmful. See his wry remarks on such matters in Chapter 3, note 62, and also his comments on the Soviet Union in a subsequent interview (1999).

But what about Korea (and China)? Of the Soviet decision to divide Germany? And the need to protect freedom in Vietnam? There are strong reasons to doubt the U.S. position on all those conflicts. See the following scholarly works: Bruce Cumings, *The Origins of the Korean War* (1981), Carolyn Eisenberg, *Drawing the Line: The American Decision to Divide Germany* (1996), and Marilyn Young, *The Vietnam Wars, 1945–1990* (1991); and see the comprehensive study of Lawrence Wittner, *Cold War America: From Hiroshima to Watergate* (1978). It will be seen that all these books postdated the "Freedom of Information Act" of 1975, which made available long-suppressed and damning documents. Thus, regarding the division of Germany, which did (and does) so much harm and brought the world so close to major war, this statement from our Ambassador to Germany to President Eisenhower in the midst of negotiations: "The difficulty under which we labor is that in spite of our *announced* position [for a united Germany] we really do not want nor intend to accept German unification in any terms that the Russians might agree to – *even though they seemed to meet most of our requirements"* (quoted in Eisenberg, 1996; emphasis added). That is, of course, exactly opposite to what the general public was told then and since.

13. Though Keynes himself had dismissed such ways of supporting the economy as foolish in *The General Theory*: akin to "paying some men to dig holes and others to fill them; or building battleships and then sinking them." Nor is it irrelevant that the first major country to adopt Keynesian theory/policy did so in that way: Hjalmar Schact, the finance minister of Nazi Germany, quite explicitly saw such policies as suiting the double aim of eliminating unemployment and preparing Germany for war. Unique to the capitalist world, by 1938 unemployment had been "conquered" in Germany, as it also prepared to strike. Joan Robinson came to call the use of Keynesian ideas after World War II "bastard Keynesianism." See Lynn Turgeon, *Bastard Keynesianism* (1996).

14. As they have been (for many years) by the industrial economist Professor Seymour Melman (Columbia University) in several books: *Our Depleted Society* (1965), *Pentagon Capitalism* (1970) and, among more recent works, *The Demilitarized Society: Disarmament and Conversion* (1988). His emphasis is on diversion of about two-thirds of scientists, engineers, and highly-skilled workers into the relatively secure and well-paying jobs in the military–industrial complex.

15. Except that of avoiding depression. But that requires an embarrassing admission: that contemporary capitalism cannot endure profitably *without* the waste and dangers of dependency upon permanently massive milex.

16. See, for example, the heavily documented but readable study by Victor S. Navasky, *Naming Names* (1980), where you will discover that among the "namers" were Ronald Reagan and Walt Disney.

17. I have written at some length on this process in my essay "Militarized Economy, Brutalized Society," *Economic Forum* (1981).

18. It is worth going back to look at Keynes's comment on the Soviet Union, as quoted in the preceding chapter: "Give them a chance." A voice in the wilderness.

19. Thus, the U.S. Senate Committee on Small Business issued a report in 1946 showing that the 100 largest industrial corporations received over two-thirds of all war contracts of World War II (with associated power over their many thousands of suppliers). In addition, and no small matter in itself, was that many existing plants were expanded and many *new* plants constructed with government funds during the war (for metals, vehicles, etc.); and after the war most of them were "sold" to the involved companies for $1: cheap at twice the price.

20. Soon after both wars, through the "Red Scare" of the 1920s and the McCarthyism of the Cold War, legislation allowed the crushing or weakening of unions.

21. By Adolph Berle and Gardiner Means. Berle was a Wall Street lawyer, and Means was an economist edging outside the mainstream. Their principal concern was the separation of ownership from management, which they saw as intrinsic to the giant corporation. Subsequent critics of giantism, as will be seen, while not disagreeing that such was so, were concerned with different issues: market power and inefficiency or, with some few, the tenuous relationship between concentrated economic power and political democracy.

22. See the final report of the TNEC for the 76th U.S. Congress: *Investigation of the Concentration of Economic Power* (1940).

23. U.S. Federal Trade Commission, *Report on the Present Trend of Mergers and Acquisitions* (1955, 7).

24. Joe S. Bain, *Industrial Organization* (1959, 92–4).

25. Also noted was that the profits (after taxes) of the 500 "rose a stunning 54 percent on a sales gain of only 8.2 percent and an employment gain of 2.6 percent." Bigger *is* better, it seems.

26. From his unpublished essay "The United States Multinational Corporation and Japanese Competition in the Pacific," which the author allowed me to use in the early 1970s (shortly after which he died in an accident). Subsequently, that essay was published as part of his M.I.T. doctoral dissertation, *A Study of Direct Foreign Investments* (1976).

27. See Ernest Mandel, *Europe vs. America* (1970, 22).

28. Joyce Kolko, *America and the Crisis of World Capitalism* (1974, 30).

29. As the most fully "capitalist" of societies, the crisis hit the United States first; by the 1980s it had surfaced in all the major nations in different ways (as will be discussed in the next chapter).

30. "Social capital" comprises both social investment and social consumption; taken together they lower the costs of production (through industrial parks, superhighways, and the like) and increase the productivity of labor (as with social insurance, public education, and grants to universities); "social expenses" are those required to maintain social harmony (such as welfare payments).

31. Corporate profits taxes fell from their high of about 30 percent (in the 1950s) to about 6 percent by the 1980s; and the personal income tax, which at the highest levels could come to 90 percent, fell steadily to 28 percent. Meanwhile, Social Security payroll taxes rose from their original 1 percent to the present 7.6 percent (up to $62,000 – and zero above that), as federal and state sales taxes and fees, along with property taxes, also steadily rose. See, for example, Joseph Pechman's *Who Paid the Taxes, 1966–1985?* (1985).

32. Poverty was estimated at about 22 percent as the 1960s began. But the official estimates then, and even more so now, are substantial understatements. The official poverty level was set at $3,000 annually for a family of four (in 1964). That figure – this is hard to believe – was derived from what it would cost to maintain a family of four *after*

a nuclear attack; moreover, the figure assumed that rent constituted a third of total expenses for a family. Quite apart from all else, rents in the United States have risen much more than other cost items and, especially for those in the bottom third of the population, now amount to 50–60 percent of household expenses. But the poverty calculation has not changed to account for that (among others of its deficiencies). In Europe, generally, the poverty level is set where a family's income is less than half of the median family income, which would add up to 50 percent to the U.S. poverty level. See Lars Osberg, *Inequality and Poverty: International Perspectives* (1991).

33. This is the title of a book of essays by Hans Magnus Enzensberger (1974). Note the year of publication. Its lead essay, "The industrialization of the Mind," is especially germane for present purposes, as witness this excerpt: "Whether we realize it or not, the mind industry is growing faster than any other, not excluding armament. It has become the key industry of the twentieth century" (6).

34. It is, of course, impossible to find an objective definition of what *should be* "pleasures." But that does not rule out the possibility of locating an area separating normal irrationalities from those that are systematically cultivated for profit. A useful examination of this matter is Tibor Scitovsky's searching critique of the treatment of pleasure in neoclassical economics, *The Joyless Economy* (1976). Like Keynes, Scitovsky (who taught at Stanford) was a leading neoclassical economist; like Keynes, having deviated from orthodoxy, he was subsequently ignored or reviled.

35. Paul Baran, "Theses on Advertising," in *The Longer View* (1969, 231; emphasis in original), a posthumous collection of his essays. As for the expansion of advertising, Baran notes (for the United States) that in 1929 advertising expenditures were $1.1 billion (1.38 percent of National Income) and had risen by the 1965 to $15 billion annually (about 4 percent of National Income). And he adds that this amount does not include the costs of market research, designing for advertising purposes, and so on, going on within the producing and selling companies (for which he suggested adding $10 billion) (1969, 225). By 1985 such expenditures had risen six-fold to $95 billion and by 1999 to $220 billion (in current dollars) – half of the entire world's advertising expenditures. See McChesney (1999, 85). A very useful book in this connection is Stuart Ewen, *Captains of Consciousness: Advertising and the Social Roots of the Consumer Culture* (1976).

36. For those not old enough to remember, there were NO credit cards in the interwar period. In the 1950s oil companies began to issue credit cards for use at gas stations, and (as had long been so) "reputable" customers had "charge accounts" at leading department stores. The current meaning of credit cards took firm hold in the 1960s in the United States and soon spread to other rich countries. Already in the 1970s, the big

change took place: one didn't have to be reputable; as was once said about being drafted into the army, one simply had to be "warm." I still remember the shock on my university campus (in 1973): card tables in front of the gym and various other buildings with signs inviting "Everyone: you don't have to be employed or have good credit standing." Soon thereafter wallets began to be made that would hold "ladders" of credit cards; in the next chapter we'll examine what that has meant regarding average levels of personal indebtedness and bankruptcies – and profits for the lenders.

37. See the article "The Media Generation: Multitask Children All Alone," in *Washington Post*, November 19, 1999, for data.

38. In his *The Needs of Strangers* (1984, 13).

39. The first (and excellent) study of the phenomenon, still worth reading, was by Howard Sherman, *Stagflation* (1977).

40. Mild inflation – say, 2-3 percent per annum – is beneficial for most business and most workers; when it goes beyond that, a result will be a redistribution of income upwards, favoring the strongest sellers of commodities and of labor. In the inflation of the 1970s, as organized labor was weakened, the net result was a redistribution confined to the top layers of businesses and personal incomes.

41. This ("arithmetic") average is calculated by dividing total incomes by total recipients. When income inequalities are high and increase, the average is systematically overstated. That it did, after 1973 and did so into the 1990s. Thus even that 1.4 percent annual increase is an overstatement for the bottom 80 percent. The foregoing data are drawn from Richard Du Boff, *Accumulation and Power* (1989, Chapters 5 and 6).

42. Here we follow economics in the United States for the most part. The history was quite different in Europe, for reasons similiar to those affecting its politics (as noted earlier). Neoclassical economics existed, but without real influence (except in the academy) up through the 1970s; reflecting the strength of social democracy in Europe, reformist and radical economists were most influential.

43. Alfred S. Eichner (ed.), *A Guide to Post-Keynesian Economics* (1978–79, 80). Joan Robinson provided a Foreword to the book, and was helpful in its work until her death. The book's table of contents aptly represent post-Keynesianism, ranging as they do from "macro-dynamics" through pricing, income distribution, fiscal economics, production theory, labor, monetary, and international markets, and natural resources. Alfred Eichner was a highly respected member of this group, and was much lamented when he fell ill and died in 1988, at the age of 50.

44. The title of Eichner's major work, *The Megacorp and Oligopoly: Micro Foundations of Macro Dynamics* (1976) is in this sense self-explanatory. His work in that area (and income distribution) was

preceded by that of Joe S. Bain, *Pricing, Distribution and Employment* (1948). Although nobody was speaking of "post-Keynesian economics at that time, Bain was teaching it. In the fall of 1947, I was his reader in "intermediate economic theory," which he taught from the manuscript for the book just noted; in 1948, I was one of his two research assistants for his next book, *Barriers to New Competition* (1956), on both of which some elements of what became post-Keynesianism depended.

45.   Stephen Rousseas, *Post-Keynesian Monetary Economics* (1992, 13–14). And see the ongoing *Journal of Post-Keynesian Economics*.

46.   It has gone through several editions; the one cited here is the third (1986). Its authors were among the founders of the Union for Radical Political Economics in 1968. The latter publishes the quarterly *Review of Radical Political Economics* and sponsors the monthly popular magazine *Dollars & Sense*, a readable collation of useful essays and data.

47.   The British "New Left" differed greatly from the "New Left" of the 1960s in the United States: though students were very much part of it, its character was given to it more by its works of scholarship – as often as not Marxist – than by its "politics." In the United States, the New Left was predominantly a student movement caught up in protests against poverty, racism, and U.S. foreign policy. Although there were Marxist and socialist elements in it, they were very much a minority.

48.   In English there are several books that present Gramsci's arguments clearly and well: John M. Cammett, *Antonio Gramsci and the Origins of Italian Communism* (1967), Carl Boggs, *Gramsci's Marxism* (1976), and Quintin Hoare and G.N. Smith, *Selections from the Prison Notebooks of Antonio Gramsci* (1971). His *The Modern Prince* is widely available in paperback.

49.   Thus, about 20 years *after* Senator McCarthy's death, at a state university in California where I was teaching, 13 of the economics faculty (half of the department) were discharged for no discernible reason connected with their professional competence. All were left of center but, except for perhaps three, as strong liberals or mild radicals. The attempt was made on eleven successive semesters to add one to that number – myself – and failed, largely because I was the oldest and least vulnerable of those targeted. The then president of the university soon joined (and remains) with a California research institute whose staff includes Milton Friedman.

50.   E.K. Hunt, *History of Economic Thought* (1979, 422). Friedman's principal inspiration was Friedrich von Hayek (in turn inspired by Ludwig von Mises), and his *Road to Serfdom* (1946). The "serfdom" of von Hayek referred to the U.S. New Deal. Friedman and von Hayek may be seen as serving as the doctrinal core of the so-called "Chicago School." That "school" was in effect founded by F.H. Knight, one of the principal theorists of U.S. neoclassicism from the 1930s into the 1950s. (F.H. was

the brother of my quite different mentor M.M. Knight.) And "los Chicago Boys" are widely seen as the economic mentors of the Pinochet regime of Chile, after 1973.

51. Among those on the sidelines were those called "institutionalists," in one way or another, the practitioners of the Veblenian tradition. They often differ as much from each other as they do from the neoclassicists or Marxists: some are empiricists and some (fewer) are theorists; some are radical, leaning a bit toward Marx; others are conservative, leaning a bit towards Friedman. Be that as it may, they have a useful journal: *The Journal of Economic Issues*.

CHAPTER 5

1. Robert Kuttner, *Everything for Sale* (1996).
2. Richard B. Du Boff, *Accumulation and Power* (1989, 128).
3. James M. Cypher, "Crisis Tendencies of the 1990s: Constraints on the Ideology of Globalization?" (1999, 2, n.p.). Professor Cypher is an international and development economist with a main focus on Latin America.
4. Walter Adams and James Brock, *The Bigness Complex* (1986, 208).
5. In the United States the leading personalities of these processes were Carl Icahn and T. Boone Pickens, Ivan Boesky and the "inventor" of the junk bond Michael Milken (from which he personally gained in spectacular ways: "earning" $500 million in one year). Both he and Boesky were caught out in nefarious deals which gave them short stays in prison. Just prior to his indictment, Boesky, at the invitation of the Business School of the University of California (Los Angeles) gave a commencement speech whose title (honestly) was "Greed is Good." He was, of course, speaking to the already converted.
6. A leveraged buyout signifies a merger between two or more companies in which the purchase price of the merger is financed by the issuance of bonds, "hostile" when initiated by "corporate raiders" (as distinct from corporate management). Usually the bonds – which came to be called "junk bonds" – bear high interest rates. And, as Du Boff points out, "Companies so restructured end up carrying less equity and far higher levels of debt, making them more vulnerable to an economic setback" (1989, 137). Just how much more vulnerable the whole economy has now become as regards debt will be treated below. Suffice it to say here that high debt loads for businesses (and consumers) were among the crucial factors in bringing the present dominance of finance over production.
7. Du Boff (1989, 134).
8. These data are taken from *Fortune*, April 22, 1991.
9. Unless otherwise noted, these data are taken from *Fortune*, August 22, 1999. *Fortune*'s provision of these data for 1999 will come forth in the summer of 2000, too late for inclusion here.

10. The sources of these data are the financial pages of the *New York Times*, in the months indicated – most usefully a partial summary of September 12, 1999.

11. Robert Samuelson, "Boom Times in the Casino: Feeling Lucky on Nasdaq," *Washington Post*, January 13, 2000. And on February 26, 2000, Sandra Sugawan reported (also in the *Washington Post*) that the NASDAQ ratio had risen to 356:1.

12. The data on hours are found in *Business Week*, December 6, 1999, p. 40; those concerning jobs in the *New York Times*, December 20, 1999.

13. More exactly, it was redefined in 1988 "as two earners working fulltime the year round with two dependents." The data are taken from Kevin Phillips, *Boiling Point* (1993, 48). The taxes noted are, of course, decided by the government; but in those same years whatever influence over such decisions had been held by organized labor had declined substantially, as it has even more since 1987.

14. What started in the United States soon spread to the strongest European economies and Japan. Moreover, in the 1980s South Korea (as also other "emerging economies") in the 1970s seen as a low-wage country, already found itself "outsourcing" to countries with lower wages (and no unions).

15. In his excellent analysis of globalization *One World, Ready or Not: The Manic Logic of Global Capitalism* (1997, 74). An excellent new book, compact and very readable, which arrived too late to be discussed here, is Robin Hahnel, *Panic Rules: Everything you Need to Know About the Global Economy* (1999).

16. Barry Bluestone and Bennett Harrison, *The Deindustrialization of America* (1982, 9–10; emphasis in original). Those processes took hold in the 1970s and 1980s. Along with the acceleration of M&As in the 1990s went rising job losses. *Business Week* (December 20, 1999) reported that since March 1998 alone 533,000 manufacturing jobs have been lost in the United States. Some telling examples include that of GE which "expanded its capital stock, but not in the United States. During the 1970s, GE expanded its worldwide payroll by 5,000, but it did so by adding 30,000 foreign jobs and reducing its U.S. employment by 25,000" (7). And they go on to cite similar cuts by RCA and Ford and GM, et al.

17. The full title is *Fat and Mean: The Corporate Squeeze of Working Americans and the Myth of Managerial Downsizing* (1996). Tragically, the author recently died for lack of a heart replacement (at the age of 51), just as his book was published.

18. Those recent data were provided in the annual executive pay survey of *Business Week* (April–May, 1998), as reported by Holly Sklar in her essay "CEO Greed is Out of Control," *Z Magazine*, June 1998. She quotes J.P. Morgan's remark that the ratio "between the top people and the rank and file should be twenty-fold, post-tax ... Beyond that, you create social tension." True, but in today's world the "creators" have had the power and the means to redirect that tension in ways that solidify rather than

harm their interests. In the *Washington Post* (November 5,1999) in an article headlined "More on the Inflated Pay of Business Titans," the author cites the latest ratio of CEO to the average worker as 419:1.

19. It should be noted that the State in Britain was exceptional in those relatively narrow tasks. Although the United States sees itself as also having had merely a "nightwatchman state" in the nineteenth century, the realities were different: the transportation system, protective tariffs, and the banking system, among other vital matters of political economy, were all decisively directed and/or subsidized through the State. And, of course, the main European economies (and that of Japan) all became "modern" in close cooperation with the State. But in no case did the State perform the functions it would under Monopoly Capitalism I.

20. *Capital*, vol. I (1967, 751).

21. In a speech delivered before the Democratic Association of Brussels, January 9, 1848, shortly before he and Engels wrote the *Manifesto*.

22. See Greider (1997, Chapter 5) for instances.

23. The term was invented by Kevin Phillips, as he sought to explain and document "The Financialization of America: Electronic Speculation and Washington's Loss of Control over the 'Real Economy.'" The foregoing is the heading of Chapter 4 of his *Arrogant Capital: Washington, Wall Street, and the Frustration of American Politics* (1994). I shall make further reference to this useful work in what follows.

24. Source: *Economic Report[s] of the President* (1991, 311, 388–9) and subsequently.

25. In the sense that contained within "corporate profits" as a category are the profits of financial corporations; moreover, the number of financial corporations as a percentage of all corporations has also increased markedly since the 1970s.

26. Emphasis added, but author's exclamation mark (1994, 79–80).

27. "Vast" as signified by the estimated $90 *trillion* circulating in that market in 1999. Because of the sums involved, it requires the miscalculations of only a few individuals to cause a large financial calamity. After all, it was one very young man who brought down the venerable Baring Brothers; and a couple of Nobel prize winners (for their work on derivatives!) to bring down Long Term Capital Management (in 1998) – saved just in time by the intervention of several of the largest banks, prodded by the Fed, to bail them out.

28. These data are regularly made available through the Bank for International Settlements.

29. The Federal Reserve System of the United States is "owned" by its member banks. It has twelve "districts" each with its own governing body, entirely appointed by the member banks and selected other representatives from business and the community. But they are presided over for many critical decisions by the Board of Governors whose seven members and whose Chair are appointed by the President, with Senate

approval. That power of appointment and approval is widely understood to be at the informal consent of the private financial community. In one variation or another, this is the practice throughout most of the world – an instance of the fox guarding the chicken coop.

30. The North American Free Trade Agreement, which links Canada and Mexico to the United States. The agreement is such that all three nations lose some of their sovereignty, in the specific sense that all of them must become increasingly open to capital and goods flowing from the others, without the restrictions earlier created in any one country. That means several things; among them, it is of course the United States that is sending capital and goods north and south, rather than Canada and Mexico; also, for example, Canada has a national health care program ("the single-payer system," where the single payer is the government) which U.S. health care companies are now allowed to penetrate, pretty much no matter what.

31. Noam Chomsky has written a substantial critical essay on the MAI: "Domestic Constituencies: MAI, the further corporatization of America and the world," in *Z Magazine* (May 1998). The MAI was first brought to light in 1995, and the target date for its approval was 1997. Substantial opposition came from outside the charmed circle of the Group of Seven and, as the issue came to be discussed publicly, also within. It has yet to be approved. As it and the current attempts to broaden the scope of the WTO come under further scrutiny, especially if there is a global slump, the likelihood of approval may well decrease.

32. Unless otherwise indicated, the data to follow are taken from that article.

33. "Syndicated loans" are those shared among many lenders. The data are taken from the *New York Times*, July 15, 1998, "Worries About Loans Revive Ghost of 1980s Debacle."

34. Data taken from *Left Business Observer*, July 21, 1998. The author (Doug Henwood) adds: "besides credit cards, poorer debtors are also fleeced by second mortgage brokers, pawn shops, finance companies 'payday' loans at an annualized rate of 2,000 percent, rent-to-own schemes ..."

35. James Cypher, in "Financial Domination in the US Economy" (1998, 68).

36. Gretchen Morgenstern (principal analyst for the financial pages of the *New York Times*) spoke to this question (June 20, 1999), in a perceptive essay entitled "U.S. Shoppers Shoulder the Weight of the World." After noting that U.S. imports were about 4 percent of the industrial world's GDP in 1995, she points out that they were 7.5 percent in 1999, and that about half of that gain was registered *after* the Asian crisis began in 1997. She goes on to argue (with support from other sources) that it was because U.S. interest rates and prices fell in consequence – but that in 1999 rates and prices have begun to rise, and that the recent annual

increase in real (not money) wages had fallen from 3 to 1.5 percent annually, that Europe's growth is only 2 percent, and that Asian and Latin American economies are "either flat or contracting." She concludes with the admonition that if growth really slows down "and gets into a more scary scenario, then the whole stock market gets into trouble." "If" or "when"?

37. The estimate is that of the Securities Industry Association. It can be seen as more bad than good news. It is the highest percentage ever for stock ownership; but it is substantially overstated in an important sense. Probably half or so of those households "owns" securities it has never "bought." It "owns" them (as I do) because their pension funds – over which they usually have no control – have invested in those securities, either in mutual funds or in particular assets, and whose lives will be much damaged to the degree that their pension funds are hit badly. As for those in the market voluntarily, the Association reports that "a vast majority" of those who have done their own buying have a "buy and hold strategy"; that is, "they are relying on stocks to reach retirement ..." These findings of the Association were quoted in the *New York Times*, October 22, 1999, in an article headed "Survey Says 78.7 million Own Stocks in United States." Also of significance is that well over a fifth of all those who do their own investing own shares in from four to seven separate funds – "suggesting that they may have taken diversification a little too far and created bookkeeping headaches as well."

38. Even before World War II, some films may be seen as indirect advertisers – of cigarettes, for example. Now that is becoming common in TV shows and in films. "A show like News Corp's *The Simpsons* ... has tie-ins with four major firms, including Pepsi-Cola and Subway Sandwiches ... Time-Warner inked a three-year deal with Frito-Lay in 1997, in which Warner Bros characters will be used exclusively in Frito-Lay point of purchase displays the world over ... In 1998 Disney's Miramax Films signed a deal with Tommy Hilfiger where the characters of a Miramax film will wear Hilfiger clothing and also appear, in character, in ads for Hilfiger jeans." Robert W. McChesney, *Rich Media, Poor Democracy* (1999, 38–9).

39. Edward S. Herman and Robert W. McChesney, *The Global Media* (1997, 104). The five largest of these giants are, in order, Time Warner, Disney, Bertelsmann, Viacom, and News Corporation. Among the others control emanates from outside the media, as with Sony, Seagram, and General Electric. As a major actor in the M&As of the past 20 years or so, Rupert Murdoch aptly expressed what underlies the processes of concentrated ownership, as quoted in *Business Week* (March 25, 1996): "We can join forces now, or we can kill each other and then join forces."

40. Robert W. McChesney (1999, 84–5).

41. The U.S. data are from a *Washington Post* article, "The Media Generation: Multitask Children All Alone" (November19, 1999), and

are based on a survey carried out by the Kaiser Family Foundation (a major HMO); the figures for the 41 nations are from Edward S. Herman and Robert W. McChesney, *The Global Media* (1997, 41).

42. This is from his *Amusing Ourselves to Death* (which, you will guess, inspired the subtitle of this section) (1985, 78).

43. In a letter to a friend, as quoted in *Albert Einstein: A Biography* (1997), by Albert Folsing, and noted in "The Contradictory Genius," by Alan Lightman, *New York Review* (April 10, 1997).

44. McChesney (1999, 288).

45. Hugh Stretton, *Economics: A New Introduction* (1999, ix). In reading his comments on economic fallacies that shortly follow in the text, it is useful to know that their author has long worked both in business and government, as well as in the academic world.

46. Stretton (1999, 63). He goes on say that "most of the mistakes are not ignorant laymen's mistakes, they are professional economists' mistakes." As regards the items concerning housing, here are some recent data for the United States: 1) in 1995, the Center on Budget and Policy Priorities (using Census data) found an all-time deficiency of 4.4 million units of affordable housing, such that two low-income renters must compete for every one unit; 2) from 1995 to 1997 (according to the Department of Housing and Urban Development), the number of "struggling renter households" increased by 3 percent, to 8.9 million; and that affordable rental units decreased by about 5 percent (372,000 units) from 1991 to 1997. In New York City, the "struggling household" ceiling is $16,000, about 30 percent of the median income for a NYC family of four. The 1990s were years of increasingly successful assaults against rent controls in the United States (*New York Times*, September 24, 1999).

47. There are about 22 million small businesses in the United States, but we have seen that a small fraction of *one* percent of businesses own 59 percent of all business assets, and that they do more than half the sales and hire 54 percent of all workers. These data, provided by William Domhoff in his recent *Power and Politics in the Year 2000* (1998), reveal that the concentration of wealth among individuals and households is replicated by that among companies. It is also relevant that a high proportion of "normal businesses" live very much like serfs, their primary (or sole) customer being a major corporation – with all the power that suggests: earlier we noted that GM alone has upwards of 40,000 businesses as its suppliers (and is responsible for 1.5 percent of total GDP). Not quite what Adam Smith or Albert Marshall had in mind when they thought of the invisible hand of market competition.

48. Hunt (1979, 420). The factors of production are land (ownership of resources), labor, and capital. The owners of each – agricultural, mining, and timber companies, workers, and owners of businesses, respectively – are assumed to be contributing to production in one degree or another. This vital argument was a giant departure from the classical political

economy of Smith and (especially) Ricardo, who saw the return to ownership as a return not to production but to power, and "labor alone as contributing to production." Marx made the most of this of course. (In this connection the *management*, as contrasted with the ownership and control, of business is seen as a form of labor.)

49. See the excellent survey by the late Lynn Turgeon, *Bastard Keynesianism* (1996), so-called by Joan Robinson, referring to the adaptation to military and commercial desires, as distinct from the overall economy's needs.

50. It is pertinent to report that the Chief Economist of the World Bank, Joseph Stiglitz, who has been critical of the IMF and related matters, as doing much harm and little good, announced his resignation in late November, 1999. He had been under considerable criticism, not only by many economists, but as well by the head of the Bank, James Wolfensohn.

CHAPTER 6

1. Karl Marx and Friedrich Engels (1967c, 38).
2. James Cypher (2001). Emphasis added.
3. See Naomi Klein (2000) and Joseph Stiglitz (2003).
4. "'Jobless Recovery' – How it's possible," *Boston Globe*, October 14, 2003.
5. "Overcapacity Stalls New Jobs," *New York Times*, October 19, 2003.
6. *New York Times*, September 4, 2003.
7. *International Herald Tribune*, October 30, 2003.
8. "China: U.S. Losing Status in Asia," *New York Times*, October 17, 2003.
9. *La Repubblica*, October 19, 2003.

EPILOGUE

1. The first is Stretton's (critical) comment (1999, 62), the second is the famous (and popular) exclamation of the coach of the Green Bay Packers, Vince Lombardi.
2. There is a small and (one hopes) enlarging minority that demurs strongly, most frequently on ecological grounds; and there are other important bases for criticism, more rarely made. Taken together, they constitute my own position and will be examined later.
3. Madrick is Editor of *Challenge*, an informative periodical on economic affairs, and he regularly contributes useful essays to the *New York Review*. His political stance can fairly be described as "liberal" – 'in the sense in which the term has been used in the United States to describe the socioeconomic policies of the New Deal and the Kennedy–Johnson 1960s.'
4. Pages 4–5. It is worth noting that the data provided by Madrick throughout his book are valuable in themselves, and his ability and

inclination to study and use those data sets him apart from most of his fellow economists.

5. That assertion is frequently made; never have I seen any qualification to the notion of "peacetime" that would seem to be called for by the annual expenditure of about $250 billion for the military.

6. One of the other important elements of growth's support discussed at some length earlier have been enormous military expenditures. Except for what is noted now, we will not explore that further: 1) the United States was very much at the forefront of such expenditures and still is; they are now budgeted to rise significantly over the next several years; 2) one of the major requirements of membership in the recent expansion of NATO (to include ex-members of the Soviet Bloc) is the creation of a modern military force, the weaponry for which must meet U.S. standards – which usually means its purchase from U.S. companies.

7. Even at five times that much, the annual income would be under $2,000 – one-eighth of the official poverty level in the United States. The figures are from the *New York Times* (June 3, 1999), "World Bank Says Poverty is Increasing." Interestingly, the *Times* notes, "The report implied that the increase was caused in part by the international rescue packages begun to help Asian countries overcome their difficulties ... packages mainly prepared by its sister institution, the International Monetary Fund." The matter of income distribution will be returned to subsequently.

8. A reputable study of the levels of waste, already in the 1980s, concluded that only about *half* of total output in the United States could be considered as non-wasteful, that is, as serving human and social needs – 'even though they classified 70 percent of milex as useful and took no account of the now widespread industrial practice – 'begun in the automobile industry in the 1920s, of "deliberate obsolescence."' The study is quoted in the useful book of readings edited by Richard C. Edwards, et al. (eds.) *The Capitalist System* (1986, Chapter 9).

9. The data are found in the United Nations Human Development Report of 1998, as reported in the *New York Times*, September 27, 1998.

10. Testimony before a 1974 U.S. Senate Committee cited the sustained involvement of GM, along with a tire and a petroleum company "in the destruction of more than 100 surface rail systems in 45 cities, including New York, Philadelphia, Baltimore, Oakland, Salt Lake City, and Los Angeles." Bradford Snell, "American Ground Transport," in *Hearings* before the Sub-Committee on Antitrust and Monopoly, 93rd Congress, 2nd Session, U.S. Senate, pp. A-2 and A-3. Just before that Snell explained the motivation for that destruction: "one bus can eliminate 15 automobiles, one streetcar, subway or rail transit vehicle can supplant 50 passenger cars; one train can displace 1,000 cars or a fleet of 150 cargo-laden trucks ..."

11. As early as 1961 Lewis Mumford pointed out that "More than a third of the Los Angeles area is consumed by ... these grotesque ... many-laned expressways ... *two-thirds* are occupied by streets, freeways, parking facilities, and garages" (*The City in History* [1961, 510]). When he wrote, Los Angeles was almost unique; now such distortion of city life is common in all quarters of the globe and is worsening. Interestingly, according to a New York City survey, there has been this version of progress: in 1907, horse-drawn vehicles moved at an average speed of 11.5 miles per hour; in the mid-1970s, cars in the city moved at an estimated average of 6 miles an hour.

12. Italy holds the European Union record for number of cars per capita, 571 for every 1,000 people, reported Eurostat "beating even the United States." *Corriere della Sera* (November 23, 1999). Earlier, Italy was reported as having the most cellular phones per capita in the world. And their TV, once entirely public and with excellent music, drama, and sports, now has found depths below those elsewhere. Who says the United States is No. 1?

13. The TV ads for these SUVs always show them driving over rough country and mountainous roads, even though the industry's own market research shows that only 13 percent of their use is outside cities. As for profits, Ford's small car, the Escort, in 1998 sold for $13,145 and yielded a profit of $2,100; its SUV, the Explorer, sold for $27,270 with a profit of $8,600. The above data and that in the text on the SUV may be found in articles in the *New York Times* of September 24, 1997; April 16, 1998; and February 14, 1999. In the article concerned with highway deaths, GM's director of advanced technology responded to the data by saying "Even if you're driving a tank down the road, you could always be hit by a locomotive." The tobacco industry could use arguments like that; indeed it has.

14. The phrase is that of the Australian Alex Carey, in his *Taking the Risk Out of Democracy* (1997). For an excellent survey and analysis of this development in the United States, see Stuart Ewen, *PR! A Social History of Spin* (1996).

15. This was done in many ways, most crudely by hiring men to speak before hundreds of semi-business clubs (for example, Elks, Rotary) to recount horror stories concerning the Germans, and the like. See Larry Tye, *The Father of Spin: Edward L. Bernays and the Birth of Public Relations* (1998).

16. "Propaganda" because the aim of advertising and public relations (whether for businesses or politicians or ideas) is to sell, to control, to deceive, to "spin" – not to provide information or understanding, but disinformation, misinformation, and confusion.

17. As for those techniques, see the important book by Jerry Mander, *Four Arguments for the Elimination of Television* (1978). He should know: in the 1960s, Mander was generally viewed as one of the stars of the

TV/advertising complex. It was his experience in that work that led him to propose the "elimination" of TV, having come to the conclusion that its dangers outweighed its values. Among those dangers, Mander shows that the technology of TV requires its programs to keep each "scene" to a desired maximum length of 2–3 seconds if it is to avoid watcher boredom. The attendant short attention span becomes habitual, and viewers become "consumers" of what is seen and heard. The content that best fits that technology consists of melodramatic versions of life, whose limits continue to be expanded, with predictable effects.

18. Note "within." Much violence has of course been used elsewhere, in the many wars since World War II – the "hot" side of the Cold War. And there is the violence accompanying racism, whether that in the United States that has placed a high percentage of (especially) young Afro-Americans in prison (themselves riddled by violence and acquiesced in by the authorities), or in Europe, against the rising tide of immigrants – a tide whose origins are less in the countries left behind than in the practices of the major powers that have disrupted the economies of those countries.

19. Postman (1985, 197).

20. And it is not a joke to say that some very high percentage of those "members" we now know to have been government agents, FBI or otherwise – reminding of the English writer G.K. Chesterton's story of a century ago, "The Man Who Was Called Thursday." That man, eager to promote revolution in England, joined a group so select that it had only seven members, each named after a day of the week. At the end of the story we find that our hero alone was working for the revolution; the other six were government agents.

21. I'll not resist a true story. When I joined the faculty at Cornell University in 1953, my broader than usual interests as an economist led me to be asked to join a new and interdisciplinary "major": American Studies. Among the many disciplines on the committee was history, represented by an eminent professor who later was President of the American History Association. We became friends. One day in 1954, as we left a committee meeting, he handed me a book – wrapped by him in plain brown paper – and said he thought I would find it worth reading. It was I.F. Stone's *Hidden History of the Korean War*, published by Monthly Review Press. Until then there was a *Monthly Review* but no press; it came into existence to publish that book, for no other publisher in the United States would do so. The book, it should be added, was not an attack on the United States, but merely an analysis of how the war began that departed from the official explanation.

22. The details and a lengthy discussion are provided by Kevin Phillips in his *Arrogant Capital* (1994, 36). Among all those lobbyists are those from interests other than business of course; but, having less money by far,

they have little clout unless backed up by significant public opinion. And the latter is also bought and paid for in the media.

23. Noted in the *New York Times* (January 8, 1999) on its editorial page under the heading "Money Warps the System." Bumpers took over the seat of William Fulbright, another honorable senator in all respects but civil rights, concerning which a politician from Arkansas in Fulbright's days could not be honorable and remain in politics.

24. The terminology changed over time, evidently in response to expressed resentments from those "backward" areas. By the 1960s it was "under-developed economies," now it is "developing economies," and "emerging market economies."

25. William Greider's *One World, Ready or Not* (1997) is useful for details on most of the countries in the world, including "the Tigers."

26. The figures are from Thomas Crampton, "Developing Nations ...," *IHT* (September 24, 1999).

27. In the past two to three decades, earlier disasters have had piled on them new and even more destructive ones: as the poorer economies have been "brought into the world economy" and their agriculture and forests made suitable for export, traditional peoples have been pushed off the land – and, in the process, made available for harsh exploitation in the cities of their own or other countries; a repetition with variations on the enclosures and related horrors of the industrial revolution. An extraordinary work of scholarship making those and related points for the western hemisphere (but which applies equally elsewhere) is Ronald Wright, *Stolen Continents* (1995). The author studied the languages and the histories of five tribes as they existed before the arrival of the Europeans and then again at present: the Cherokee and Iroquois in North America, and the Aztec, Inca, and Maya in Latin America.

28. It was because he pointed his finger at the IMF in these regards that Joseph Stiglitz was castigated, and for which (as noted earlier) he resigned as the World Bank's chief economist.

29. See the essay "Good News for Vultures," by Gregg Wirth, in *LBO* #81 (January 21, 1998).

30. There have been many works putting forth positions compatible with what is to follow, and in considerable detail. Two that seem to me to be particularly appropriate, written wholly or in part by Herman Daly, are these: Herman E. Daly and John B. Cobb Jr., *For the Common Good* (1989) and Herman E. Daly, *Beyond Growth: The Economics of Sustainable Development* (1996). Daly was long on the research staff of the World Bank; like Joseph Stiglitz, he has returned to the university.

31. From the "Preface to the Critique of Political Economy," found in many editions, taken here from Marx and Engels, *Selected Works* (1967, 183).

Bibliography

Adams, Walter and Brock, James W. 1986. *The Bigness Complex: Industry, Labor, and Government in the American Economy*. New York: Pantheon.

Adelman, M.A. 1973. *The World Petroleum Market*. Baltimore: Johns Hopkins University Press.

Allen, G.C. 1946. *A Short Economic History of Modern Japan: 1867–1937*. London: Macmillan.

Arendt, Hannah. 1958. *The Human Condition*. Chicago: University of Chicago Press.

Arnold, Thurman. 1941. *The Folklore of Capitalism*. Garden City, NY: Doubleday.

Ashworth, William. 1987. *A Short History of the World Economy since 1850*. London: Longman.

Bagdikian, Ben. H. 1983. *The Media Monopoly*. Boston: Beacon Press.

Bain, Joe S. 1948. *Pricing, Distribution and Employment: Economics of an Enterprise System*. New York: Holt.

—— 1956. *Barriers to New Competition*. Cambridge, Mass.: Harvard University Press.

—— 1968. *Industrial Organization* (revised edition). New York: John Wiley.

Baran, Paul. 1957. *The Political Economy of Growth*. New York: Monthly Review Press.

—— (with Paul Sweezy) 1969. "Theses on Advertising," in *The Longer View*. New York: Monthly Review Press.

Baran, Paul, and Sweezy, Paul. 1966. *Monopoly Capital: An Essay on the American Economic and Social Order*. New York: Monthly Review Press.

Barber, Benjamin. 2001. *Jihad vs. McWorld: Terrorism's Challenge to Democracy*. New York: Ballatine Books.

Baritz, Loren (ed.). 1977. *The Culture of the Twenties*. New York: Bobbs-Merrill.

Barnet, Richard, and Cavanagh, John. 1994. *Global Dreams: Imperial Corporations and the New World Order*. New York: Simon and Schuster.

Bentham, Jeremy. *See* Stark, William.

Berle, A.A. and Means, Gardner. 1932. *The Modern Corporation and Private Property*. New York: Macmillan.

Bernays, Edward. 1952. *Public Relations*. Norman: University of Oklahoma Press.

Blackburn, Robin (ed.).1973. *Ideology in Social Science: Readings in Critical Social Theory*. New York: Vintage.

Blair, John. 1972. *Economic Concentration*. New York: Harcourt Brace Jovanovich.

—— 1976. *The Control of Oil*. New York: Vintage Books.

Block, Fred. 1977. *The Origins of International Economic Disorder*. Berkeley: University of California Press.

Bluestone, Barry, and Harrison, Bennett. 1982. *The Deindustrialization of America*. New York: Basic Books.

Boggs, Carl. 1976. *Gramsci's Marxism*. London: Pluto Press.

Bowden, Witt, Karpovitch, Michael, and Usher, Abbott Payson. 1937. *An Economic History of Europe since 1750*. New York: American Book Co. (Republished, 1969. New York: Howard Fertig, Inc.).

Boxer, C.R. 1965. *The Dutch Seaborne Empire*. New York: Knopf.

Brady, Robert A. 1933. *The Rationalizaton Movement in German Industry*. Berkeley: University of California Press.

—— 1937. *The Spirit and Structure of German Fascism*. New York: Viking Press.

—— 1943a. "The Economic Impact of Imperial Germany." *Journal of Economic History*. (Summer).

—— 1943b. *Business as a System of Power*. New York: Columbia University Press. (Republished, 1999. Piscataway, NJ: Transaction Publishers.)

Braudel, Fernand. 1949/1994. *The Mediterranean and the Mediterranean World in the Age of Philip II*. London: Fontana Press.

—— 1979/1992. *The Structures of Everyday Life*. Berkeley: University of California Press.

Braverman, Harry. 1974. *Labor and Monopoly Capital: The Degradation of Work in the Twentieth Century*. New York: Monthly Review Press.

Brebner, J.B. 1948. "Laissez-faire and State Intervention in Nineteenth Century Britain." *Journal of Economic History* (Spring).

Breitman, Richard. 1998. *What the Nazis Planned, What the British and the Americans Knew*. New York: Hill & Wang.

Brenan, Gerald. 1943. *The Spanish Labyrinth: An Account of the Social and Political Background of the Spanish Civil War*. New York: Cambridge University Press.

Brittain, John. 1972. *The Payroll Tax for Social Security*. Washington: The Brookings Institution.

Burkitt, Brian. 1984. *Radical Political Economy: An Introduction to the Alternative Economics*. New York: New York University Press.

Business Week, various issues.

Cammett, John M. 1967. *Antonio Gramsci and the Origins of Italian Communism*. Stanford: Stanford University Press.

Carey, Alex. 1997. *Taking the Risk Out of Democracy*. Sydney: University of New South Wales Press.

Carroll, Lewis. 1865, 1872. *Alice's Adventures in Wonderland* and *Through the Looking-Glass*. New York: Oxford University Press.

Carson, Rachel. 1962. *Silent Spring*. Greenwich, Conn.: Fawcett Publications.

Chamberlin, Edward. 1933. *The Theory of Monopolistic Competition*. Cambridge, Mass.: Harvard University Press.

Childe, V. Gordon. 1946. *Man Makes Himself*. London: Penguin.

Chomsky, Noam. 1993. *Year 501: The Conquest Continues*. Boston: South End Press.

—— 1998. "Domestic Constituencies: MAI, the further corporatization of America and the world." *Z Magazine* (May 1998).

Chomsky, Noam, and Herman, Edward S. 1988. *Manufacturing Consent: The Political Economy of the Mass Media*. New York: Pantheon.

Clark, G.N. 1947. *The Seventeenth Century*. London: Oxford University Press.

Clark, John Bates. 1899/1965. *The Distribution of Wealth: A Theory of Wages, Interest and Profits*. New York: A.M. Kelley.

Clark, J.M. 1923. *Studies in the Economics of Overhead Costs*. Chicago: University of Chicago Press.

Cockroft, James D., Frank, André Gunder, and Johnson, Dale L. 1972. *Dependence and Underdevelopment*. New York: Doubleday.

Cole, G.D.H. 1927. *A Short History of the British Working Class Movement*. London: Macmillan.

—— and Postgate, Raymond. 1956. *The Common People*. London: Macmillan.

Collins, Chuck, Leondar-Wright, Betsy, and Sklar, Holly. 1999. *Shifting Fortunes: The Perils of the Growing American Wealth Gap*. Boston: United for a Fair Economy.

Conrad, Joseph. 1978 (1892). *The Heart of Darkness*. New York: Signet Classics.

Cordell, Alexander. 1960. *The Rape of the Fair Country* (New York: Bantam).

Cumings, Bruce. 1981. *The Origins of the Korean War*. Princeton: Princeton University Press.

—— and Halliday, Jon. 1988. *Korea: The Unknown War*. New York: Pantheon.

Cypher, James. 1987. "Military Spending, Technical Change, and Economic Growth." *Journal of Economic Issues* (March).

—— 1990. *State and Capital in Mexico: Development Policy Since 1940*. Boulder, Col.: Westview Press.

——1998. "Financial Domination in the US Economy," in Fayasmanesh, S. and Tool, M. (eds.) *Institutionalist Theory and Applications*. Cheltenham, UK: Edward Elgar.

—— 1999. "Crisis Tendencies of the 1990s: Constraints on the Ideology of Globalization." Unpublished.

—— 2001. "Nafta's Lessons: From Economic Mythology to Current Realities." *Labour Studies Journal* (Spring).

Daly, Herman E. and Cobb, John B. Jr. 1989. *For the Common Good: Redirecting the Economy toward Community, the Environment, and a Sustainable Future*. Boston: Beacon Press.

—— 1991. *Steady-State Economics*. Washington, D.C.: Island Press.

—— 1996. *Beyond Growth: The Economics of Sustainable Development*. Boston: Beacon Press.

Davis, Mike. 1998. *Ecology of Fear: Los Angeles and the Imagination of Disaster.* New York: Henry Holt.

de Castro, Josue. 1952. *The Geography of Hunger.* New York: Monthly Review Press.

Dewey, John. 1922. *Human Nature and Conduct.* New York: Henry Holt & Co.

Dillard, Dudley. 1948. *The Economics of John Maynard Keynes.* Englewood Cliffs, NJ: Prentice-Hall.

Dobb, Maurice. 1937. *Political Economy and Capitalism.* London: Routledge and Kegan Paul.

—— 1946. *Studies in the Development of Capitalism.* London: Routledge.

—— 1966. *Soviet Economic Development Since 1917.* London: Routledge and Kegan Paul.

Domhoff, William. 1998. *Power and Politics in the Year 2000.* New York: Oxford University Press.

Dowd, Douglas (ed.). 1958. *Thorstein Veblen: A Critical Reappraisal.* Ithaca, N.Y.: Cornell University Press.

—— 1964a. *Thorstein Veblen.* New York: Washington Square Press. (Republished 1999. Piscataway, NJ: Transaction Publishers.)

—— 1964b. "Second Thoughts on the Common Market." *Yale Review* (Spring).

—— 1964c. "On Veblen, Mills ... and the Decline of Criticism." *Dissent* (Winter).

—— 1967. "America Fouls its Dream." *Nation* (February).

—— 1971. *The State, Power and the Industrial Revolution.* Ann Arbor: Union for Radical Political Economics.

—— 1976. "Stagflation and the Political Economy of Monopoly Capitalism." *Monthly Review* (September).

—— 1977. *The Twisted Dream: Capitalist Development in the United States Since 1776.* Boston: Winthrop Publishers.

—— 1982a. "Marxism for the Few: Or, Let 'Em Eat Theory." *Monthly Review* (April).

—— 1982b. "Militarized Economy, Brutalized Society." *Economic Forum.* (Summer).

—— 1989. *The Waste of Nations.* Boulder, Col.: Westview Press.

—— 1993. *U.S. Capitalist Development Since 1776: Of, By, and For Which People?* Armonk, NY: M.E. Sharpe, Inc.

—— 1994. "Against Decadence: The Work of Robert A. Brady. (1901–1963)." *Journal of Economic Issues.*

—— 1997a. *Blues for America: A Critique, A Lament, and Some Memories.* New York: Monthly Review Press.

—— 1997b. *Against the Conventional Wisdom: A Primer for Current Economic Controversies and Proposals.* Boulder, Col.: Westview Press.

Du Boff, Richard. 1989. *Accumulation and Power: An Economic History of the United States.* Armonk, NY: M.E. Sharpe.

Duus, Peter. 1976. *The Rise of Modern Japan*. Boston: Houghton Mifflin.

Economic Report of the President. Various years. Washington, D.C., U.S. Government Printing Office.

Edwards, Richard, C., Reich, Michael, and Weisskopf, Thomas E. (eds.) 1986 (third edition). *The Capitalist System: A Book of Readings*. Englewood Cliffs, NJ: Prentice-Hall.

Eichner, Alfred S. 1976. *The Megacorp and Oligopoly: Micro Foundations of Macro Dynamics*. New York: Cambridge University Press.

—— (ed.) 1978/1979. *A Guide to Post-Keynesian Economics* (with a Foreword by Joan Robinson). Armonk, NY: M.E. Sharpe.

Eisenberg, Carolyn. 1996. *Drawing the Line: The American Decision to Divide Germany, 1944–49*. New York: Cambridge University Press.

Eliot, T.S. 1936. *Collected Poems: 1909–1935*. London: Faber & Faber.

Engels, Frederich. 1950. *The Condition of the Working Class in England in 1844*. London: George Allen & Unwin.

Engler, Robert. 1961. *The Politics of Oil*. Chicago: University of Chicago Press.

Ensenzberger, Hans Magnus. 1974. *The Consciousness Industry*. New York: Seabury Press.

Ewen, Stuart. 1976. *Advertising and the Social Roots of the Consumer Culture*. New York: McGraw-Hill.

——- 1996. *PR! A Social History of Spin*. New York: Basic Books.

Faulkner, Harold U. 1947. *The Decline of Laissez-Faire, 1897–1914*. New York: Rinehart.

Feis, Herbert. 1930. *Europe, the World's Banker, 1870–1914*. London: New York: A.M. Kelley.

Finnegan, William. 1998. *Cold New World: Growing up in a Harder Country*. New York: Random House.

——- 1999. "The Invisible War," *New Yorker*, January, 25.

Folbre, Nancy, et al. 1995. *The New Field Guide to the U.S. Economy: A Compact and Irreverent Guide*. New York: The New Press.

—— 1996. *The War on the Poor: A Defense Manual*. New York: The New Press.

Folsing, Albert. 1996. *Albert Einstein: A Biography*. New York: Viking.

Fortune Magazine, various issues.

Foster, John Bellamy. 1986. *The Theory of Monopoly Capitalism*. New York: Monthly Review Press.

Franklin, Michael. 1988. *Rich Man's Farming: The Crisis in Agriculture*. London: Routledge.

Friedman, Milton. 1962. *Capitalism and Freedom*. Chicago: University of Chicago Press.

Frumkin, Gregory. 1951. *Population Changes in Europe since 1939*. New York: United Nations.

Fussell, Paul. 1875. *The Great War and Modern Memory*. London: Oxford University Press.

Galbraith, John Kenneth. 1956. *American Capitalism: The Theory of Countervailing Power*. Boston: Houghton Mifflin.

—— 1958. *The Affluent Society*. Boston: Houghton Mifflin.

—— 1967. *The New Industrial State*. Boston: Houghton Mifflin.

Gans, Herbert. 1995. *The War against the Poor: The Underclass and Antipoverty Policy*. New York: Basic Books.

George, Susan. 1976. *How the Other Half Dies*. London: Penguin.

—— 1979. *Feeding the Few: Corporate Control of Food*. Washington, D.C.: Institute for Policy Studies.

—— 1984. *Ill Fares the Land: Essays on Food, Hunger, and Power*. Washington, D.C.: Institute for Policy Studies.

—— 1988. *A Fate Worse than Debt: The World Financial Crisis and the Poor*. New York: Grove Weidenfeld.

—— 1994. (with Fabrizio Sabelli) *Faith and Credit: The World's Secular Empire*. Boulder, Col.: Westview Press.

Gerschenkron, Alexander. 1943. *Bread and Democracy in Germany*. Berkeley: University of California Press.

Gilder, George. 1981. *Wealth and Poverty*, New York: Basic Books.

Ginzberg, Eli. 1964. *The House of Adam Smith*. New York: Octagon Books.

Glaser, Bernard (ed.). 1987. *The Green Revolution Revisited: Critiques and Alternatives*. London: Allen & Unwin.

Gordon, David M. 1996. *Fat and Mean: The Corporate Squeeze of Working Americans and the Myth of Managerial Downsizing*. New York: Free Press.

Gordon, Robert Aaron. 1974. *Economic Instability and Growth: The American Record*. New York: Harper & Row.

Gramsci, Antonio. 1967. *The Modern Prince and Other Writings*. New York: New World Paperbacks.

Greider, William. 1987. *Secrets of the Temple*. New York: Simon and Schuster.

—— 1994. *Who Will Tell the People?* New York: Simon and Schuster.

—— 1997. *One World, Ready or Not: The Manic Logic of Global Capitalism*. New York: Simon and Schuster.

Gross, Bertram. 1980. *Friendly Fascism: The New Face of Power in America*. New York: M. Evans.

Gurley, John. 1979. *Challengers to Capitalism: Marx, Lenin, Stalin, and Mao*. New York: W.W. Norton, Inc.

Hahnel, Robin. 1999. *Panic Rules: Everything you Need to Know About the Global Economy*. Cambridge, MA: South End Press.

Hammond, J.L. and Barbara. 1911. *The Village Labourer*. London: Guild Books.

—— 1926. *The Rise of Modern Industry*. New York: Harcourt, Brace.

—— 1930. *The Age of the Chartists: 1832–1854: A Study of Discontent*. London: Macmillan.

Handlin, O. 1981. *The Uprooted*. Boston: Atlantic Monthly Press.

Hansen, Alvin. 1938. *Full Recovery or Stagnation?* New York: Norton.

—— 1939. *Fiscal Policy and Business Cycles*. New York: Norton.

—— 1949. *Monetary Theory and Fiscal Policy*. New York: Norton.

—— 1953. *A Guide to Keynes*. New York: McGraw-Hill Book Company.

Heckscher, Eli. 1935, *Mercantilism*. (2 vols.) New York: Macmillan.

Henderson, W.O. 1958. *The State and the Industrial Revolution in Prussia, 1740–1870*. London: Macmillan.

—— 1959. *The Zollverein*. Chicago: Quadrangle.

Henwood, Doug. 1997. *Wall Street: How It Works and for Whom*. New York: Verso.

—— 1998. *Left Business Observer* (July).

Herman, Edward S. 1981. *Corporate Control, Corporate Power*. New York: Cambridge University Press.

Herman, Edward S. and McChesney, Robert W. 1997. *The Gobal Media: The New Missionaries of Global Capitalism*. London: Cassell.

Hess, John. 1987. "Malthus Then and Now." *Nation*, April, 18.

Hill, Christopher. 1967. *Reformation to Industrial Revolution*. Harmondsworth: Penguin.

Hoare, Quintin and Smith, G.N. (eds.). 1971. *Selections from the Prison Notebooks of Antonio Gramsci*. London: Lawrence & Wishart.

Hobsbawm, E.J. 1964. *Labouring Men: Studies in the History of Labour*. London: Weidenfeld and Nicolson.

—— 1968. *Industry and Empire*. New York: Pantheon.

—— 1984. *Worlds of Labour: Further Studies in the History of Labour*. London: Weidenfeld and Nicolson.

—— 1990. *Nations and Nationalism since 1780*. New York: Cambridge University Press.

Hobson, J.A. 1902. *Imperialism*. London: Allen & Unwin.

Hoffmann, Ross J.S. 1933. *Great Britain and the German Trade Rivalry*. Philadelphia: University of Pennsylvania Press.

Hunt, E.K. 1979. *History of Economic Thought: A Critical Perspective*. Belmont, CA: Wadsworth.

—— and Schwartz, Jesse (eds.). 1972. *A Critique of Economic Theory*. Baltimore: Penguin.

Huxley, Aldous. 1931. *Brave New World*. New York: Harper & Bros.

Hymer, Stephen. 1976. *A Study of Direct Foreign Investments*. Cambridge: M.I.T. Press.

—— 1979. *The Multinational Corporation: A Radical Approach*. New York: Cambridge University Press.

Ignatieff, Michael. 1984. *The Needs of Strangers*. London: Chatto & Windus, Hogarth Press.

Isherwood, Christopher. 1932. *Berlin Stories*. London: Faber & Faber.

Ivins, Molly. 1998. "Debt-Ridden Americans are Sinking Deeper." *SF Chron*, July, 20.

Jeffers, Robinson. 1925. *Selected Poems*. New York: Random House.

Jevons, William. 1871. *Theory of Political Economy*. London: Macmillan.

Josephson, Matthew. 1934. *The Robber Barons*. New York: Harcourt Brace Jovanovich.

Kalecki, Michal. 1972. *The Last Phase in the Transformation of Capitalism*. New York: Monthly Review Press.

Kemp, Tom. 1967. *Theories of Imperialism*. London: Dobson.

Kennan, George F. 1998. "Letter from Germany." *New York Review of Books*, December, 3.

—— 1999. "The US and the World: An Interview." *New York Review of Books*, August, 8.

Kennedy, Paul. 1989. *The Rise and Fall of the Great Powers*. New York: Vintage.

Keynes, John Maynard. 1919. *The Economic Consequences of the Peace*. London: Macmillan.

—— 1930. *A Treatise on Money*. New York: Harcourt, Brace, and Company.

—— 1931. *Essays in Persuasion*. London: Macmillan.

—— 1936. *The General Theory of Employment, Interest and Money*. New York: Harcourt Brace.

Klein, Naomi. 2000. *No Logo*. New York: St. Martins Press.

Knight, Frank. H. 1921. *Risk, Uncertainty, and Profit*. New York: Houghton Mifflin.

Knight, Melvin M. 1926. *Economic History of Europe, To the End of the Middle Ages*. Boston: Houghton Mifflin.

Kofsky, Frank. *Harry S. Truman and the War Scare of 1948*. New York: St. Martin's Press.

Kohn, Alfie. 1986. *No Contest: The Case against Competition*. Boston: Houghton Mifflin.

Kolko, Gabriel. 1970. "The Decline of American Radicalism in the Twentieth Century" (in Weinstein, James and Eakins, David [1970]).

—— 1976. *Main Currents in American History*. New York: Pantheon.

Kolko, Joyce. 1974. *America and the Crisis of World Capitalism*. Boston: Beacon Press.

—— 1988. *Restructuring the World Economy*. New York: Pantheon.

Kuttner, Robert. 1991, *The End of Laissez-Faire: National Purpose and the Global Economy after the Cold War*. New York: Knopf.

—— 1996. *Everything for Sale: The Virtues and Limitations of Markets*. New York: Knopf.

LaFeber, Walter. 1976. *America, Russia and the Cold War*. New York: Wiley.

Laski, Harold. 1936. *The Rise of European Liberalism*. London: Allen & Unwin.

La Tourette, Kenneth. 1918. *The Development of Japan*. New York: Macmillan.

Leffler, Mervyn P. 1992. *A Preponderance of Power: National Security, the Truman Administration, and the Cold War*. Stanford, CA: Stanford University Press.

Left Business Observer, various issues.

Lekachman, Robert. 1966. *The Age of Keynes*. New York: Random House.

Leontief, Wassily. 1951. *The Structure of the American Economy, 1919–1939*. Cambridge, Mass.: Harvard University Press.

Leven, Maurice, Moulton, H.G., and Warburton, Clark. 1934. *America's Capacity to Consume*. Washington, D.C.: Twentieth Century Fund.

Levi, Carlo. 1965. *Christ Stopped at Eboli*. New York: Penguin.

Levi, Primo. 1985. *If Not Now, When?* New York: Pantheon.

Lewis, Cleona. 1938. *America's Stake in Foreign Investments*. Washington, D.C.: Twentieth Century Fund.

Lewis, W. Arthur. 1949. *Economic Survey, 1910–1939*. London: Allen and Unwin.

Lichtman, Richard. 1982. *The Production of Desire: The Integration of Psychoanalysis into Marxist Theory*. New York: Free Press.

List, Friedrich. 1841, 1983. *National System of Political Economy*. London: Frank Cass.

Livingston, Jon, Moore, Joe, and Oldfather, Patricia (eds.). 1973. *Imperial Japan: 1800–1945*. New York: Pantheon.

Lockwood, William. 1964. *The Economic Development of Modern Japan*. Princeton, N.J.: Princeton University Press.

Luxemburg, Rosa. 1964. *The Accumulation of Capital* (with an introduction by Joan Robinson). New York: Monthly Review Press.

McChesney, Robert W. 1999. *Rich Media, Poor Democracy: Communication Politics in Dubious Times*. Champaign, Ill.: University of Illinois Press.

Madrick, Jeffrey. 1995. *The End of Affluence: The Causes and Consequences of America's Economic Dilemma*. New York: Random House.

—— 1998 "Waiting for the Revolution," *New York Review of Books*, 2.

Magdoff, Harry. 1968. *The Age of Imperialism: The Economics of U.S. Foreign Policy*. New York: Monthly Review Press.

Malthus, Thomas Robert. 1970. *An Essay on the Principle of Population*. Baltimore: Penguin.

Malraux, André. 1927. *Man's Fate*. New York: Vintage.

—— 1938. *Man's Hope*. New York: Modern Library.

Mandel, Ernest. 1970. *Europe vs. America*. New York: Monthly Review Press.

Mander, Jerry. 1978. *Four Arguments for the Elimination of Television*. New York: Morrow.

Mann, Thomas. 1901. *Buddenbrooks*. New York: Knopf.

Mannheim, Karl. 1936. *Ideology and Utopia: An Introduction to the Sociology of Knowledge*. London: Routledge & Kegan Paul.

Mantoux, Paul. 1906. *The Industrial Revolution in the Eighteenth Century*. London: Cape.

Markusen, Ann, and Yudken, Joel. 1992. *Dismantling the Cold War Economy*. New York: Basic Books.

Marshall, Alfred. 1890. *Principles of Economics*. London: Macmillan.

Marx, Karl. 1844/1963. *Early Writings* (translated and edited by T.B.

Bottomore. Foreword by Erich Fromm). New York: McGraw-Hill.

—— 1867/1967a. *Capital: A Critique of Political Economy* (3 vols). New York: International Publishers.

—— 1863/1967b. *Theories of Surplus Value* (3 vols.). New York: International Publishers.

Marx, Karl, and Engels, Friedrich. 1967c. *Selected Works*. New York: International Publishers.

—— 1859/1973 *Grundrisse: Foundations of the Critique of Political Economy* (translated and Foreword by Martin Nicolaus). New York: Vintage Books.

Mathias, Peter. 1987. *The First Industrial Nation: The Economic History of Britain, 1790–1914*. London: Routledge.

Melman, Seymour. 1965. *Our Depleted Society*. New York: Holt, Rinehart and Winston.

—— 1970. *Pentagon Capitalism*. New York: McGraw-Hill.

—— 1888. *The Demilitarized Society: Disarmament and Conversion*. Nottingham: Spokesman.

Menger, Carl. 1871. *Principles of Economics*. London: Macmillan.

Meszaros, Istvan. 1970. *Marx's Theory of Alienation*. New York: Harper Torchbooks.

—— 1998. "The Uncontrollability of Globalizing Capital." *Monthly Review*, February.

Miliband, Ralph. 1969. *The State in Capitalist Society*. New York: Basic Books.

Mill, John Stuart. 1909 (1848). *Principles of Political Economy*. London: Macmillan.

Mills, C. Wright. 1951. *White Collar*. New York: Oxford University Press.

—— 1956. *The Power Elite*. New York: Oxford University Press.

—— 1967. *The Sociological Imagination*. New York: Oxford Press.

Minsky, Hyman. 1975. *John Maynard Keynes*. New York: Columbia University Press.

—— 1982. *Can "It" Happen Again? Essays on Instability and Finance*. Armonk, N.Y.: M.E. Sharpe.

—— 1986. *Stabilizing an Unstable Economy*. New Haven: Yale University Press.

Mintz, Morton and Cohen, Jerry S. 1976. *Power, Inc*. New York: Viking.

Mishel, Lawrence, Bernstein, Jared, and Schmitt, John. 1998. *The State of Working America, 1998–99*. Armonk, N.Y.: M.E. Sharpe.

Mitchell, Broadus. 1947. *Depression Decade. From New Era through New Deal, 1920–1941*. New York: Rinehart.

Mitchell, Wesley Claire. 1927. *Business Cycles: The Problem and its Setting*. New York: National Bureau of Economic Research.

Mumford, Lewis. 1961. *The City in History*. New York: Harcourt Brace.

Navasky, Victor, S. 1980. *Naming Names* (New York: Viking).

Nef, J.U. 1940. *Industry and Government in France and England, 1540–1640*. Ithaca, N.Y.: Cornell University Press.

Nordholdt, W. Schulte. 1970. *The People That Walk in Darkness*. New York: Ballantine.

Norman, E.H. 1940. *Japan's Emergence as a Modern State*. New York: Institute of Pacific Relations.

O'Connor, James. 1973. *The Fiscal Crisis of the State*. New York: St. Martin's Press.

—— 1984 *Accumulation Crisis*. New York: Basil Blackwell, Inc.

Oglesby, Carl and Shaull, Richard. 1967. *Containment and Change*. London: Macmillan.

Ollman, Bertell. 1976. *Alienation: Marx's Conception of Man in Capitalist Society*. Cambridge: Cambridge University Press.

Origo, Iris. 1979. *The Merchant of Prato: Francesco di Marco Datini*. New York: Octagon Books.

Orwell, George. 1948. *1984*. London: Destino.

—— 1962. *Homage to Catalonia*. New York: Harcourt, Brace.

Osberg, Lars (ed.). 1991. *Inequality and Poverty: International Perspectives*. Armonk, N.Y.: M.E. Sharpe.

Parry, J.H. 1965. *The Spanish Seaborne Empire*. New York: Knopf.

Pechman, Joseph. 1985. *Who Paid the Taxes, 1960–1985?* Washington: The Brookings Institution.

—— 1989. *Tax Reform, The Rich and the Poor*. Washington: The Brookings Institution.

Phillips, Kevin. 1991. *The Politics of Rich and Poor: Wealth and the American Electorate in the Reagan Aftermath*. New York: Harper Perennial.

—— 1993. *Boiling Point: Democrats, Republicans and the Decline of Middle-Class Prosperity*. New York: Harper Perennial.

—— 1994. *Arrogant Capital: Washington, Wall Street, and the Frustration of American Politics*. New York: Harper Perennial.

Piven, Frances Fox, and Cloward, Richard. 1971. *Regulating the Poor*. New York: Pantheon.

Pizzo, Stephen, et al. 1989. *Inside Job: The Looting of America's Savings and Loans*. New York: McGraw-Hill.

Polanyi, Karl. 1944. *The Great Transformation*. New York: Rinehart.

Postman, Neil. 1985. *Amusing Ourselves to Death: Public Discourse in the Age of Show Business*. New York: Viking Penguin.

Power, Eileen. 1941. *The Wool Trade in English Medieval History*. Oxford: Oxford University Press.

Ratner, Joseph (ed.). 1939. *Intelligence in the Modern World: John Dewey's Philosophy*. New York: Modern Library.

Ravenscraft, David J., and Scherer, F.M. 1987. *Mergers, Sell-Offs, and Economic Efficiency*. Washington: The Brookings Institution.

Reed, John. 1917, 1977. *Ten Days that Shook the World.* New York: Penguin.

Remarque, Erich Maria. 1928/1996. *All Quiet on the Western Front.* New York: Fawcett.

Ricardo, David. 1817, 1911. *Principles of Political Economy and Taxation.* London: J.M. Dent.

Ridgeway, James. 1973. *The Last Play: The Struggle to Monopolize the World's Resources.* New York: Dutton.

Rima, Ingrid H. (ed.) 1991. *The Joan Robinson Legacy.* Armonk, N.Y.: M.E. Sharpe.

Robbins, Lionel. 1932. *The Nature and Significance of Economic Science.* London: Macmillan.

Robinson, Joan. 1933. *The Economics of Imperfect Competition.* London: Macmillan.

—— 1942. *An Essay on Marxian Economics.* London: Macmillan.

—— 1950–79. *Collected Economic Papers* (5 vols.). Oxford: Blackwell.

—— 1952. *The Rate of Interest and Other Essays.* London: Macmillan.

—— 1953. *On Re-reading Marx.* Cambridge: Students' Bookshop Ltd.

—— 1956. *The Accumulation of Capital.* London: Macmillan.

—— 1962. *Economic Philosophy.* Chicago: Aldine.

—— 1970. *Freedom and Necessity.* New York: Pantheon.

Roediger, David. 1991. *The Wages of Whiteness: Race and the Making of the American Working Class.* New York: Verso.

Rogin, Leo. 1956. *The Meaning and Validity of Economic Theory.* New York: Harper.

Roll, Eric. 1946. *A History of Economic Thought.* Englewood Cliffs: Prentice-Hall.

Ross, Robert J.S. and Trachte, Kent C. 1990. *Global Capitalism.* Albany: State University of New York Press.

Rousseas, Stephen. 1991. *Capitalism and Catastrophe: A Critical Appraisal of the Limits to Capitalism.* Cambridge: Cambridge University Press.

——- 1991. *Post Keynesian Monetary Economics.* Armonk, N.Y.: M.E. Sharpe.

Salvemini, Gaetano. 1936, 1967. *Under the Axe of Fascism.* New York: H. Fertig.

——- 1973. *The Origins of Fascism in Italy.* New York: Harper.

Sampson, Anthony. 1975. *The Seven Sisters.* New York: Viking.

Samuelson, Paul. 1947. *Economics.* New York: McGraw-Hill.

—— 1947. *The Foundations of Economic Analysis.* Cambridge, Mass.: Harvard University Press.

Schiller, Herbert. 1971. *Mass Communications and American Empire.* Boston: Beacon Press.

—— 1973. *The Mind Managers.* Boston: Beacon Press.

—— 1976. *Communications and Cultural Domination.* Boston: Beacon Press.

Schmidt, Carl. 1938. *The Plough and the Sword: Labor, Land, and Property in Fascist Italy.* New York: Columbia University Press.

—— 1939. *The Corporate State in Action*. New York: Oxford University Press.

Schor, Juliet. 1991. *The Overworked American*. New York: Basic Books.

—— 1998. *The Overspent American*. New York: Basic Books.

Schumpeter, Joseph. 1934. *The Theory of Economic Development: An Inquiry into Profit, Capital, Credit, Interest, and the Business Cycle*: Cambridge, Mass.: Harvard University Press.

—— 1939. *Business Cycles: A Theoretical, Historical, and Statistical Analysis of the Capitalist Process*. 2 vols. New York: Macmillan.

—— 1943 [1976]. *Capitalism, Socialism and Democracy* (Introduction by Tom Bottomore). London; Allen & Unwin.

—— 1946. *Mathematics for Economists*. New York: Oxford University Press.

—— 1951a. *Ten Great Economists, from Marx to Keynes*. New York: Oxford University Press.

—— 1951b. *Imperialism and Social Classes*. New York: Oxford University Press.

—— 1954. *History of Economic Analysis*. London: Allen & Unwin.

Scitovsky, Tibor. 1976. *The Joyless Economy*. New York: Oxford University Press.

Seabrook, Jeremy. 1996. "An English Exile," in *GRANTA* (Winter).

Sen, Amartya. 1981. *Poverty and Famine: An Essay on Entitlement and Deprivation*. Oxford: Clarendon Press.

Sender, Ramon. 1936, 1961. *Seven Red Sundays* (New York: Liverright).

Sherman, Howard. 1977. *Stagflation*. New York: Harper & Row.

Silone, Ignazio. 1934. *Fontamara*. New York: Macmillan.

Singer, Daniel. 1999. *Whose Millennium? Theirs or Ours?* New York: Monthly Review Press.

Sklar, Holly. 1998. "CEO Greed is Out of Control," *Z Magazine* (June).

Smith, Adam. 1776/1937. *An Inquiry into the Nature and Causes of the Wealth of Nations*. New York: Modern Library.

Soule, George. 1947. *Prosperity Decade. From War to Depression*. New York: Rinehart.

Stark, W. (ed.). 1954. *Jeremy Bentham's Economic Writings*. London: Allen & Unwin.

Stavrianos, L.S. 1981. *Global Rift: The Third World Comes of Age*. New York: Morrow.

—— 1989. *Lifelines From Our Past: A New World History*. Armonk, N.Y.: M.E. Sharpe.

Steindl, Joseph. 1952. *Monopoly and Stagnation in American Capitalism*. New York: Monthly Review Press.

Stiglitz, Joseph E. 1993. *Principles of Microeconomics*. New York: W.W. Norton, Inc.

—— 2003. *Globalization and Its Discontents*. New York: W.W. Norton.

Stocking, George W. and Watkins, Myron. 1951. *Monopoly and Free Enterprise*. Washington, D.C.: Twentieth Century Fund.

Stretton, Hugh. 1999. *Economics: A New Introduction*. London: Pluto Press.

Sward, Keith. 1948. *The Legend of Henry Ford*. New York: Rinehart.

Swedberg, Richard (ed.). 1991. *Joseph A. Schumpeter: The Economics and Sociology of Capitalism*. Princeton: Princeton University Press.

Sweezy, Paul. 1938. *Monopoly and Competition in the English Coal Trade: 1550–1850*. Cambridge: Harvard University Press.

—— 1941. *The Theory of Capitalist Development*. New York: Oxford.

Tanzer, Michael. 1969. *The Political Economy of Oil and the Underveloped Countries*. Boston: Beacon Press.

—— 1974. *The Energy Crisis: World Struggle for Power and Wealth*. New York: Monthly Review Press.

Tawney, R.H. 1912. *The Agrarian Problem in the Sixteenth Century*. London: Macmillan.

—— 1925. *The British Labour Movement*. London: Macmillan.

—— 1926. *Religion and the Rise of Capitalism*. New York: Harcourt, Brace.

—— 1931. *Equality*. New York: Harcourt Brace & Co.

Taylor, A.J.P. 1961. *The Course of German History: A Survey of the Development of Germany since 1815*. London: Methuen.

Terkel, Studs. 1974. *Working: People Talk About What They Do All Day and How They Feel About What They Do*. New York: Pantheon.

—— 1982. *Hard Times: An Oral History of the Great Depression*. New York: Pantheon.

—— 1984. *The Good War: An Oral History of World War Two*. New York: The New Press.

—— 1992. *Coming of Age: The Story of Our Century By Those Who've Lived It*. New York: The New Press.

Terrill, Ross. 1973. *R.H. Tawney and His Times: Socialism as Fellowship*. Cambidge, Mass.: Harvard University Press.

Thompson, E.P. 1968. *The Making of the English Working Class*. New York: Vintage.

Totten, George O., III. 1966. *The Social Democratic Movement in Prewar Japan*. New Haven: Yale University Press.

Tucker, Robert C. (ed.) 1978. *The Marx-Engels Reader*. New York: W.W. Norton.

Turgeon, Lynn. 1996. *Bastard Keynesianism: The Evolution of Economic Thinking and Policymaking since World War II*. Westport, Conn.: Greenwood Press.

Tye, Larry. 1998. *The Father of Spin: Edward L. Bernays and the Birth of Public Relations*. New York: Crown Publishers.

Ullmann, John (ed.) 1983. *Social Costs in Modern Society*. Westport, Conn.: Quorum Books.

U.S. Congress, 93rd. 1974. *U.S. Senate Hearings*, Sub-Committee on Antitrust and Monopoly.

U.S. Federal Trade Commission. 1940. *Report on the Automotive Industry*.

—— 1955. *Report on the Present Trend of Corporate Mergers and Acquisitions.*

Vatter, Harold G. 1963, *The U.S. Economy in the 1950s.* New York: W.W. Norton.

Veblen, Thorstein. 1899. *The Theory of the Leisure Class.* New York: Macmillan.

—— 1904. *The Theory of Business Enterprise.* New York: Scribner's.

—— 1914. *The Instinct of Workmanship.* New York: B.W. Huebsch.

—— 1915. *Imperial Germany and the Industrial Revolution.* New York: Macmillan.

—— 1917. *An Inquiry into the Nature of Peace and the Terms of its Perpetuation.* New York: Macmillan.

—— 1918. *The Higher Learning in America: A Memorandum on the Conduct of Universities by Businessmen.* New York: Huebsch (reprinted by Sagamore Press, 1957).

—— 1919a. *The Place of Science in Modern Civilization.* New York: B.W. Huebsch.

—— 1919b. *The Vested Interests and the Common Man.* New York: B.W. Huebsch. (reprinted by Viking, 1956).

——1923. *Absentee Ownership and Business Enterprise in Recent Times.* New York: B.W. Huebsch.

—— 1934. *Essays in Our Changing Order.* (Ed. by Leon Ardzrooni.) (Reprinted 1964): New York: Augustus Kelley.

von Hayek, Friedrich. 1944. *The Road to Serfdom.* Chicago: University of Chicago Press.

Walras, Leon. 1868. *Elements of Pure Economics.* London: Macmillan.

Weinstein, James and Eakins, David. 1970. *Toward a New America.* 1970. New York: Vintage.

Williams, William Appleman. 1964. *The Great Evasion.* New York: Quadrangle Press.

—— 1969a. *The Roots of the Modern American Empire.* New York: Random House.

—— 1969b. "The Large Corporations and American Foreign Policy." In Horowitz, David (ed.). 1969. *The Corporations and the Cold War.* New York: Monthly Review Press.

—— 1980. *Empire as a Way of Life.* New York: Oxford University Press.

Wills, Garry. 1988. *Reagan's America.* New York: Penguin.

Wittner, Lawrence. 1978. *Cold War America: From Hiroshima to Watergate.* New York: Holt, Rinehart and Winston.

Wolff, Edward N. 1987. *Growth, Accumulation and Unproductive Activity.* New York: Cambridge University Press.

—— 1995. *Top Heavy: A Study of Increasing Inequality of Wealth in America.* New York: Twentieth Century.

Wright, Ronald. 1992. *Stolen Continents: The Americas Through Indian Eyes Since 1492.* Boston: Houghton Mifflin.

Young, Marilyn Blatt. 1991. *The Vietnam Wars: 1945–1990*. New York: HarperCollins.

Zinn, Howard. 1996. *A People's History of the United States*. New York: The New Press.

Index